WHITEWATER; QUIETWATER

A Guide to the Wild Rivers of
Wisconsin, Upper Michigan, and NE Minnesota

Bob & Jody Palzer

To River Lovers Everywhere
This edition is dedicated to all river lovers. Special thanks to our readers, without whose enthusiastic response, this edition would not have been possible.

—Bob & Jody

Acknowledgements

This book is based in part on two Wisconsin Hoofer Outing Club booklets; the "Guide to Whitewater in the Wisconsin Area," by Andy Peekna, and the "Water Safety Code," by myself. I wish to thank the Hoofers for their support and permission to incorporate information from those sources, and to include club photographs in this book.

I would also like to thank the following people for their generous assistance;
Jody, my wife and co-worker who helped translate a dream into reality.
Mr. and Mrs. Hugo Palzer, and Mr. and Mrs. Gordon Cairns, our parents.
Tom, my brother.
Ray and Mary Kent
Terry Spennetta
Al and Ginny Stamm
John Strahler
Gail Toman
Fred Young
Roy Campbell, Fred Dreher, Ed Oakes, Gurth Hendrickson, and C. L. R. Holt, of the U.S.G.S.
Prof. Arthur Robinson of the U.W. Cartography laboratory.
Donna Jungans of the aerial photo division of the U.S. Soil Conservation Service.
Edward Faber and Bud Parker of the Wisconsin DNR.
Paul Pequinot, the late director of the Michigan Tourist Council.
Bill Beverly and Frank Turkeimmer of the John Muir chapter of the Sierra Club.
Chuck Bader, Glen Bostad, Walt Brummand, Ken Evans, Don Fritz, Leighton Matsuyama, Rod McCormick, John Nelson, Eric Olsen, Andy Peekna, and Jim Stolmquist.

Bob Palzer
Spring 1973

Photo & Other Credits

Cover: Photo, Al Stamm; Design, Jody Palzer.
Chapter 3: Photo 1, Lowell Klessig; Photo 2, Al Stamm.
Chapter 4: Photos 1-4 and 6, Al Stamm; Photo 5, Wisconsin DNR.
Chapter 5: Photos 1 and 3, Wisconsin DNR; Photos 2, 4-11 and 13, John Strahler; Photo 12, Wisconsin Hoofers; Photo 14, Al Stamm.
Chapter 6: Photo 1, Wisconsin DNR; Photo 2, Martin Begun; Photo 3, Al Stamm.
Chapter 7: Photos 1 and 2, Al Stamm; Photo 3, Paul Kromholz.
Chapter 8: Photos 1, 2, 8, 18, 19, 25, 27, 29, 30, 49, and 50, Bob Palzer; Photos 3-7, 9-16, 22, 24, 31, 36, 38-41, 44-48, 51, 55, and 56, Wisconsin DNR; Photos 17, 20, 21, 32, 35, 42, 43, 52-54, Al Stamm; Photos 23, 33, 34, and 37, Paul Kromholz; Photos 26 and 28, Lowell Klessig.
Inside Back Cover: Left Photo, Al Stamm; Right Photo, Wisconsin DNR.
Maps and illustrations: Jody Palzer.

The following people generously donated the notes used to describe the following runs:
Chapter 8: Jim Stohlmquist: Black River (Sections 1&2)
Bob Kline: Black (Sections 3&4) and Montreal rivers.
Terry Spennetta: Black (East Fork), Brule, and Tomahawk rivers; Mirror Lake and the Wisconsin Dells.
Al Stamm: Cloquet and Kickapoo rivers.
Chapter 9: Fred Young, Dave Anglin, and Andy Westerhaus: Brule River. Terry Spennetta: Crystal and Jump Rivers.
Eric Olsen: Embarrass River.
Andy Peekna and Steve Ransburg: Vermilion River.

Sixth Edition, 1992
ISBN 0-89732-086-7
Library of Congress Catalog Card Number: LC 83-80899

Contents

1 How to Use This Guide

Rivers are listed alphabetically in two categories: those with maps, and those with descriptions only. The mapped sections are numbered. Letters have been used to designate the others. An index map showing the relative location of these runs can be found on the outer back cover.

Each river run is described as a one-day trip between landings accessible by car. Extended trips of a week or longer can be made by combining a series of adjoining runs. Match lines are provided on overlapping maps.

The following useful information is given for each run in standard format: the recommended starting point or put-in, the recommended ending point or take-out, the length of the run in river miles, the time for a leisurely run in hours, the river width in feet, the gradient (steepness) in feet per mile, the drainage area (watershed) in square miles, the hazard rating according to the International Scale of River Difficulty (see introduction), and the water conditions in terms of canoeability. In addition there are comments about the scenery, geology, fishing potential, campgrounds, and history of the area.

All maps share a common self-explanatory legend. The scale varies with the action. Runs having numerous rapids and falls are generally shorter to allow ample time for scouting and possible rescue. Maps of such runs cover fewer miles and are somewhat more detailed. The scale of miles is given for each map.

Rapids, falls, campsites, and other interesting features are pinpointed on our maps and described in downstream order in the text. The designations left or right refer to the direction when facing downstream. Cumulative mileages are given for alternate landings and other numbered points of interest. Trip length can be varied with ease.

We used trip notes and aerial photographs to pinpoint rapids, falls, and other permanent hazards on our maps. Although we have taken great pains to be accurate, we are not infallible. Use your own descretion to avoid being caught in any potentially dangerous situation. **When in doubt, stop to scout!** (See technique section.)

We have included warnings about hazards that may no longer be present. Barbed wire, downed trees, and low-slung footbridges come and go. Rivers are one of natures most constantly changing quantities. In **Life on the Mississippi,** Mark Twain has written at length about the meanderings of the Mississippi River, such that a town would be in Mississippi one day and in Arkansas the next. Nothing quite like that happens on our smaller rivers, nevertheless they are constantly changing. Banks erode, trees fall, boulders roll, rains fall, and snow and ice melt. The river runner must constantly be alert to these changes.

Our maps show most convenient car-access points to the river. Many of these landings are reachable only by secondary roads not shown on most state highway maps. The best shuttle routes (to avoid having to paddle back upstream after a run) are described in the text when not readily obvious from our maps. Cities, major highways, and other reference points are included, and all our maps have been drawn with north facing upwards so they can be readily compared with others.

A state highway map and this guide should provide all the information you need for a successful trip. However, for those who desire additional information, we have listed all of the county, forest service, USGS, and other maps that cover each run. The date listed indicates the edition we used to prepare our maps. More recent editions of some of these maps are now available (see appendix E). Unless otherwise indicated, all the USGS maps listed are topographic. The overview maps are of the 1:250,000 series in which one inch equals approximately four miles. The other topographic maps are more detailed as indicated.

We have identified those portions of river shoreline that are in public hands. Our primary objective is to show how little river shoreline the public has title to, even along rivers flowing through many state and national parks and forests. We have listed our sources along with the date obtained. Real-estate transactions in the interum may have altered the public status of some of these holdings.

Rivers have been apportioned into sections according to the time and skill required to make the run. Rivers with a relatively uniform hazard rating, have been divided into sections of approximately equal length. Rivers that alternate between quitewater and difficult whitewater have been divided into sections according to the skill-level required. Novice runs have been separated from expert ones. Most sections are intended to provide a good day's run.

Unlike most other types of boating, river cruising is highly dependent upon water levels. Under water conditions, we have indicated the canoeability of a run at different water levels. By digging through flow records we have come up with guidelines that can be used to predict the water level and canoeability throughout the canoeing season, which we consider to be from April through September.

We have also expressed canoeability in terms of a 10%/90% flow duration ratio. (This concept is discussed more fully in the section on practical hydrology.) In short, the lower the ratio, the higher the ground water contribution to a river and the more uniform its flow throughout the year. Rivers having a ratio of 3 or less are generally runnable at all times. The higher the 10%/90% ratio the less likely a river will have sufficient water to be runnable except during periods of very high water.

For some rivers we have listed numbers to call for up-to-date river touring information.

Appendix's A and B are tables that list the difficulty, length, time required, and canoeability (10%/90% ratio) of each run in this book. If you are about to take a trip, but are undecided where to go, you can use those tables to help make your choice. Let's say you are looking for a less than 10 mile long trip on a quietwater river that is likely to be runnable in August. A quick glance at the summary tables will show you which sections qualify. Once you have narrowed down the possible choices, you can read the individual descriptions to select the most appealing run. The index map on the back cover and a state highway map should tell you how to get to the river from your present location. Now all that's left is to load the car, make any last minute preparations, and you can be on your way.

2 Introduction

Whitewater, Quietwater was not just a necessity, it was a labor of love. Five years have gone into the creation of this guide to the finest canoe streams and rivers in Wisconsin, Upper Michigan, and northeastern Minnesota. The waterways we have detailed, described, and mapped have been personally run, noted, and remembered. We have sweated and thrilled to these streams and rivers until we have established a relationship with them. We have found these experiences meaningful and worthy of being shared with others who would like to have similar feelings of happiness and strength, confidence and contact, respect and love. These can all be experienced on a fine day with a good canoe, perfect water conditions, and several friends.

We consider canoeing a body contact sport. Therefore, we have avoided mention of highly polluted waterways unless they are exceptional in other regards. Likewise we have not listed those areas in which motor boating predominates.

Canoeing is a sport of silence and gut energy. We have shared waterways with motor-powered boats, but only when we have had no other choice. We are primarily interested in those waters that are still mainly for canoes only. Wide rivers, lakes, and flowages are not included. For those who are interested in this type of boating, most state highway maps indicate the necessary access points. An almost limitless variety of trips are possible on such waterways with little need for a guidebook to point them out.

There are several other intentional omissions in this book. We have excluded streams that are not generally runnable most of the year unless they are otherwise exceptional.

This area is a river curiser's heaven. We have spent thousands of pleasurable hours touring this area by canoe, kayak, and raft, and yet there are still many fine paddleways we have yet to explore. Unless otherwise noted, every mile of river described in this book has been personally run by us. The other descriptions were compiled from notes generously provided by fellow paddlers and upon whose reliability we can vouch for.

We have attempted to be objective and consistent in our assignment of hazard ratings. All hazards have been rated according to the International Scale of River Difficulty. According to this scheme, rapids and other hazards are rated from grade I, easy, to grade VI, the upper limit of navigability. Navigability and safety are the factors considered. In some instances, the hazard rating depends on the type of equipment used. If a particular stretch of river cannot be characterized properly for all boats, the lower rating is for decked craft (see equipment section) and the higher one for open canoes; for example, I-II indicates grade I for decked boats and grade II for open canoes. We have included a few runs in which one or a few short stretches are appreciably more difficult than most of run. If these hazards can be easily portaged, this is indicated by a grade with a subscript; for example, II_5 is used to denote a grade II run having at least one easily avoidable grade V drop.

Changes in water level may alter any given hazard rating. Rule of thumb: **Most rivers in this area (except most quietwater runs) can be considered to be about one grade higher in difficulty in the spring over their usual summer rating.** Our maps list the usual summer hazard rating except for spring (or high water) only runs. In the latter case, the spring ratings are given, and this is so indicated in the text.

Below is a brief description of grades Q thru VI.

(Grade Q - There are no rapids, although there may be minor riffles. Although this is not actually an ISRD designation, we felt that Q stretches should be identified for all boaters.)

Grade I - Very easy rapids that have small, uniform waves with clear channels. If there are obstacles (i.e., rock gardens) that require maneuvering to avoid, there is little current to interfere or to increase the hazard of a mistake. Grade I rapids should cause no problem for novices in open canoes.

Grade II - These are relatively easy rapids with only intermediate difficulty or with longer, more continuous stretches of easy rapids. Novices with decked craft should have few problems with grade II rapids, which can also be handled by persons of intermediate ability using open canoes.

Grade III - These are difficult rapids with numerous, large, irregular waves. Intricate maneuvering, physical strength, and canoeing know-how are all necessary to get through grade III rapids. We recommend using only decked boats, thereby avoiding all chance of swamping. Some experts are able to run grade III rapids in open boats; however, we recommend against this (see equipment and safety sections).

Grade IV - These are very difficult rapids with very large waves powered by an irregular current. The speed of the water and its force require difficult maneuvering around obstacles. Only experts and fools venture down grade IV rapids, the former with decked boats and great skill and the latter with the grace of God.

Grade V - These are extremely difficult rapids that have long, extensive stretches of rapids with large waves, steep gradients, powerful hydraulics, and souse holes. Needless to say, grade V rapids are restricted, by wisdom and logic, to only experts in decked craft. We have rated all such rapids as mandatory portages.

Grade VI - These are rapids with exceedingly difficult problems. Experts using the best equipment and all the experience in the world still risk their lives when they try to run grade VI rapids. We have rated all such rapids as mandatory portages.

Since we did not feel qualified to rate the very few grade V and grade VI drops that exist on the rivers in this guide book, we have designated these rapids and unnavigable falls as mandatory portages. Respect those designations.

There are places on some rivers where falls cannot be seen or heard until the canoeist is right on top of them and by then it may be too late to react. Those rivers that have falls or unnavigable rapids have been detailed to include various landmarks and river features that anticipate the coming of difficult rapids and ominous falls. When **Whitewater, Quietwater** indicates that scouting is suggested or required, it would be wise to heed the warning. Nothing can ruin what was to be a beautiful run down a good river more than an unfortunate, avoidable accident. Canoeing can be somewhat like skydiving and underwater exploration. Details and cautionary reasoning may be lost in the euphoria of running a fine section of whitewater. Pay attention to our warnings. Don't wind up flotsam and jetsam.

Whitewater, Quietwater is based on the priniciple that there is more to running a river than just getting in a canoe and setting off with book and paddle in hand. Therefore it contains a great deal of practical information about equipment, technique, and safety and a working glossary of canoeing terminology (excluding profanity). We have also included a section on the practical hydrology of river running, that is, what to consider when preparing for a trip.

We have described trips that we consider a reasonable day's run. Only when limited road access has forced us, have we joined extensive quietwater sections with hairy whitewater runs. We have stayed away from the formats of other guide books -- unlimited mapping of rivers through towns, flowages, dams, and unrealistic portages. What you see is what you get, for there is a map to accompany most descriptions, with little page-turning required to read the text and see the map.

Other guide books have used maps that were prepared by state or federal agencies, but we have felt from the beginning that this method sorely limits us as canoeists. We knew that there was only a certain amount of information that we would like to see when planning a trip or running a river. Either too much visual or not enough written information has always been our major problem with other guide books. Roads cut off arbitrarily to fit the text and lack of standard format have made other guide books difficult to use. The eventual result was that we had to compile our own maps from scratch using topographical maps, county maps, our own notes, and aerial photographs.

We also decided that it was essential to present information so the reader can easily find and use it. There is a map index to enable you to locate a specific river. The maps are numbered alphabetically. The points of interest on a map are always numbered from upstream to downstream, usually starting with a put-in and ending with a take-out. A common legend accompanies each map. There is a table of all the rivers listing rivers according to hazard rating, scenery, gradient, watershed area, and length and time of run, as well as a listing of sources for additional information. In this manner rivers can be readily compared. We have attempted to make **Whitewater, Quietwater** one of the most easy to use and informative guides to this area of the United States. With only a state highway map and this book as a guide, the prospective canoeist, kayakist, or rafter should be able to plan an enjoyable and challenging river trip.

The descriptions of the rivers include the locations of nearby campgrounds, both developed and undeveloped, and where known, we have located those campsites that are accessible only from the river itself. In addition, portions of the shoreline that fall into the category of public land -- land owned by the U.S. government, state, county, or township -- are indicated. Furthermore, for each river there is an estimate of the time required for a casual trip, including running, portaging, scouting, and lunch stops. Where possible we have provided names, addresses, and phone numbers which can be used to obtain information concerning water levels, as well as the best levels at which to run the river. For fishermen we have mentioned those sections of rivers and entering creeks that are noted for fishing and the kind of fish you can hope to catch.

Some of the areas we cover are relatively unknown and remote. To some that may be a disadvantage, but we feel **Whitewater, Quietwater** should run the gamut of canoeing experiences. We have included popular stretches of river such as the Wisconsin Dells. But we have also included trips into the boondocks, acknowledging our preference. There is a refreshing feeling in finding a place where one can be truly alone, surrounded by only wilderness. No traffic, no competition, no motors--just the canoe, the paddle, and the quiet world of trees and flowers and deer, of beaver, muskrat, blue herons, bald eagles, brown trout, and clean water. All these are reasons to include the rare areas of solitude.

There is yet another reason why we have included some lesser-known rivers in this book. We hope the inclusion of such rivers, will encourage others to discover what it is like to be in a remote and truly wild area. Unless more people become aware of these unique areas and help join the struggle for their preservation, commercial exploitation is likely to destroy what was once beautiful and alive when left alone. Wilderness is being destroyed at an alarming rate under the guise of progress. We fear that the time is coming when the only way anyone will know about our wild rivers is to read about them. "Grandad, was it really like that, way back when, with all those animals and trees and bears and birds and fish and clean, clear water. What happened? How come they are all gone now? Why didn't you do anything to stop it?" These are questions we would rather not have to answer in our autumn years. In the following section we will consider several proposals for the preservation of our wild rivers through legislation, donation, and common sense.

---

3 Equipment

OPEN CANOES

The traditional open canoe (Figures 1 & 2) comes in a variety of styles and lengths and is constructed from a number of different materials. In choosing a canoe, the basic characteristic to consider is the hull shape, since it determines paddling ease and maneuverability. In general, the greater the ratio of length to width the faster the canoe and the better it will hold its course, but the harder it will be to turn. A 15-foot canoe is primarily suitable for a solo boater with little duffel. A 17-foot canoe is ideal for two people with a small amount of duffel. Longer models are available, but they are not recommended for pleasure cruising on rivers. Long boats are less maneuverable and heavy to portage. These models, however, are fine for lake boating or when a large amount of duffel must be carried. Also, because they are faster, longer models tend to be preferred for racing. Remember that a canoe is primarily intended to carry two persons. A third person, even a child, should not be carried while negotiating any rapids.

Rocker is the curvature of the keel from bow to stern. The greater the rocker the more banana-shaped the boat and the more readily maneuverable it will be. Boats with lots of rocker usually lack a keel. A keel provides tracking, the ability to hold a straight course. A keel is desirable for lake boating where emphasis is on tracking rather than maneuverability. However, the river canoe should have either a shoe-keel or better yet, no keel. A keel reduces the effective draft of a canoe -- a serious drawback in shallow areas -- and currents striking a keel will tend to overturn a boat. Furthermore, boats with keels are harder to turn and consequently less maneuverable, a distinct disadvantage in rapids boating.

The shape of the hull is important. The shape of the hull at the water line should be a smooth curve from bow to stern. Any indentation, or cheek, in this curvature will make the canoe act like a barge when paddled at any appreciable speed.

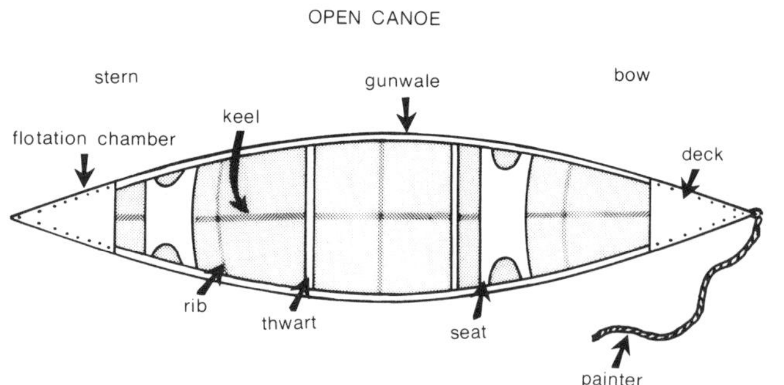

Figure 1.

All canoes should have built-in flotation tanks in both the bow and the stern. If not, flotation at both ends (styrofoam, inner tubes, or air mattresses) should be securely tied in. A kneeling position provides the lowest center of gravity and the greatest control of the canoe. Avoid canoes with low seats that can trap a kneeling canoeist in the event of a tipover. Most experts remove the bow seat of open canoes and replace it with a thwart before use on rapids because there is usually insufficient leg clearance below these seats. Also, the canoeist would do well to invest in a pair of knee pads similar to those used by gardeners.

Most aluminum canoes and some fiberglass models have ribs. Ribs provide strength. In general, the more ribs the stronger the canoe. A light canoe with many ribs may be as strong or stronger than a heavier canoe with few ribs. Thwarts impart lateral strength to a canoe and provide lashing posts for duffel. They are not intended to be used as alternate seats. However, thwarts provide a back rest for the solo boater who kneels in the center or the bow man in a boat from which the front seat has been removed.

Canoes made of aluminum or fiberglass will withstand gravel and rocks much better than the cedar-planked, canvas-covered models. Boats constructed of other materials, while perhaps esthetically pleasing, lack the strength required for river running. For this purpose, it is largely a matter of personal preference as to whether aluminum or fiberglass is best. Fiberglass slides off of rocks more easily than aluminum, which tends to grab onto rocks. This tendency can be partly avoided by waxing the hull of an aluminum canoe with floor or car body wax. Fiberglass is also less noisy and may be preferred by fishermen. A well-designed aluminum canoe is generally stronger than fiberglass models of comparable weight. However, once an aluminum canoe develops a leak, usually at a seam, it is nearly impossible to make a totally leak-proof patch, although tar and pitch can be used with some degree of success. In my early days of running rapids in aluminum canoes with the Hoofers, our canoe fleet was commonly referred to as the "tar babies" for obvious reasons. While fiberglass canoes of comparable weight are more easily damaged than aluminum models, they are also more easily repaired both on the river (with grey tape) and off the river (with a permanent fiberglass patch).

An open canoe provides a large number of sitting and kneeling positions, thus allowing greater comfort on longer trips. Because it is undecked, an open canoe can easily accommodate fishing and camping gear. Although it is advisable to tie in duffel on extended quietwater trips, it is best, when running rapids, to either portage the duffel or leave it loose in the canoe. A capsized canoe full of tied-in duffel is nearly impossible to salvage in a rapids.

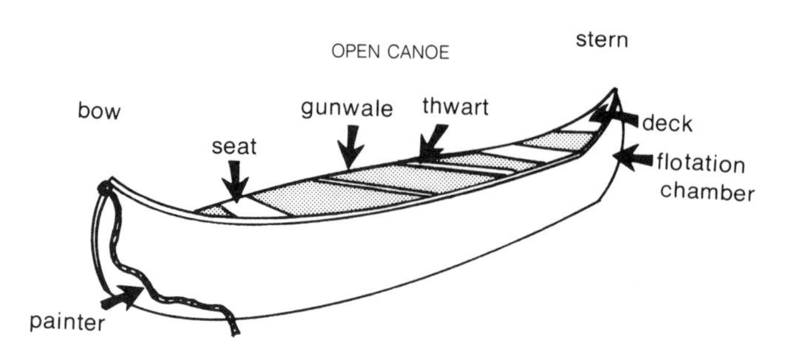

Figure 2.

Duffel encased in waterproof units (plastic litter bags enclosed in duffel bags) floats free following capsize and can either be picked up immediately by other members of the party, or if it floats into an eddy, can be picked up later.

All canoes should be equipped with a painter which is useful in rescue. However, when not in use painters should be tied in so there are no loose ends that could entangle a dunker in turbulent water.

DECKED BOATS

One- and Two-man Canoes (C-1 and C-2)

For the purposes of this guide, a decked canoe is not an open canoe which has been modified to include a temporary deck, but rather is a specially designed fiberglass canoe suitable

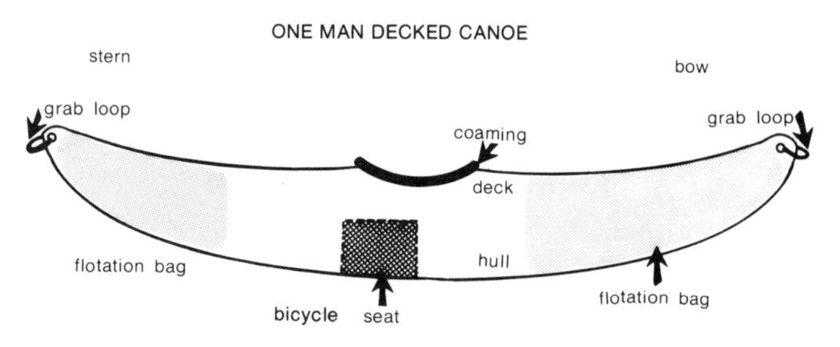

Figure 3.

for use on whitewater. Sometimes referred to as "not a kayak," the decked or whitewater canoe exists in two versions. The one-man canoe (C-1) is about 13 feet long and contains a single cockpit (Figure 3). The two-man canoe (C-2) is about 15 feet long and may contain two or three cockpits (Figure 4). The center cockpit

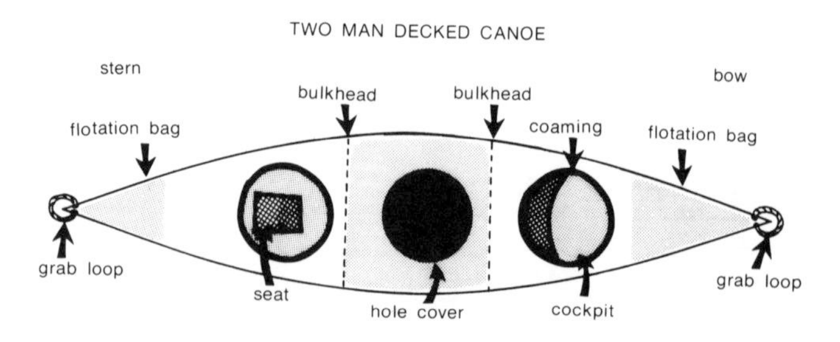

Figure 4.

of the three-holed C-2 may be used for solo paddling or for storage of duffel. Aside from the permanent deck, the canoe is characterized by a high degree of rocker and the absence of a keel. A single-bladed paddle is used to propel this craft. The hull is designed for maximum maneuverability. Less emphasis is placed upon its ability to hold a straight course or its static stability (stability on quietwater). The bilges are much more rounded than those found in the open canoe. This feature makes the decked canoe more unstable in quietwater and yet much less likely to tip in turbulent water, meaning it has greater dynamic stability.

Whitewater canoes are made of fiberglass, which makes repair a very simple matter (a technique all too soon learned by all whitewater boaters). Decked fiberglass boats are much stronger

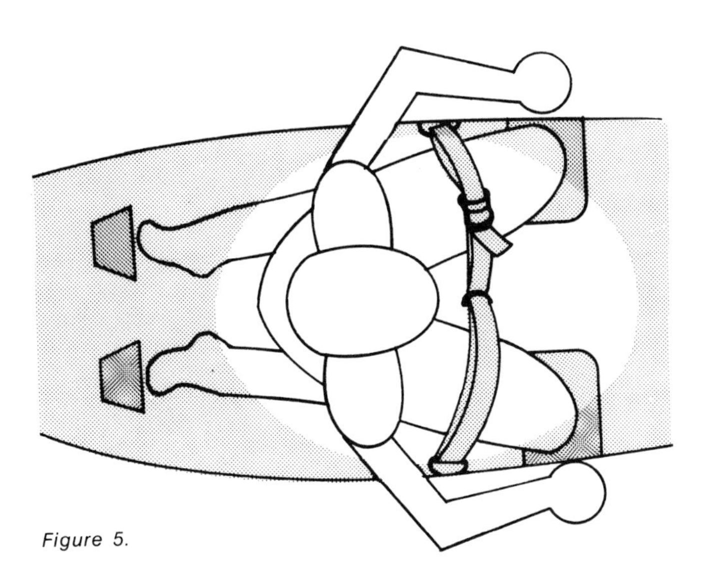

Figure 5.

than open fiberglass boats since the cross section is oval, which adds rigidity. Fiberglass lends itself to home construction, giving a boater the opportunity to build his own canoe or kayak. Fiberglass construction facilitates design changes and permits a boater to customize his boat. The cockpit has a rim or coaming which permits a nearly water-tight seal between the deck and the spray skirt.

The seating arrangement permits little flexibility. The canoeist kneels with the toes pushing against toe blocks (Figure 5). Knee straps which pass over the boater's thighs are attached to the hull and bilges of the canoe. These "braces" enable the canoeist to use his legs and hips to exert positive control over the lean of the boat. During capsize, the boater need only straighten his legs and the knee straps slip off easily, permitting rapid exit. To succeed in an Eskimo roll, the "inverted canoeist" must remain in the bracing. If he fails to remain in a crouched position, he will instantaneously fall out of the bracing and out of the canoe itself. Such a person is referred to as a dunker. Knee pads are permanently installed. The seat, or more properly, the buttocks-rest, may consist of canvas attached to the coaming (bow of Figure 4), a bicycle-type stump resting on the hull (stern of Figure 4), or a hinged thwart attached to the bilge. Most fixed thwart seats are to be avoided unless they provide sufficient leg clearance for a rapid exit in case of a tipover.

Kayaks

The best kayaks (Figure 6) are constructed of fiberglass or high-impact plastic. We do not consider boats made of collapsible materials suitable for whitewater. A kayak (Figure 6) is about 13 feet long and 2 feet wide, slightly narrower than the C-1 (Figure 3). The hull is shaped with rounded bilges, a pronounced rocker, and no keel, making handling easy in turbulent water with heavy currents.

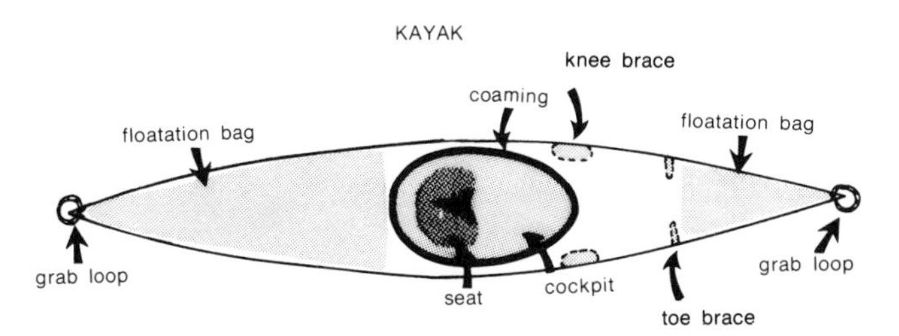

Figure 6.

To compensate for a narrow beam and its inherent instability, the kayakist sits low in the boat with his legs extended forward. The feet rest against toe blocks or a foot bar. The knees press against braces attached to the deck. This arrangement permits the kayakist to control the lean of the boat with his hips and legs. A spray skirt is worn to keep out the water and a double-bladed paddle is used. The double-bladed paddle provides added advantages. First a paddle blade is always immediately available to brace against a possible tipover to either side. Secondly, a double bladed paddle requires little effort to hold a straight line while backpaddling.

Although the kayak is the most unforgiving of miscalculations, it is also the easiest boat to Eskimo roll. Early mastery of the Eskimo roll (even before learning how to paddle) adds immeasurably to the development of good kayak technique and to the fullest pleasure of kayaking.

A kayak should be equipped with maximal flotation extending from the stern to just behind the cockpit and from the bow to the kayakist's feet. Specially designed form-fitting vinyl air bags are available commercially (see sources). Because of its small size, the kayak has very little duffel-carrying capacity. Furthermore, the kayakist has the disadvantage of sitting low in the boat which reduces visibility, thus making it more difficult to "read the water" than from a canoe. However, the ease of backpaddling more than compensates for this disadvantage.

Maximal Flotation

To equip a boat with maximal flotation is to prevent a capsized boat from filling with water. Thus flotation provides the least submerged surface for the current and obstructions to strike or pin the craft. Water in a boat without flotation makes it more dangerous since the dunker can be pinned by the boat against obstacles as it broadsides in heavy current. A boat full of water with the open face upstream to a moderate current presents a force of up to 8,000 pounds against any object (hopefully not the dunker) pinned between it and a rock. Rescue is difficult, and potential damage to dunker and boat are great.

Maximal flotation can be provided by large form-fitting vinyl air sacks that fill all of the boat except the cockpits. Such bags are now available commercially (see sources). Some newer bags permit gear to be stored inside the air bag, which can then be sealed and inflated. Inner tubes and air mattresses do not fill all available space and are easily dislodged. Their use is therefore discouraged. For three-holed C-2's, bulkheads can be placed between the first and third cockpits (Figure 4) in lieu of an air bag. Thus when the boat is used by two people, the middle cockpit (which must be covered with a hole cover) is filled with air. If the canoe is being soloed then the two end cockpits are covered and become air chambers. A pliable synthetic waterproof material called "Ethafoam" (see sources) makes suitable bulkheads when installed with resin or contact cement. This material is also satisfactory for making knee pads and bicycle-type seats.

RAFTS

The use of inflated rafts constitutes an entirely different approach to river travel. Minimal skill is required to use this type of craft. Hence, rafts are suitable for those who do not wish to take the time and trouble to acquire canoe or kayak skills, or for those whose main interest is a leisure float-fishing trip. A raft is also a good family craft since it permits the transportation of non-paddlers.

For most of the rivers described in this guide book, the optimal size for a raft is approximately 6 x 9 feet with an outer tube section that is approximately 16 inches across. Larger rafts do not permit easy passage through the relatively narrow spaces between boulders in rapids, and smaller rafts are too easily swamped by standing waves. A raft full of water is nearly as unwieldly as a swamped open canoe.

Although less skill is required to run a raft on a river, there are certain precautions that must be taken. All rafters should WEAR lifejackets when negotiating rapids. Even though a fully inflated raft is essentially unsinkable, this is of little solace to the person who falls out and becomes separated from the raft. Rafters should not sit on the upstream tube of a raft in heavy rapids. A person so positioned can be flipped off backwards even if there is no tipover. Also as with any swamped craft in a current, a rafter should never hang onto the downstream side. We know of at least one person whose back was broken when a swamped raft slammed her into a rock while she was holding onto the downstream side. We know of many more fatalities involving rafts than we do of those involving canoes or kayaks. Falls and rapids with large standing waves, souse holes, and backrollers are particularly hazardous for rafters.

A falls is more likely to be a problem primarily because even though the rafter recognizes the hazard and attempts to avoid it, the reduced maneuverability of the raft may not allow enough time to pull out and safely get to shore. Souse holes and backrollers (see technique section) are an even greater risk to life and limb largely because most rafters don't recognize these hazards as dangerous and therefore rarely attempt to avoid them. This can be quite dangerous as rafts can be violently overturned. Also, rafts are prone to being held by these hydraulic phenomenon, sometimes for hours. Needless to say, all large souse holes and backrollers should be avoided at all times.

DECKED VERSUS UNDECKED?

While we do not wish to argue the relative advantages and disadvantages of kayak versus decked canoe, the distinctions between an essentially quietwater craft and a whitewater craft are worthy of comparison. Perhaps the best way to illustrate the superiority of an open canoe on quietwater would be to relate a kind of Aesopian story, not unlike "The Tortoise and the Hare." It concerns our first encounter with the Namekagon back in the mid-1960's.

This was the time of the early attempts to pass the National Wild and Scenic Rivers Act. Wisconsin's Senator Gaylord Nelson was one of the prime movers of the legislation, and he was scheduled to be a guest of honor at a Namekagon canoe-in to promote the National Wild and Scenic Rivers Act. There were to be more than 100 of us interested canoeists making the trip from Cable to Hayward. A bunch of Hoofers decided to make the trip, but we showed up after everybody else had started downriver.

Confident in our ability to run the river quickly, we took to our decked whitewater canoes ready to make up for lost time in the rapids. We were sure that the slowpokes downstream, being typical novices, were just hanging up on rocks. Our early run was proving us right. We passed quickly through the first easy rapids, overtaking a number of inexperienced paddlers who were hopelessly hung up in the shallow, grade I rapids. The quietwater sections would take some work, but we were sure doing well with the rapids.

It wouldn't be entirely accurate, but you might say we were a little cocky. Then came the two little old ladies in tennis shoes, probably remembering the old days on Wingra. When we first came up to them, they were stalled in some shallows and passing the time by passing a jug. Well, this certainly was one way of running the Namekagon, but not our way, and we shot by the old canoe queens. Senator Nelson was just a little farther ahead, and our decked canoes were going to make the day.

There was one stretch of relatively slow quietwater. We were doing OK. Then out of the corners of our sweaty eyes we caught sight of the two little old ladies just paddling right by us. There might have been a slightly obscene wave of the hand, but they were obviously having a grand old time.

Photo 1. A tipover at Meyer's Falls on the Pine.

Moral: If you want to beat little old ladies, or just time on the Namekagon, don't run the river in decked whitewater canoes. Largely because these boats have more rocker, they are slower and harder to keep going in a straight line than open canoes. The possible sitting or kneeling positions are severely limited, and appreciable stamina is required to endure the discomfort experienced whenever these boats are paddled for long distances at a time. Furthermore, it is difficult to carry a water bottle so that it is readily accessible, let alone other substitute liquids. In addition, whitewater boats don't usually have sufficient room for all of the essentials required for a pleasant camping or fishing trip.

Photo 2. Requiescat in pace.

When it comes to rapids however, pictures speak louder than words. Photo 1 shows a near disastrous encounter which occurred at Meyer's Falls, a grade III drop on the Pine River. In this potentially dangerous situation, the dunker is downstream of a swamped open canoe that is broadside to the current. The dunker could easily have been pinned against a rock. An open canoe in even a moderate current can exert as much as 8,000 pounds of force on any object pinned between it and a rock. Fortunately in this instance both boater and boat escaped unharmed, but others have been less lucky. Photo 2 shows the last earthly remains of an aluminum canoe fished out of Shotgun Rapids in the summer when this rapids rates grade II. The unfortunate owner (or rather fortunate, for we found no blood) had to abandon the canoe in the river because it was tightly wrapped around a rock. It took our party of 10 strong, healthy boaters an hour to remove this very dangerous obstacle from the river. A decked canoe equipped with maximal flotation will float high in the water and is not likely to become pinned against a rock as illustrated in Photo 3. This photo was taken at Ralton's Rips Rapids, a grade II rapids on the Peshtigo.

Photo 3. A decked canoe with maximum flotation will ride high.

Photo 4. A kayakist in Horserace Rapids on the Peshtigo, grade IV.

Decking prevents water from swamping a boat. Photo 4 shows a kayakist under full control. This photo was taken in high water at Horserace Rapids on the Peshtigo River. This grade IV water is recommended only for experts equipped with decked boats.

PADDLES

Canoe

For quietwater a sturdy but lightweight paddle is best. Pine or basswood paddles are satisfactory, but they do not hold up as well as paddles made of ash. For rapids canoeing you must have a sturdy paddle, even if it is heavy. It must not break when subjected to great stress, such as that required for draw strokes and paddle braces (see technique section). Wooden paddles made of ash and with an 8 to 9 inch blade are satisfactory, but heavy. When selecting a wooden paddle, look for even grain in the wood and a not-too-narrow shaft near the throat (see Figure 7), since that's where most paddles break. Proper length is about chin height. However, most rapids boaters prefer a somewhat shorter paddle for use with decked whitewater boats. A short paddle facilitates fast acceleration.

Paddles with a shaft made of hollow aluminum covered with fiberglass tape and with blades of fiberglass or high-impact plastic combine light weight with strength. These paddles are superb for most types of canoeing, although the shaft may bend during a pry stroke made in any canoe having a sharp gunwale edge. Wood laminate paddles that alternate spruce or pine with mahogany or red cedar also combine strength with light weight and are equally suitable for most types of canoeing. Both of these types of paddles, however, are rather expensive.

Kayak

A feathered (blades at right angles to one another) double-bladed paddle is best. Normal length is 78 to 84 inches depending on your arm span. Paddles with an aluminum shaft and fiberglass blades, while expensive, are superior. Most wooden paddles are either too heavy or don't hold up very well. Either the shaft breaks or the blades crack or are splintered off. Some wood laminates which have recently appeared on the market appear to be satisfactory.

A kayak paddle may have flat blades, like a canoe paddle, or the blades may be curved (Figure 8). The flat-bladed paddle is somewhat easier for the novice to use. Many experts, however, prefer a curved-bladed paddle since it permits greater speed and control. These paddles require a bit more dexterity to handle properly. Since the blades are feathered, one hand grips the paddle firmly in a fixed position on the shaft for one stroke, and then for the next stroke the paddle is rotated a quarter turn in the loosely gripped palm of the other hand. When selecting a curved-

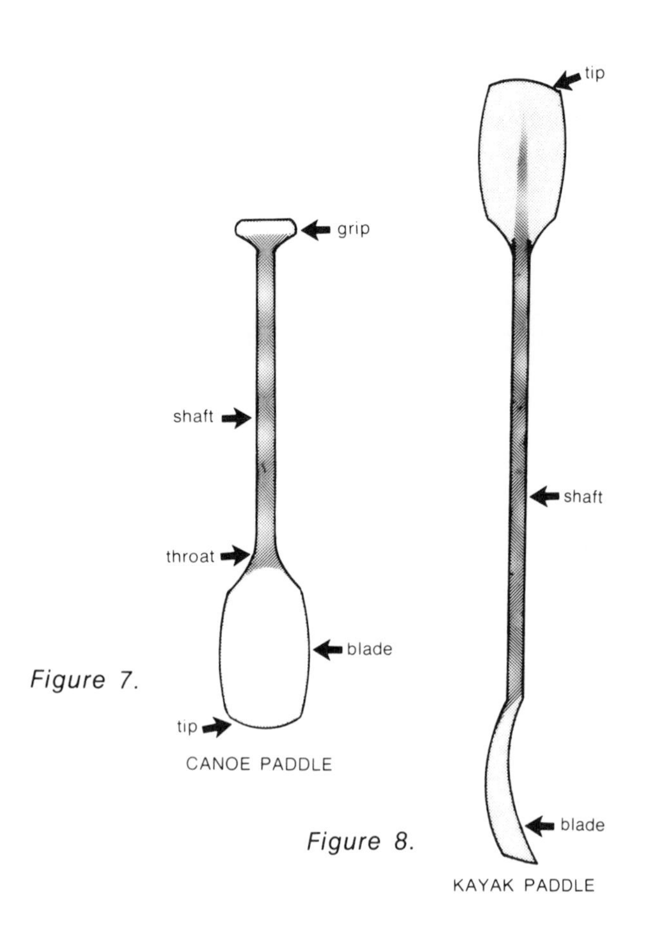

Figure 7.

Figure 8.

Kayak

A feathered (blades at right angles to one another) double-bladed paddle is best. Normal length is 78 to 84 inches depending on your arm span. Paddles with an aluminum shaft and fiberglass blades, while expensive, are superior. Most wooden paddles are either too heavy or don't hold up very well. Either the shaft breaks or the blades crack or are splintered off. Some wood laminates which have recently appeared on the market appear to be satisfactory.

A kayak paddle may have flat blades, like a canoe paddle, or the blades may be curved (Figure 8). The flat-bladed paddle is somewhat easier for the novice to use. Many experts, however, prefer a curved-bladed paddle since it permits greater speed and control. These paddles require a bit more dexterity to handle properly. Since the blades are feathered, one hand grips the paddle firmly in a fixed position on the shaft for one stroke, and then for the next stroke the paddle is rotated a quarter turn in the loosely gripped palm of the other hand. When selecting a curved-bladed paddle you must specify whether you hold the paddle with the grip fixed firmly with the left or right hand.

Some kayak paddles are detachable into sections. These paddles are inherently weak at the connecting joint and tend to twist or come apart. These paddles are only suitable as spares.

Spare

A spare paddle may be attached to a boat in several ways so as to be readily available in an emergency. It can be attached to the thwart of an open canoe with tape that is slightly adhesive or with a quick release knot. With decked boats, the spare can be inserted into loops of elastic shock cord that has been run through holes drilled in the boat deck (Photo 6). Other systems can be devised to permit quick access.

Paddles that are securely taped or tied in a boat are seldom available in an emergency. This point was driven home to yours truly some years back. I once lost a paddle just above the approach to First Drop on the Peshtigo, a solid grade III rapids. I was paddling an open canoe at the time with the spare paddle securely tied in. With some gymnastics and lots of luck, it was an eventful, but successful run. Paddles stuffed under the air bags of a decked boat are also useless in emergency situations.

LIFEJACKETS

Lifejackets are the seat belts of the waterways. When and only when they are worn they are an invaluable safety aid to the whitewater boater. "Lifejacket" is actually a misnomer. In reality a lifejacket is only a flotation aid and is no substitute for boating and swimming ability. On quietwater, common sense dictates that nonswimmers and weak swimmers should wear a lifejacket at all times. **We recommend that all boaters and rafters wear a lifejacket while negotiating all rapids.**

The U.S. Coast Guard has three categories of life-saving devices. Those categorized as "life preservers" are intended for ocean-going vessels where rescue may be a long time in coming. The minimum buoyancy is 33 lbs. and there are other rigid design specifications. This type of lifejacket is generally too bulky for the river boater. A second U.S.C.G. category is "special purpose device." This category includes ring buoys and seat cushions and need not concern us. The third category, "buoyant vests," more appropriately applies to the river rat. The minimum buoyancy is 15 1/2 lbs. At least 70% to 75% of the buoyant material must be in front to assure an upward turning moment.

The canoeist, kayakist, and rafter require a lifejacket that has some unique characteristics. The primary requirement is that the flotation be sufficient to bring the dunker swiftly to the surface following tipover, but not so bulky that it impairs paddling or swimming movement. The paddler must be able to see behind him without hindrance to arm movement. Occasionally a lifejacket is worn for up to 10 hours of continuous paddling; therefore it must be comfortable and not chafe. The flotation should have a positive righting moment that will tend to float the unconscious dunker face up. A snug form-fitting vest is best for the rapids boater. These vests do not entrap water. Consequently swimming and Eskimo rolling are readily accomplished while these safety aids are worn. Lifejackets should have a minimum number of straps which can catch on obstacles such as submerged rocks and tree limbs. Zippers work best, but buckles of the quick-release type are acceptable if all the loose ends are securely tucked away. Crotch straps are a nuisance, and side straps or a tight cut under the armpits are preferred to keep the vest properly in place. The lifejacket should also be lightweight and brightly colored.

Buoyancy is achieved by a number of materials. Kapok is commonly used as filler material. However, kapok sealed in vinyl bags is generally not acceptable to the canoeist. Jackets made with this material are usually rather bulky and although the dry weight of kapok filler is usually 2 to 3 lbs., once the vinyl coating has ruptured and the kapok gets soaked the weight often soars to 7 to 10 lbs. Buoyancy is not impaired, but under these circumstances the jackets become unbearably heavy. Unicellular plastic foam cut into small panels forms a close-fitting vest which serves the needs of the canoeist admirably. Some lifejackets achieve buoyancy through 100 to 300 air cells sealed in vinyl tubing. These vests are lightweight and comfortable. However, care must be taken to avoid puncturing the air cells; otherwise the jacket will not be fully functional. This type of flotation has also been known to lose air from the cells after as little as one season of use.

As of October 1, 1975, all canoes and kayaks, irregardless of length, and all other boats less than 16 feet in length, must carry one U.S. Coast Guard-approved Type I, II, III, or IV personal flotation device for each person on board while traveling on any federal waters. Boats 16 feet or longer (except canoes and kayaks) must carry at least one additional Type IV (throwable) personal flotation device per boat. The above requirements are now in effect for **all** waterways under the jurisdiction of the State of Wisconsin. Other states are adopting similar requirements.

PROTECTIVE AIDS: THE HEAD AND FEET

Protective headgear(Photo 6) is an essential piece of whitewater equipment. If you are paddling through turbulent water, the possibility of a bump on the head cannot be ignored. Even a slight bump on the unprotected head can knock the dunker unconscious. A suitable helmet should be rounded, like a football helmet. A rimmed or visored helmet can be hazardous in turbulent water because a current can pull on it. Helmets with a collapsible nonresilient lining are the only ones that provide adequate protection to a dunker who must survive impacts of from 10 to 15 miles mph. Helmets designed for surfing or rock climbing provide good protection and are lightweight and comfortable. Hockey helmets provide inadequate protection against impact. A motorcycle helmet should never be worn. Your helmet must allow you to hear upcomming rapids and falls.

The whitewater boater should never go without some sort of foot protection, whether it is tennis shoes, river sandals, or neoprene footwear. The river boater never knows for sure when, where or how he will get out of his boat. Tipovers are generally unplanned. Usually it is painful, if not impossible, to walk along the riverbed or shoreline in bare feet. Furthermore, a dunker can swim a rapids most safely if he assumes a feet-first position. Needless to say, it is more pleasant to ward off rocks with feet that are protected by footwear.

WET SUITS

The properly equipped cold water boater always wears a neoprene wet suit until the water temperature is up to at least 50° (see Photo 5). Ice water can sap the dunker's strength very quickly and may make him immobile so that he will be unable to hold onto a rescue line or swim. The initial shock of immersion in cold water invariably makes him unable to breathe for a while. Cold water saps body heat and aggravates the already tiring experience of being tossed about by turbulent water. Mental confusion often follows. Since even an excellent lifejacket does not always keep the dunker's head above water in waves and turbulence, a drowning is possible. People who scoff at such safety precautions should select a moderately difficult short stretch of rapids with a quiet section following, station rescue personnel below, try to swim through wearing a lifejacket when the water temperature is below 50°, and then decide if they'd care to repeat the experience.

A wet suit keeps the dunker warm because a thin layer of water inside the suit is warmed by the body and helps insulate the paddler from the otherwise unbearably cold water. Gloves, boots, and a hood can also be worn. A wet suit is made of neoprene and is shaped to fit an individual's body contours so as to produce a snug fit. However, the wet suit must fit loosely enough at the shoulders for freedom of arm movement. A wet suit made of eighth-inch neoprene provides reasonable protection from the cold and is sufficiently flexible that the paddler does not become unduly fatigued. A quarter-inch neoprene suit is much warmer, but it is too thick for comfortable paddling.

Neoprene wet suits also provide supplemental flotation, but the amount is never sufficient to replace the lifejacket. A neoprene jacket with long sleeves (1/8") will provide about 3 1/2 lbs. buoyancy; a vest (1/8") about 2 lbs.; trousers (1/8") about 3 lbs. Trapped air in a full wet suit usually raises the buoyancy to about 7 to 10 lbs., depending on sleeve length. For more information on the hazards of cold water see the spring boating section in the technique section.

Photo 5. Wet suits recommended! Bad River downstream of Cooper Falls State Park.

WELL EQUIPPED BOATERS

Photograph 6 shows a properly equipped two-man decked canoe. Note that the boaters are wearing protective helmets (1) and lifejackets of the kapok filled (2) and air cell type (6). The boat has spare paddle (3) attached with quick-releasing elastic straps. A hole cover (4) seals the unused cockpit. The boaters are wearing spray skirts (5) and are using paddles of the aluminum-shafted, fiberglass-bladed variety (7). Also note that the boater in the bow is doing an excellent high brace. This boat is also equipped with grab loops (8) to facilitate rescue in the event of a tipover. This picture was taken at Ralton's Rips, a grade II rapids on the Peshtigo River.

Photo 6. Well-equipped rapids boaters.

5 Technique

PRACTICAL HYDROLOGY

We have included a discussion of practical hydrology in this section because proper boating technique requires working with the river current rather than fighting it. It is essential to understand the factors influencing water flow to have a successful, or perhaps equally important, to have an enjoyable run on whitewater. Factors required for the formation of rapids are also included to facillitate the detection of rapids and falls even though such hazards are usually more appropriately recognized by direct audible and visual warnings. When traveling down an unknown river, even the quietwater boater must know how to spot rapids and falls so that he can avoid them as required.

Water Cycle

The influence of the environment on stream flow is best understood by considering the movement of water from the atmosphere to the earth and back to the atmosphere again. This is referred to as the water cycle.

Water that has fallen on a watershed travels over three routes. Part runs over the surface of the land directly into rivers as **surface runoff;** part is retained by the soil where it is absorbed by plants or lost by evaporation **(evaportranspiration);** and part seeps down into the ground and moves laterally as ground water until it is discharged into springs, rivers, and swamps as **ground-water runoff.** In general, the greater the amount of water that follows the subsurface route as ground-water runoff the higher the flow during dry periods and the more likely the stream will have sufficient water to permit canoeing most of the year.

In this region the average annual amount of precipitation is approximately 26 to 32 inches per year. Usually 1 to 2 inches per month fall as snow in the winter and 2 to 4 inches per month fall as rain during the rest of the year. Evapotranspiration usually ranges from 14 to 20 inches per year. The remaining 6 to 12 inches are divided between surface runoff and ground-water runoff, which varies considerably from river to river.

Seasonal Variations in Canoeability

Variations in discharge (water flow rate) on undammed rivers are caused by variations in precipitation, snow melt, and evapotranspiration. Highest discharge normally occurs during the spring snowmelt. The maximum discharge depends on the water content of the snow, amount of frost in the ground at the time of snowmelt, rate of melting, permeability of the soil, ground cover and slope of the land surface. Discharge usually declines during the late spring, reaching a minimum during the summer months when growing plants use up (transpire) large quantities of water. This is also the period when relatively high temperatures cause increased evaporation. Also, since the ground is not saturated, rain water sinks in rather than runs-off. Killing frosts in the fall reduce transpiration and usually cause a slight increase in discharge. Much of the winter precipitation is in the form of snow and does not reach the river until the following spring. Thus, discharge declines during the winter months. Unusually intense rains at any season may cause high rates of discharge.

Seasonal variations in discharge are common to all rivers in this area, but the magnitude of the variations ranges widely. These variations generally result from differences in the relative amounts of water derived from surface runoff and ground-water discharge. The quality of the watershed (drainage area) rather than its size determines the ground-water surface-water relationship, and this in turn determines whether a river will be runnable at most times of the year.

Aspects of the watershed such as permeability of the soil, topography of the land, and amount and type of vegetative cover determine the relationship among surface runoff, ground-water runoff, and evapotranspiration. Air temperature directly influences the rates of evaporation and transpiration, which are highest in the summer. Higher rates of evapotranspiration are found in areas with relatively impermeable soils such as clay or in areas where there is little soil above the bedrock. Highly packed soils hold greater amounts of moisture by capillary action than do the more porous sandy soils and consequently more water is available for evaporation and transpiration.

The nature of the glacial deposits and the type of soil in a watershed affect the rates of infiltration which in turn determine the route by which precipitation reaches a river. In areas of silt, clay, or exposed bedrock, there is little permeability and most of the water travels to the river as surface flow. On the other hand, in regions composed chiefly of sand, gravel, and other porous materials, much of the water travels as ground-water runoff.

Surface runoff reaches the river a short time after rains (or snowmelt), usually within a few hours. After reaching the peak discharge, surface runoff declines rapidly. Ground-water runoff is slower to reach the stream and slower to decline after reaching a peak. It is ground-water runoff that keeps the river flowing during rainless periods. In general, the greater the component of ground-water discharge the more uniform the flow.

The amount of water which enters the river via surface or ground-water discharge is reflected by flow durations. Flow durations indicate the percentage of the time that a specified discharge is equalled or exceeded. By relating the discharge that is equaled or exceeded 10 per cent of the time to the 90 per cent figure, an estimate can be made of the contribution of ground-water discharge to total river flow. For example, the Bois Brule is typical of a river with a very high component of ground-water discharge. The total discharge of the Bois Brule is at least 115 cfs 90 per cent of the time and exceeds 260 cfs 10 per cent of the time. The ratio of 10 per cent/90 per cent is 2.2. As a rule of thumb, a river with a 10 per cent/90 per cent ratio of 3 or less has a high percentage of ground-water discharge and is runnable most of the year. By way of contrast, the Jump River, as its name implies, is a very flashy stream. The discharge is mostly surface water and the

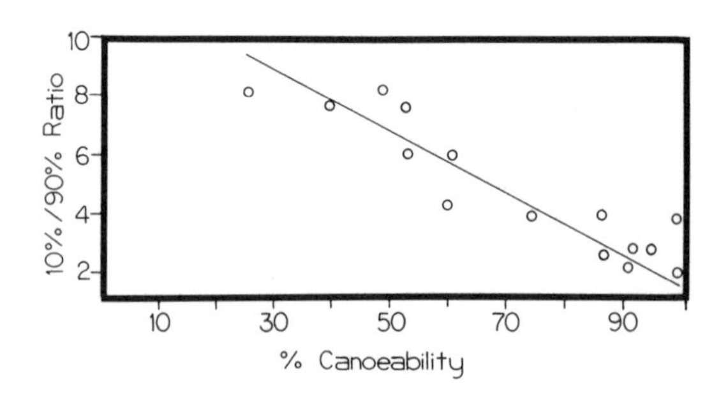

Figure 1.

runoff is quite rapid. The discharge is at least 40 cfs 90 per cent of the time and 1,500 cfs 10 per cent of the time. The ratio is 38. If the ratio exceeds 10-15, the river is not runnable except during very brief periods during spring runoff or after prolonged periods of heavy rains. Figure 1 shows the relationship of the 10 per cent/90 per cent flow duration ratio to canoeability. Canoeability is the percentage of the time during the canoeing season that the river flow equals or exceeds what we consider to be the minimum for a pleasurable run. In this area the canoeing season extends from April through September. The flow duration-canoeability relationship is an unreliable indicator of canoeability on rivers having higher ratios. For the most part such rivers are usually not runnable. It is perhaps more than mere coincidence that rivers with a low ratio are cooler, have a more stable flow, and usually have abundant populations of trout.

Formation of Rapids

Rivers differ from man-made channels of uniform cross section. The width, depth, gradient, and composition of the riverbed varies (sometimes dramatically) at different sites along the river. Rapids, falls, and other potential hazards may result from such variations even on rivers that consist essentially of quietwater. A practical knowledge of river hydrology will enable you to anticipate hazards likely to be encountered in river running. Hopefully this information will enable you to prepare accordingly.

There are three major components of stream flow--discharge, velocity, and stage. **Discharge** is the volume of water moving past a given cross section of river per unit of time. In this book the units used to express this measurement are cubic feet per second (cfs). **Velocity** (river current) is the speed of water movement (in feet per second). **Stage** is the height (in feet) of the water level above an arbitrary zero point. All of these components are interrelated; when water levels are up, so are the volume and speed of flow.

The most practical method used to determine discharge is to measure the stage of the river and to use a conversion table that relates stage to discharge. This relationship depends on the configuration of the stream bed and differs for each river and for each section of the same river. In this book we have provided a conversion table relating discharge to stage under "water conditions" for each river section for which we have this information.

The velocity or current speed at a given discharge depends on two factors--gradient and cross-sectional area of the stream bed. The profile or **gradient** of a river refers to its fall in feet per mile from source to mouth or within given sections. The steepness of gradient influences canoeability chiefly by modifying the velocity of stream flow. Where the gradient of a river increases, the velocity of stream flow increases.

Normally the profile of a river is relatively steep in the headwaters and relatively flat near the mouth. However, this general relation is modified within any given section by the geology of the river basin. Where topography permits, local steepening of gradient occurs where rivers cut across exposed bedrock or beds of stony outwash because these materials are more resistant to erosion than the rest of the riverbed. Beds of dense clay in outwash deposits may also resist erosion and cause a steeper gradient. Gradients of most of the rivers included in this guide book range from 0.5 to 60 feet per mile.

In addition to gradient, the second factor that determines current speed is the cross-sectional area of the river channel. For a given flow rate (discharge), velocity increases when the cross-sectional area of the channel decreases. This occurs either when the river becomes shallower or when the river narrows. The increased velocity that results from a shallow or narrow channel frequently results in riffles or rapids. In regions where the channel is deep, stream bed materials are of little significance to the boater. However, rapids are usually found where the river passes over shallow regions of erosion-resistant outwash or exposed bedrock. Riverbeds having large boulders with water moving at a relatively high velocity produce rapids with a high hazard rating.

Variations in current speed are likely within any given channel. Current speed is influenced by obstacles such as rocks and vegetation found along the river-bed which slow down the flow rate. Therefore the current is usually fastest in the middle and slowest along the sides and bottom. Figure 2 shows the cross-sectional view of a hypothetical river channel. The current ranges from more than 4 feet per second in the upper center of the channel to less than 1 foot per second near the bottom and sides of the channel.

Another generalization that frequently holds is that the current is usually greatest at the outside of turns. Fast current tends to scour out the outer channel, so that's usually where the water is deepest. The significance of this phenomenon will be discussed more fully in Chapter 6 (sieve-like obstacles).

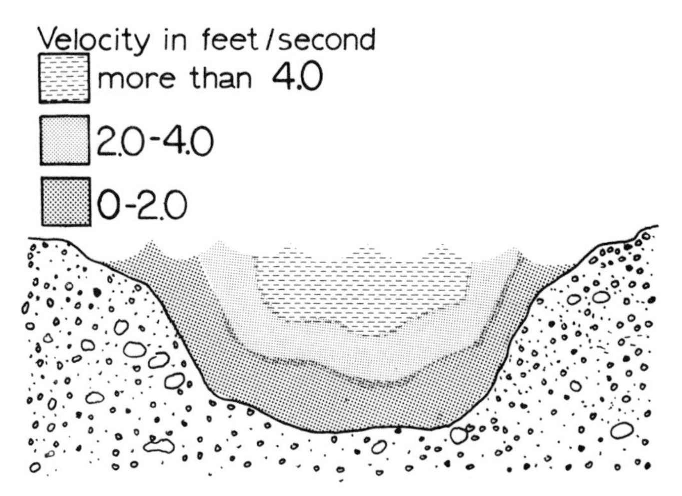

Figure 2.

RIVER READING AND HYDRAULICS

Chutes

River reading involves recognition of obstacles and evaluation of the water flow so that an appropriate course can be chosen. A good route through obstructions in a rapids is called a **chute.**

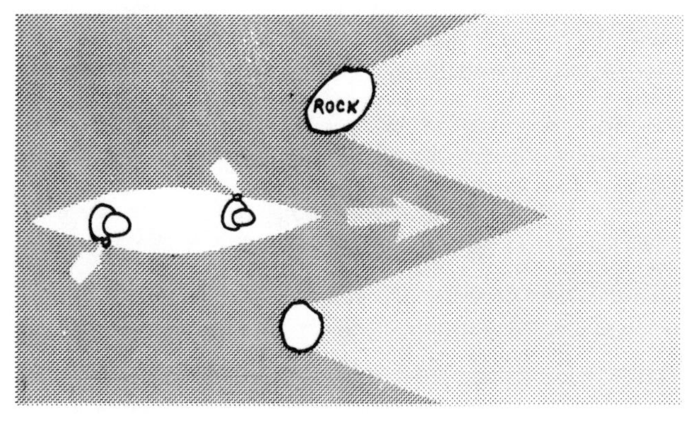

Figure 3.

Photo 1. Cedar Rapids on the Flambeau - grade II.

Chutes are usually characterized by smooth water in which surface riffles suggest the letter "V" with the point downstream (Figure 3). Conversely, surface ripples that suggest the letter "V" with the point upstream indicate a rock at the point of the "V" and must be avoided. In Figure 3, the dark area represents smooth water and the light area represents riffles or other turbulence. Can you spot the two obvious chutes in Photo 1? The canoe is in one chute (making the chute less obvious) and an imaginary line that connects arrows 1, 2, and 3 illustrates a second navigable channel. The canoeists have chosen a good route. The second chute is equally satisfactory because it avoids the rocks that are downstream of arrows 5 and 6 and the ones that are upstream of arrows 7 and 8. Notice the downstream "V" at arrow 2 and the upstream "V's" at arrows 7 and 8.

Eddies

Rocks in the river bed, unless they protrude above the surface, are recognized by the nature of the turbulence downstream. Figures 4 and 5 show a hypothetical river profile at low and high discharge, respectively. The turbulence (hydraulics) below the rocks is related to the gradient, discharge, and size of the obstruction.

During periods of low discharge (Figure 4), both of the large rocks (4-B and 4-C) protrude well above the surface and are readily obvious from upstream. Eddies occur below both of these obstructions. An **eddy** is an area immediately downstream of an obstacle in a river where the current is relatively calm or may actually flow upstream. The eddy results from water filling the void behind the obstacle as the main current flows past (Figure 6). Eddies provide a place for rest stops in the midst of even the most difficult rapids. The significance of eddies and techniques used to enter and leave them will be discussed later in this section. In Figure 4, discharge is relatively low and the increase in gradient has little effect on the nature of the eddy below rock 4-C compared to the one behind rock 4-B.

Rocks submerged just below the surface of the water (Figure 4-A) can be recognized by a smooth hump that is formed by the fast-moving water as it follows the contour of the rock. This smooth hump of dark water is often followed by white turbulence downstream. Be careful since the turbulence may be several feet downstream of the rock. Such rocks are hard to spot. In slow-moving water, the hump may not show. In commonly paddled areas these rocks can sometimes be identified by their shiny coat of aluminum left by previous boaters.

Souse Holes and Backrollers

Since the gradient is larger, the water flowing over rock 4-D falls a greater distance and produces more turbulence below it than below the similar sized obstacle 4-A. The water flowing over the rock piles up on itself creating small waves. If the water falls steeply enough, the first wave may curl back on itself creating a back wave or **backroller.** Water will also flow around the rock creating an eddy. The combination of eddy and backroller creates the hydraulic known as the **souse hole.** In a souse hole the water enters the depression from all sides--from upstream over the rock, from downstream (backroller), and from the sides (eddy action). At low flows such as depicted in Figure 4-D, the mini-souse hole is merely a mildly turbulent eddy. In Photo 1, arrow 8 shows a mini-souse hole with the smooth hump upstream. The situation at arrow 7 is slightly different. This hydraulic is more properly a mini-backroller formed by the water flowing over the rock at arrow 6 and the rock to the right (in the background) of this one. The difference between a souse hole and a backroller is one of dimensions. A backroller forms below a broad ledge (a natural dam) or a string or rocks as in Photo 1 arrow 7 while a souse hole forms below a narrower obstacle.

At higher flow rates such as depicted in Figure 5, the situation changes considerably. All of the rocks are covered with water. The large rock on the left (5-B) can be recognized by a smooth hump of dark water while the small rock (5-A) is sufficiently submerged that it is of no significance to the boater.

The souse hole shown in 5-C is identical to that depicted in 4-D except that it is larger. Large souse holes such as the one shown in Photo 2 can be hazardous. This team of expert canoeists (Photo 2) is playing in a moderate-sized souse hole. Such holes are potentially very dangerous. Experts and only experts should even approach let alone willingly enter one.

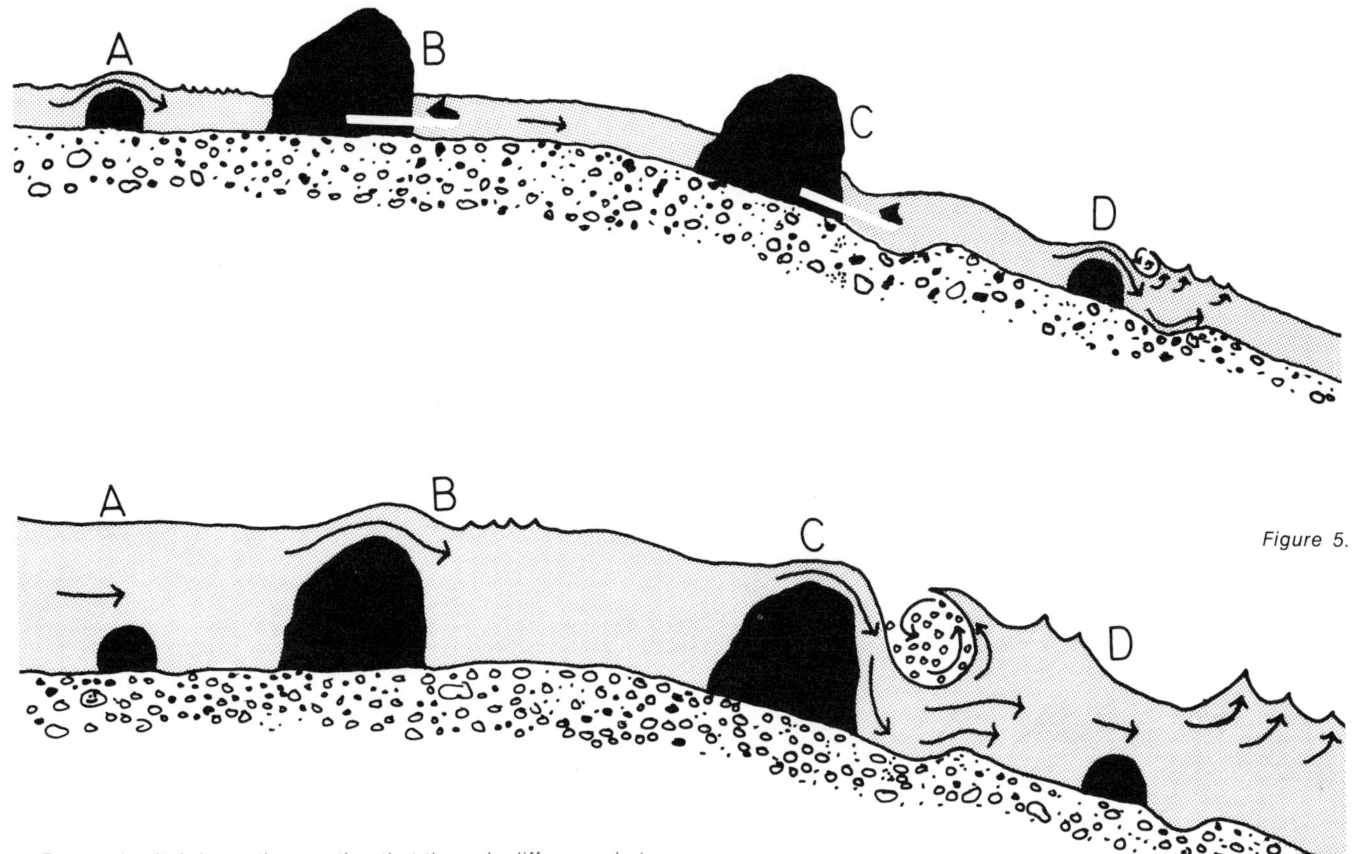

Figure 4.

Figure 5.

For emphasis it is worth repeating that the only difference between the souse hole at arrow 8 in Photo 1 and the one in Photo 2, just as between the souse holes in Figures 4-D and 5-C, is one of dimensions. The larger the souse hole the greater the hazard rating. The hazards of souse holes will be discussed more fully later in the section on safety.

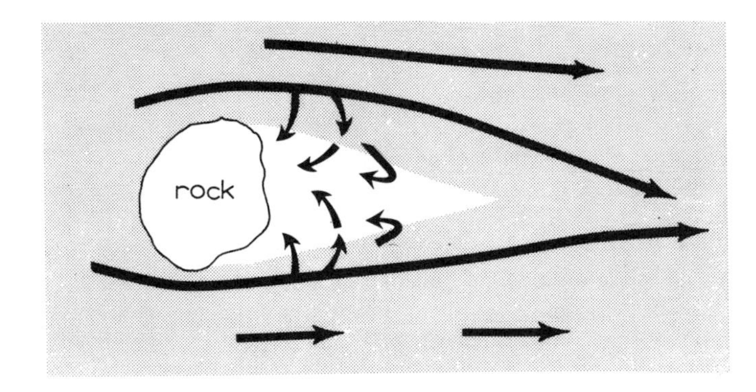

Figure 6.

Standing Waves

Standing waves result from the slowing down of a fast current and are usually associated with deep water. In Figure 5-D the water flowing over the rock is piling up on itself creating a series of interconnecting standing waves or haystacks. Thus, the eddy or mini-souse hole of Figure 4-D is converted into a series of standing waves as a result of the higher flow rate. If the discharge of this hypothetical river were increased even more, standing waves would develop below rock 5-C also. Because of the increased depth required to produce standing waves, they provide a good rock-free ride through a rapids. Standing waves are found between arrows 2 and 3 in Photo 1. Although these are not particularly large waves, note that a similiar sized wave (arrow 4) is coming over the left gunwale of the canoe. Photo 3, taken below Little Bull Falls on the Popple River, shows some larger standing waves. This rapids rates grade II-III. The higher rating is for open canoe because they are almost certain to swamp unless they avoid the largest waves. Occasionally troublesome insufficiently submerged rocks may be concealed among the standing waves. Their presence can usually be identified by the irregularity of the waves.

Photo 2. Upper Teakettle Rapids on the Wolf - grade III.

Standing waves also form downstream of any constriction in the width of a river channel. For example, standing waves are frequently encountered at a point where the river widens below a narrow canyon. Conditions necessary to form standing waves do not require much gradient if there is adequate discharge.

River reading is an art that must be mastered slowly and sometimes with much bumping and scraping. The topography of the river bed is revealed much more clearly from the bottom of the rapids than from the top. It is often helpful to look back upstream after running a rapids and try to relate these two completely different views or to scout a rapids from below before running it.

Photo 3. Standing waves - below Little Bull Falls on the Popple.

PADDLE STROKES

The primary objective of this section is to show the relationship of one paddle stroke to another and the net effect in turning the boat. Additional information can be found in several technique manuals (see Appendix E). However, proper paddling technique is best acquired under the supervision of a competent instructor.

In all of the illustrations the bow of the boat is pointed toward the top of the page. The shaded arrow indicates the direction in which that end of the boat turns when the paddler moves his paddle in the water in the direction depicted by the solid black arrow. The dotted line indicates paddle retrieval (above the water) between strokes. Note that in all of these diagrams the boat moves as a unit that pivots about the middle. A stroke that moves the bow toward the left moves the stern to the right, and the boat rotates counterclockwise. With a two-man boat the canoeists should paddle on opposite sides. This arrangement facilitates steering and also provides a paddle on each side for use as an emergency "brace." If one paddler changes sides, the other should do likewise. Occasionally it is desirable for canoeists to paddle on the same side. For example, if the canoe is caught sideways in a backroller both paddlers should brace on the downstream side.

All paddle strokes are intended to move the BOAT and not the paddle. Ideally the paddle is stationary in the water while the boat is either pulled toward or pushed away from this "immovable object." Because the force of the paddle can never be directed completely through the center keel line of the boat, all paddle strokes will turn the canoe, some more than others. When paddling forward or backward, the stroke should be made parallel to the center line of the canoe. If the paddle follows the gunwale line, some of the force of the stroke is wasted in turning the canoe to the side rather than in pulling the canoe forward. In all strokes, the upper hand is held over the top of the grip. This grip is designed to permit positive control over the angle of the blade. The lower hand should grasp the paddle shaft low at the throat to permit greater leverage and thus impart more power to the stroke.

There are different strokes for different folks. Some strokes are done only from the bow, some only from the stern, and some from both positions. Remember, however, that when paddling backwards the bowman performs stern strokes and **vice versa.**

Canoe

J-stroke, stern of Figure 7: The J-stroke is a steering stroke used only when paddling in the stern. Insert the powerface of the paddle in the water as far forward as possible and pull to your hip. As you continue to move the paddle towards the stern, rotate the powerface away from you and turn the thumb of your upper hand

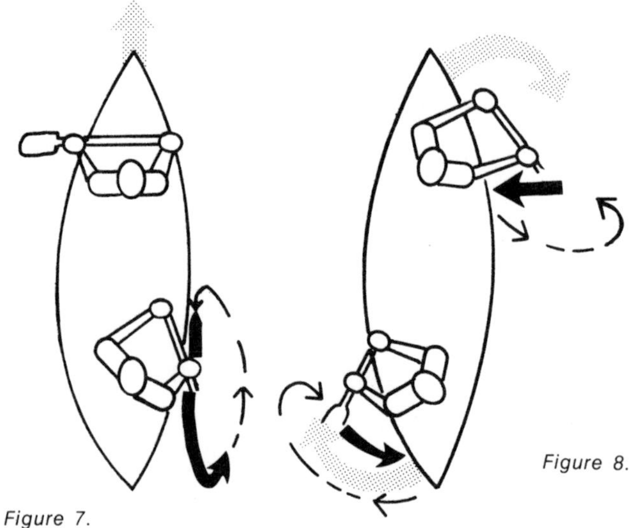

Figure 7.

Figure 8.

down while using the lower hand to push the powerface away from the stern. This movement suggests the letter "J." To recover, lift paddle edgewise and rotate the nonpowerface flat to the water while swinging forward in an arc out to the side of the boat until the paddle is as far forward as you can reach. Now you are ready to repeat the stroke.

Novices who are unfamiliar with this stroke will find that unless they frequently change paddle sides, the boat will continue to turn in a direction away from their paddle side.

Draw in the bow, **Sweep** in the stern Figure 8: In this figure the boat turns clockwise as the result of the combination of a draw in the bow with a sweep in the stern. Both of these strokes can be used from either the bow or the stern. A sweep is useful in making a gradual turn while paddling forward, whereas the draw is used only for turning.

The **Draw** stroke is used to move the end of the boat to the paddle side. The upper hand is held above the head and the torso is turned sideways from the waist. This stroke is made by reaching out as far as possible from the canoe with the lower hand. The powerface of the paddle on the surface of the water will keep you from tipping over. As you push out with the upper hand and then pull in with the lower hand, use the lower hand as a fixed pivot point; the canoe will be pulled toward the paddle blade. To recover: just before the canoe hits the paddle, use the lower hand as a pivot point at the gunwale and push the upper hand down and forward toward the bow while swinging the blade up out of the water. If the paddle should get caught against the canoe, immediately release the paddle with the upper hand and pull the paddle free with the lower hand. Resist the temptation to remove the paddle from the water by raising the shaft vertically. This attempted maneuver has caused many tipovers. Another method of recovery, useful when a number of draw strokes are done in rapid succession, is to rotate the paddle shaft 90° with the upper hand and slice the blade through the water out to the initial position.

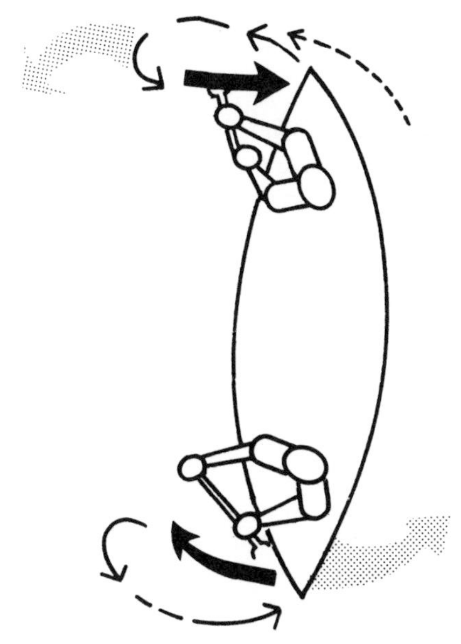

Figure 9.

The **Forward Sweep** provides forward power with moderate turning force. When done from the stern, the stern is pulled to the paddle side, turning the canoe to the nonpaddle side. The paddle is inserted in the water just out from the hip with the shaft at a 45° angle. The paddle is swept back in a wide arc until the blade reaches the stern. Recovery is the same as for the J-stroke. The - **Forward Sweep** from the bow (no diagram) will force the bow of the canoe to the nonpaddle side. Reach as far forward as possible and insert the paddle blade near the bow. Sweep out and back until the paddle is even with the hip. Sweeping past this point contributes very little toward turning the canoe.

Cross-bow draw and **Reverse Sweep,** Figure 9: The **cross-bow draw** is done only from the bow. Without changing the position of the hands on the shaft, swing the blade of the paddle all the way across the bow to the opposite side of the canoe by rotating the torso at the hips as far as possible. Do not cross arms. The upper hand is kept close to the hip with the elbow at the side. With the lower arm fully extended, insert the blade in the water narrow edge up and at about a 45° angle from the bow. By pushing out with the upper hand and using the lower hand as a pivot, you will pull the bow toward the paddle. Note, however, that the shaft is not held vertically as with the draw stroke. To recover, push down with the upper hand and lift the paddle up when it reaches the bow.

The **reverse sweep** is a stern-only stroke. This stroke is started by reaching as far back as possible and inserting the paddle in the water near the stern. With the blade tilted so the top edge is slightly forward, sweep the paddle out and forward in a wide arc. The upper hand is held low and near the gunwale on the paddle side. The forward tilt permits the canoeist to place his weight on the paddle as the stern is pushed away. The stroke ends with the shaft at 45° to the keel line and with the canoeist crouched down near the gunwale in order to maintain his balance. Do not continue this stroke beyond a point where the paddle is at more than a 45 ° angle to the stern. To do so is essentially backpaddling and therefore contributes little to turning. (An extension of this stroke is the low brace which will be discussed later.) With open canoes, repeated short strokes are more effective than a single long one. To recover, move the torso over the center of the canoe and kneel erect. The paddle is now in position for a forward paddle stroke.

Both paddlers doing the **Pry Stroke,** Figure 10: The **Pry** is a short, quick, and powerful turning stroke. It is much preferred to the forward sweep or cross-bow draw for turning to the nonpaddle side in turbulent water. The forward sweep is less powerful and with the cross-bow draw there is a period of instability when the paddle side is changed. The pry loses its effectiveness, however, in shallow water. It is essentially the reverse of the draw stroke. Insert the paddle with the blade near and slightly under the canoe with the shaft in an almost vertical position. Use the lower

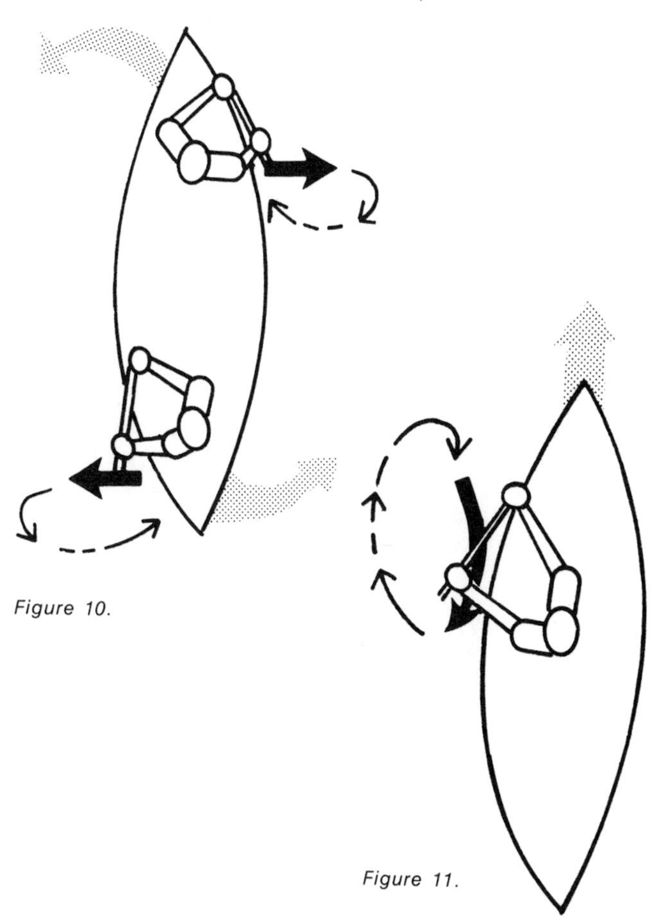

Figure 10.

Figure 11.

hand to pivot the throat of the paddle against the gunwale while pulling in with the upper hand. The paddle is thus used as a lever to pry the boat away from the paddle. Caution: don't pinch your fingers between the paddle and the gunwale. To recover, rotate the paddle shaft 90° and slice back to the starting position; repeat if necessary. The throat is held against the gunwale at all times during the stroke and recovery. Because of the tremendous leverage of this stroke, most paddles have a decided tendency to break (or bend) at the throat when the pry is used with unbridled enthusiasm to turn an open canoe having a sharp gunwale. Paddle damage, however, is not a problem with decked boats which turn more easily.

Basic C-1 Stroke (Inverted C-Stroke), Figure 11: Solo boating differs from the two-man situation. You no longer need to wonder what your partner is doing; you choose the route; there is no need to coordinate strokes with another; and of course there is no one to blame if something goes wrong. The solo boater positions himself in the middle of the boat, near or slightly fore of the pivot point. The strategy is to move the middle (rather than the bow) in the right direction. This approach is desirable for two reasons. The first is that there is no partner to help you move the boat great distances. The second reason is that a solo boat turns more easily than one occupied by two men because the mass (ie, the boater) is positioned in the center.

The **Inverted C-Stroke** combines a draw stroke with the pry-stroke. At the start, the paddle is positioned in the water near the bow and about 12-18 inches out from the gunwale (bilge). The paddle is first moved toward the gunwale, then back, and then away from it. The net effect is to move the paddle in an arc that circumscribes the letter 'C."

Kayak

The kayakist has fewer strokes to master than the canoeist. Because he has a paddle blade immediately available on both sides of the boat, there is no need for the J-stroke, the cross-bow, or the pry. On the other hand, the kayakist has to be bracing continuously to stabilize this tippy craft. Each of the turning strokes requires a heavy lean to achieve maximum efficiency because the kayak is designed to turn most easily when on its side. Although disconcerting initially, this technique is quickly learned. The kayakist literally "wears" his boat from the waist down. As discussed under bracing, the kayakist leans on the paddle with his torso while controlling the lean of the boat with his knees, feet, and hips.

The kayak paddle itself presents a problem alien to the canoeist. Because the blades are feathered and there is no grip as with a canoe paddle, basic paddle handling differs. The shaft is held with the hands about 3 to 4 feet apart with the thumbs pointing toward each other. One hand firmly grips the shaft at all times and controls the blade angle for all strokes. This is the fixed hand. There are no special problems when paddling on the fixed side. For strokes on the opposite side, rotate the paddle shaft 90° by loosening the grip of the nonfixed hand and dropping the wrist of the fixed hand down so the shaft is above the forearm. At the end of the stroke, loosen the grip with the nonfixed hand and rotate the shaft back to the initial position with the fixed hand.

The forward paddle stroke is done with the shaft at a 45° angle to the water. With the upper hand at shoulder height, push out with the upper hand as if throwing a punch while pulling back with the lower hand. To backpaddle, just reverse this action using the opposite face of the blade. Backpaddling is much easier in a kayak than in a canoe. In order to maintain a straight course, the kayakist may have to do an occasional sweep on one side while paddling "straight" on the other. In the sweep stroke, move the paddle in a wide arc from the bow to the stern while leaning the boat to the paddle side. The motion and weight shift is the same as that described for the reverse sweep in the canoe, whether the kayakist is doing a forward or a reverse sweep (also called a low-brace turn); only the direction is changed.

In the draw stroke, extend the paddle out as far as possible and lean on it. As the boat is drawn toward the paddle, gradually shift the lean of the kayak back to a vertical position. This lean enables the kayakist to obtain a greater extension from the boat resulting in a more powerful stroke. A draw stroke followed by a forward paddle stroke is essentially the same as the solo-canoeist's inverted C-stroke.

Another extension of the draw stroke is the high brace (Duffek) turn. This stroke is used for crossing current differentials such as required for eddy turns. In this maneuver the kayakist inserts his paddle into the eddy current while holding the paddle vertically with the powerface of the blade turned slightly away from the bow. This paddle position is coupled with an extreme lean of the kayak. Although the paddle is positioned nearly vertically, the kayakist is supported by the force of the current differential. The kayakist merely pulls on the paddle while the mainstream carries the kayak downstream, across the current differential, and into the eddy. This sequence is similiar to reaching out and grabbing a sign post while running down the street. The centrifugal force swings you around while you continue to remain in an upright position.

Bracing

A relatively recent innovation which has revolutionized whitewater boating is the paddle brace. This technique evolved out of the necessity to fully utilize the potential of the decked whitewater craft. However, these bracing strokes are useful for open canoes as well. A paddle brace provides the boater with a powerful tool that can be used to stabilize a boat in turbulent and calm water. These braces provide a far superior approach toward maintaining boat stability than simply shifting body weight or "balancing through" turbulence.

With this technique, the paddle is used as an outrigger onto which the paddler places a significant portion of his body weight. To maximize the effectiveness of a paddle brace, a heavy lean must be exerted on the paddle. When a paddle brace is used to prevent a tipover, the boater leans **toward** the direction he is tipping. In Figure 12 an arrow indicates the direction of the upward force of the water on the paddle that is capable of supporting the boater's weight. The boater places his weight on his fully extended lower arm. The grip then acts as the pivot point while the upper hand is pushed upward. At the same time the hips must be shifted in the opposite direction to keep the boat from tipping. This is done by pushing down with the knee opposite the paddle side and by pulling upward with the other knee. Knee bracing is required for maximum effect (see equipment section). Once the boat has been righted, the boater can safely raise his torso to an erect position and be ready to paddle onward.

A high brace (bow of Figure 12) is made with the paddle shaft positioned almost vertically with the thumb of the upper hand pointing downward as in the draw stroke. On the other hand, the low brace (stern of Figure 12) is executed with the paddle shaft positioned horizontally with the thumb of the upper hand pointing upward as in the reverse sweep. The low brace is the more powerful of the two when used to right a tipping boat, but it sacrifices forward momentum to gain stability.

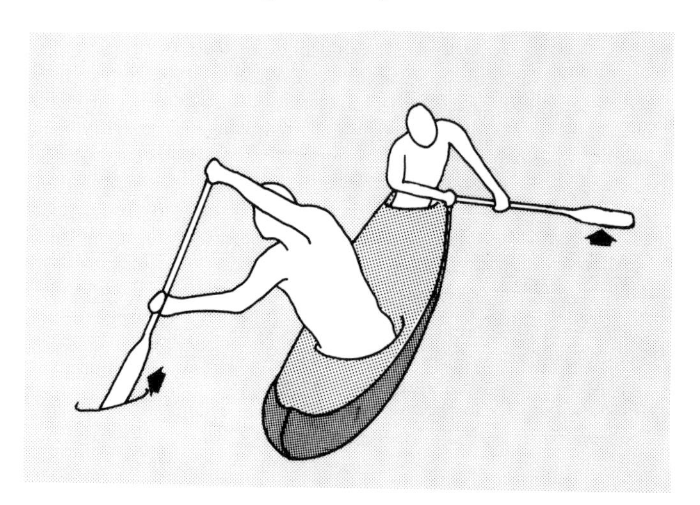

Figure 12.

A boater's body weight cannot be supported by a paddle unless there is an opposing force capable of supporting this weight. If the paddle is flat on the surface of the water it will support some downward force initially but the paddle will gradually sink. Continuous support can be achieved and the paddle will remain on the surface whenever there is relative motion between the paddle blade and the water, provided the paddle is moving at a climbing angle. Figure 13 shows how a paddle moving from right to left will remain on the surface if held at a climbing angle (13-A) or will sink if held at a diving angle (13-B). The upward force that keeps the blade on the surface in 13-A can also support a boater's weight. Remember that a climbing angle and, therefore, an upward force on the blade depends on the relative motion between the paddle and the water. Thus if both the paddle and the current are moving in the same direction and the paddle moves faster than the current, the blade should be tilted forward in the direction of the stroke (Figure 13-C). If, on the other hand, the paddle is moving slower than the current (e.g., the paddle is held stationary while the boat is hung up on a rock), the blade should be tilted in the opposite direction (Figure 13-D). The paddle will dive in 13-C if the paddle moves slower than the current or in 13-D if the paddle moves faster than the current. Also note that if there is no current, a climbing angle will be maintained in 13-C and a diving angle in 13-D. Sculling is accomplished by moving the paddle back and forth at climbing angles while the boat remains stationary.

The amount of upward force and consequently the amount of weight you can put on the paddle depends on the angle of the blade and the relative motion between paddle and current. The more relative motion between paddle and current, the greater the climbing angle possible and the greater the weight which can be supported. Experience is the best teacher of the blade angle that provides maximum support in each situation.

Also note that with strokes in which the paddle is positioned vertically such as with the high brace (Figure 12) a climbing angle is maintained by placing the leading edge of the paddle blade away from the direction in which the boat is headed relative to the water movement.

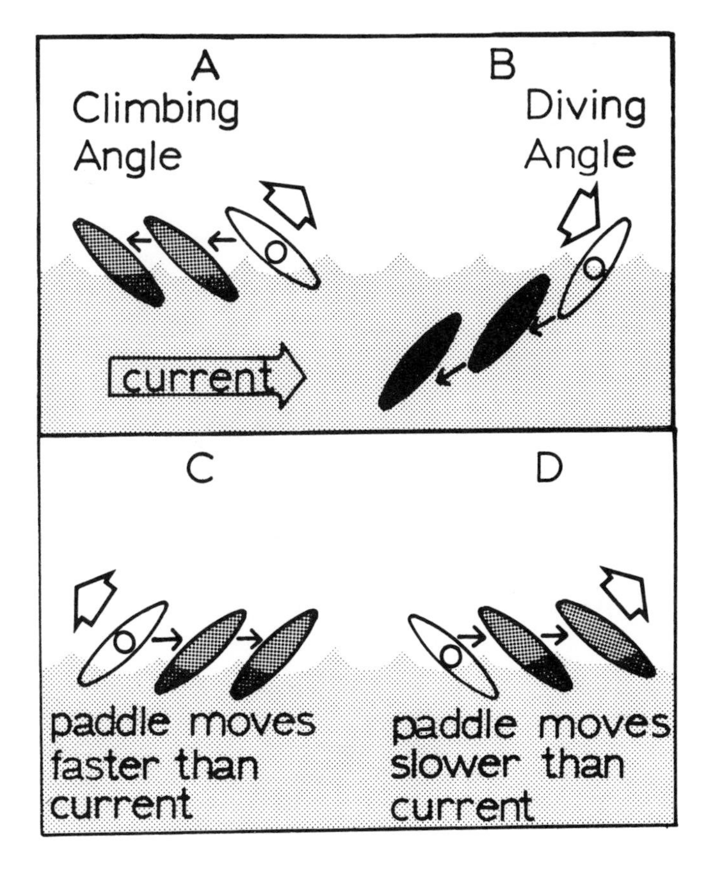

Figure 13.

Eskimo Roll

Note: This maneuver can only be performed in decked boats equipped with spray skirts and suitable bracing. The spray skirt must always be adjusted so that it is readily removable whenever the boater wishes to exit.

An Eskimo roll is the logical extension of a brace. A successful Eskimo roll is a matter of coordination, not strength. The roll can be divided into two parts: first the boat is turned right side up, and second the body is lifted from the water. If the boater tries to lift the body from the water first, the roll will require considerable strength and will at best be unreliable.

The essence of any successful roll lies in proper body coordination during the first segment of the roll. The correct body motion, termed the **hip snap,** can be practiced by holding on to an immovable object (e.g., edge of a pier) at the surface of the water. For a roll to the right, grasp the immovable object with your right hand while you are in a canoe or a kayak. To overturn the boat, rotate the hips to the right (into the support). Very little force need be exerted with the right arm to maintain your left shoulder on the surface. A hip snap is done by lifting up with the right knee while quickly shifting the hips to the left. If done properly, this action will raise the boat upright. It is important to keep your head and shoulders stationary on the surface of the water. Do not lift your head until the boat is three-quarters of the way upright, at which time it is easy to lift your head and move your torso to an upright position.

The **put-across** is basically an extension of the low brace discussed earlier in this section, see Figure 12. While the boater is upside down, the paddle blade closest to the boat is placed against the chest with the left hand and the paddle is gripped with the right hand which is extended at a comfortable distance down the shaft (Photo 4). Cock the right wrist upward. When you are upside down, hold the paddle vertically and hold the right arm upright. Bend to the left while shifting the hips to the right, and work the paddle (narrow edge up) to the surface of the water. Then rotate the paddle 90° until it is flat on the surface. Perform a hip snap while lifting the paddle up with the left hand and pushing down with the right hand (Photos 5 and 6). Notice that the head and shoulders remain parallel to the surface and do not rise out of the water until the hip snap has been completed and the boat is three-quarters of the way upright (Photo 6). While pulling the paddle inward and pushing downward on it, you can shift the shoulders towards the bow, enabling you to raise your body out of the water to a completely upright position (Photo 7). This entire sequence, but particularly the latter portion, should be done in one smooth, coordinated motion; otherwise you may roll over again in the opposite direction once you get up. The chin should be tucked against the chest at all times during the roll. If done correctly, the extended paddle blade remains near the surface and perpendicular to the boat throughout the roll. Note that the grip required to position the paddle properly to begin this roll (Photo 4) differs from a normal paddling position.

A second type of Eskimo roll, the **screw roll,** can be initiated without changing the grip from the normal paddling position and therefore is the preferred type of roll to use on a rapids. With this

Photos 4-7. The Put-Across Roll.

roll the paddle is less likely to be pulled from the boater's hands by turbulence or by rocks that are brushed against while he is upside down. Furthermore, after the roll has been completed the boater is immediately in position to paddle onward. The screw roll, however, is slightly more difficult to master than the put-across. The hip snap is identical; only the paddle and torso motions are different.

To do the screw roll, move the paddle in a wide arc extending from the bow to the stern with the blade held at a climbing angle. A well-coordinated hip snap rights the boat. To envision this roll, consider your hip to be the shaft of a large screw and the paddle motion to represent movement of the paddle up the incline of the thread. The paddle is inserted into the groove of the thread so it remains stationary as the hip moves upward as the "screw" is rotated. This movement is equivalent to lifting up one side of a car with a screw-type jack.

For a roll on the right side, the inverted paddler must shift his hips to the right while he leans forward. Hold the paddle parallel to the boat with the extended blade resting flat on the surface near the bow. With the right arm fully extended and the left arm bent at the elbow, sweep the paddle in a wide arc so that the blade closest to you is out of the water, just far enough that it clears the hull (Photo 8). A hip snap must also be done as you move the paddle in its arc (Photos 9 and 10). Timing and coordination are important. The head and shoulders must remain parallel to the surface until the boat is nearly upright (Photo 11). Then and only then should you raise the head and straighten the torso. Note that the extended paddle blade remains on the surface at all times throughout this roll. If the right wrist is not bent upright sufficiently at the start and throughout the roll, the paddle will sweep downward at a diving angle and the roll will fail. Also, if the paddle is not moved in a wide enough arc there may be insufficient lifting power to permit a successful roll. Finally, the most likely cause of failure of this roll is if the boater's head and shoulders are lifted too soon, before the boat is three-quarters upright.

Photos 8-11. The Screw Roll.

MANEUVERING IN A RAPIDS

The basic principle that relates current flow (hydraulics) to boat stability is that whenever a boat is perpendicular to a current, the current exerts a force on the boat which tends to overturn it in an upstream direction. In Photo 12 the current is flowing from right to left. The boat is about to tip over because the boaters failed to lean the boat downstream while crossing the current. Water is entering the canoe as the upstream gunwale dips below the surface. Properly equipped decked boats will not swamp, but they may nevertheless overturn because the current will roll the boat as indicated by the arrow. To counterbalance the tipping effect of the current you should always lean the boat downstream when crossing a current. The downstream lean is most effective when accompanied by a paddle brace made on the downstream side of the boat. Photo 13 shows a kayakist using good technique. He is using a low brace to maintain stability as he leans downstream. The arrows in the photograph indicate the direction of water flow.

Photo 12. An upstream lean - a No-No.

Rule of thumb: for maximum stability while maneuvering down a river, your boat should always be kept parallel to the main current (to avoid the tipping effect), unless you are performing other maneuvers such as eddy turns or ferries. In those cases WATCH YOUR LEAN POSITION!

Photo 13. The downstream lean - Yellow Bridge Rapids on the Pike - grade II-III.

When crossing a current differential, the lean is always downstream relative to the current you are **entering.** Thus when crossing an eddy line, the current in the eddy is moving upstream relative to the main current and the lean must then be upstream (relative to the main current) once you cross the eddy line. Timing is important. When do you reverse your lean? The answer can only be found by experience. You can feel the force of the current on the boat and when this force shifts to the opposite side, REVERSE YOUR LEAN. Rules of thumb: **When perpendicular to the current, lean downstream. When turning across a current differential, lean into the turn. When crossing a current differential, reverse your lean.**

Figure 14.

Eddy Turns

One of the most convenient methods of stopping in a rapids is to turn into an eddy with the bow pointing upstream. You can accomplish this by aiming the boat so that the bow will be pointed alongside and slightly downstream of the obstacle causing the eddy (See Figure 14). The shaded outlines indicate the path the boat takes when turning into an eddy.

Paddle forward so that the bow enters the eddy. As you cross the eddy line you must lean the boat upstream (lean into the turn). Allow the current to swing the stern around and paddle forward to secure the boat in the shelter of the eddy. Remember that the current in the eddy is opposite to that in the mainstream. Eddy turns are not difficult, but you must paddle decisively to effect a 180° turn while checking the boat's downstream momentum. If the eddy is large and you are positioned properly, it will take little or no effort to maintain your boat in this position indefinitely. When you wish to leave an eddy, point the bow out into the current and lean the boat downstream as you cross the eddy line and enter the mainstream.

Upstream Ferry

When you are moving your boat perpendicular to the mainstream (as when going from one shore to another) the current exerts considerable force on the boat, and in shallow rocky rivers it is easy for the boat to be forced upon rocks. This may lead to a possible upset and cause damage to the boat. You can prevent this by ferrying. An upstream ferry (Figure 15) is accomplished by aiming your boat upstream with the bow pointed toward the shoreline for which you are headed. You must paddle upstream to overcome the current. The amount of upstream paddling and the angle of the boat required are a function of the current force; the greater the current the harder you must paddle and the more nearly parallel to the current you must point your boat. The boat must be leaned toward the side to which you are heading; otherwise the current can grab the upstream gunwale and cause a tipover. The force of the current against the hull pushes the boat sideways. When done properly, a ferry will allow you to go from shore to shore with little or no downstream movement and with maximum stability. Remember that if you are entering an eddy at the end of the ferrying maneuver, you must reverse the lean of the boat as you cross the eddy line (Figure 16).

Figure 15.

Downstream (Back) Ferry

The downstream ferry is similar to the upstream ferry. In this instance the boat is aimed downstream with the bow angled away from the direction of travel, and the boater must backpaddle to overcome the current. This technique eliminates the need to have the boat pointed perpendicular to the current at any time. Consequently, there is more stability. This maneuver is useful for getting into an eddy or for minor course adjustments to the side. Furthermore, since you are positioned properly for downstream cruising, river reading is much easier. For these reasons it is worthwhile to master this technique. You can also use the downstream ferry to enter an eddy as shown in Figure 16. The boaters must lean slightly to their left (downstream) until they cross the eddy line and reverse their lean.

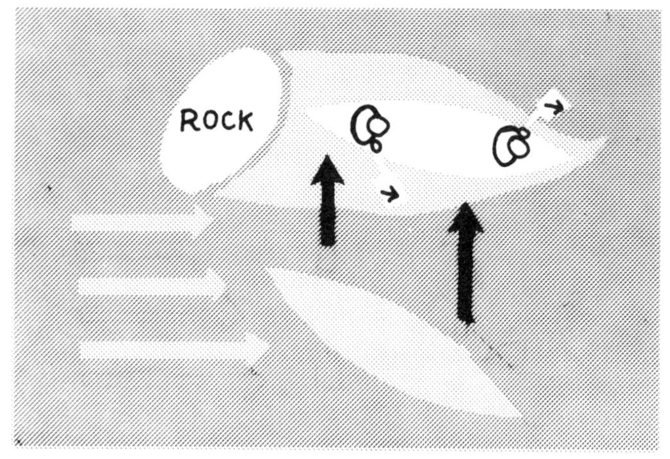

Figure 16.

Surfing

Surfing is a refinement of the upstream ferry that can be used to cross a powerful current without being swept downstream or just to have fun. With the bow pointed upstream the goal is to position the boat on the upstream side of a wave so that gravity pulls you upstream while the current pulls the boat downstream. If you achieve the proper balance between these opposing forces, you can sit there for minutes without using your paddle except perhaps for an occasional brace. To move across the river, point the bow of the boat slightly in the direction you wish to go and lean on a brace to the downstream side of the boat. It's less tiring than ferrying since the current does the work. In very strong currents, surfing may be the only alternative for crossing the river. Photo 14, shows a kayakist surfing across a backroller. The kayakist is well aware that his boat must be kept parallel to the main current since this backroller is large enough to hold a boat that inadvertently gets turned sideways in it.

Photo 14. Surfing at Ducksnest Rapids on the Wolf - grade III.

Running Standing Waves

When running a series of standing waves in an open canoe, you should not head the canoe directly into the waves but rather approach them at a slight angle. The bow will bury less and less water will be taken in. The angle should not be so great as to risk broaching, however. Lean the canoe into the wave as it goes over the upstream side. If in doubt as to whether there is a rock in the waves, run through the edge of the waves.

Bibliography

River Hydrology

1. Curtis, George W., **Statistical Summaries of Illinois Stream Flow Data,** U.S. Geological Survey, 1969.
2. Hendrickson, G. E., and Doonan, C. J., **Hydrology and Recreation on the Cold-water Rivers of Michigan's Southern Peninsula,** U.S. Geological Survey, 1972.
3. Knutilla, R. L., **Flow Characteristics of Michigan Streams,** U.S. Geological Survey, 1967.
4. Mann, William B. IV, **Flow Characteristics of Minnesota Streams,** U.S. Geological Survey, 1971.
5. Oakes, E., Field, J., and Seegar, L. P., **The Pine-Popple Basin: Hydrology of a Wild River Area, Northeastern Wisconsin,** U.S. Geological Survey, 1970.
6. **Surface Water Records of Illinois,** U.S. Geological Survey Annual Reports, 1961 through 1969.
7. **Surface Water Records of Michigan,** U.S. Geological Survey Annual Reports, 1961 through 1970.
8. **Surface Water Records of Minnesota,** U.S. Geological Survey Annual Reports, 1961 through 1970.
9. **Surface Water Records of Wisconsin,** U.S. Geological Survey Annual Reports, 1961 through 1971.
10. Young, K. B., **Flow Characteristics of Wisconsin Streams,** U.S. Geological Survey, 1963.
11. Young, K. B., **Supplement to Report on Flow Characteristics of Wisconsin Streams,** U.S. Geological Survey, 1965.

Technique

1. McNair, Robert, **Basic River Canoeing,** American Camping Association, 1969.
2. Urban, John, **A Whitewater Handbook for Canoe and Kayak,** Appalachian Mountain Club, 1965.

6 Hazards and Safety

As with any sport, boating safety involves recognition and avoidance of situations likely to be hazardous. Appropriate equipment and technique are essential to safe boating. Since those subjects have already been discussed, this section is limited to hazardous situations likely to be encountered in river running.

Wisconsin DNR records of river boating accidents prove that rapids and falls and other river hazards rarely present a danger to anyone except the uninformed, poorly equipped, or inexperienced boater. Wisconsin statue 30.67(2) (a) requires that any boating accident which "...results in death or injury to any person or total property damage in excess of $100 ..." must be reported to Wisconsin Department of Natural Resources, Box 450, Madison, Wisconsin 53701.

SCOUTING RECOMMENDED

Always scout an unfamiliar rapids. Photo 1 shows an unrunnable drop which is preceeded by the most innocent looking easy rapids. An arrow in the photograph points out an observer on the left bank.

We recommend scouting any rapids that are not readily visible from upstream or whenever your ability or preparedness suggests caution. Rules of thumb: **If you aren't prepared to swim a rapids, don't run it. Also, never run any substantial rapids unless you have a support crew of at least two other boats available for rescue.** An expert river cruiser is a cautious boater who uses good judgment. He stops and scouts frequently. Whenever there is any possible risk to life and limb, he portages. In this way, wise expert's reach old age with dignity, fools usually strike out on both counts.

Photo 1. Copper Falls on the Bad - unrunnable.

When you prepare to scout, stop at a safe point above the rapids and make certain you secure your boat and equipment to the shore. If you decide to run a difficult rapids, position boaters to man rescue ropes. Also have a manned boat located downstream that can be used to pick up any dunkers, loose paddles, or boats. Rescue ropes should be positioned so that the dunker will have time to see the rope as it is thrown and so that he will have sufficient time to grab it and be pulled in (if possible) before having to swim any additional rapids.

LINING THROUGH A RAPIDS

If after scouting a rapids you decide not to run it, you have two options. One is to portage. The other is to line your boat down. The second method is only suitable for rapids where the drop is not too severe and the shoreline is relatively free of obstructions. Figure 1 shows two boaters lining their boat down a rapids. (If only one line is used it should be attached to the upstream end of the canoe.) One advantage of this technique is that the boat floats high because it is free of occupants and duffle. Thus, it is less likely to ship water or become hung up in the shallows. Also, since lines are attached to the boat while the boaters themselves are on the shoreline, the boat can be eased slowly through rather intricate passages of turbulent water with precision. If you use this technique properly, you will discover that for the most part the current tends to direct the downstream end of the boat through the best passage. The upstream line is used primarily to overcome the tendency of the boat to turn broadside in the current--a real no-no.

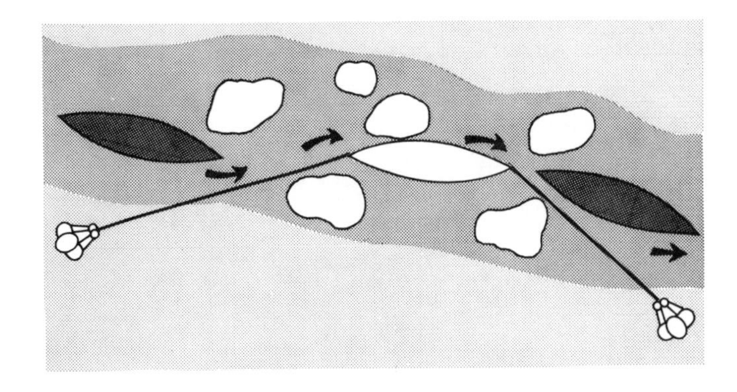

Figure 1. Lining through a rapids.

BROACHING ON OBSTACLES

If your boat hangs up in a rapids, you should act promptly. Prompt action will prevent most tipovers of stranded boats. Try to point the boat in a direction parallel to the water flow, even if this means running the rest of the rapids backwards. If your boat should become perpendicular to the current, remember that the force of water that flows under a broadsided boat will tend to overturn it in an upstream direction. To counterbalance this tendency, you should immediately **lean the boat downstream.**

Survey the situation. Estimate where the boat will go when it is freed and act accordingly. If gentle rocking, backpaddling, or careful weight shifting is insufficient to free the boat, it is generally prudent for one person to get out quickly, but carefully. CAUTION!! If you get out on the downstream side, you risk being pinned against a rock by the boat should it suddenly become free. On the other hand, if you leave on the upstream side in fast, deep water, you risk being swept off your feet and forced under the boat. Both of these potentially dangerous situations can be avoided by getting out in a very shallow spot or in one where you have adequate footing.

Make sure you hold onto the boat as you get out, as the increased buoyancy may free the stranded craft. If after you have gotten out the boat remains stranded, ease it off gently. Make certain you have positioned the boat properly before you get back in.

Be prepared to bail out your boat if needed. Water in a boat will cause it to ride lower, be harder to manage, and be almost impossible to balance properly.

TIPOVERS

In the event of a tipover, be aware of your responsibility to assist your partner. If the water is not too swift or too cold, it is often helpful to stay with your boat as it makes rescue much easier. The boat may provide added buoyancy in heavy waves or serve as a buffer against rocks. If conditions allow, hold onto your paddle. However, if there are any questions about your safety, leave the boat immediately.

If you leave your boat, try to swim to shore. But remember, since your feet may serve as excellent shock absorbers and your head will not it is best to float downstream on your back with your feet first, using them to ward off rocks. You can maintain this position by sculling with your hands until you get to a quieter section where you can either wade or swim to shore. Be calm, but don't be complacent.

Be on the alert for a rescue rope. (If you are throwing a rescue line, make certain boaters are expecting it before it is tossed; otherwise it is likely to be missed.)

After boaters have been rescued, recover boats and equipment. Decked boats should be kept upside down until they are emptied. The air pocket thus created will prevent the boat from taking in more water, making it easier to rescue and less likely to be damaged.

SOURCES OF DANGER

While rapids boating is a relatively safe sport (much safer than downhill skiing, for instance) there are a number of potential dangers which should be understood. In most instances trouble can be avoided with a little foresight and understanding.

Horizontal and Sieve-like Obstacles

Fallen trees found on the outside of river bends present a particularly hazardous situation as their presence is usually the result of the gouging action of the current which eroded the river bank and caused the trees to fall initially. This same current will tend to force a boat into them, and this in turn can cause a possible upset or entanglement (Figure 2). Rescue is often very difficult and sometimes impossible. Thus, it is wise to give a wide berth to fallen trees. Low bridges, brush, fences, or any other obstacles with water flowing through or under them present similar dangers.

In Figure 3, the boaters avoid the fallen tree by taking the inside of the turn. Decisive forward paddling while crossing the current is required to prevent being swept sideways. An alternative method of crossing to the inside of the turn is to back ferry (see technique section). Use this maneuver immediately if there is any chance of being swept into any sieve-like obstacle such as the tree shown in Figure 2. Rule of thumb: **The current tends to be swiftest (and deepest) on the outside of bends.** To avoid the largest waves in high water, stay on the inside of turns. Alternatively, in summer or other periods of low water, stick to the outside of turns for the deepest water, provided there are no obstacles.

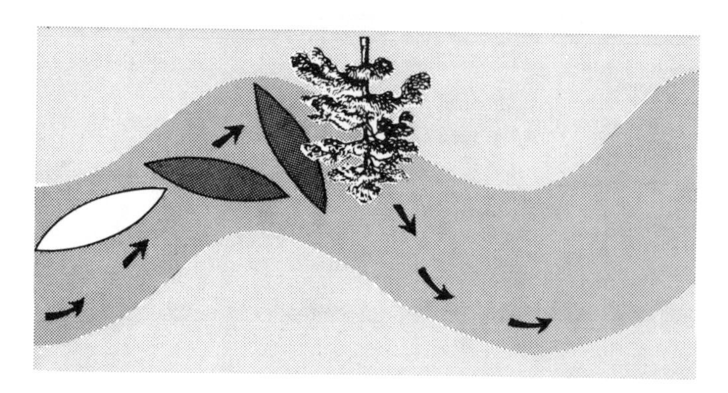

Figure 2. The boat (shading) could not make the turn - Danger!

Figure 3. The high water route. At low water, follow the current (the deep channel) if there is no obstacle.

Souse Holes and Backrollers

Although unrunnable backrollers and souse-holes exist in this area, they are relatively uncommon. Water flowing over a natural or man-made dam, may create a dangerous uniform backroller that can easily trap a swimmer or a boat. These backrollers often look deceptively innocent, but they must be avoided as they are responsible for countless drownings. A backroller or souse-hole is no place for an open canoe, and only experts in decked craft should even consider running them. The main danger of either of these hazards lies in the difficulty of exit once the boater has entered. A backroller is a wave that curls back on itself. The water is highly aerated and it flows upstream. Aerated water will not support a paddle. Consequently bracing is impossible unless the paddle is dug deep into the downstream current flowing under the backroller. The best method of escape from a backroller is to paddle to the side until you get out. If this fails, a deliberate tipover may permit you to escape if you dig your paddle deep into the downstream moving current. As a last resort, exit the boat and dive down toward the bottom where hopefully current will wash you out. It is easy to lose your orientation while being tossed and rolled about, but resist the tendency to fight to the surface. The circulating water will alternately bring you to the surface and then back down again. Assist the current by diving DOWN. The deeper you go, the better your chances of being washed out. Although it is difficult to dive down while wearing a lifejacket, don't shed yours unless absolutely necessary since the lifejacket will come in handy if there are any rapids downstream of the backroller.

The souse-hole (see Chapter 5) is generally less than a boat width in length, so if you must exit the boat hold onto the grab loops and try to push the boat out of the hole. Once the boat is out, it will usually pull you out with it. If not, then dive down as discussed above. Remember, the downward force of the water is usually sufficient to carry you beneath a backroller or souse-hole even if you are wearing a lifejacket. If caught in a backroller STAY COOL or better yet DON'T GET CAUGHT--PORTAGE around these hazards.

The difficulty in assessing the dangers of souse-holes and backrollers is illustrated in Photos 2 and 3. The risk to a well equipped expert canoeist going over the 15 foot drop in Photo 2 is not much different than swimming close to the dam in Photo 3. At this flow rate at least (Photo 2), the backroller at the bottom is irregular and unlikely to trap either boater or boat should a tipover result. Running this grade V drop is risky for everyone, including well-equipped expert boaters.

Neither the boater in Photo 2 nor the other members of his party could tell for sure if this was a killer drop until the first boat went over. Only after much deliberation and after rescue precautions were taken did the first canoeist venture forth. A boat was stationed below the drop and a rescue line was in readiness to assist him should he become trapped. However, because of the potential danger from a mistake, we strongly recommend against running any such drops.

Photo 2. A fifteen-foot drop taken in stride by an expert canoeist.

In contrast, the backroller formed by the less than two-foot drop shown in Photo 3 looks pretty innocuous, doesn't it? Well, it isn't. This has been the site of several drownings of unfortunate swimmers who were unaware of its dangers. This uniform backroller is regular and can hold a person with little chance for escape. Such backrollers have been known to hold a dunker's body for hours.

Because the dunker is constantly buffeted around in a backroller, the danger of slamming the head against the ledge is great. An unconscious dunker caught in a uniform backroller has little chance for survival. Consequently the use of helmets is an additional safety precaution.

RIVERS IN FLOOD

The most serious dangers to the canoeist, kayakist, or rafter occur during spring flood. Rivers are swollen with the recent snowmelt and are cold. Discharge is large and the current fast.

Photo 3. A two foot drop with a uniform backroller - a danger to the unwary swimmer.

The following incidents, a near-fatal mishap and several drownings, illustrate what can happen during spring boating.

The first incident occurred on the S-Curve Rapids on the Peshtigo River in the spring of 1960. The water was high and extremely cold, and many boaters in the party had swamped, some several times. All of the canoeists had open boats and were not wearing wet suits. They were all cold and eager to get off the river as quickly as possible, and so did not scout the drop before running it. One canoe swamped and the dunker was in serious trouble for he had neither a lifejacket to support him nor a wet suit to insulate him from the cold water. For a brief moment the dunker was pinned to the river bottom by his sunken canoe, but with strength born of desperation he managed to push the canoe off. By the time he surfaced, the exertion and numbing cold water had exhausted him. Before he could reach shore, he lost consciousness and went under in the turbulent water. Some of his companions ran downstream along the river bank frantically trying to spot him. He was found several hundred yards from the point of upset and was pulled out. Fortunately, there were persons trained in first aid in the party, and thanks to artificial respiration he is alive today. He and his party had disregarded many safety rules, but adherence to the American Whitewater Affiliation credo "Never Boat Alone" saved his life.

A second incident had a more tragic ending. A young man--the third person in an open canoe--drowned on Garfield Rapids on the Wolf River in May of 1961. Following capsize of their open canoe, all three dunkers quickly tired as they experienced the continuous buffeting of the rapids. The two dunkers wearing lifejackets made it to shore, but the third man, a weak swimmer without a lifejacket, didn't. A similar drowning involving one of two men in an open canoe occurred on the Little Wolf River in the spring of 1973. Again the victim was wearing neither lifejacket nor wet suit. Others, even those wearing lifejackets, have died in similiar incidents within the last few years. It is ironic that most if not all of these tragedies could easily have been prevented if reasonable safety precautions were taken. For this reason, we have included the following discussion on the hazards of spring boating.

The character of many rivers, especially of those with a high 10 per cent /90 percent flow duration ratio, changes dramatically during spring flood. The Vermillion River in Illinois is an example of such a river. While events seem to happen slowly, they usually occur with awesome force. Most rapids are washed out, causing standing waves to be replaced with huge moving waves which travel slowly downstream. Under these conditions the unwary boater experiences abrupt changes in position and elevation. Boats occasionally stand on end, and a "slow motion" tipover usually results. Most eddies are washed out and the remaining few have a frothy, irregular transitional zone several feet wide. Experienced boaters using decked craft and wearing wet suits and lifejackets can find these conditions pleasantly exciting. But there are dangers. A capsize of a boater without a sure Eskimo roll usually means a long tiring swim in icy water. The dunker's head may be inundated by large waves, sometimes for long intervals. Boat recovery is difficult for decked boats with maximal flotation, and nearly impossible for open canoes which are almost certain to swamp under these conditions.

In the spring there is an additional hazard of entanglement with tree branches along the flooded shoreline. This is a particularly serious hazard on narrow rivers, small streams, and creeks which are generally unrunnable in the summer, but which may become raging torrents in the spring.

Rivers flowing over beds with large boulders or ledges provide an additional hazard in high water; large powerful backrollers and souse-holes develop which can easily trap a boat or dunker. Even rivers with a low 10 percent / 90 percent flow duration ratio such as the Wolf and the Peshtigo develop large souse-holes and backrollers during the spring.

COLD WATER: DROWNING AND HYPOTHERMIA

The early spring (and late fall) boater is confronted with the most serious hazard a river has to offer--COLD WATER. Sudden immersion in cold water may produce serious consequences. Immediate death may result from drowning or cardiac arrest. Exposure to cold water for anywhere from a few minutes to an hour or more leads to hypothermia, a lowering of the core body temperature (measured by rectal not oral thermometers). Unconsciousness and consequently a risk of drowning occur whenever the core body temperature is reduced appreciably. A further lowering of body temperature inevitably leads to death.

Sudden immersion in water colder than 50° causes immediate and intense difficulty in breathing. Gasping and inability to control breathing may cause the dunker to panic within a few minutes following a cold water tipover. Whenever the head of a gasping dunker is covered by a wave (even if only for a few seconds), he is likely to inhale water and possibly drown, Gasping and rapid breathing can produce hyperventilation within 10 seconds, and this can lead to unconsciousness. Consequently the likelihood of drowning increases because even the best lifejacket cannot be expected to hold the head of an unconscious dunker above the water in turbulence.

In addition to the breathing difficulties associated with cold water immersion, the dunker's body rapidly loses heat at a rate MUCH FASTER THAN THE DUNKER REALIZES. Depending on skin thickness and the amount and kind of protective clothing worn, the dunker's core body temperature drops from a normal value of 98.6° F to about 96° F within 2 to 10 minutes. At these low core body temperatures, useful work becomes difficult and often impossible. Consequently the dunker is unable to swim or in any other way assist in his own rescue. A drop in core temperature to 88° F leads to unconsciousness, and a further drop to about 77° F usually results in immediate death.

To understand hypothermia, consider how the body gains, conserves, and loses body heat. The human body is heated in two ways, externally and internally. Heat is produced internally by the oxidation of food (metabolism) which occurs at one rate in a resting individual and at a higher rate during exercise. Shivering is an involuntary form of muscular exercise that produces heat at the expense of body food stores. The body can also receive external heat from the surroundings (sun, fire, another body, etc.). Body heat is conserved by the insulative layer of subcutaneous fat and by constriction of the blood vessels to the extremities. Body heat is lost by exhalation of warm air, by sweating, and by radiation, convection, and conduction from exposed body surfaces. To the boater, convection and conduction are the most important means of heat loss.

Rapids boaters are generally subjected to continual wetting even in the absence of tipovers. Wet clothing drains heat from a boater's body at an alarming rate because water conducts heat away from the body at a rate 20 times faster than air. Complete immersion is an even more serious hazard to the boater. Within seconds after immersion, clothing loses its insulative properties; these are due primarily to trapped air which prevents heat loss by reducing convection. Unless a garment is waterproof, wet clothing cannot prevent the rapid circulation of cold water past the skin (convection). Within minutes, the skin temperature of the dunker who is not wearing waterproof clothing will drop to within a few degrees of the water temperature. The dunker's body automatically responds by cutting off blood circulation to the skin in an attempt to conserve heat. Reduced blood circulation prevents the transport of energy stores required by the muscles to perform voluntary work. Thus voluntary movement of the extremities becomes increasingly difficult, sapping body strength and incapacitating the dunker.

Muscular activity on the part of the dunker creates a dilemma. Muscular activity is needed for the dunker to rescue himself, but it also increases the rate of heat loss since blood forced to the extremities is cooled rapidly by the cold water. In short, the dunker should ALWAYS GET OUT OF COLD WATER AS QUICKLY AND WITH AS LITTLE EXERTION AS POSSIBLE. If feasible, he should lie on his back in a feet-first position and let the current carry him downstream as he works his way to the shore. He should forget about saving his boat and rescuing other equipment. Unconsciousness can occur within 5 minutes after immersion in cold water. Scientific experiments and personal experience have shown that even good swimmers cannot swim a distance of 200 yards when the water temperature is less than 40° to 45° F. Differences in skin thickness, basal metabolic rate, and other physiological parameters produce variability in the **timing** of an individual's response to immersion in cold water. Therefore, the following table should be considered only as a rough guide. We can't tell you how long YOU will last in cold water. Physical fitness is not an indicator. The physically fit person may be the first to go because body fat provides protection against cold.

Water Temperature	Useful Work	Unconscious
32.5°	**less than 5 min.**	**less than 15 min.**
40°	**7.5 min.**	**30 min.**
50°	**15 min.**	**60 min.**
60°	**30 min.**	**2 hr.**
70°	**45 min.**	**3 hr.**

Adapted from Davidson, A.F.: "Survival - The Will To Live," AWA vol. XII, No. 1, Summer 1966.

Protection against the serious consequences of cold water immersion may be obtained either by acquiring a substantial layer of body fat or by wearing protective clothing. The above table lists estimates for a person clothed appropriately for the air temperature. Wearing waterproof outer layers extends these times somewhat, but wearing a neoprene wet suit extends them considerably. Woolen underwear worn under a wet suit (and lifejacket) provides the best protection against cold water that we know of.

Paddlers who have been wearing wet clothing for several hours may experience a mild case of hypothermia. This causes a reduction in the times listed in the above table. Consequently, be on the alert for signs of hypothermia in yourself and your companions. Symptoms include a lack of coordination, thickness of speech, irrationality, blueness of skin, dilation of pupils, and decrease in heart and respiratory rate. These symptoms are similar to those of a drunken person, and the judgment of a hypothermic boater is generally equally irrational.

Treatment: At least two persons in every boating party should be versed in mouth-to-mouth resuscitation and external cardiac massage, so that if one of the first-aiders becomes the victim there will be another available to provide assistance. Whenever a boater has been in the water for more than 10 minutes, hypothermia is almost certain. Under these conditions artificial respiration should be given only if breathing has stopped completely, and then it should be applied "at no more than half the normal rate."[1] Otherwise the would-be rescuer may cause the victim to become hyperventilated since during hypothermia metabolism is slower and less oxygen is consumed.

The hypothermic victim must be supplied with external heat as rapidly as possible. Removal of wet clothing facilitates heating. If the victim has experienced only a relatively mild case of hypothermia, replacement of wet clothing with dry apparel usually suffices. However, in instances of extreme hypothermia, external heat must be applied since the victim is incapable of generating enough heat himself regardless of the amount of dry clothing supplied. A bath of warm water is the best source of external heat, but since it

1 Keatinge, W.R.: Survival in Cold Water: The Physiology and Treatment of Immersion Hypothermia and of Drowning: Blackwell Scientific Publications, Oxford, 1969, p. 73.

is not generally available other heat sources should be used. A fire or another warm body can be used if necessary.

It should be apparent from the above that the spring boater runs the most risks. A spring boating trip is not the time to practice new maneuvers learned from books over the winter months. It is not the time to introduce your friends to canoeing. It is not the time to make a spur of the moment trip **alone** because the rivers are high and you can't round up suitable companions to shoot the rapids.

Expert boaters prefer spring boating and are well prepared to protect themselves against its hazards. Know your limitations and equip yourself properly. If you have any doubts about your ability to safeguard yourself, wait for warmer weather.

7 Getting With It

CLUBS AND ORGANIZATIONS

There is safety in numbers. On trips through wilderness areas or on rivers where there are rapids, we strongly recommend that you never boat alone. Three boats (not boaters) are considered a minimum. One way to find other boaters is to join a canoeing organization. In the address section we have listed a number of such groups already in existence, and we hope more such organizations will soon be forthcoming. Some groups provide instruction in boat handling and safety techniques and may even share club-owned equipment. Other groups provide less opportunity for formal instruction, but nevertheless new techniques and equipment are usually the topics of "bull sessions" between members. In any event, the advantages of joining such a group usually far outweigh any conceivable disadvantages.

NAVIGABILITY, LANDOWNERS AND FISHERMEN

The exact definition of a navigable stream varies somewhat from state to state, and the fine points of such definitions face continuous interpretation. In Wisconsin, however, a boater cannot legally scout or portage around any rapids if he is trespassing on private land without the owner's consent. Along a navigable stream the owner's property line begins at the normal high water mark. Some rivers have barbed wire strung across them. Although barbed wire is a dangerous obstruction, do not cut it. Currently there is no legal prohibition against such obstructions.

We strongly urge all boaters to comply with the requests of shoreline owners and do whatever is reasonable to promote good will. Note: Our maps indicate areas of shoreline in public ownership; other lands can be considered privately held. Also, in the river descriptions, we have indicated places where we have encountered barbed wire strung across a river.

Most of the rivers we have described are prime fishing grounds as well as great canoe streams. We would recommend that all boaters cooperate with fishermen by avoiding possible hostile encounters (i.e., give wide berth to the wading fisherman). It is mutually beneficial to have cooperation between fishermen and boaters. These groups can form a powerful lobby that can join together to protect our wild rivers.

COMPETITION

As with all recreational activities, competition is strong and ever growing on the paddling scene. Canoe and Kayak racing falls into two general categories: downriver and slalom. A downriver race is a test of strength, endurance, and the boater's ability to select the fastest channel in the river. Downriver racing is subdivided into two categories: quietwater and whitewater. A quietwater race is usually 20 miles or longer and may require one or more portages. Open canoes generally fare best in this type of race. On the other hand, the whitewater race is usually less than 10 miles in length and frequently is much shorter. The course is run mainly through rapids. There are usually separate classes for kayaks and one- and two-man canoes as well as for novices and experts. There are also separate classes for men and women.

Slalom racing differs from downriver racing in that a high premium is placed on precision maneuvering. It is somewhat similar to a downhill ski slalom. The course is a sequence of 25-30 gates hung from wires above a short stretch of rapids (see Photo 2). To make things difficult, the course may require the paddler to pass through the gates either while paddling forward or backward and entering from either the upstream or downstream sides. Unlike the ski slalom, however, it is not sufficient to pass through the gates in the correct sequence and from the proper direction: penalty seconds are added to the score for each gate touched or otherwise negotiated improperly (e.g., upside down, sideways, or missed). It takes most boaters about two to five minutes to run most courses before penalty seconds are added on for mistakes (from 10 seconds for hitting one pole of a gate to 50 seconds for missing a gate entirely). Penalties can add up rapidly, and precision is very important.

For more information on downriver and slalom racing consult the racing schedules published by the national canoe organizations listed in appendix E. Whitewater races are listed in publications of the United States International Slalom Canoe Association and the American Whitewater Affiliation and the American Canoe Association. Quietwater races are listed in the publications of the United States Canoe Association and the American Canoe Association.

Photo 2. Slalom at Hanson's Rips on the Wolf.

8 Rivers With Maps

BAD RIVER

SECTION 2

Bad River: Ashland County, Wisconsin.
Topo map(s): Mellen (1:62,500) 1967 and Odanah (1:62,600) 1964.
Overview map(s): Ashland (1953).
Public lands: Ashland County plat book (1969).
Section 1: See Marengo River (Map 23).
Section 2: (Section 1 of this river starts on the Marengo River, See map 23.)
Start: Elm Hoist Trail Bridge.
End: First bridge upstream of Odanah.

	SEC. 2
Difficulty (high water)	Qp
Difficulty (usual summer flow)	Qp
Length	19
Time	10
Width	50-200
Gradient	3
Drainage area	611

Water Conditions: There is a U.S.G.S. gauge located at the Elm Hoist Trail Bridge. This river has a rather uneven flow and is prone to flooding, thus the name Bad River. The river is best run in the spring when the water is higher. A gauge reading is turned in weekly to the U.S.G.S. Rice Lake Field Headquarters, P.O. Box 506, Rice Lake, Wisconsin 54868. Phone (715) 234-4015.

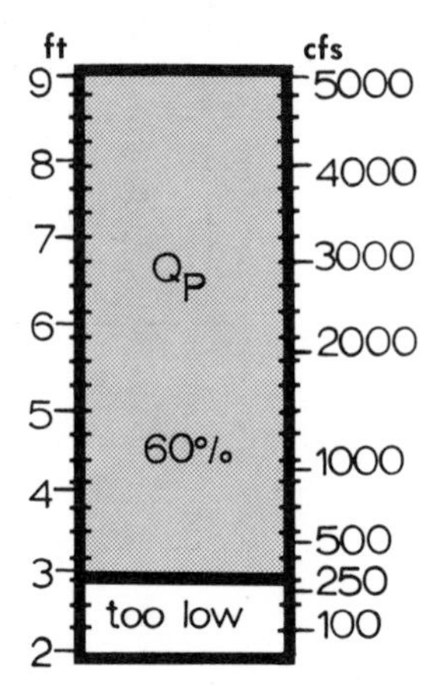

Canoeable Days Per Month

month	Apr	May	June	July	Aug	Sep
days	30	31	24	9	3	12

Scenery: The scenery is excellent. There has been virtually no development of the shoreline. There are a few areas of red sandstone cliffs. Large elms, maples, and other hardwoods in addition to "popples" make this area particularly colorful in the fall. Wildlife is common. Occasionally one can find Indian artifacts along the shoreline.

Geology: The geology of this river is very similar to that of the lower section of the Bois Brule and White Rivers. The bedrock consists of Lake Superior sandstone that is heavily overlayed with clay, which makes the river muddy. The steep river banks are highly susceptible to erosion.

History: This area underwent very extensive logging during the 1920's and 1930's. Although most of this area falls within the boundary of the Bad River Indian Reservation, an examination of land records indicates that a considerable portion of the land holdings are held by numerous commercial, corporate interests.

Fish: This river is noted for its excellent walleye fishing, particularly during the annual spring spawning run that occurs shortly after the ice moves out.

Campgrounds: See the description accompanying map 23.

Points of Interest: The numbered points of interest are continued from the Marengo River (map 23).

7 (12.4 miles) **Elm Hoist Trail Bridge.** This is the recommended put-in for this section. The roads in this area are primarily of dirt and clay: consequently during the spring thaw or during periods of unusually heavy rains, they are best traveled with four-wheel drive vehicles. This stretch of river consists primarily of quiet water, but there are two sets of rapids. Both of these rapids can be portaged, or the boats can be lined down.

8 (14.2 miles) **Rapids.** This rapids rates a grade II, when it is navigable, but during most periods it is too shallow and rocky to run. There are some very spectacular red sandstone cliffs in this location.

9 (15.7 miles) **Bad River Falls.** A powerline and a number of very large islands signal the approach of a series of sandstone and shale ledges. These ledges generally do not have a runnable chute. **They must be portaged or lined down.** There is a foot path on the right bank that can be used as a portage trail. This trail also extends to the Birch Hill Trail Road.

10 (20.4 miles) **Camerons Creek.** Enters from left.

11 (20.0 miles) **Sugarbush Creek.** Enters from right.

12 (26.6 miles) **Powerline.** Crosses river.

13 (31.2 miles) **Bridge.** This first bridge upstream of Odanah is the recommended take-out.

14 (32.2 miles) **Confluence with the White River.** The Chicago and Northwestern Railroad bridge is also located here.

15 (33.5 miles) **U.S. Highway 2 bridge.** This is an optional take-out. There are four more miles of river left before it enters Lake Superior. There is no access road at the mouth, only big, old Lake Superior in all its seasonal glory.

Photo 1. Rock Ledges above Bad River Falls.

Photo 2. Bad River Falls during early Spring.

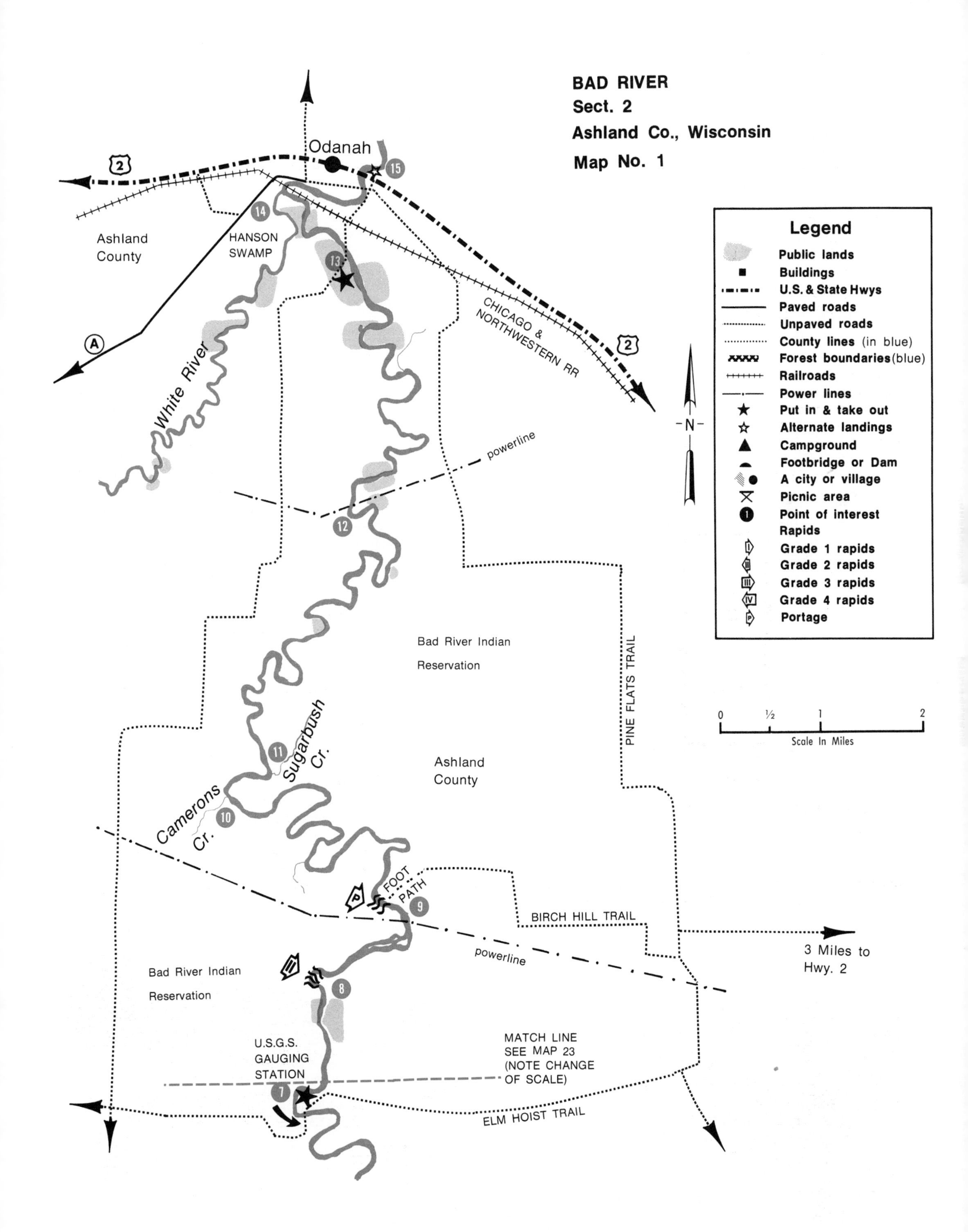
BAD RIVER
Sect. 2
Ashland Co., Wisconsin
Map No. 1
Legend
Public lands
Buildings
U.S. & State Hwys
Paved roads
Unpaved roads
County lines (in blue)
Forest boundaries(blue)
Railroads
Power lines
Put in & take out
Alternate landings
Campground
Footbridge or Dam
A city or village
Picnic area
Point of interest
Rapids
Grade 1 rapids
Grade 2 rapids
Grade 3 rapids
Grade 4 rapids
Portage
Odanah
2
Ashland County
HANSON SWAMP
A
White River
CHICAGO & NORTHWESTERN RR
N
powerline
Bad River Indian Reservation
PINE FLATS TRAIL
0
½
1
2
Scale In Miles
Ashland County
Sugarbush Cr.
Camerons Cr.
FOOT PATH
BIRCH HILL TRAIL
3 Miles to Hwy. 2
Bad River Indian Reservation
U.S.G.S. GAUGING STATION
MATCH LINE SEE MAP 23 (NOTE CHANGE OF SCALE)
ELM HOIST TRAIL
7
8
9
10
11
12
13
14
15

BLACK RIVER

SECTIONS 1 & 2

Black River: Gogebic County, Michigan.
Topo map(s): Ironwood (1:62,500) 1955, and Wakefield (1:62,500) 1955.
Overview map: Ashland (1953).
Public lands: Michigan DNR map of west part of Gogebic County, Michigan (1968).
Section 1
Start: County Highway 513 bridge 6 miles south of Bessemer.
End: Park in Ramsey, Michigan.
Section 2
Start: Park in Ramsey, Michigan.
End: U.S. Highway 2 bridge.

	SEC. 1	SEC. 2
Difficulty (high water)	I2	II-III
Difficulty (usual summer flow)	I2	II
Length	8	1.5
Time	6	0.5
Width	20-100	10-150
Gradient	8	20
Drainage area	77	120

Water Conditions: Section 1 is usually runnable except during periods of rather low flow. **Section 2** is not runnable except during high water. The flow in both of these sections depends on the amount of water discharged from the dam upstream. A U.S.G.S. gauge is located in Gogebic County, Michigan, on the right bank about 500 feet downstream of Powder Hill Creek and about 2.5 miles northwest of Bessemer. We have insufficient information at this time to indicate minimum water levels for a pleasurable run.

U.S.G.S. Gauge Conversion Table

ft.	cfs
0.5	12
0.8	33
1.1	68
2.0	262
3.0	565
6.0	2,020
8.0	3,300
9.0	4,200

Scenery, Geology, Fish and Campgrounds: See the description accompanying map 3.

Points of Interest:

Section 1

1. (0.0 miles) **County Highway 513 bridge.** This is the recommended put-in for Section 1. It is located six miles south of Ramsey.

2. (1.0 miles) **Devils Creek.** Enters from the right.

3. (2.5 miles) **Granite Rapids.** This is a rather straightforward three-foot drop that rates grade II. Novices may want to scout this rapids as it is decidedly more difficult than the other rapids on this stretch of river.

4. (3.7 miles) **Hasking Creek.** Enters from the right.

5. (4.0 miles) **Sunset Creek.** Enters from the right.

6. (6.2 miles) **Ramsey Dam.** Just above the dam is the recommended take-out for **Section 1** and put-in for **Section 2.** This old sluice dam is runnable.

Section 2 has fairly continuous grade II rapids. The river is fast and flows through a small canyon with high banks.

7. (7.7 miles) **U.S. Highway 2 bridge.** This is the recommended take-out for **Section 2.**

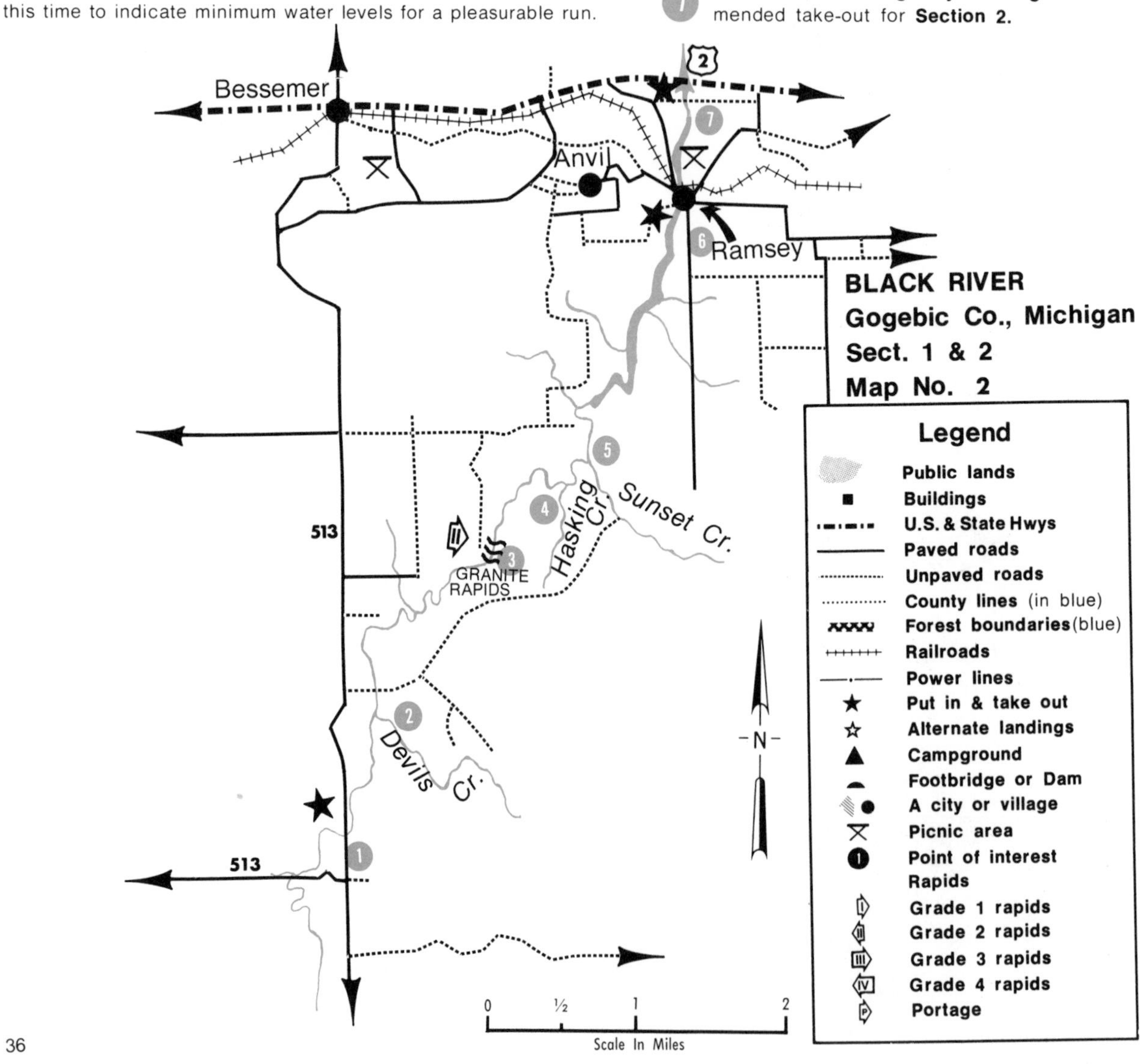

BLACK RIVER

SECTIONS 3 & 4

Black River: Gogebic County, Michigan.
Topo map: North Ironwood (1:48,000) 1956.
Overview map: Ashland (1953).
Public lands: Michigan DNR map of west part of Gogebic County, Michigan (1968).
Section 3
Start: The Narrows roadside park.
End: Road near Copper Peak Ski Jump.
Section 4
Start: Road near Copper Peak Ski Jump.
End: Campground at Lake Superior.

	SEC. 3	SEC. 4
Difficulty (high water)	III	IVp
Difficulty (usual summer flow)	Not runnable in low water	
Length	4	6
Time	3	5*
Gradient	--	60

***There are many portages so time for run depends on how fast you walk.**

Water Conditions: This is one of Michigan's wildest rivers. **Once you are on the river expect the worst.** You will find some calm stretches, but for the most part it is a fast stream with numerous waterfalls that must be portaged. There are no cut portages. You'll have to find your way between trees and up and down steep banks.

Scenery: The scenery is quite outstanding. There are numerous falls that must be portaged. All however are most attractive. The shoreline is heavily forested, and there are steep rocky hills.

Geology: The bedrock of this river consists of granite and other igneous rocks.

Fish: Rainbow and brook trout are in abundance.

Campgrounds: There is a developed campground at Black River Harbor State Park, located at the mouth of the Black River on the shore of Lake Superior. There are 24 sites, and a small fee is charged for their use.

Points of Interest:

Section 3

8 (17.6 miles) **The Narrows.** This roadside park is the put-in for **Section 3.** It is located on County Highway 513 seven miles north of Bessemer. Just below the put-in there is an island that is approximately a quarter of a mile long. Be on the lookout for possible log jams in either of these channels. Below this, Copper Peak Ski Jump comes into view for the first time. Below this point there are continuous boulder-strewn rapids, and it is not always easy to get to the shore.

9 (18.1 miles) **Whelp Creek.** Enters from the right.

10 (18.9 miles) **Reed Creek.** Enters from the left.

11 (19.6 miles) **Greys Creek.** Enters from the right. **Beware of low strung steel cable that crosses river near here.**

12 (20.8 miles) **Chippewa Falls.** Runnable by experts during high water. Somewhere below this point there is another low-strung **steel cable** crossing the river. Be on the lookout for it.

13 (21.4 miles) **Unnamed road.** This is the take-out for **Section 3** and beginning of **Section 4.**

(Continued on Page 38)

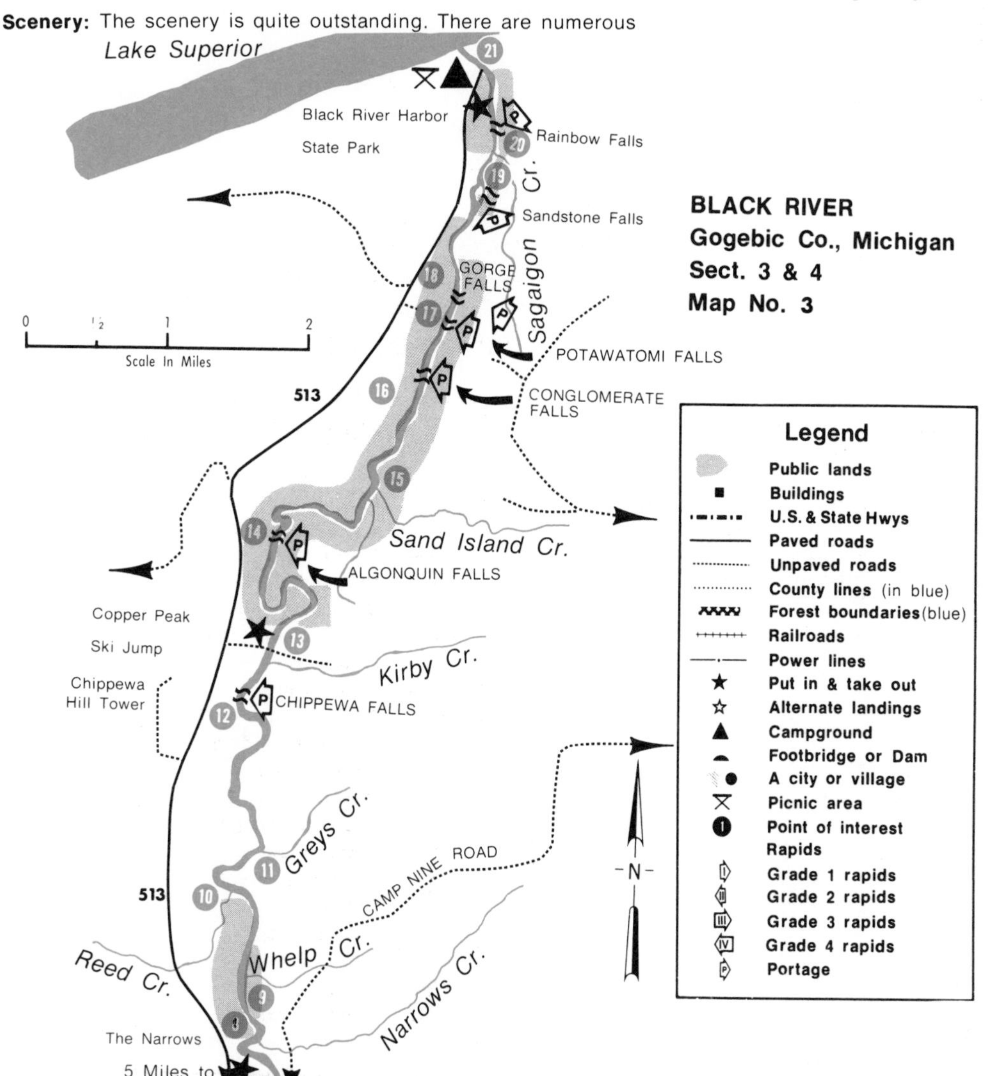

(Continued from Page 37)

Section 4 is best scouted but not paddled. It is much nicer and more beautiful from the shore than from a boat. If you do run this section the left bank provides the best route around all falls.

14. (22.8 miles) **Algonquin Falls. PORTAGE!**
15. (24.2 miles) **Sand Island Creek.** Enters from the right.
16. (25.0 miles) **Conglomerate Falls. Portage left.** A chunk of conglomerate rock sticking up in the middle of the river marks the beginning of this falls. There is a 25-foot drop here.
17. (25.6 miles) **Potawatomi Falls. Portage left -** 1/2 mile long. Recognized by two platforms erected on the west shore for spectators.
18. (25.8 miles) **Gorge Falls. Portage.**

BLACK RIVER (EAST FORK)

Black River (East Fork): Jackson and Clark Counties, Wisconsin.
Topo maps: Hatfield (1:48,000) 1958 planimetric and City Point (1:48,000) 1957 planimetric.
Overview map: Eau Claire (1953).
Public lands: Jackson County plat book (1968).
Section 1
Start: First bridge west of the village of City Point.
End: Bridge directly north of Pray.
Section 2
Start: Bridge directly north of Pray.
End: Black River Forest Campground near Lake Arbutus.

	Sec. 1	Sec. 2
Difficulty (high water)	II[3]	II
Difficulty (usual summer flow)	II	II
Length	8	11
Time	6	7
Width	20-100	30-150
Gradient	4	4
Drainage area	180	---

Scenery: This is one of those trips that make time stand still. All along the river there is a very pleasant mixture of red pine and oak trees. If you look closely you will see the blue heron which frequent the area, and if you listen carefully you will hear all kinds of hawks. Evidently the deer believe the place to be good, for they walk around with easy grace and confidence.

Campgrounds: Lake Arbutus Campground. There are two separate developed campgrounds at Lake Arbutus with a total of 55 sites. Jackson County charges a small fee for their use. For further information write County Park Administration, Black River Falls, Wis. 54165, or phone (715) 284-0224.

Black River Forest Campground. This campground is maintained by the Wisconsin DNR. There are 24 sites and a minimal user fee is charged. For more information write to the Wisconsin DNR, West Central District Headquarters, 910 Highway 54 East, Black River Falls, Wisc. 54615.

Points of Interest:
Section 1

1. (0.0 miles) **Put-in.** The recommended **put-in** is at the first bridge downstream of the village of City Point.
2. (2.5 miles) **Landing.** There is road access to the river at this site which is located north of Spaulding. There is another good landing on a paved road about one and a half miles downstream of here. It is recognized from the river by a cabin on the left bank. One and a half miles below this landing are 2 sections of grade I riffles.
3. (6.0 miles) **Falls.** At a point where the river bends to the left, there is a rapids in two pitches with an island midstream. The first pitch is rocky but easy. The second pitch has a three-foot falls that rates grade III when it is runnable; usually this last drop is too shallow to run. - **Portage** on the right bank.

Section 2

4. (8.0 miles) **Take-out** for Section 1 and **put-in** for Section 2. There is access on a road that runs north of the village of Pray.
5. (12.0 miles) **Unnamed creek.** Enters from the right.
6. (13.5 miles) **Unnamed creek.** Enters from the left.
7. (16.0 miles) **Rapids.** This rapids is recognized by a house on the left bank at a point where the river bends to the left. It rates grade II.
8. (18.5 miles) **Black River Forest Campground.** This is the recommended **take-out** for Section 2.

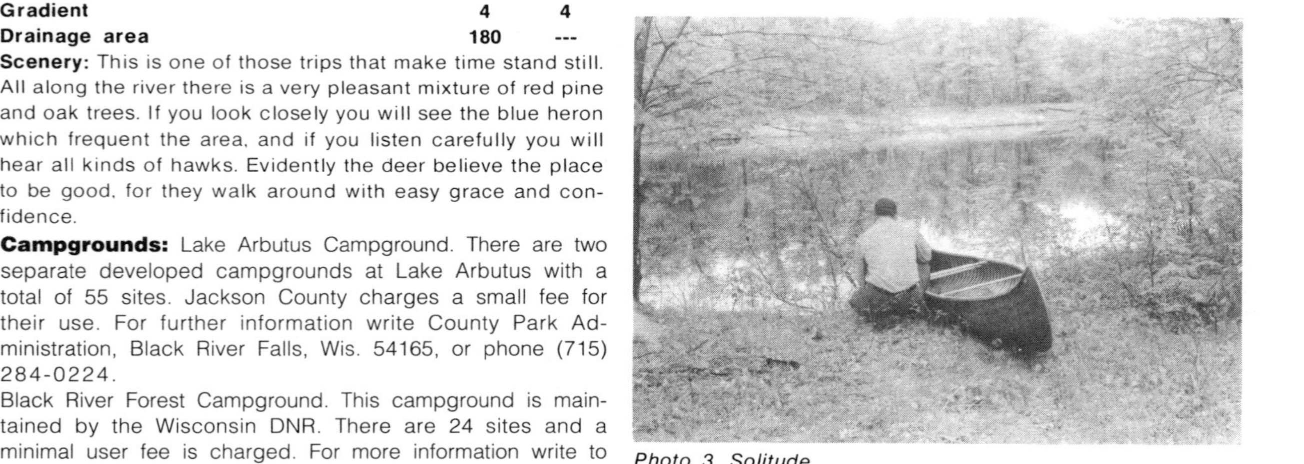

Photo 3. Solitude.

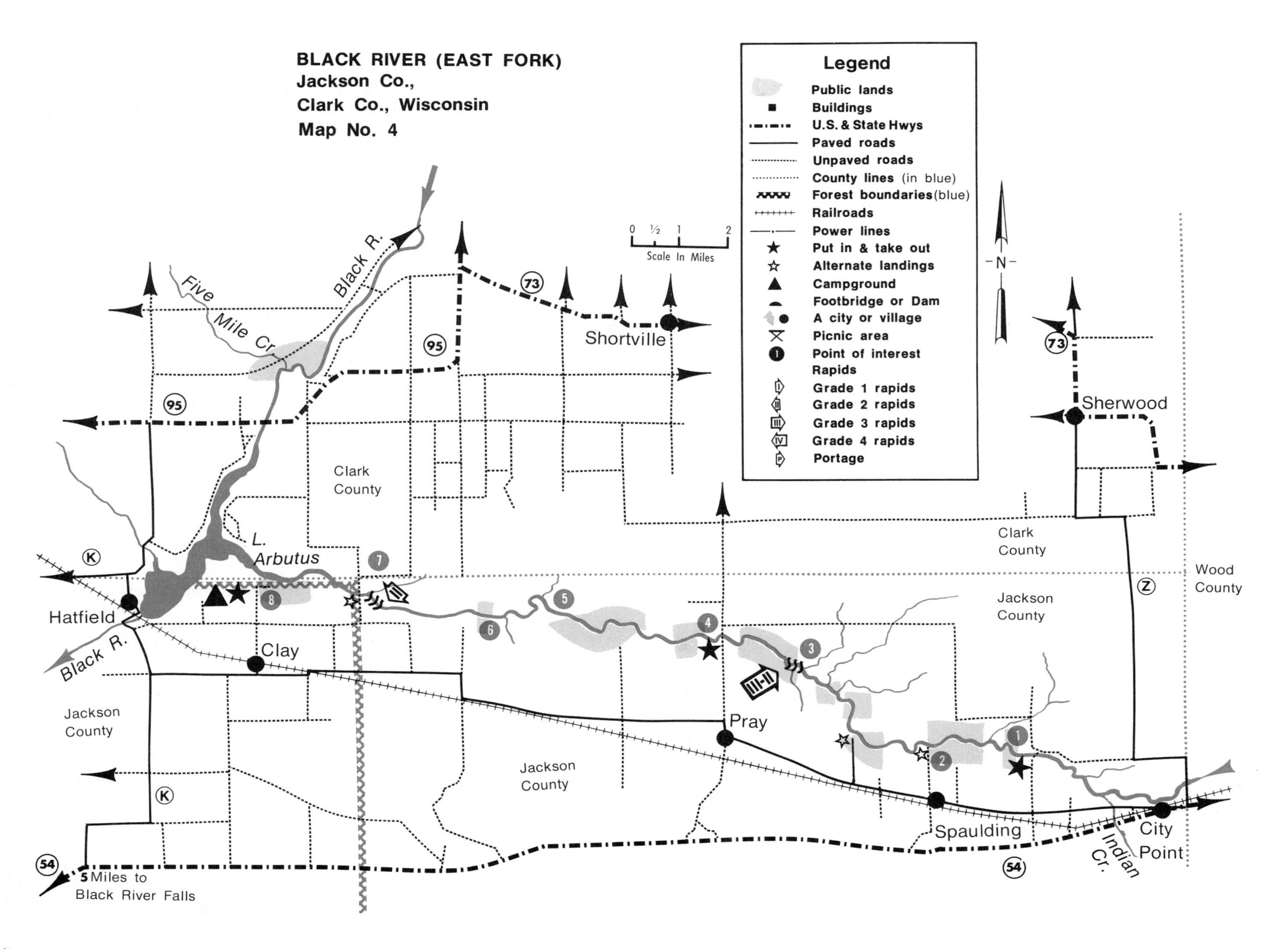

BLACK RIVER (EAST FORK)
Jackson Co.,
Clark Co., Wisconsin
Map No. 4
Legend
Public lands
Buildings
U.S. & State Hwys
Paved roads
Unpaved roads
County lines (in blue)
Forest boundaries (blue)
Railroads
Power lines
Put in & take out
Alternate landings
Campground
Footbridge or Dam
A city or village
Picnic area
Point of interest
Rapids
Grade 1 rapids
Grade 2 rapids
Grade 3 rapids
Grade 4 rapids
Portage
N
0 ½ 1 2
Scale In Miles
Five Mile Cr.
Black R.
Shortville
Sherwood
Clark County
Wood County
Jackson County
L. Arbutus
Hatfield
Clay
Pray
Spaulding
City Point
Indian Cr.
5 Miles to Black River Falls
73
95
54
K
Z

BOIS BRULE RIVER
SECTIONS 1 & 2

Bois Brule River: Douglas County, Wisconsin.
Topo maps: Brule (1:62,500) 1961 and Ellison Lake (1:62,500) 1961.
Overview map: Ashland (1953).
Public lands: Douglas County plat book (1973).
Section 1
Start: County Highway S bridge (Stone's Bridge).
End: County Highway B bridge near Winneboujou.
Section 2
Start: County Highway B bridge.
End: U.S. Highway 2 bridge at Brule.

	SEC.1	SEC. 2
Difficulty (high water)	I	II
Difficulty (usual summer flow)	I	I-II
Length	9	4
Time	4	2
Width	30-100	30-50
Gradient	4	17
Drainage area	27	

Water Conditions: There is nearly always enough water for a pleasant run. (See the description accompanying maps 6 and 7 for more details.) A U.S.G.S. gauge is located on the right bank of the river, 1.4 miles downstream of Nebagamon Creek, and 1.7 miles downstream from the Little Bois Brule River. For gauge information contact: Brule Ranger Station, Brule, Wisc. 54820.

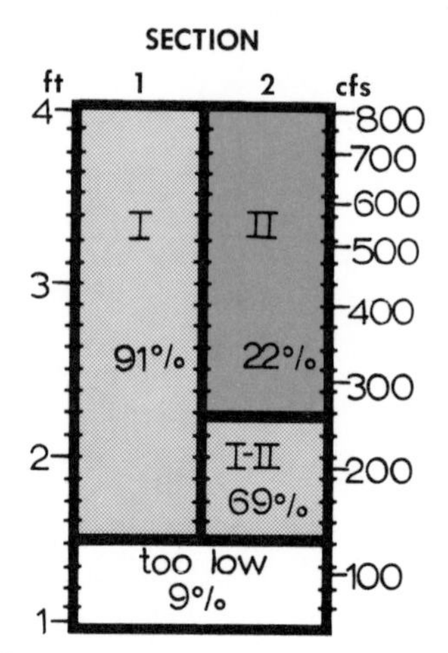

Canoeable Days Per Month

month	Apr	May	June	July	Aug	Sep
days	30	31	30	25	22	27

Scenery: It is worth seeing even though there are numerous cabins located within sight of the river. Motor boats are prohibited everywhere except at the mouth of the river. The map indicates how little shoreline is currently in public ownership even though the entire river flows within the boundaries of the Brule River State Forest. The upper stretches of river flow through numerous spruce and tamarack bogs. Downstream there are record-size white and Norway pines, wild orchids, and various species of land birds such as warblers and eagles, as well as deer and waterfowl.

Geology: The bedrock is of Pre-Cambrian age. Lake Superior sandstone is found in all of these sections with Keweenawan igneous rocks, gabbro, and basalt predominating in the first ten miles of Section 4. Near the end of Section 4, the river banks have large clay bluffs which experience continual erosion, contributing to the high turbidity of the water in this stretch.

History: This river was once part of an early fur trade route that connected the Great Lakes with the Gulf of Mexico via the Bois Brule, St. Croix, and Mississippi Rivers.

Fish: This is an internationally known trout stream.

Campgrounds: Brule River Campground close to the ranger station near the city of Brule. There are 37 sites at this developed campground that has road access. Wisconsin DNR charges an admission and user fee. For more information contact the Ranger Station, Brule, Wisc. 54870.

Lucius Woods State Park. There are 28 developed sites in this Wisconsin DNR campground. There are entrance and user fees. For more information write St. Croix Lake, Route 2, Box 435, Superior, Wisc. 54801.

Points of Interest:
Section 1

1 (0.0 miles) **Stones Bridge.** The put-in for this stretch of river is where County Highway S crosses the river. The bridge is named in memory of a Judge Stone, whose cabin was located nearby. We have not mapped the upper stretch of river as it is frequently too shallow for enjoyable canoeing.

2 (1.8 miles) **McDougal Springs.** This was once a privately owned trout pond but is now in public ownership. There are picnic areas at this location.

3 (4.0 miles) **Cedar Island Estate.** This can be recognized by a cedar board-covered building, followed by the boat house, the caretaker's residence, and then the estate itself. This site was the 1928 summer White House of President Calvin Coolidge. Presidents Hoover and Eisenhower were guests at this lodge during their terms of office.

4 (4.5 miles) **The Falls and Little and Big Twin Rapids.** All three are easy grade I rapids.

5 (5.0 miles) **Big Lake.** There are picnic areas on both sides of this natural impoundment of the river. There is a spring on the right bank near the picnic area. Wildcat Rapids is an easy grade I rapids connecting this lake with Lucius Lake.

6 (6.1 miles) **Lucius Lake.** This lake is another natural impoundment of the river. There is a small grade I rapids at the outlet.

7 (6.9 miles) **Spring Lake.** This is the last of the lakes on the Brule River. There is a nice spring located here.

8 (8.1 miles) **Little Bois Brule River.** This tributary of the main river connects on the right bank. Below this point is an easy grade I rapids called Station Rapids, named after a railroad depot, once located near this site.

Section 2

9 (8.9 miles) **County Highway B bridge near Winneboujou.** This is the recommended take-out for Section 1 and put-in for Section 2. This village is named in honor of an Indian god. Section 2 has more difficult rapids than Section 1; the first of these is Williamson Rapids, and it begins immediately downstream. It rates grade I-II.

10 (9.4 miles) **Hall Rapids.** Fast current is found in this rapids which is spanned by a footbridge. Two sharp turns are required in fast current, but they are not particularly difficult to execute, except perhaps for the novice. This rapids rates grade I, a rating contrary to information given by other guide books.

11 (9.7 miles) **Nebagamon Creek.** This trout stream is the outlet of Nebagamon Lake. The three pitches of Nebagamon Rapids are located near here, and all three rate grade I.

12 (10.9 miles) **Little Joe Rapids.** This is a short rapids that rates grade I-II. This rapids is a bit tougher than the others on this stretch. It may rate as high as grade II-III in high water -- the higher rating is for open canoes due to rather large waves which develop here.

13 (11.5 miles) **Brule River State Forest Campground.** There is an alternate landing at this site in addition to a developed campsite. The Brule River Ranger Station and the U.S.G.S. gauge are located nearby.

14 (12.5 miles) **U.S. Highway 2 bridge.** The landing is on the left bank upstream of the bridge. This is the recommended take-out for Section 2 and the put-in for Section 3. Limited parking is available.

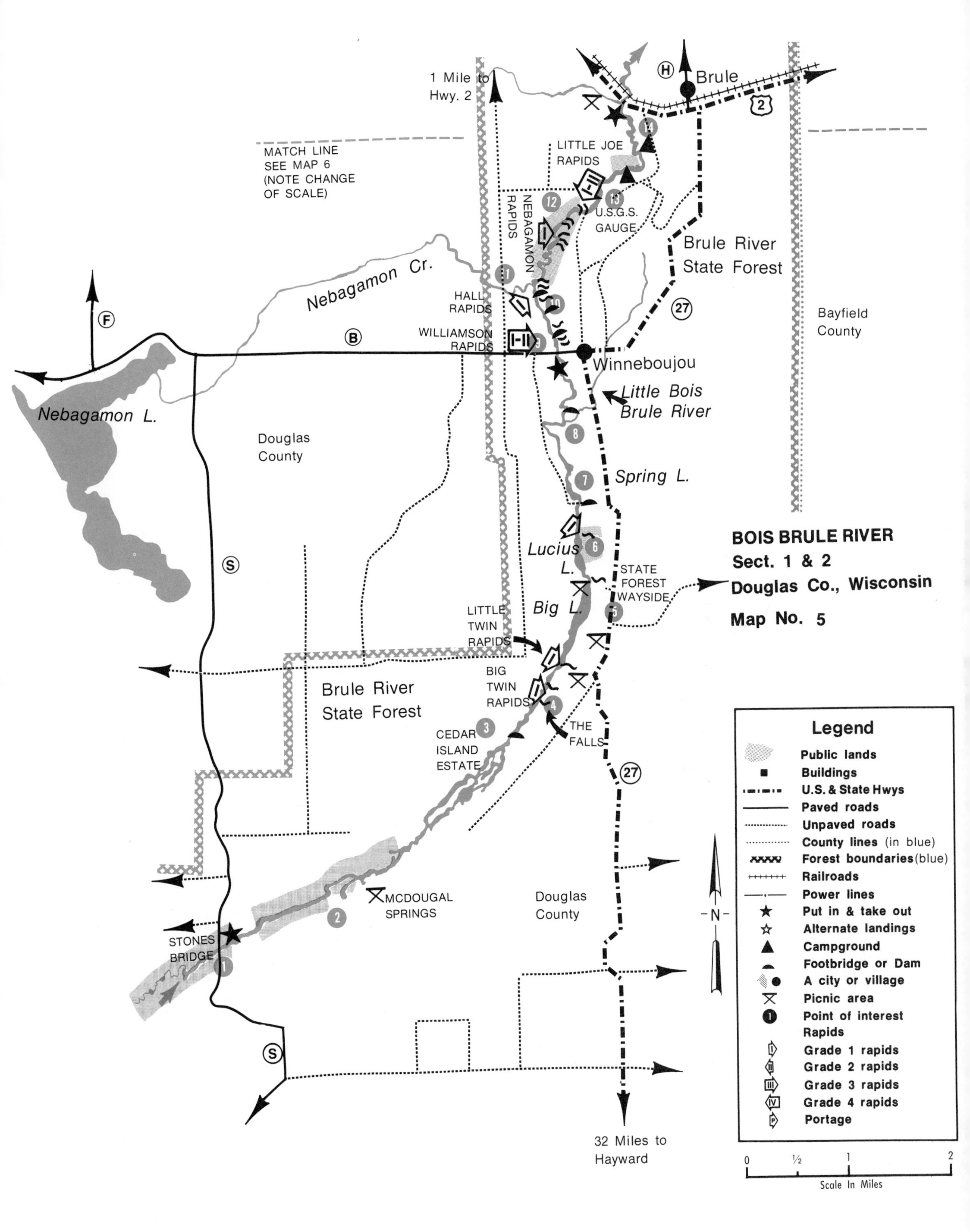

BOIS BRULE RIVER
Sect. 1 & 2
Douglas Co., Wisconsin
Map No. 5
1 Mile to Hwy. 2
Brule
MATCH LINE SEE MAP 6 (NOTE CHANGE OF SCALE)
LITTLE JOE RAPIDS
NEBAGAMON RAPIDS
U.S.G.S. GAUGE
Brule River State Forest
Nebagamon Cr.
HALL RAPIDS
WILLIAMSON RAPIDS
Winneboujou
Little Bois Brule River
Bayfield County
Nebagamon L.
Douglas County
Spring L.
Lucius L.
STATE FOREST WAYSIDE
LITTLE TWIN RAPIDS
Big L.
BIG TWIN RAPIDS
THE FALLS
Brule River State Forest
CEDAR ISLAND ESTATE
MCDOUGAL SPRINGS
Douglas County
STONES BRIDGE
32 Miles to Hayward
Legend
Public lands
Buildings
U.S. & State Hwys
Paved roads
Unpaved roads
County lines (in blue)
Forest boundaries (blue)
Railroads
Power lines
Put in & take out
Alternate landings
Campground
Footbridge or Dam
A city or village
Picnic area
Point of interest
Rapids
Grade 1 rapids
Grade 2 rapids
Grade 3 rapids
Grade 4 rapids
Portage
N
Scale In Miles

BOIS BRULE RIVER

SECTIONS 3 & 4

Bois Brule River: Douglas County, Wisconsin.
Topo map: Brule (1:62,500) 1961.
Overview map: Ashland (1953).
Public lands: Douglas County plat book (1973) supplemented with Wisconsin DNR records.
Section 3
Start: U.S. Highway 2 bridge at Brule.
End: Copper Range Campground.
Section 4
Start: Copper Range Campground.
End: Highway 13 bridge.
Section 5
Start: Highway 13 bridge.
End: Mouth of Bois Brule at Lake Superior.

	SEC. 3	SEC. 4	SEC. 5
Difficulty (high water)	Q	II-III	I
Difficulty (usual summer flow)	Q	II	Q
Length	8	8	7
Time	4	5	4
Width	30-50	30-50	30-50
Gradient	5	25	15
Drainage Area	175	(at FF bridge)	

Water Conditions: At 140 cfs there is sufficient water to run the ledges in Section 4. Above 250 cfs is high water for this river and therefore should be considered spring conditions. At this level, the ledges in Section 4 approach grade III. Look at rapids at County Highway FF bridge if you have doubts about your ability to handle this stretch. A rather unique combination of a small watershed, a high ground-water contribution, and numerous springs produces a river with a basically uniform water flow during all seasons. The flow rate ranges from a low of 130 cfs in August on a very dry summer to 500 cfs during the spring snow-melt runoff. However, the basic character of the river does not change appreciably at either of these extremes. At low water levels rock scraping is more of a nuisance than usual, but nevertheless the river is still quite runnable. See the canoeability chart accompanying map 7 for more details.

Scenery: High quality. Although there are numerous cabins along the shoreline, most of these developments are not particularly offensive. Most of Section 3 consists of bogs and elder thickets. Section 4 is primarily second-growth aspen with pines, spruce, birch and maple. Deer and waterfowl abound. Fishermen and their trappings are quite common, too.

Geology: (See the description that accompanies map 5.)

History: For a short history of this area see map 5.

Campgrounds: Copper Range Campground. There are 17 sites in this Wisconsin DNR developed campground. There is an entrance and user fee. For more information write: Brule Ranger Station, Brule, Wisc. 54820. For information about two other nearby campgrounds see map 5.

Points of Interest:

Section 3

14 (12.5 miles) **U.S. Highway 2 bridge.** The recommended put-in is at the public access located on the right bank just upstream of the bridge. This is a very lazy stretch of river. For eight miles, the river meanders slowly through elder thickets and pastures. There may be an occasional log obstruction. The gradient is only 5 feet per mile, as compared with 33 feet per mile for the start of Section 4.

15 (15.2 miles) **Rocky Run Creek.** This tributary stream enters from the right.

16 (15.7 miles) **Casey Creek.** Enters from the left.

17 (20.5 miles) **Copper Range Campground.** (formerly called Co-op Park). There is a take-out above these grade I rapids of the same name. You can also use the recommended take-out on the left bank upstream of the bridge, below this rapids. Percival Creek enters the river just downstream of this point.

Section 4

18 This is clearly the most difficult stretch of river, although it does not rate above grade II during usual water flows. There are nearly continuous grade I-II rapids until the Lenroot Ledges.

19 (23.0 miles) **Lenroot Ledges.** Two ledges in sight of one another. Identified by cabins on both sides of river. Scouting from the right bank is recommended, because the proper route is not obvious from upstream. These ledges are grade II and may rate as high as grade II-III in high water (>250 cfs). In low water (<125 cfs), there is not enough water to run either these ledges or the May Ledges downstream, below Johnson Bridge.

20 (23.3 miles) **Johnson Bridge.** This is the County Highway FF bridge. There is a landing with parking on the left below the bridge. The rapids by this bridge are typical of this stretch. It's worthwhile to look them over if you are unfamiliar with this river.

21 (23.8 miles) **May Ledges.** Three ledges of copper-range sandstone are within sight of one another. **Scouting is recommended.** The right bank is best for scouting and portaging. The second ledge of the three is the hardest. These rapids rate grade II at most times, but they may rate as high as grade II-III during high water. In low water these ledges may not be runnable. The rest of this stretch alternates between grade I-II rapids and quiet sections.

22 (28.3 miles) **Highway 13 bridge.** Take out on the right bank upstream of the bridge. A short walk up a steep cliff is required. There is ample room for parking. If you don't like hill climbing there is an alternate take-out on the left bank several hundred yards upstream of the Highway 13 bridge.

Photo 4. A typical rapids on Section 4 of the Bois Brule.

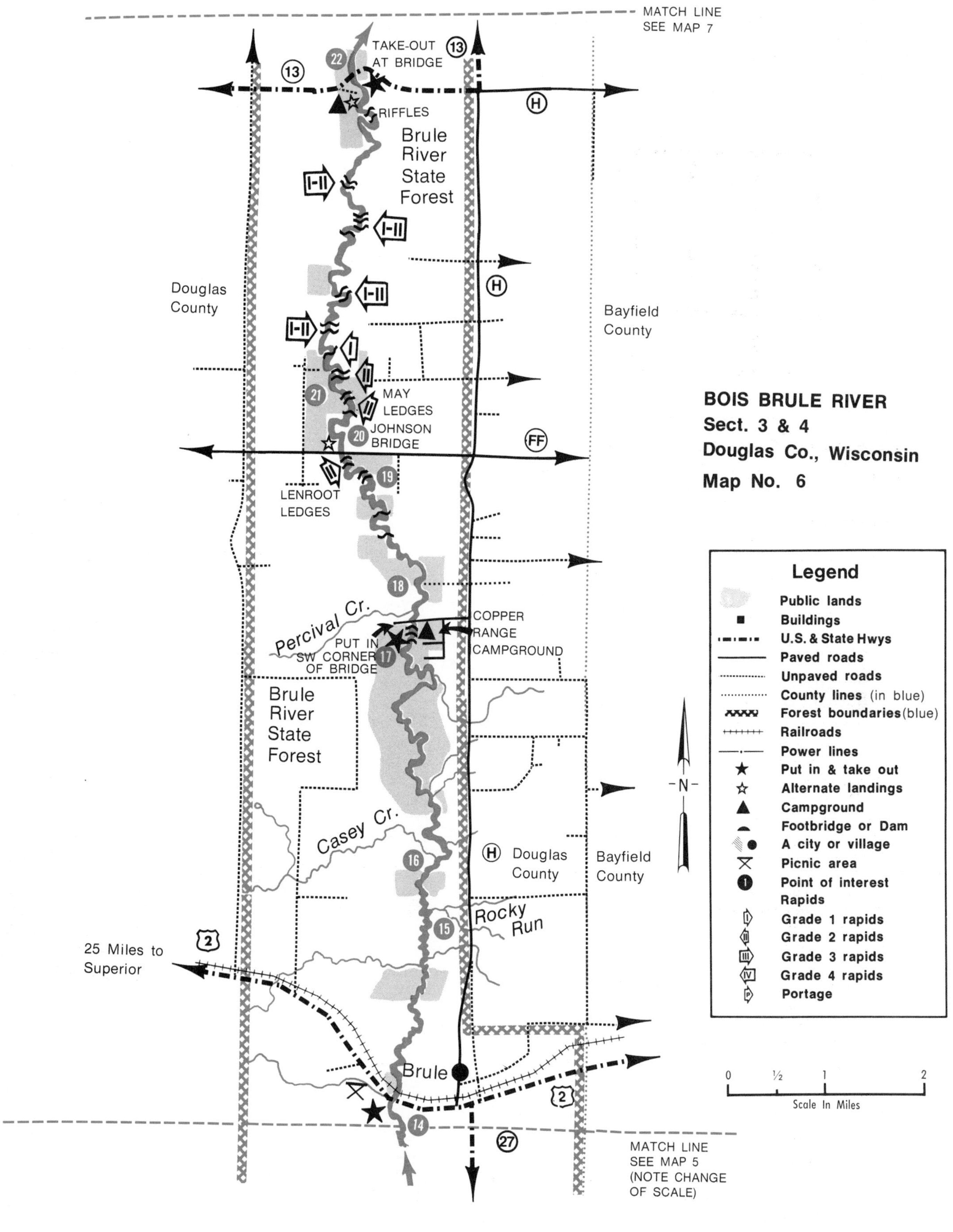
MATCH LINE
SEE MAP 7
TAKE-OUT
AT BRIDGE
13
H
RIFFLES
Brule
River
State
Forest
I-II
Douglas
County
Bayfield
County
I
II
MAY
LEDGES
JOHNSON
BRIDGE
FF
LENROOT
LEDGES
Percival Cr.
PUT IN
SW CORNER
OF BRIDGE
COPPER
RANGE
CAMPGROUND
Brule
River
State
Forest
Casey Cr.
Douglas
County
Bayfield
County
Rocky
Run
25 Miles to
Superior
2
Brule
27
MATCH LINE
SEE MAP 5
(NOTE CHANGE
OF SCALE)
BOIS BRULE RIVER
Sect. 3 & 4
Douglas Co., Wisconsin
Map No. 6
Legend
Public lands
Buildings
U.S. & State Hwys
Paved roads
Unpaved roads
County lines (in blue)
Forest boundaries (blue)
Railroads
Power lines
Put in & take out
Alternate landings
Campground
Footbridge or Dam
A city or village
Picnic area
Point of interest
Rapids
Grade 1 rapids
Grade 2 rapids
Grade 3 rapids
Grade 4 rapids
Portage
N
0 ½ 1 2
Scale In Miles

BOIS BRULE

SECTION 5

For additional details see the description accompanying map 6.

Water Conditions: This section has numerous riffles and is generally runnable. See the description accompanying map 5 for the gauge location.

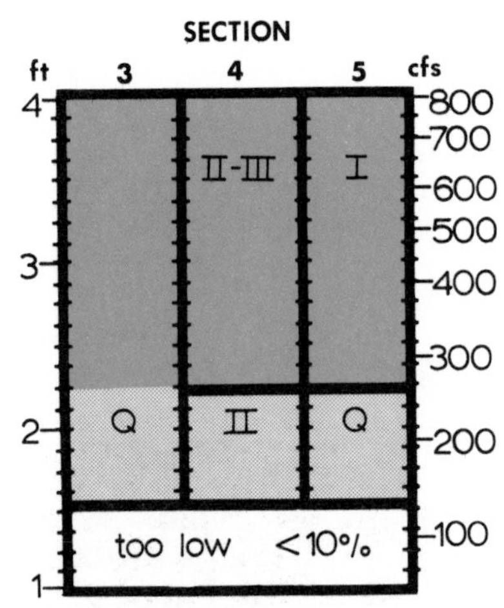

Canoeable Days Per Month

month	Apr	May	June	July	Aug	Sep
days	30	31	30	25	22	27

Points of Interest:

Section 5

(22) (28.3 miles) **Highway 13 bridge.** This is the put-in for Section 5. This stretch has good current with numerous riffles, and there is only one real rapids.

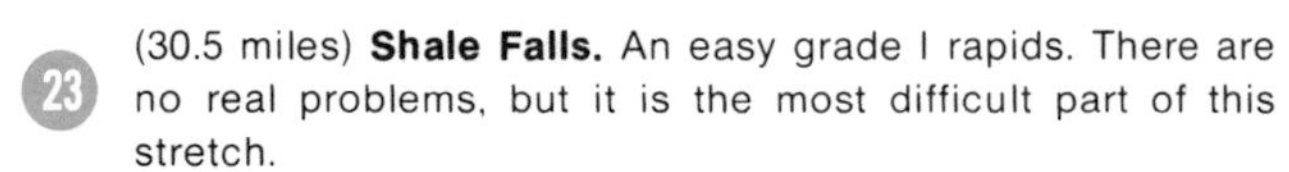

(23) (30.5 miles) **Shale Falls.** An easy grade I rapids. There are no real problems, but it is the most difficult part of this stretch.

(24) (31.0 miles) **McNeil Landing.** This is a marginal, optional take-out. The quality of the access road is seasonally variable. There are nearly continuous riffles downstream.

(25) (34.5 miles) **Trask Creek.** Enters from the right.

(26) (35.2 miles) **Electric Lamprey Weir.** A **portage** on the right bank is required here when this weir is in operation. The weir uses an electric field to steer fish into cages where the lamprey can be counted and killed and the fish released. The weir was constructed to see how effective various control measures were in eliminating the lamprey, which came into the Great Lakes when the St. Lawrence River was opened to ocean vessels.

(27) (35.6 miles) **Mouth of Bois Brule landing.** This landing provides the take-out for this trip. You might want to allow time to beachcomb for agates or driftwood, or just take a nice walk on the shoreline of Lake Superior. There is a picnic area here, but camping is not permitted.

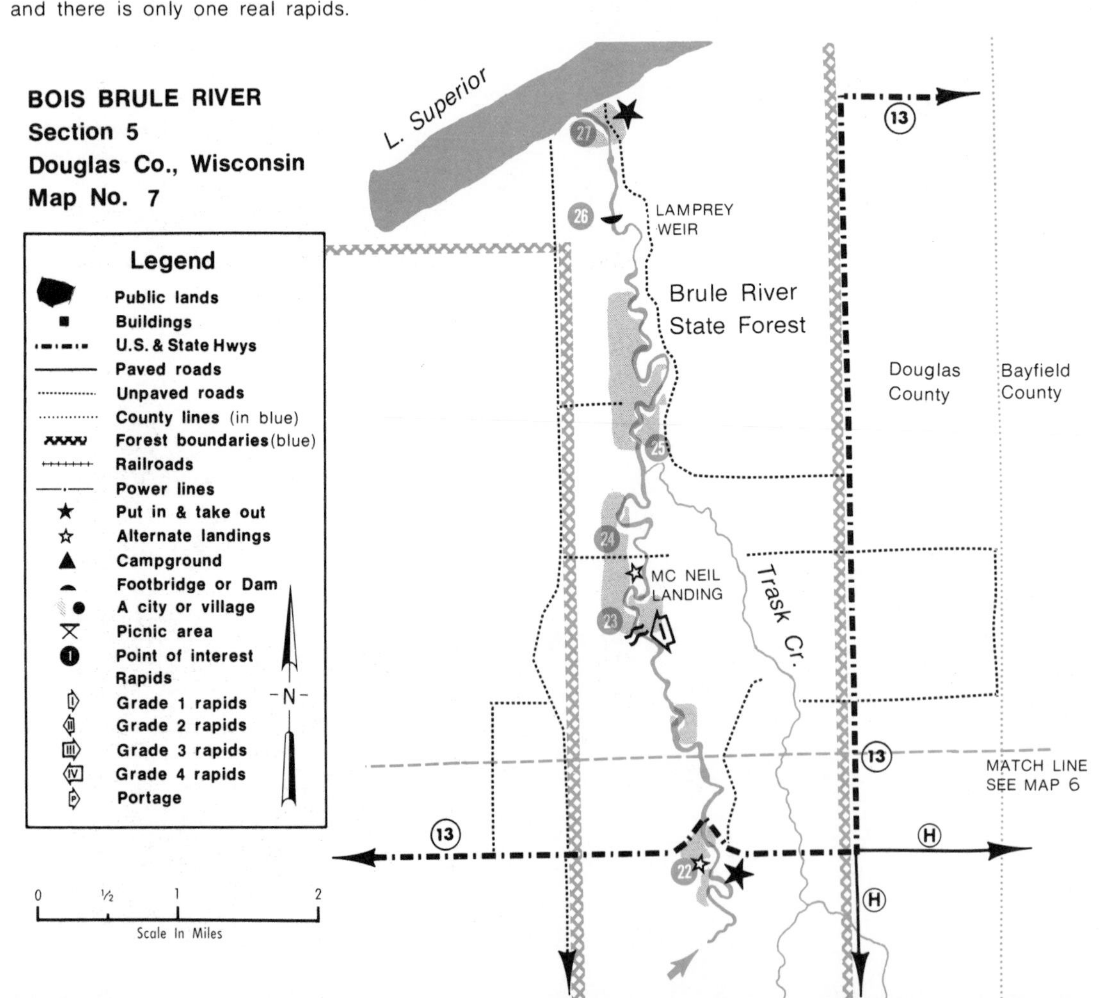

Photo 5. The landing at Stone's Bridge - the put-in for Section 1 of the Bois Brule.

Photo 6. "Let's make camp here."

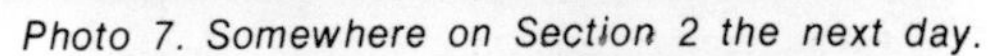

Photo 7. Somewhere on Section 2 the next day.

BRULE RIVER
SECTIONS 1 & 2

Brule River: Forest and Florence Counties, Wisconsin.
Topo map(s): Fortune Lake (1:24,000) 1944, Gaastra (1:24,000) 1944, Long Lake (1:48,000) 1939 planimetric and Beechwood (1:62,500) 1956.
Overview map(s): Iron River (1958) and Iron Mountain (1954).
Public lands: Forest (1966) and Florence (1971) Counties, Wisconsin plat books and Iron (1968 and 1969) County, Michigan DNR maps.
Section 1
Start:Wisc. Hwy. 55 (Mich. Hwy. 73) near Nelma, Wisc.
End: Wisconsin Highway 139 bridge (Michigan 189).
Section 2
Start: Wisconsin Highway 139 bridge (Michigan 189).
End: FS 2150 (Rainbow Trail) bridge.

	SEC. 1	SEC. 2
Difficulty (high water)	I	II
Difficulty (usual summer flow)	I	I-II
Length	14	11
Time	8	6
Width	20-100	40-125
Gradient	13	17
Drainage area	116	229

Water Conditions: The river is quite runnable when there are 400 cfs of flow, and it may be runnable as low as 200 cfs, which means this river probably always has enough water. The gauge is located at the Washburn bridge, one mile upstream of the confluence of the Paint River. See map 9 for exact location.

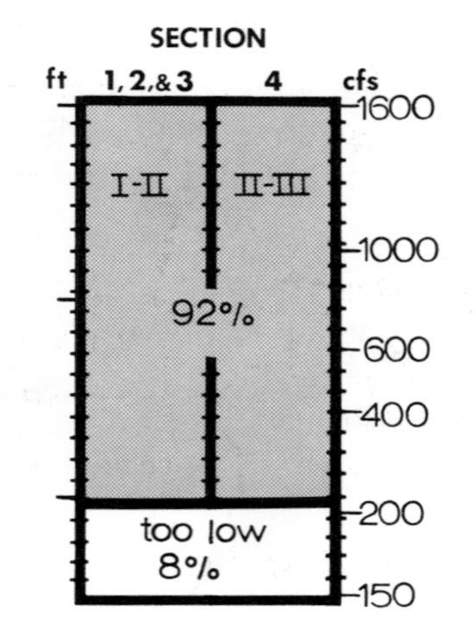

Canoeable Days Per Month

month	Apr	May	June	July	Aug	Sep
days	30	31	30	22	28	27

Scenery: See description accompanying map 9.
Geology: Pre-Cambrian metamorphic bedrock is covered with a layer of glacial drift that varies from a thin almost nonexistent layer to a very thick one.
Campgrounds: The Brule River Campground is in the Nicolet National Forest, located one-quarter mile before the river on Wisconsin Highway 55 (Michigan 73). There are 11 developed campsites. For more information write U.S. Forest Service, Eagle River, Wisc. 54521. Along the river there are occasional, primitive camping spots.
Points of Interest:
Section 1

1. (0.0 miles) **Brule River Campground.** This is located near the put-in and is maintained by the U.S. Forest Service. There are 11 developed campsites.

2. (0.5 miles) **Wisconsin Highway 55 (Michigan 73) bridge.** This is another possible put-in. Hagerman Creek enters from the left.

3. (6.0 miles) **FS 2172 landing.** Not far upstream of Wilson Creek is another possible put-in.

4. (9.0 miles) **Allen Creek.** Trout stream enters from the right. One mile downstream the outlet of Plover Lake enters from the left. A mile above Huff Creek the outlet of Mud Lake enters from the left.

5. (13.0 miles) **Huff Creek.** Trout stream enters from the right. Just downstream an unnamed stream enters from the right.

6. (14.7 miles) **Wisconsin Highway 139 (Michigan 189) bridge.** There is a developed parking area on the right bank, just upstream of the bridge. This is our recommended take-out for Section 1 and put-in for Section 2.

Section 2
There are numerous grade I rapids on this stretch.

7. (21.0 miles) **Wisconsin Creek.** Trout stream enters from the right.

8. (21.5 miles) **Iron River.** Enters from the left and is frequently rather muddy.

9. (22.2 miles) **FS 2152 landing.** There is no bridge at this location.

10. (22.5 miles) **Olsens Creek.** Trout stream enters from the left.

11. (24.0 miles) **Unnamed Rapids.** There are two grade I-II rapids located about a mile apart. In both cases they are located at a point where the Chicago and Northwestern Railroad approaches the river (left bank).

12. (27.0 miles) **FS 2446 bridge at Pentoga.** Alternate landing. Stay on the right side above the bridge as the left side has the remains of an old dam. Shortly downstream is the mouth of LeRoy Creek. This is a trout stream.

13. (29.6 miles) **Grade II ledges.** There is a two-foot drop over a rocky ledge. A path just to the right of center is usually best, but be careful of waves which may swamp open canoes. Immediately downstream of the ledge, the current pulls toward the right shore. Stay left to avoid getting hung up in the bushes on that shore. See map 9 for the remainder of this section.

14. (32.0 miles) **FS 2150 (Rainbow Trail) bridge.** This is the recommended take-out for Section 2 and put-in for Section 3. There is an extensive marshy area located downstream.

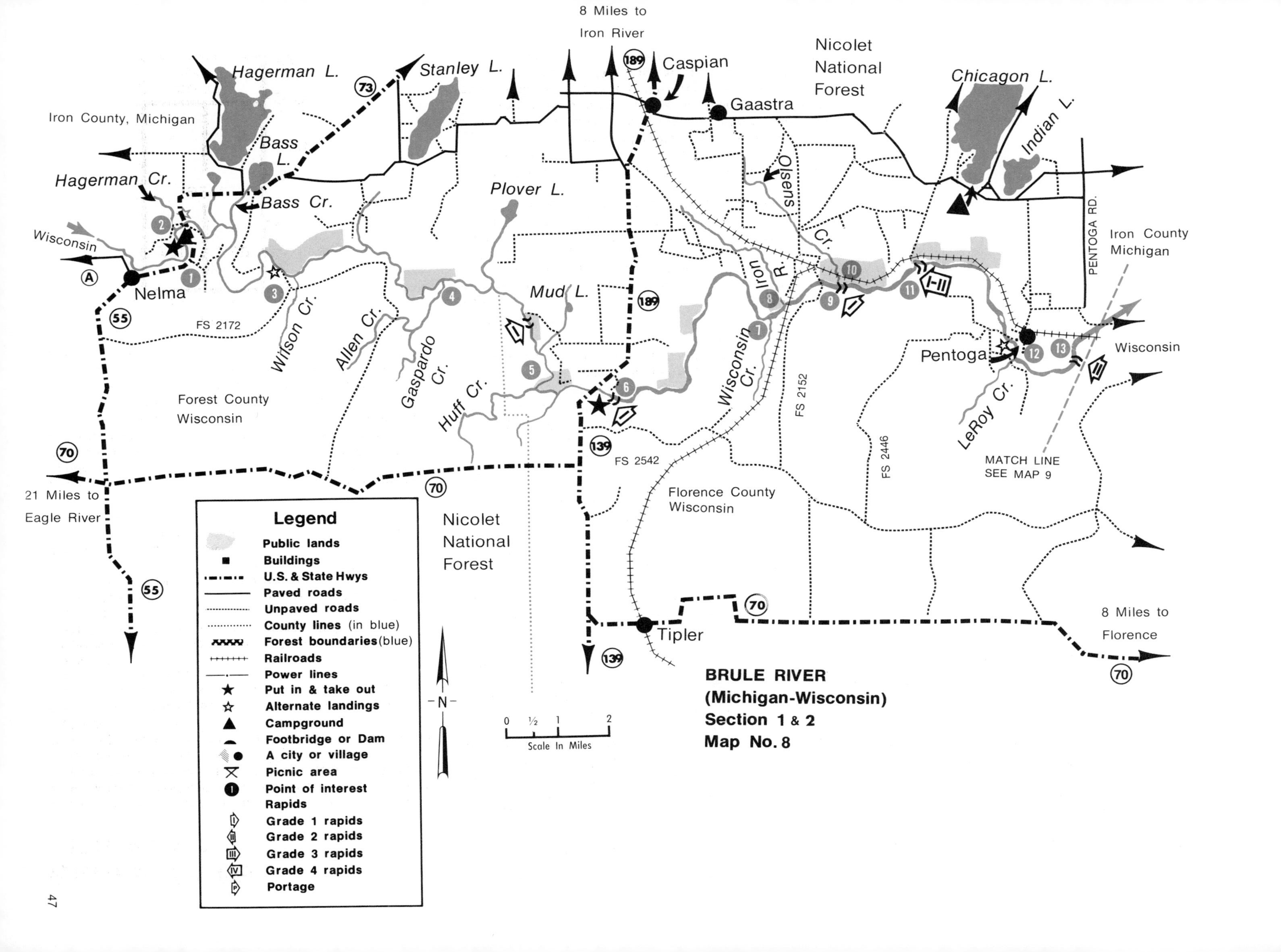

BRULE RIVER
(Michigan-Wisconsin)
Section 1 & 2
Map No. 8
8 Miles to
Iron River
Caspian
Gaastra
Nicolet
National
Forest
Hagerman L.
Stanley L.
Chicagon L.
Indian L.
Iron County, Michigan
Bass
L.
Hagerman Cr.
Bass Cr.
Plover L.
Olsens
Cr.
Wisconsin
Nelma
FS 2172
Wilson Cr.
Allen Cr.
Gaspardo
Cr.
Huff Cr.
Mud L.
Iron
R.
Wisconsin
Cr.
FS 2152
FS 2446
FS 2542
Pentoga
LeRoy Cr.
PENTOGA RD.
Iron County
Michigan
Wisconsin
MATCH LINE
SEE MAP 9
Forest County
Wisconsin
21 Miles to
Eagle River
Nicolet
National
Forest
Florence County
Wisconsin
Tipler
8 Miles to
Florence
Legend
Public lands
Buildings
U.S. & State Hwys
Paved roads
Unpaved roads
County lines (in blue)
Forest boundaries(blue)
Railroads
Power lines
Put in & take out
Alternate landings
Campground
Footbridge or Dam
A city or village
Picnic area
Point of interest
Rapids
Grade 1 rapids
Grade 2 rapids
Grade 3 rapids
Grade 4 rapids
Portage
N
0 ½ 1 2
Scale In Miles

BRULE RIVER

SECTIONS 3 & 4

Brule River: Florence County, Wisconsin and Iron County, Michigan.
Topo map(s): Florence East (1:24,000) 1962, Florence West (1:24,000) 1962, Naults (1:24,000) 1962, Fortune Lake (1:48,000) 1944, and Gaastra (1:24,000) 1944.
Overview map(s): Iron River (1958) and Iron Mountain (1954).
Public lands: Florence County plat book (1971) and Michigan County map (1967).
Section 3
Start: FS 2150 (Rainbow Trail) bridge.
End: (Washburn Bridge) Landing near junction of Paint and Brule Rivers.
Section 4
Start: Below Brule River Dam.
End: Landing six miles downstream of Brule River Dam.

	SEC. 3	SEC. 4
Difficulty (high water)	II	III
Difficulty (usual summer flow)	I-II	II-III
Length	14	6
Time	6	3
Width	40-150	100-300
Gradient	22	8
Drainage area	389*	1500**

*The U.S.G.S. gauge is located on the left bank, one mile upstream of the confluence of the Paint River and five miles upstream of the confluence with the Michigamme River.
**The U.S.G.S. gauge is located on the left bank, 0.5 miles downstream of the confluence of the Brule and Michigamme Rivers and 3.5 miles northeast of Florence.

Water Conditions: The water flow is greatly influenced by the release from the numerous upstream dams. Therefore canoeability may vary considerably from one day to the next. See chart accompanying map 8.

Scenery: The scenery is excellent. This would be a good choice for designation as a wild river. The shoreline of this river is covered with pines, various hardwoods, aspen, and birch. Marshlands break into the woodlands providing range for deer, blue herons, beaver, and various species of waterfowl.

Fish: There is good trout fishing in some of the spring-fed rapids of the river itself and in the numerous tributary streams. The reservoir is open to motor boats and the fishermen go after bass, northerns, and pan fish.

Campgrounds: See the description accompanying map 8.

Points of Interest:
Section 3

14 (32.0 miles) **FS 2150 (Rainbow Trail) bridge.** This is the recommended put-in for this stretch. There is an extensive marshy area located downstream and evidence of beaver colonies.

15 (33.2 miles) **Mouth of Armstrong Creek.** Trout stream enters from the left.

16 (33.5 miles) **Mouth of Riley Creek.** Trout stream enters from the right. This is the boundary of the Nicolet National Forest.

17 (36.2 miles) **Landing.** On the Michigan side there is a trail which may serve as an emergency exit.

18 (38.2 miles) **McGovern's Creek.** Enters from the left.

19 (41.8 miles) **Chicago and Northwestern Railroad.** Just upstream of this bridge Montagne Creek enters from the right. This is a trout stream.

20 (42.8 miles) **U.S. Highway 2 and 141 bridge.** There is an alternate landing on the left side downstream of the bridge.

21 (45.8 miles) **La Chapelle Rapids.** Rates grade I-II.

22 (46.5 miles) **Washburn Bridge.** This is the recommended take-out for Section 3. There is a U.S.G.S. gauge located here.

23 (47.5 miles) **Landing above the flowage.** This is near the mouth of the Paint River.

24 (47.6 miles **Brule River Flowage.** Has walleye, bass, northern pike, and pan fish. Flowage may be run; if so, take out at the dam. However, permission and cooperation from the dam keeper are necessary; he is needed to open the fence gate around the dam.

Section 4

This section of the Brule River is ideal for the adventurous canoeist who is comfortable in large streams with extremely rapid current and gigantic waves.

25 (49.6 miles) **Brule River Dam.** Below this dam on the right bank is the recommended put-in for this section of river.

26 (50.0 miles) **Fisher Creek.** Trout stream enters from the right.

27 (53.6 miles) **Michigamme River.** There is a U.S.G.S. gauge located here. At this point the Brule, having joined the Paint and Michigamme Rivers is now called Menominee. The water flow (cfs) is more than triple that of the Brule above the flowage on Section 3.

28 (54.6 miles) **Big Bull Rapids.** This grade III rapids is the major attraction on this section of river. **Scouting** from the large island near the right bank is **strongly recommended.** This rapids consists mostly of large waves developing at the upstream point of the island. The narrow channel on the right side of the island is not runnable due to tight turns and brush obstacles. The left channel has the majority of water flow and is usually a straight-through run except for some large rocks close to the island halfway down. Open canoes are easily swamped and this rapids is not recommended for those faint of heart or weak swimmers.

29 (55.6 miles) **Landing.** This is our recommended take-out.

30 (57.6 miles) **Alternate landing.**

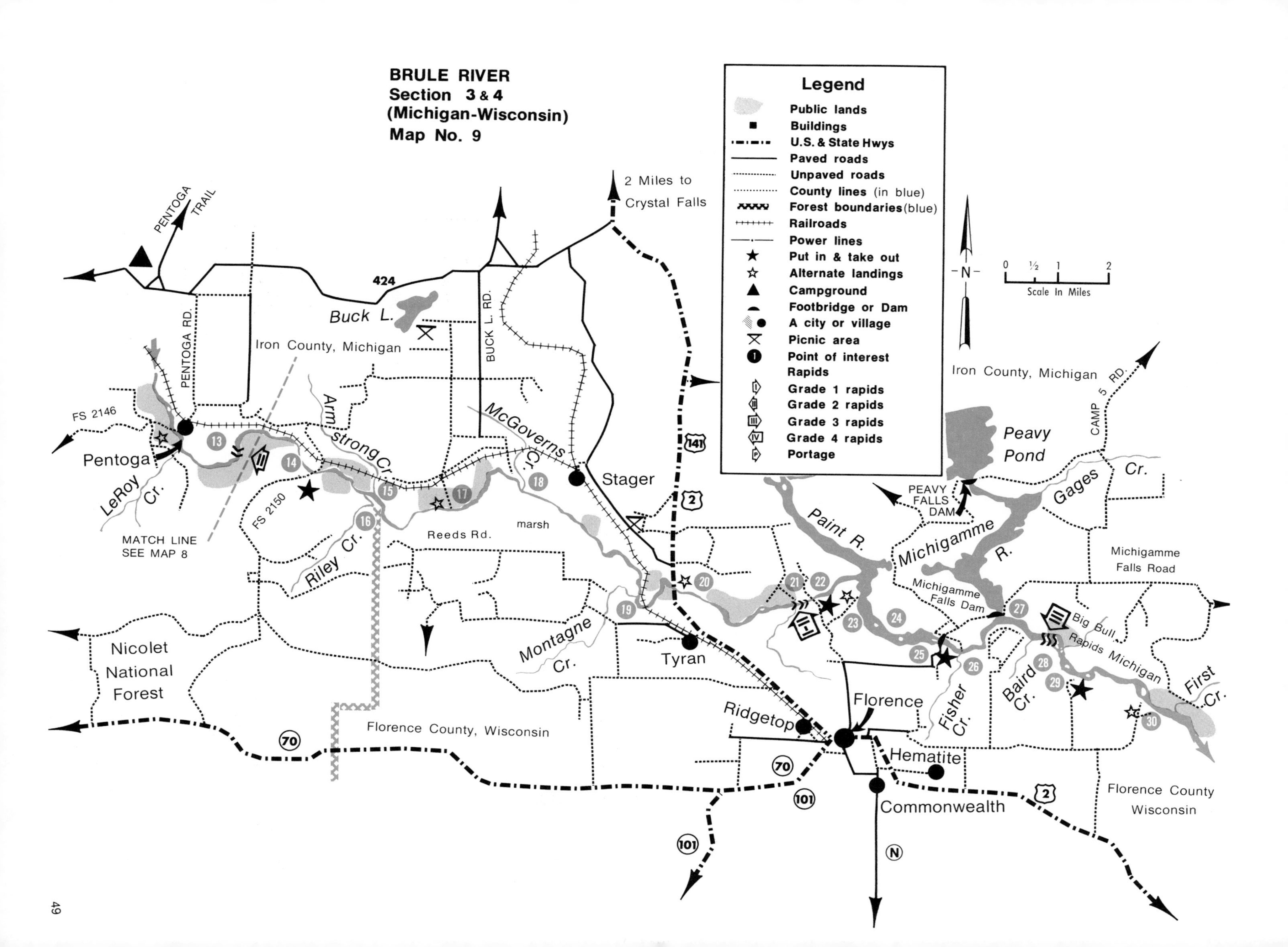
BRULE RIVER
Section 3 & 4
(Michigan-Wisconsin)
Map No. 9
Legend
Public lands
Buildings
U.S. & State Hwys
Paved roads
Unpaved roads
County lines (in blue)
Forest boundaries (blue)
Railroads
Power lines
Put in & take out
Alternate landings
Campground
Footbridge or Dam
A city or village
Picnic area
Point of interest
Rapids
Grade 1 rapids
Grade 2 rapids
Grade 3 rapids
Grade 4 rapids
Portage
N
0 ½ 1 2
Scale In Miles
2 Miles to Crystal Falls
PENTOGA TRAIL
424
Buck L.
BUCK L. RD.
PENTOGA RD.
Iron County, Michigan
FS 2146
Pentoga
LeRoy Cr.
MATCH LINE
SEE MAP 8
Armstrong Cr.
McGoverns Cr.
Stager
FS 2150
Riley Cr.
Reeds Rd.
marsh
Montagne Cr.
Tyran
141
2
Paint R.
Michigamme R.
PEAVY FALLS DAM
Peavy Pond
Gages Cr.
CAMP 5 RD.
Iron County, Michigan
Michigamme Falls Road
Michigamme Falls Dam
Big Bull Rapids
Michigan
First Cr.
Fisher Cr.
Baird Cr.
Florence
Ridgetop
Hematite
Commonwealth
Florence County, Wisconsin
Florence County Wisconsin
Nicolet National Forest
70
101
N
13
14
15
16
17
18
19
20
21
22
23
24
25
26
27
28
29
30

CLOQUET RIVER

Cloquet River: St. Louis County, Minnesota.
Topo maps: Brookstone (1:24,000) 1953, Independence (1:24,000) 1953, and Alborn (1:24,000) 1953.
Overview map: Duluth (1953).
Public lands: not done.
Start: U.S. Highway 53 bridge.
End: U.S. Highway 2 bridge (on St. Louis River).

Difficulty (high water)	**I-II**
Difficulty (usual summer flow)	**I**
Length	**11**
Time	**4**
Width	**100-200**
Gradient	**7**

Water Conditions: The water flow is controlled by the output of the Island Lake Reservoir Dam.
Scenery: This fairly wide, peaceful river is a pleasant trip through banks of woods punctuated by an occasional bluff. There is minimal development along the shores.

Geology: The rock in this area is mainly slate and dark-colored schist.
Campgrounds: See State Highway maps for campgrounds at Savanna Portage State Park and Cloquet Valley State Forest.
Points of Interest:

1. (0.0 miles) **Highway 53 bridge at Independence.** This is the recommended put-in for this river.
2. (2.9 miles) **Bridge.** The mouth of Chalberg Creek is located a short distance downstream from this bridge.
3. (4.5 miles) **Beartrap Creek.** This creek, like the outlet from Sunset Lake, enters from the left.
4. (5.0 miles) **Highway 7 bridge.**
5. (5.4/5.7 miles) **Railroad bridge and Highway 694 bridge.**
6. (8.0 miles) **Lake outlets.** The outlets of two unnamed lakes enter on opposite banks of the river.
7. (9.5 miles) **Confluence with the St. Louis River.**
8. (10.5 miles) **U.S. Highway 2 bridge.** This is the recommended take-out for this stretch of the river.

KETTLE RIVER

WATER CONDITIONS (MAP NO. 20)

Water Conditions: There is a stage marker located at the Highway 23 bridge. This gauge reads in feet. Below a reading of 1 the water level is too low for enjoyable canoeing. At a reading of 2 this section is suitable for persons experienced in open canoes and persons with decked boats having intermediate ability. Above a reading of 3, this river should only be run by experienced people with decked boats. This river has been run at a reading as high as 9 by experts but this is not recommended. The river has been known to change by two feet in one day, which means it has a very fast run-off. Because of the length of the first series of rapids, self-rescue can be difficult in high water when numerous large waves, souse holes, and cold water tire a swimmer. There have been several drownings and near drownings of inexperienced boaters and rafters, and even experts have had some difficulty reaching shore after capsizing. This section should only be run in the company of other boaters competent to perform rescue in high water and should not be attempted in open canoes during high water because of the additional probability of swamping and destruction of the boats.

The gauge indicated in the canoeability chart is the stage marker at the Highway 23 bridge. There is also a recently added U.S.G.S. Gauge at Sandstone, but we have insufficient information to correlate these two gauges or to indicate the percentage of the time the water flow exceeds the indicated gauge heights.

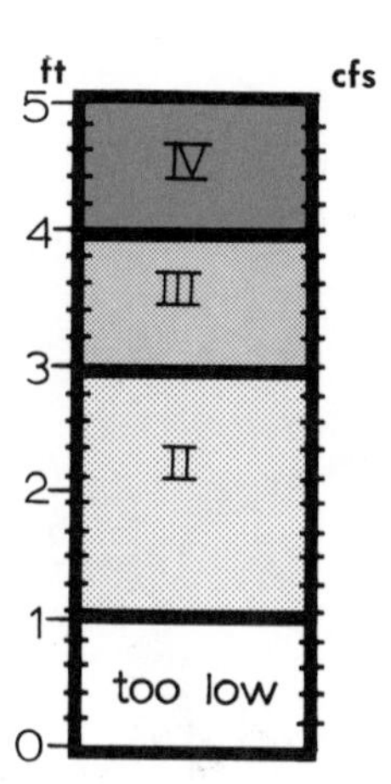

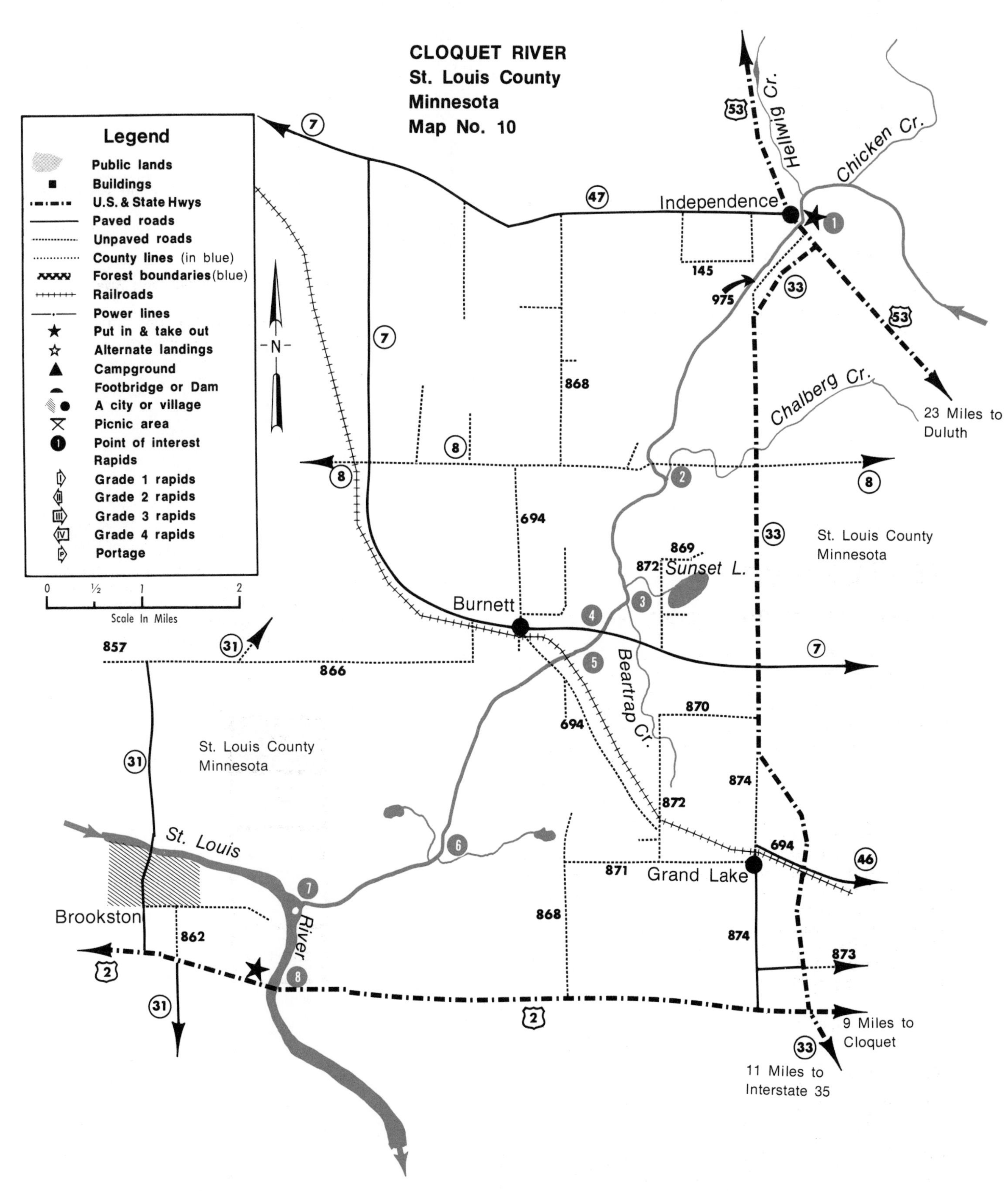

CLOQUET RIVER
St. Louis County
Minnesota
Map No. 10
Legend
Public lands
Buildings
U.S. & State Hwys
Paved roads
Unpaved roads
County lines (in blue)
Forest boundaries (blue)
Railroads
Power lines
Put in & take out
Alternate landings
Campground
Footbridge or Dam
A city or village
Picnic area
Point of interest
Rapids
Grade 1 rapids
Grade 2 rapids
Grade 3 rapids
Grade 4 rapids
Portage
0
½
1
2
Scale In Miles
N
Independence
Hellwig Cr.
Chicken Cr.
Chalberg Cr.
23 Miles to Duluth
145
975
868
694
869
872
Sunset L.
Burnett
Beartrap Cr.
St. Louis County Minnesota
857
866
870
874
872
871
Grand Lake
St. Louis
River
Brookston
862
873
9 Miles to Cloquet
11 Miles to Interstate 35

EAU CLAIRE RIVER

Eau Claire River: Douglas County, Wisconsin.
Topo map(s): Ellison Lake (1:62,500) 1961, Chittamo (1:48,000) 1947 planimetric, and Minong (1:62,500) 1965.
Overview map(s): Ashland (1953).
Public lands: Douglas County plat book (1973).
Start: Below Mooney Dam at the lower Eau Claire Lake.
End: Gordon Ranger Station.

Difficulty (high water)	**I-II**
Difficulty (usual summer flow)	**I**
Length	**14**
Time	**7**
Width	**15-50**
Gradient	**6**
Drainage area	**107**

Water Conditions: There is no gauge on this river, but as with the Bois Brule, there is a rather steady flow and usually enough water for a nice trip.

Scenery: The primarily undeveloped shoreline is very pleasing to the eye. Bald eagles soar above, along with a wide variety of waterfowl. This river's source is the Eau Claire Lake (elev. 1,120 feet), which is quite clear and clean. The riverbed is largely gravel.

Geology: This area has undergone extensive glacial activity. The oldest rocks here are Pre-Cambrian metamorphic and volcanic formations. In most places this bedrock is covered by Cambrian sandstone and other glacial clays, sands, silts, and gravels.

Fish: No catch reports available, but possibilities look promising. Trout hang around the rapids all along the river, and bass and northern pike have been known to frequent other quieter stretches of the river. The latter are particularly fond of the flowage above the dam.

Campgrounds: Lower Eau Claire Dam campsite is owned by the county, which charges a minimal fee. For more information, write to: Douglas County Conservation Department, Solon Springs, Wisc. 54873. A Wisconsin DNR developed campground, Lucius Woods State Park, is located at Solon Springs, and there is a user's fee. See state highway map for location.

Points of Interest:

1. (0.0 miles) **Mooney Dam.** This is located at the site of an old logging dam and is the recommended put-in for this stretch.

2. (1.2 miles) **Bridge.** There is an optional access at this point but the parking facilities are poor.

3. (2.8 miles) **Power Line.** A power line crossing above the river signals the approach of a long grade I rapids which is about half a mile downstream.

4. (3.1 miles) **Six Mile Dam.** Ruins of this old logging structure remain. We recommend a careful approach to this obstacle, which can be run with little difficulty.

5. (4.3 miles) **McCumber Bridge.** This could serve as a possible alternate landing, but it does not have a developed parking area. Shortly downstream of this bridge, there is an easy grade I rapids. Be on the lookout for **barbed wire** crossing the river in this area.

6. (6.3 miles) **Outlet of Sauntrys Pocket Lake.** There is an easy grade I rapids located a few hundred yards downstream of the outlet of this lake.

7. (7.3 miles) **Lindberg Bridge.** This is another possible access point with no developed parking area. There are two minor grade I rapids located further downstream.

8. (9.0 miles) **Bridge.** This bridge signals the start of an annex to the Brule River State Forest. There is an easy grade I rapids located just downstream from here.

9. (11.0 miles) **Eau Claire Flowage.** There are bass and northern pike in this impoundment.

10. (11.5 miles) **Eau Claire Dam.** This **must be portaged** on the left bank. The river conditions downstream are dependent on the amount of water that is released from the dam. If there is only a small volume of water being released, it is recommended that you take out here.

11. (12.6 miles) **Confluence with the St. Croix River.**

12. (14.0 miles) **Gordon Ranger Station.** This is our redommended take-out (left bank). Overnight camping is permitted at this location with no charge to river travelers. However, first seek permission at the ranger station.

Photo 8. Meandering through the brush.

Photo 9. Although photographed elsewhere this scene is reminiscent of the area below the confluence of the Eau Claire and St. Croix Rivers.

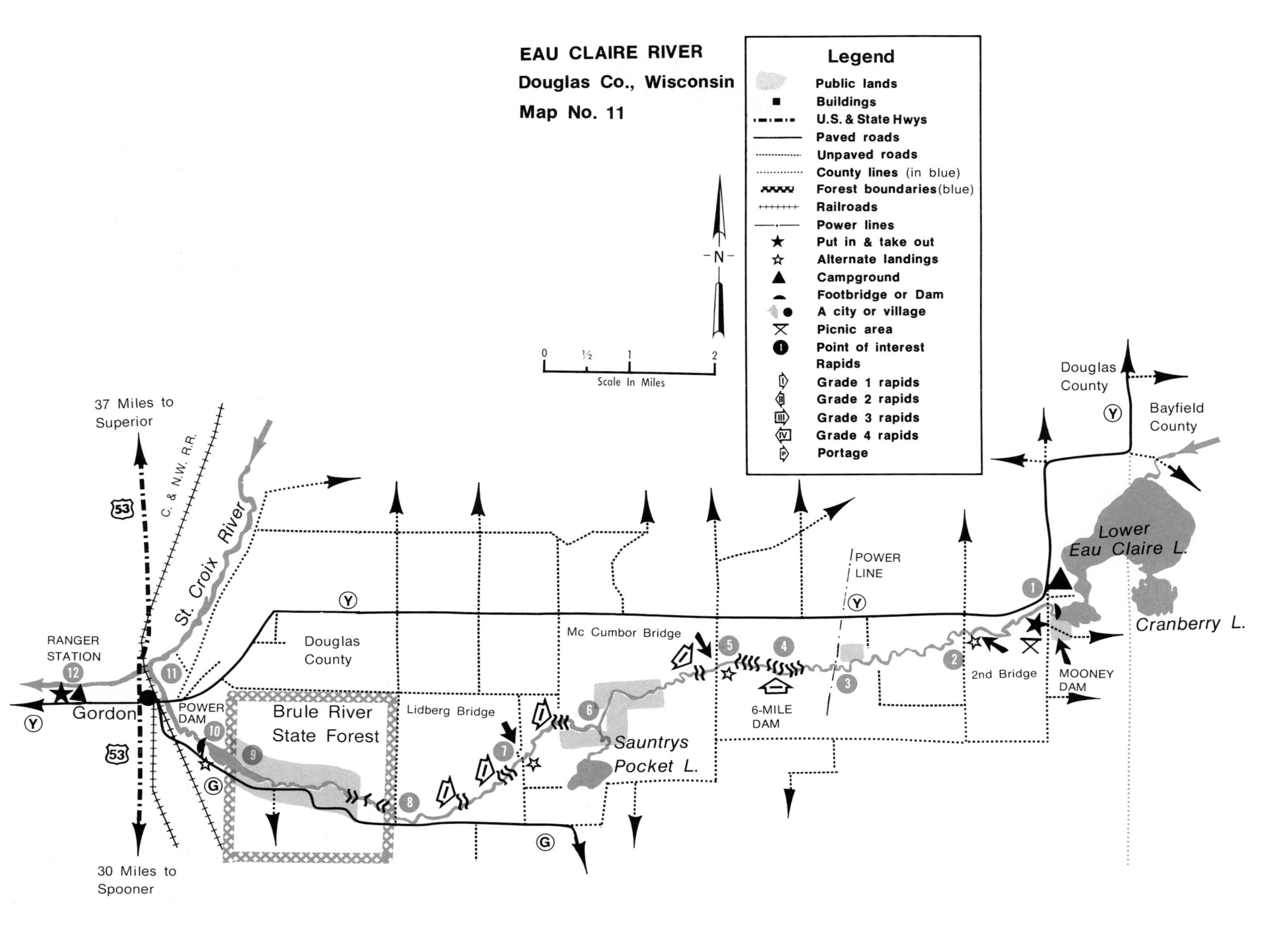

EAU CLAIRE RIVER
Douglas Co., Wisconsin
Map No. 11
Legend
Public lands
Buildings
U.S. & State Hwys
Paved roads
Unpaved roads
County lines (in blue)
Forest boundaries (blue)
Railroads
Power lines
Put in & take out
Alternate landings
Campground
Footbridge or Dam
A city or village
Picnic area
Point of interest
Rapids
Grade 1 rapids
Grade 2 rapids
Grade 3 rapids
Grade 4 rapids
Portage
N
0 ½ 1 2
Scale In Miles
37 Miles to Superior
30 Miles to Spooner
C. & N.W. R.R.
St. Croix River
RANGER STATION
Gordon
POWER DAM
Brule River State Forest
Douglas County
Lidberg Bridge
Mc Cumbor Bridge
Sauntrys Pocket L.
6-MILE DAM
POWER LINE
2nd Bridge
MOONEY DAM
Lower Eau Claire L.
Cranberry L.
Douglas County
Bayfield County

EAU CLAIRE RIVER

Eau Claire River: Marathon County, Wisconsin.
Topo map(s): Doering (1:48,000) 1951 planimetric and Hatley (1:62,500) 1964.
Overview map(s): Green Bay (1955).
Public lands: Marathon County plat book (1971).
Section 1
Start: Bridge over Spring Brook near Hogarty, Wisconsin.
End: State Highway 52 bridge at Hogarty.
Section 2
Start: Foot of low dam upstream within sight of County Highway Y bridge.
End: First bridge downstream of County Highway Z bridge.

	SEC. 1	SEC. 2
Difficulty (high Water)	II	II3
Difficulty (usual summer flow)	II	II3
Length	3	5
Time	3	4
Width	30-70	10-100
Gradient	18	19
Drainage area	276	291

Water Conditions: There is a U.S.G.S. gauge located on the right bank 50 feet downstream of the County Highway SS bridge near Kelly, Wisconsin, where the drainage area is 326 square miles. Do not be misled by the relatively deep water at the County Highway Y bridge. The river becomes much wider and shallower about two-thirds of a mile downstream. Weekly readings are sent to the Merrill Field Office of U.S.G.S. For more information write to Merrill Field Headquarters, 1029 1/2 E. Main St., P.O. Box 151, Merrill, Wisc. 54452, or phone (715) 536-2200.

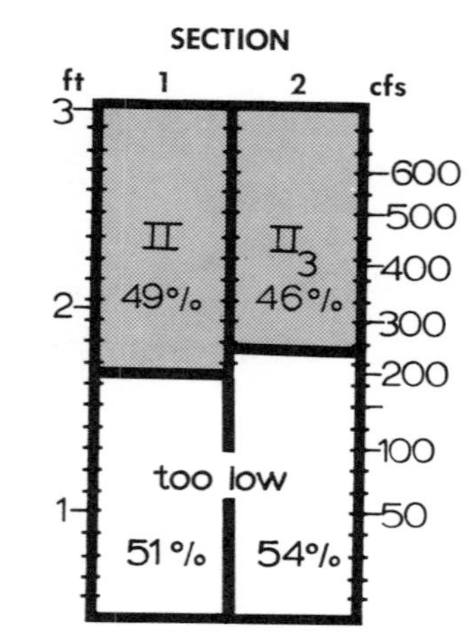

Canoeable Days Per Month

month	Apr	May	June	July	Aug	Sep
days	30	28	11	3	1	11

Scenery: Although not as grand or spectacular as other areas, this section of the Eau Claire River is quite pleasant. The only development seen during the trip is some stretches of cultivated or cleared farm land along the shoreline.
Geology: The bedrock of this river consists of granite and other igneous and metamorphic rocks of the pre-Cambrian era.
Campgrounds: There is a partially developed campground located at the dells of the Eau Claire River.
Points of Interest:
Section 1

1. (0.0 miles) **Spring Brook.** The recommended put-in is the bridge over Spring Brook located a few hundred yards upstream of its junction with the Eau Claire River.

2. (1.0 miles) **Master Ledges.** There are two sloping ledges within sight of one another. These rate grade II and are not particularly difficult. Novices may wish to scout them when the water level is low.

3. (1.5 miles) **Bader Ledges.** In the last half of this section, there is another double-ledge combination. The first ledge is preceeded by a slight bend of the river to the left, and it is easy to spot. The second ledge is located within sight of the first. Both of these ledges and the rapids between are the most difficult of this section, although they only rate grade II. The route over the lower ledge is by no means obvious from upstream. **Scouting** is **recommended** even for experienced boaters.

4. (2.75 miles) **Skulen Pond Creek.** Enters from the right.

5. (3.0 miles) **Highway 52 bridge at Hogarty.** This is the recommended take-out for this section. The next four miles downstream, until the recommended put-in for section 2, consist primarily of quiet water.

Section 2

6. (8.0 miles) **Dam.** This impoundment is used locally for various water sports. A portage may be required.

7. (8.2 miles) **County Highway Y bridge.** The recommended put-in for section 2 is located on the right bank below an old dam that is just upstream of this bridge. This bridge is the best location to **scout** the rapids located in the dells. This shallow rocky rapids rates high grade III. It descends 65 feet in a distance of one and a half miles. Just downstream of the bridge is the Dells County Park. Camping is permitted at this partially developed campground. There is a scenic overlook trail above the dells and a footbridge that spans the river.

8. (9.7 miles) **S-Curve Rapids.** At a point about a mile downstream of the dells the river makes the first abrupt turn to the left. Here you will find rapids of somewhat greater difficulty than the rest. **Scouting** is **advisable.** Danger: **barbed wire** may be strung across the river at this location. Use extreme caution.

9. (10.5 miles) **County Highway Z bridge.**

10. (11.0 miles) **Barnard Rapids.** At this spot a large island divides the river into two channels, both of which have rapids. The right channel is usually best. **Scouting** is **recommended.** These rapids are 700 yards long and have a total drop of 15 feet.

11. (14.0 miles) **Jody Creek.** Enters from the left shortly downstream. The recommended take-out is located on the right bank at a point where Old Wausau Road approaches the river. However, there is no developed landing here.

Photo 10. Dells of the Eau Claire.

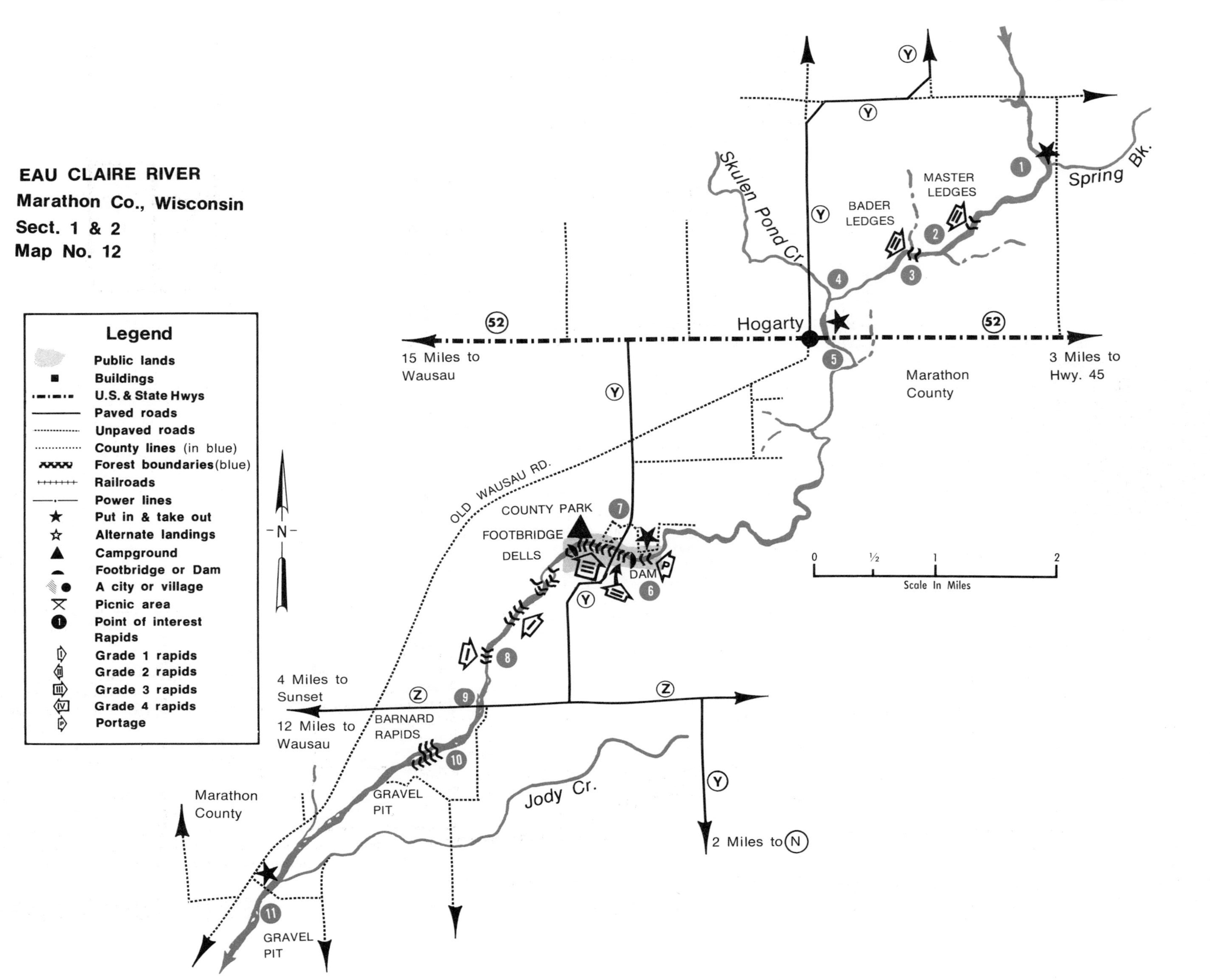
EAU CLAIRE RIVER
Marathon Co., Wisconsin
Sect. 1 & 2
Map No. 12
Legend
Public lands
Buildings
U.S. & State Hwys
Paved roads
Unpaved roads
County lines (in blue)
Forest boundaries (blue)
Railroads
Power lines
Put in & take out
Alternate landings
Campground
Footbridge or Dam
A city or village
Picnic area
Point of interest
Rapids
Grade 1 rapids
Grade 2 rapids
Grade 3 rapids
Grade 4 rapids
Portage
N
Spring Bk.
MASTER LEDGES
BADER LEDGES
Skulen Pond Cr.
Hogarty
52
15 Miles to Wausau
3 Miles to Hwy. 45
Marathon County
Y
OLD WAUSAU RD.
COUNTY PARK
FOOTBRIDGE
DELLS
DAM
0
½
1
2
Scale In Miles
4 Miles to Sunset
12 Miles to Wausau
Z
BARNARD RAPIDS
GRAVEL PIT
Jody Cr.
2 Miles to N
Marathon County
GRAVEL PIT

ESCANABA RIVER

Escanaba River: Marquette and Delta Counties, Michigan.
Topo map(s): Watson (1:62,500) 1963 and Gladstone (1958).
Overview map(s): Escanaba (1954).
Public lands: Marquette (1967) and Delta (1967). County maps prepared by the Michigan DNR.
Section 1
Start: Swimming Hole Creek Campground.
End: Boney Falls Dam.
Section 2
Start: Below Boney Falls Dam.
End: County Highway 519 bridge at Cornell. (A third section starting at the Highway 519 bridge and ending at County Highway 420 bridge near Carrol Corner can be run.)

	SEC. 1	SEC. 2
Difficulty (high water)	I-II	II3
Difficulty (usual summer flow)	I	I
Length	11	7
Time	4	4
Width	100-200	75-250
Gradient	9	15
Drainage area	748	779

Water Conditions: There is a U.S.G.S. gauge located 50 feet downstream of the take-out for Section 2. The average flow at this site for 26 years has been 896 cfs. The flow in Section 1 is primarily dependent on the output of the power plant at Gwinn controlled by the Boney Falls Power plant. This plant usually generates around the clock, giving a steady flow. When one turbine is working at full capacity, there is just barely enough water for an enjoyable run on Section 2. If two turbines are running, the water depth is less marginal. When all three turbines are running at full capacity and water is being spilled through the flood gate as well, standing waves are produced in this section that could swamp an open canoe. The rapids on this river are quite unique — there are no large boulders that must be avoided. Fast current and some standing waves allow large distances to be covered in a short time.

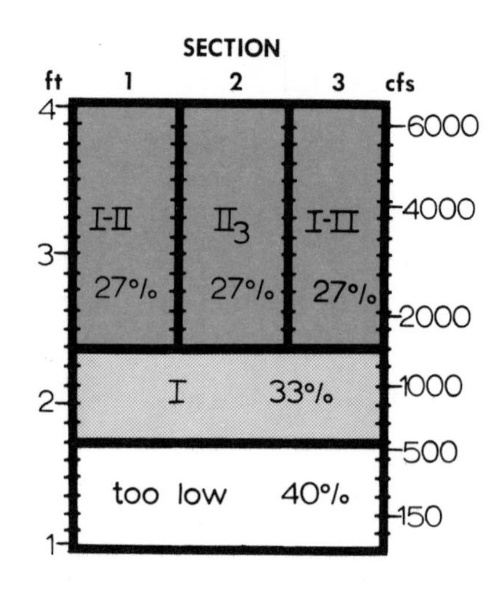

Canoeable Days Per Month

month	Apr	May	June	July	Aug	Sep
days	30	31	27	9	3	9

Scenery: There are interesting small rock cliffs located in the upper part of Section 2. Further downstream, the river runs through farmlands along the shoreline and through numerous marshy areas.

Geology: The bedrock of this river consists of Black River and Platteville-Galena dolomite with some limestone. The bottom consists of gravel and sand.

Fish: There are trout in the river above the Boney Falls flowage and bass in the flowage itself. This river makes a great float fishing trip.

Campgrounds: In addition to the Escanaba State Forest Campground (six sites) located at the put-in for Section 1, there are scattered primitive campsites along the river.

Points of Interest:

Section 1

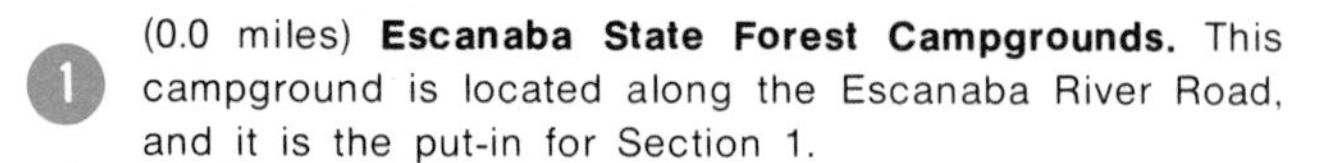

1. (0.0 miles) **Escanaba State Forest Campgrounds.** This campground is located along the Escanaba River Road, and it is the put-in for Section 1.

2. (2.8 miles) **Unnamed Creek.** Enters from the left.

3. (3.1 miles) **Unnamed Creek.** Enters from the right.

4. (6.1 miles) **Unnamed Creek.** Enters from the left.

5. (7.5 miles) **Unnamed Creek.** Enters from the left.

6. (8.5 miles) **Pipeline.** There is a cleared area where a pipeline crosses the river at this location. The road runs near here and can be used as a take-out if you wish to avoid the dead water of the flowage.

Section 2

7. (10.5 miles) **Boney Falls Dam.** The recommended take-out for Section 1 is on the river bank above the dam. The recommended put-in for Section 2 is located on the right bank, downstream of the dam.

8. (12.7 miles) **Squaw Creek.** Enters from the left.

9. (13.0 miles) **Indian Creek.** Enters from the left.

10. (14.2 miles) **Hunters Brook.** Enters from the right.

11. (14.6 miles) **Ledges. Scouting is recommended** here because this area has some irregular sloping ledges that could cause difficulties for those people using open canoes. Take out early, on the left bank, because it is easy to underestimate the force of the current above these ledges. This rapids usually rates a grade II.

12. (15.8 miles) **Mosquito Creek.** Enters from the left.

13. (16.6 miles) **Bobs Creek.** Enters from the right.

Section 3

14. (17.1 miles) **County Highway 519 bridge at Cornell.** This is the recommended take-out for this stretch. The U.S.G.S. gauge is located 50 feet downstream of this location. For those boaters interested in a longer trip, it is possible to continue another 10.5 miles downstream to the County 420 bridge located 3 miles due west of Gladstone. This stretch of river has a gradient of 7 feet per mile and is probably similar to Section 1 of this river. We have not run this section of the river, however, and have not mapped it.

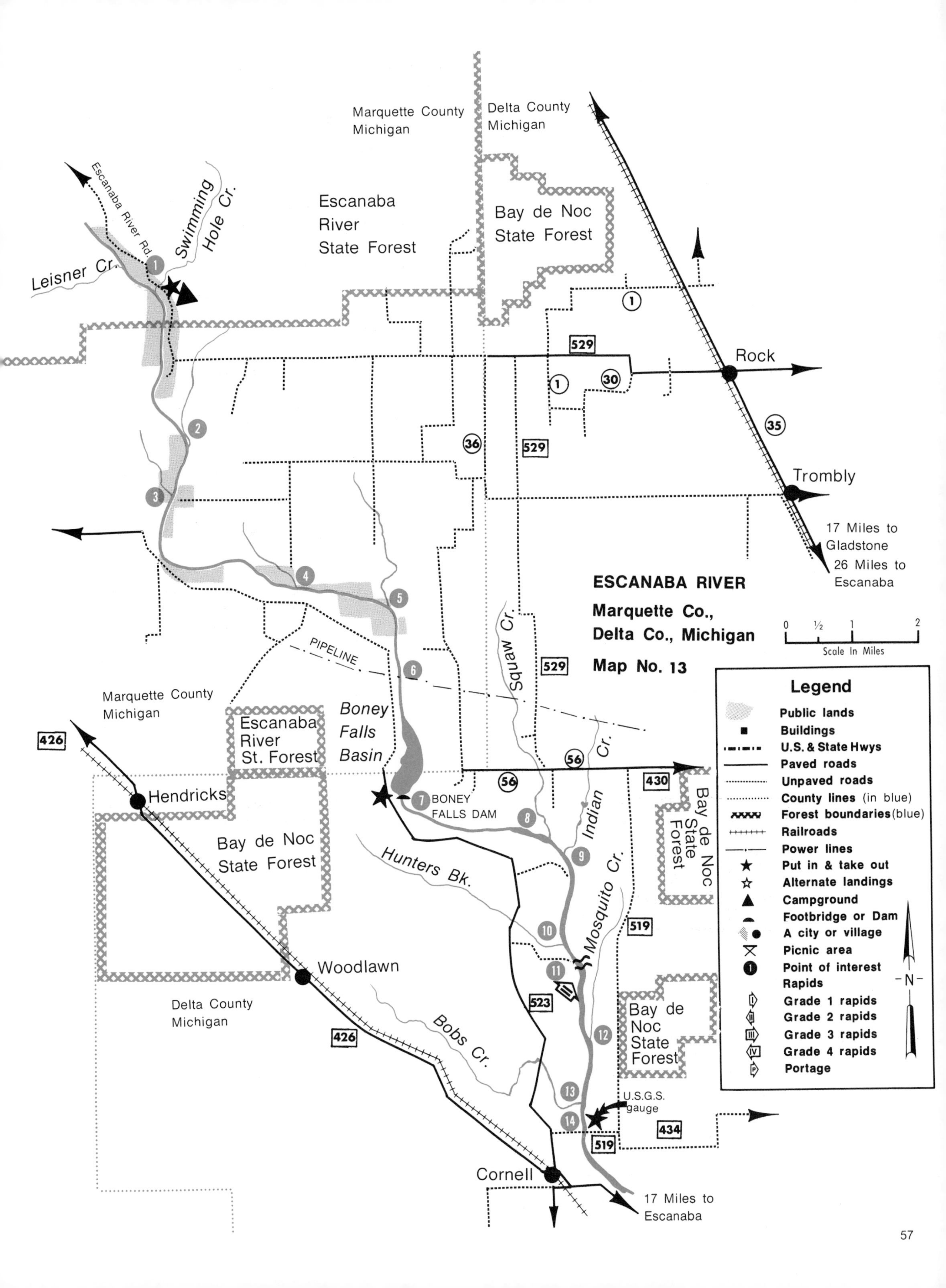
ESCANABA RIVER
Marquette Co.,
Delta Co., Michigan
Map No. 13
Marquette County
Michigan
Delta County
Michigan
Escanaba River Rd.
Swimming Hole Cr.
Leisner Cr.
Escanaba
River
State Forest
Bay de Noc
State Forest
Rock
Trombly
17 Miles to
Gladstone
26 Miles to
Escanaba
PIPELINE
Squaw Cr.
Boney
Falls
Basin
Escanaba
River
St. Forest
BONEY
FALLS DAM
Indian
Cr.
Hunters Bk.
Mosquito Cr.
Hendricks
Bay de Noc
State Forest
Woodlawn
Delta County
Michigan
Bobs Cr.
U.S.G.S.
gauge
Cornell
17 Miles to
Escanaba
Scale In Miles
Legend
Public lands
Buildings
U.S. & State Hwys
Paved roads
Unpaved roads
County lines (in blue)
Forest boundaries(blue)
Railroads
Power lines
Put in & take out
Alternate landings
Campground
Footbridge or Dam
A city or village
Picnic area
Point of interest
Rapids
Grade 1 rapids
Grade 2 rapids
Grade 3 rapids
Grade 4 rapids
Portage
N

FLAMBEAU RIVER (NORTH FORK)

SECTIONS 1 & 2

Flambeau River (North Fork): Sawyer and Price Counties, Wisconsin.

Topo map(s): Draper (1:48,000) 1944 planimetric and Kennedy (1:48,000) 1941 planimetric.

Overview map(s): Rice Lake (1953).

Public lands: Sawyer County (1968) and Price County (1968) plat books, updated to January 1973 with Wisconsin DNR records.

Section 1

Start: Mouth of nine Mile Creek.

End: Highway 70 bridge at Oxbo.

Section 2

Start: Highway 70 bridge at Oxbo.

End: Babbs Island Ranger Station (County Highway W bridge).

	SEC. 1	SEC. 2
Difficulty (high water)	I	I
Difficulty (usual summer flow)	I	I
Length	9	7
Time	5	4
Width	40-100	50-100
Gradient	3	4
Drainage area	--	1,000

Water Conditions: See the description accompanying map 15.

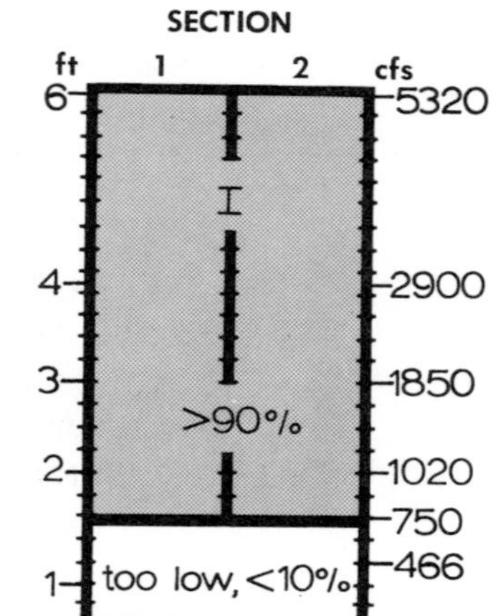

Scenery: An excellent scenic trip, with little development and plenty of public land. There are waterfowl, beaver, deer, bald eagles, and other wildlife which form a natural welcoming committee.

Geology: Bedrock consists of granite and other igneous rocks.

Campgrounds: Numerous primitive sites along the river with no car access. There is no charge for these one-night-only campsites. There is road-access camping at Connor Lake and Lake of the Pines. Wisconsin DNR charges both user and admission fees for these sites.

Shuttles: Car shuttles are generally three-quarters of an hour to two hours long. County roads are recommended since the back roads are generally poor, especially in bad weather. The shuttles for both forks of the Flambeau River are long, and it is therefore impossible to show them on the accompanying maps. In those cases the suggested shuttle is given.

Shuttle (for Section 2): Start at the State Highway 70, bridge at Oxbo and go west until you are just past Draper, then go south on County Highway M, and east on County Highway W to the river.

Points of Interest:

Section 1

1. (0.0 miles) **Nine Mile Creek.** Enters from the left. The mouth of this creek is the recommended put-in for this stretch of river. With the exception of one minor grade I rapids, this entire stretch consists of quiet water. The Flambeau River State Forest begins near this location.
2. (1.0 mile) **Barnaby Rapids.** An easy grade I rapids.
3. (2.5 miles) **Butternut Creek.** Trout stream enters from the right.

Photo 11. A fishing rod, a canoe and the Flambeau.

4. (3.0 miles) **Deadman's Slough.** Named after an early logger who met his demise at this site. This is an alternate landing.
5. (6.0 miles) **Rock Creek.** Enters from the left.
6. (7.0 miles) **Pine Creek.** Enters from the right. The mouth of this creek is located just downstream of the Price-Sawyer county line.

Section 2

7. (9.8 miles) **Highway 70 bridge.** This is the take-out for Section 1 and the put-in for Section 2.
8. (10.5 miles) **Log Creek.** Trout stream enters from the right.
9. (13.2 miles) **Mason Creek.** Enters from the left. Approximately halfway between Mason Creek and Long Creek, Bear Creek enters from the right.
10. (15.2 miles) **Long Creek.** Enters from the left.
11. (17.2 miles) **County Highway W bridge.** This is the recommended take-out for Section 2 and put-in for Section 3. There is a DNR Ranger Station and U.S.G.S. gauge on the right bank slightly downstream of here.

Photo 12. Flambeau River State Forest - This land is your land - Use it or loose it.

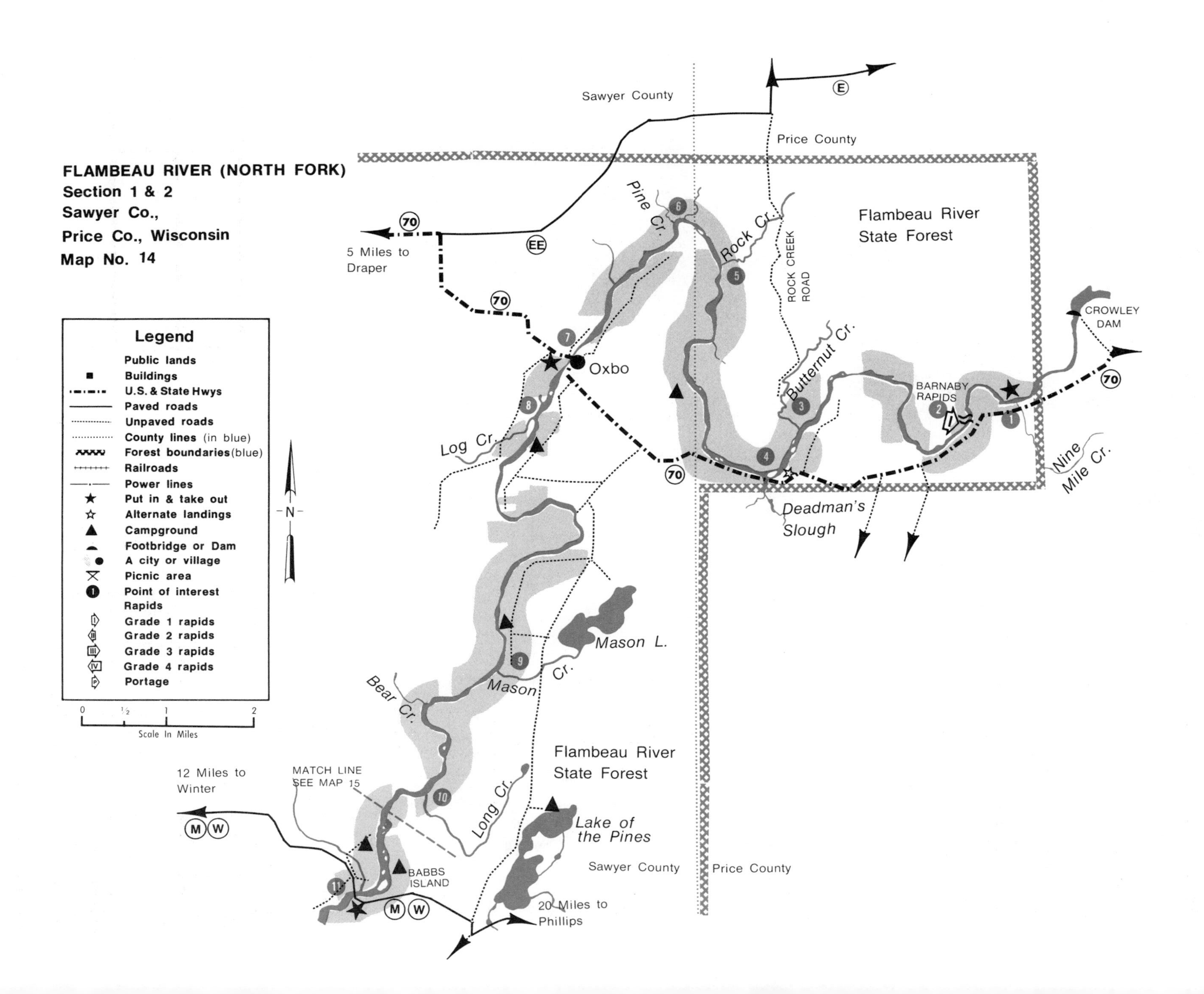

FLAMBEAU RIVER (NORTH FORK)
Section 1 & 2
Sawyer Co.,
Price Co., Wisconsin
Map No. 14
Legend
Public lands
Buildings
U.S. & State Hwys
Paved roads
Unpaved roads
County lines (in blue)
Forest boundaries(blue)
Railroads
Power lines
Put in & take out
Alternate landings
Campground
Footbridge or Dam
A city or village
Picnic area
Point of interest
Rapids
Grade 1 rapids
Grade 2 rapids
Grade 3 rapids
Grade 4 rapids
Portage
0
½
1
2
Scale In Miles
N
Sawyer County
Price County
E
70
EE
5 Miles to
Draper
Pine Cr.
Rock Cr.
ROCK CREEK
ROAD
Butternut Cr.
Flambeau River
State Forest
CROWLEY
DAM
BARNABY
RAPIDS
Oxbo
Log Cr.
Deadman's
Slough
Nine
Mile Cr.
Mason L.
Mason
Cr.
Bear Cr.
Long Cr.
Flambeau River
State Forest
Lake of
the Pines
Sawyer County
Price County
12 Miles to
Winter
MATCH LINE
SEE MAP 15
BABBS
ISLAND
M
W
20 Miles to
Phillips

FLAMBEAU RIVER (NORTH FORK)

Section 3

Flambeau River (North Fork): Sawyer and Rusk Counties, Wisconsin.
Topo map(s): Draper (1:48,000) 1944 planimetric and Ingram (1:48,000) 1946 planimetric.
Overview map(s): Rice Lake (1953).
Public lands: Sawyer County (1968) and Rusk County (1968) plat books, updated to January 1973 with Wisconsin DNR records.
Section 3
Start: Babbs Island Ranger Station (County Highway W bridge).
End: Hervas Landing.

	SEC. 3
Difficulty (high water)	I-II
Difficulty (usual summer flow)	I-II
Length	14
Time	6
Width	100-200
Gradient	3

Water Conditions: Gauge at put-in. River flow is relatively consistent. There is nearly always enough water for an enjoyable run.

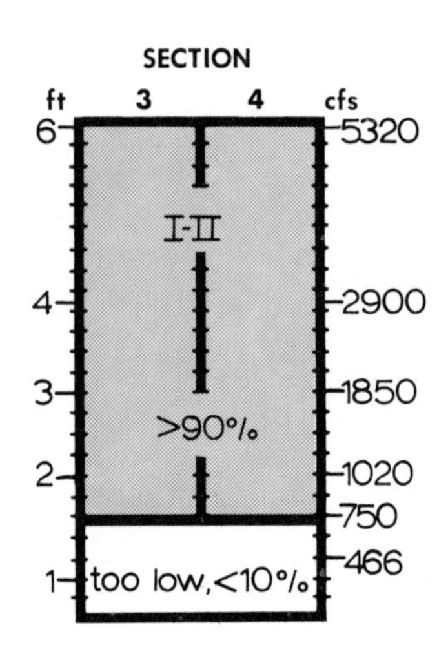

Scenery: Excellent scenery, with virtually no development along the heavily wooded shoreline. There is some virgin timber. Deer, waterfowl, and other wildlife romp and fly.
Geology: The bedrock consists of granite and other igneous rocks.
Fish: Muskie, walleye, and smallmouth bass take bait.
Campgrounds: Developed campsites with road access are located at Lake of the Pines and Connor Lake. There are numerous primitive campsites along the river for which there is no fee, but a one-day limit.
Shuttle (from Babb's Island to Hervas Landing): West on County Highway W to Winter, west on tate Highway 70 to Ojibwa, south on State Highway 27 to Ladysmith, east on U.S. Highway 8 to Glen Flora, and north on County Highway B. When B turns keep going straight to Hervas Landing.
Points of Interest:

11 (17.2 miles) **County Highway W bridge.** This is the recommended put-in for this section. The Babbs Island Ranger Station and the U.S.G.S. gauging station are also located near this site.

12 (19.8 miles) **Deer Creek.** Enters from the right.

13 (20.8 miles) **Connor Creek.** Enters from the left. This is the outlet of Connor Lake.

14 (22.8 miles) **Porcupine Rapids** (First Pitch). This rapids rates grade I, as does the Second Pitch, which is just downstream.

15 **Big Block.** This area has several hundred acres of mature hardwood and hemlock.

16 (24.5 miles) **Porcupine Rapids** (Third Pitch). This rapids rates grade I.

17 (25.0 miles) **Camp 41 landing.** This is an alternate landing with limited camping facilities; the site of a logging camp until the mid-1930's.

18 (27.5 miles) **Wannigan Rapids.** This is a rapids in two pitches, both of which rate grade I-II.

19 (28.5 miles) **Flambeau Falls.** This is a rapids in two pitches, One pitch is above Dodes Island and the second is below the island. Both pitches rate grade I-II.

20 (29.5 miles) **Confluence with the South Fork of the Flambeau River,** which enters from the left.

21 (31.2 miles) **Hervas Landing.** This camp was named after four brothers who were trappers in this area in the mid-1930's. This is our recommended take-out for Section 3. However, in periods of wet weather the road is poor (grade IV)!

Photo 13. Wannigan Rapids - second pitch.

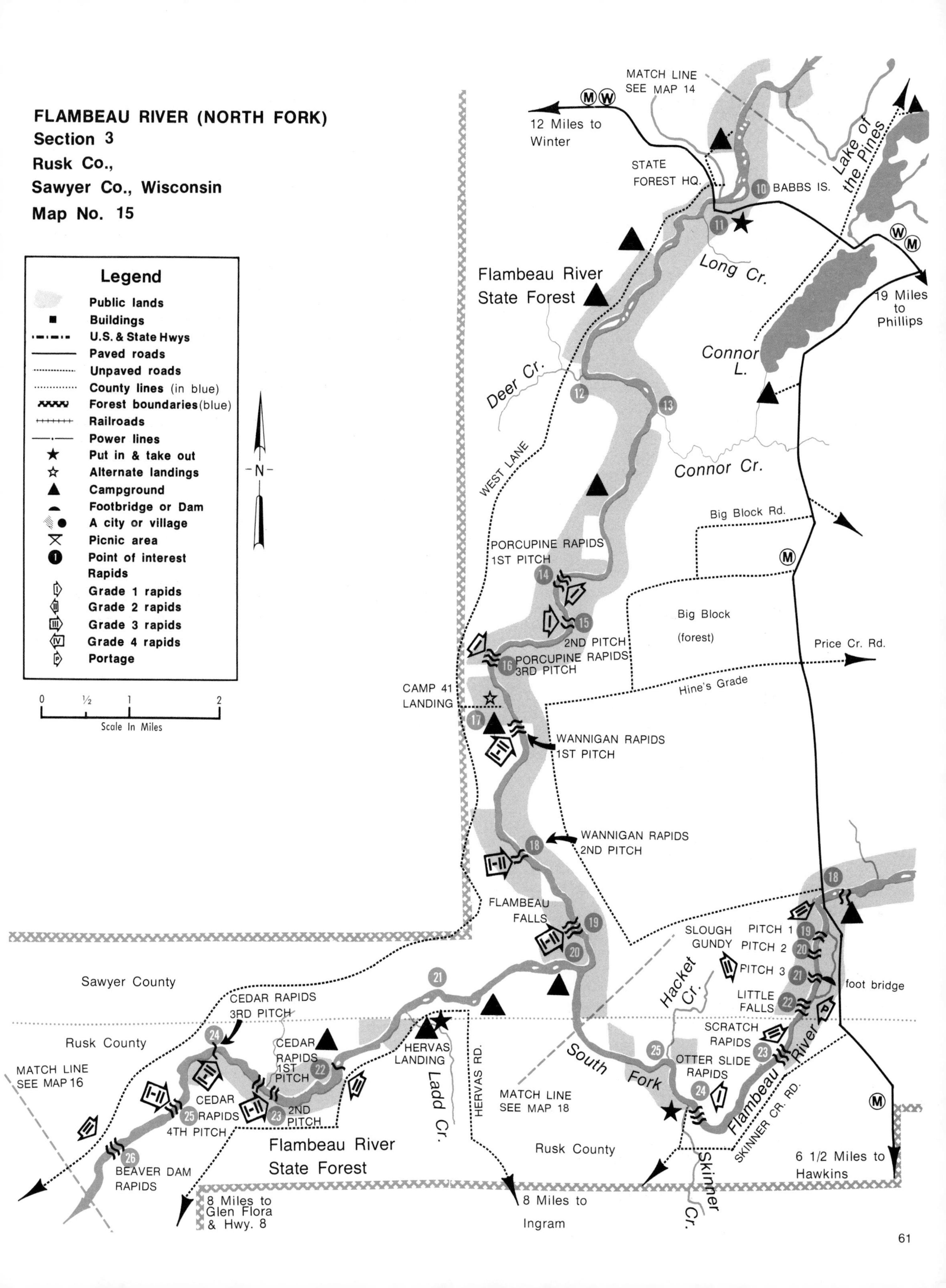
FLAMBEAU RIVER (NORTH FORK)
Section 3
Rusk Co.,
Sawyer Co., Wisconsin
Map No. 15
Legend
Public lands
Buildings
U.S. & State Hwys
Paved roads
Unpaved roads
County lines (in blue)
Forest boundaries (blue)
Railroads
Power lines
Put in & take out
Alternate landings
Campground
Footbridge or Dam
A city or village
Picnic area
Point of interest
Rapids
Grade 1 rapids
Grade 2 rapids
Grade 3 rapids
Grade 4 rapids
Portage
Scale In Miles
N
MATCH LINE
SEE MAP 14
12 Miles to
Winter
STATE
FOREST HQ.
BABBS IS.
Lake of
the Pines
Long Cr.
Flambeau River
State Forest
19 Miles
to
Phillips
Connor
L.
Deer Cr.
WEST LANE
Connor Cr.
Big Block Rd.
PORCUPINE RAPIDS
1ST PITCH
2ND PITCH
PORCUPINE RAPIDS
3RD PITCH
Big Block
(forest)
Price Cr. Rd.
Hine's Grade
CAMP 41
LANDING
WANNIGAN RAPIDS
1ST PITCH
WANNIGAN RAPIDS
2ND PITCH
FLAMBEAU
FALLS
SLOUGH
GUNDY
PITCH 1
PITCH 2
PITCH 3
foot bridge
LITTLE
FALLS
Hacket
Cr.
Sawyer County
Rusk County
CEDAR RAPIDS
3RD PITCH
CEDAR
RAPIDS
1ST
PITCH
HERVAS
LANDING
HERVAS RD.
Ladd Cr.
South
Fork
SCRATCH
RAPIDS
OTTER SLIDE
RAPIDS
Flambeau River
SKINNER CR. RD.
MATCH LINE
SEE MAP 16
CEDAR
RAPIDS
4TH PITCH
2ND
PITCH
MATCH LINE
SEE MAP 18
BEAVER DAM
RAPIDS
Flambeau River
State Forest
Rusk County
8 Miles to
Glen Flora
& Hwy. 8
8 Miles to
Ingram
Skinner
Cr.
6 1/2 Miles to
Hawkins

FLAMBEAU RIVER (MAIN BRANCH)

SECTION 4

Flambeau River (Main Branch): Rusk County, Wisconsin.
Topo map(s): Ingram (1:48,000) 1946 panimetric.
Overview map(s): Rice Lake (1953).
Public lands: Rusk County (1968) plat book, updated to January 1973 with Wisconsin DNR records.
Section 4
Start: Skinner Creek Landing (at Otter Slide Rapids on the South Fork)
End: Flambeau River Lodge

	SEC. 4
Difficulty (high water	**II**
Difficulty (usual summer flow)	**I-II**
Length	**15**
Time	**7**
Gradient	**6**

Water Conditions: See description accompanying map 15.
Campgrounds: There are campsites at Connor Lake, Lake of the Pines, Big Falls Dam, and at the Flambeau Lodge. User fees are charged at all of these sites except the one at Big Falls Dam.
Shuttle: From Skinner Creek Landing, go southwest to County Highway B, south on B to Glen Flora, west on U.S. Highway 8 to Tony, and north on County Highway 1 across the Flambeau River. One and a half miles after crossing the river County Highway 1 becomes gravel. At the first crossroad (a blind corner) go right and follow the road approximately three miles to the Flambeau River Lodge.
Points of Interest: Our suggested put-in is Skinner Creek Landing on the South Fork of the Flambeau (see map 18). You could also start at Hervas Landing on the North Fork, but that landing is hard to find and the roads are usually poor.

Section 4
Map 15

24 (23.0 miles) **Skinner Creek Landing.** This is the start for this section as well as the recommended take-out for Section 3 of the South Fork.

25 (23.5 miles) **Hacket Creek.** Enters from the right. The numbered points of interest and cumulative mileages below are continued from the North Fork. See map 15.

20 (29.5 miles) **Confluence** of the north and south forks of the Flambeau River.

21 (31.2 miles) **Hervas Landing.** This is an alternate landing. However, during prolonged periods of wet weather the roads are rather poor. There is a primitive campsite with a spring on the right bank just upstream of Cedar Rapids.

22 (32.0 miles) **Cedar Rapids** (First Pitch). This rapids rates grade II. The left channel is the best route, but it has standing waves that could swamp open canoes in high water (see technique section). Those wishing to avoid the large waves should take the shallower, rocky, right channel. This is a spring on the left side of the second pitch of Cedar Rapids.

23 (32.8 miles) **Cedar Rapids** (Second Pitch). This rapids rates grade I-II.

24 (33.8 miles) **Cedar Rapids** (Third Pitch). This rapids rates grade I-II. There is a spring on the right side of the river.

Map 16

25 (34.5 miles) **Cedar Rapids** (Fourth Pitch). This rapids rates grade I-II.

26 (35.0 miles) **Beaver Dam Rapids.** A grade II rapids. The river forms a natural dam at this location. In very high water a backroller develops. See the technique section for precautions. A memorial near this site marks a **drowning** that occured here in 1928. A spring is located on the right side.

27 (36.0 miles) **Little Cedar Rapids.** This grade I rapids is also known as Pine Island Rapids.

28 (37.0 miles) **An unnamed creek** signals the end of the Flambeau River State Forest.

29 (40.0 miles) **Flambeau River Lodge.** This is the recommended take-out. There is a parking fee. The proprietor of this lodge will provide a shuttle for a fee. There is also a campground at this location. Phone (715) 532-5392, or write Route 2, Ladysmith, Wisc.

30 (40.5 miles) **Big Falls Dam.** An alternate landing with a take-out on the left bank. Free camping is permitted at this site, which is maintained by the Lake Superior District Power Company. Before the dam was completed in the 1920's, this rapids was runnable by skilled boaters. Portage left if you are continuing downstream.

Photo 14. Cedar Rapids - first pitch.

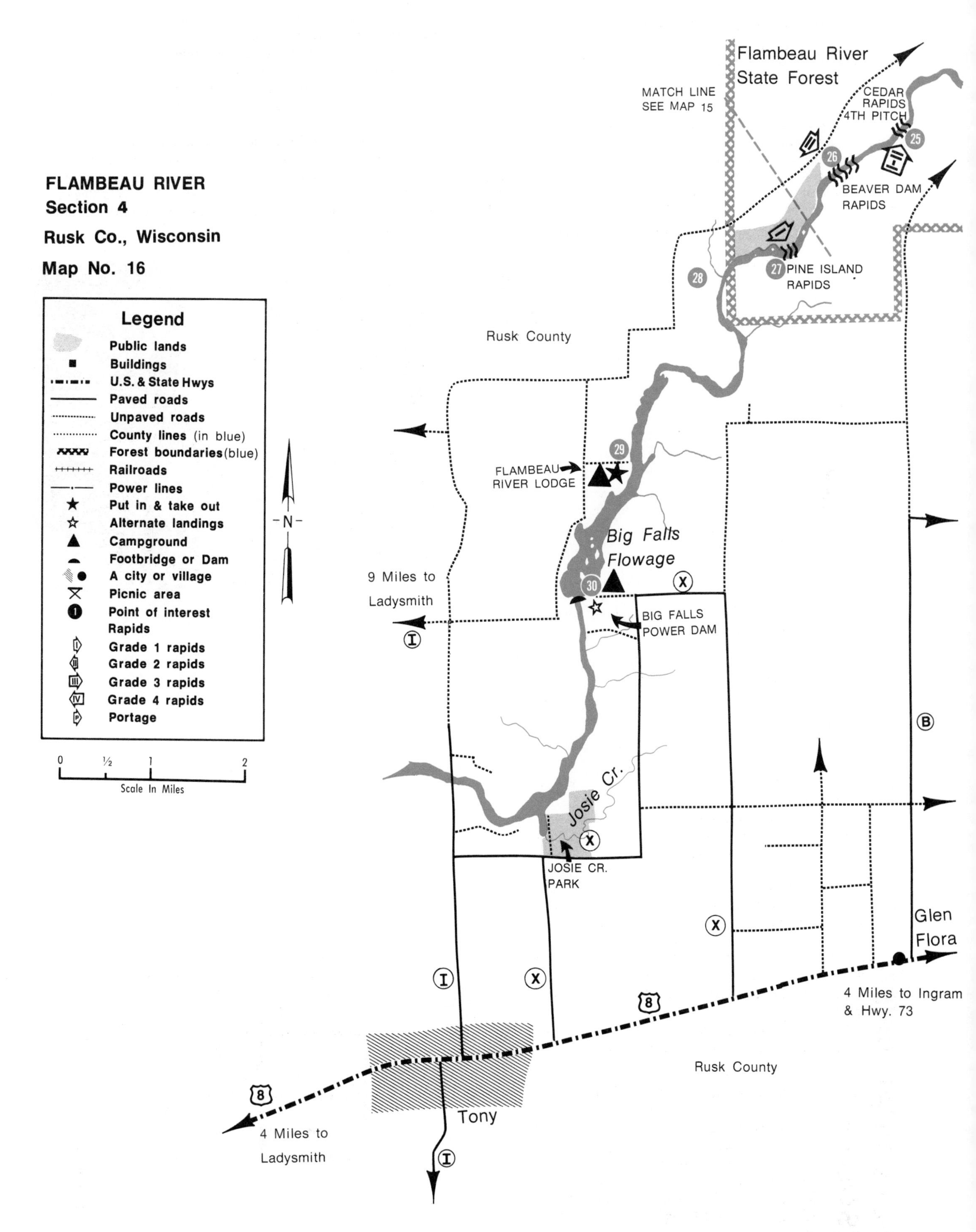
FLAMBEAU RIVER
Section 4
Rusk Co., Wisconsin
Map No. 16
Legend
Public lands
Buildings
U.S. & State Hwys
Paved roads
Unpaved roads
County lines (in blue)
Forest boundaries (blue)
Railroads
Power lines
Put in & take out
Alternate landings
Campground
Footbridge or Dam
A city or village
Picnic area
Point of interest
Rapids
Grade 1 rapids
Grade 2 rapids
Grade 3 rapids
Grade 4 rapids
Portage
0 ½ 1 2
Scale In Miles
N
Flambeau River
State Forest
MATCH LINE
SEE MAP 15
CEDAR
RAPIDS
4TH PITCH
BEAVER DAM
RAPIDS
PINE ISLAND
RAPIDS
Rusk County
FLAMBEAU
RIVER LODGE
Big Falls
Flowage
9 Miles to
Ladysmith
BIG FALLS
POWER DAM
Josie Cr.
JOSIE CR.
PARK
Glen
Flora
4 Miles to Ingram
& Hwy. 73
Rusk County
Tony
4 Miles to
Ladysmith

FLAMBEAU RIVER (SOUTH FORK)

SECTION 1

Flambeau River (South Fork): Price County, Wisconsin.
Topo maps: Kennen (1:48,000) 1941 planimetric and Kennedy (1:48,000) 1941 planimetric.
Overview map: Rice Lake (1953).
Public lands: Price County plat book (1968), updated to January 1973 with Wisconsin DNR records.
Section 1
Start: County Highway F bridge near Lugerville.
End: County Highway W bridge.

	SEC. 1
Difficulty (high water)	**II**
Difficulty (usual summer flow)	**I-II**
Length	**10**
Time	**6**
Width	**40-100**
Gradient	**5**

Water Conditions: The water level fluctuates much more so than on the North Fork.

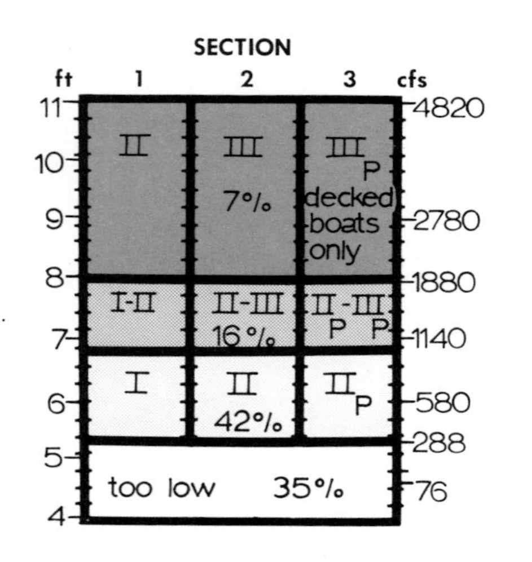

Canoeable Days Per Month

month	**Apr**	**May**	**June**	**July**	**Aug**	**Sep**
days	30	31	28	9	9	12

Scenery: Very good stretch, with not too much development. The shoreline is wooded and wildlife is abundant.
Fish: Smallmouth bass, muskie, and walleye call the river their home.
Campgrounds: There are campsites at Connor Lake and Lake of the Pines. A user fee is charged at both of these Wisconsin DNR developed campgrounds. There is no charge for the numerous primitive campsites located along the river. However, there is a one day limit for these overnight sites.
Shuttle: Head southeast on County Highway F from Lugerville to State Highway 13, south on Highway 13 to Phillips, and west on County Highway W from Phillips to the river.
Points of Interest:
Section 1

1. (0.0 miles) **County Highway F bridge** near Lugerville. This is the recommended put-in.
2. (0.5 miles) **Mt. Pelee Creek.** Enters from the left. The mouth of this creek signals the start of Kashinski Rapids, which is an easy grade I rock garden.
3. (1.5 miles) **Little Stonewall Rapids.** This is a grade II rapids that takes its name from the abrupt bluff on the left bank.
4. (2.5 miles) **River Road landing.** There is an alternate landing on the left bank. The mouth of Smith Creek is located several hundred yards downstream. It is a trout stream which enters from the right.
5. (3.8 miles) **Rock Ledge Rapids.** There is a primitive campsite located at the grade I-II rapids.
6. (4.5 miles) **Davis Rapids.** This rapids rates grade I-II.
7. (5.8 miles) **Clubhouse Rapids.** There are some easy grade I rapids at this location.
8. (6.0 miles) **Nelson Creek.** Enters from the right.
9. (7.0 miles) **Carl's Rapids.** This rapids rates grade I-II.
10. (9.0 miles) **Mouth of the Elk River.** Enters from the left. This river has both brook and brown trout.
11. (9.5 miles) **County Highway W bridge.** Just downstream of this bridge, on the left bank, is the recommended **take-out** for Section 1 and **put-in** for Section 2. Approximately a half mile downstream from the County Highway W bridge is a partially developed, primitive campsite on the left bank. This site is only accessible from the river.

Photo 15. Tranquility Base.

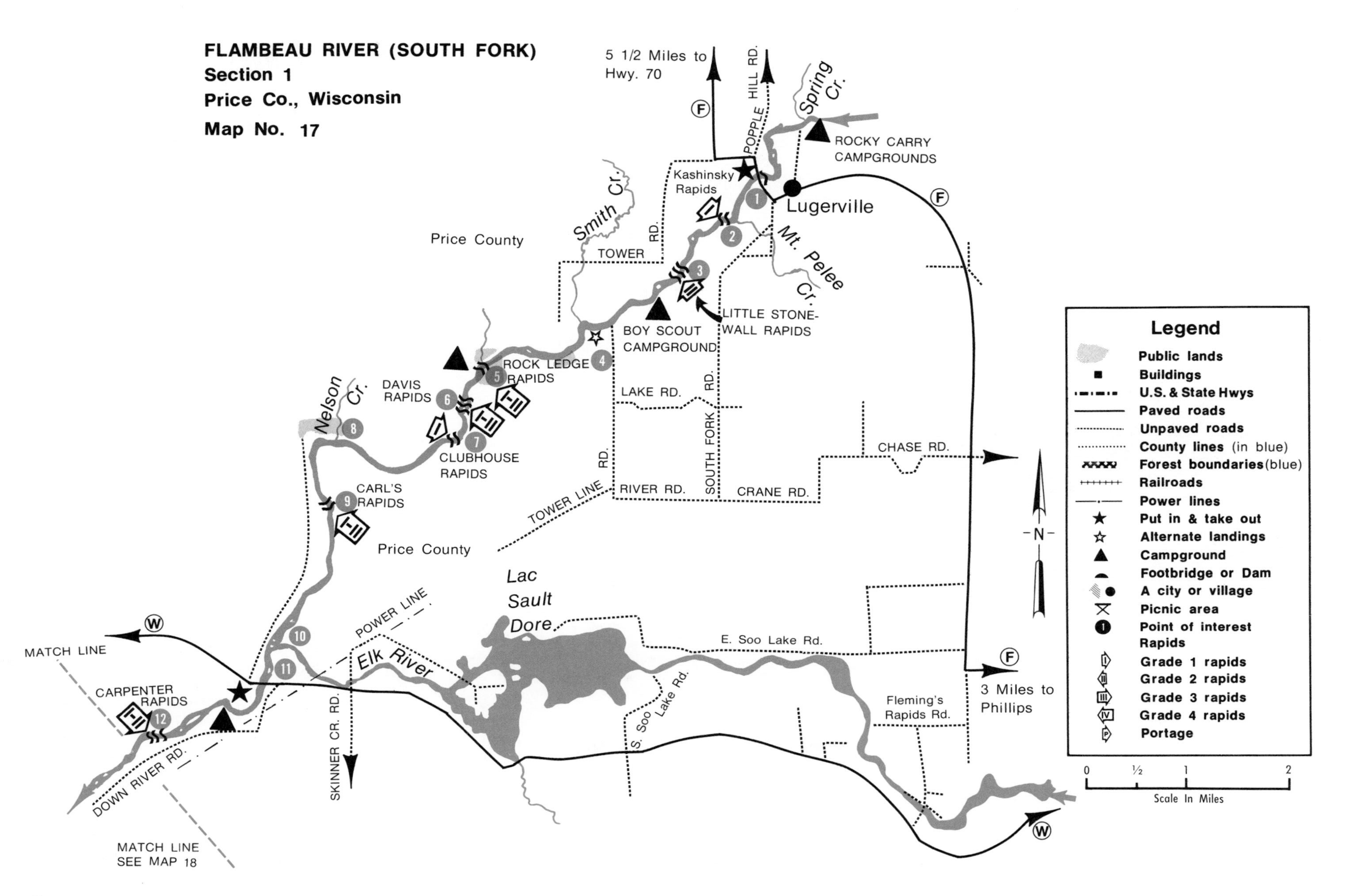
FLAMBEAU RIVER (SOUTH FORK)
Section 1
Price Co., Wisconsin
Map No. 17
5 1/2 Miles to Hwy. 70
POPPLE HILL RD.
Spring Cr.
ROCKY CARRY CAMPGROUNDS
Kashinsky Rapids
Lugerville
Smith Cr.
TOWER RD.
Mt. Pelee Cr.
Price County
LITTLE STONE-WALL RAPIDS
BOY SCOUT CAMPGROUND
ROCK LEDGE RAPIDS
DAVIS RAPIDS
Nelson Cr.
LAKE RD.
SOUTH FORK RD.
CLUBHOUSE RAPIDS
CHASE RD.
RIVER RD.
CRANE RD.
CARL'S RAPIDS
TOWER LINE RD.
Price County
Lac Sault Dore
POWER LINE
Elk River
E. Soo Lake Rd.
S. Soo Lake Rd.
MATCH LINE
CARPENTER RAPIDS
SKINNER CR. RD.
Fleming's Rapids Rd.
3 Miles to Phillips
DOWN RIVER RD.
MATCH LINE SEE MAP 18
-N-
Legend
Public lands
Buildings
U.S. & State Hwys
Paved roads
Unpaved roads
County lines (in blue)
Forest boundaries (blue)
Railroads
Power lines
Put in & take out
Alternate landings
Campground
Footbridge or Dam
A city or village
Picnic area
Point of interest
Rapids
Grade 1 rapids
Grade 2 rapids
Grade 3 rapids
Grade 4 rapids
Portage
0 ½ 1 2
Scale In Miles

FLAMBEAU RIVER (SOUTH FORK)

SECTIONS 2 & 3

Flambeau River (South Fork): Sawyer and Rusk Counties, Wisconsin.
Topo maps: Kennen (1:48,000) 1941 planimetric and Ingram (1:48,000) 1946 planimetric.
Overview map: Rice Lake (1953).
Public lands: Sawyer County (1968) and Rusk County (1968) plat books, updated to January 1973 with Wisconsin DNR records.
Section 2
Start: County Highway W bridge.
End: County Highway M bridge.
Section 3
Start: County Highway M bridge.
End: Skinner Creek Landing.

	SEC. 2	SEC. 3
Difficulty (high water)	**II-III**	**IIIp**
Difficulty (usual summer flow)	**II**	**IIp**
Length	**10**	**4**
Time	**5**	**2**
Width	**40-100**	**40-100**
Gradient	**7**	**-**
Drainage area	**615**	**-**

Water Conditions and Canoeability Table: See description accompanying map 17.
Campgrounds: There are campsites at Connor Lake, Lake of the Pines, and Flambeau River State Forest. There is a user fee at all of these campsites.
Shuttle: Section 2. Go west from the County Highway W bridge and south on M to the river.
Section 3. From the put-in go south on County Highway M, west on Skinner Creek Road just past Skinner Creek, turn right, and park in the empty field by the creek and river (Skinner Creek Landing).
Points of Interest:
Section 2

11 (9.5 miles) **County Highway W bridge.** This is the put-in for this stretch. Open canoes should avoid this section in high water (above 2,000 cfs). Large standing waves develop at the major rapids.

12 (11.2 miles) **Carpenter Rapids.** This is a rapids in two pitches: the first rates grade I and the second rates grade II.

13 (14.2 miles) **Mouth of Stony Brook.** Enters from the left. This trout stream has been dammed just upstream of its mouth.

14 (15.2 miles) **Cornsheller Rapids.** An island signals the start of this grade II rapids. The right channel is the easiest. Large waves develop in the left channel during higher water.

15 (16.2 miles) **Price Creek.** Enters from the right.

16 (16.2 miles) **Big Bull Rapids.** This rapids rates grade II.

17 (18.0 miles) **Bergeron Rapids.** This is a rapids in three pitches: the first two rate grade I, and the third pitch rates grade II. The latter pitch is also known as Prison Camp Rapids. It is a grade I rock garden in low water.

18 (19.0 miles) **County Highway M bridge.** This is the recommended take-out for Section 2 and the put-in for Section 3. The State Prison Forestry Camp is located on the right bank just downstream of this bridge.

Section 3: All persons with open canoes should avoid this section in high water.

19 (19.5 miles) **Slough Gundy** (First Pitch). This pitch usually rates grade II; it rates grade III in high water. All three pitches of Slough Gundy are located in the right channel around a large island. In the past, the left channel has had a low footbridge which must be portaged. During high water (above 1,500 cfs) high standing waves develop. At 3,000 cfs, these rapids provide a fantastic, but very wet ride for persons in decked boats. This run could be suicidal for open canoes in high water due to the proximity to Little Falls.

20 (20.0 miles) **Slough Gundy** (Second Pitch). This pitch also rates grade II and rates grade III in high water. A rather large sidecurler develops at high water levels.

21 (20.2 miles) **Slough Gundy** (Third Pitch). This pitch develops the largest waves at very high water. This rapids rates grade II; it rates grade III in high water.

22 (20.5 miles) **Little Falls.** Although this falls has been run successfully, a **portage** is **recommended.** Occassionally there is a chicken route on the right bank that is runnable in high water. In low water, portage over the island in the middle, but in high water use the left bank. There is an alternate take-out at this location if you are willing to carry your boat approximately 500 yards on a service road with a locked gate. This road is located on the left bank of the river, just above the falls.

23 (21.0 miles) **Scratch Rapids.** As with Slough Gundy Rapids, this rapids is shallow and rocky in low water and develops large standing waves in high water. This rapids rates grade II; it rates grade III in high water.

24 (23.0 miles) **Skinner Creek Landing.** The recommended take-out is located on the left bank. It is preceded by Otter Slide Rapids which is a grade I rapids. If you wish to continue downstream, see map 15 this is the suggested put-in for Section 4 of the Flambeau River (Main Branch).

25 (23.5 miles) **Hacket Creek.** Enters from the right.

26 (25.2 miles) **Confluence with the North Fork.** See map 15 if you are continuing downstream.

Photo 16. Little Falls of the Flambeau - an unrunnable drop.

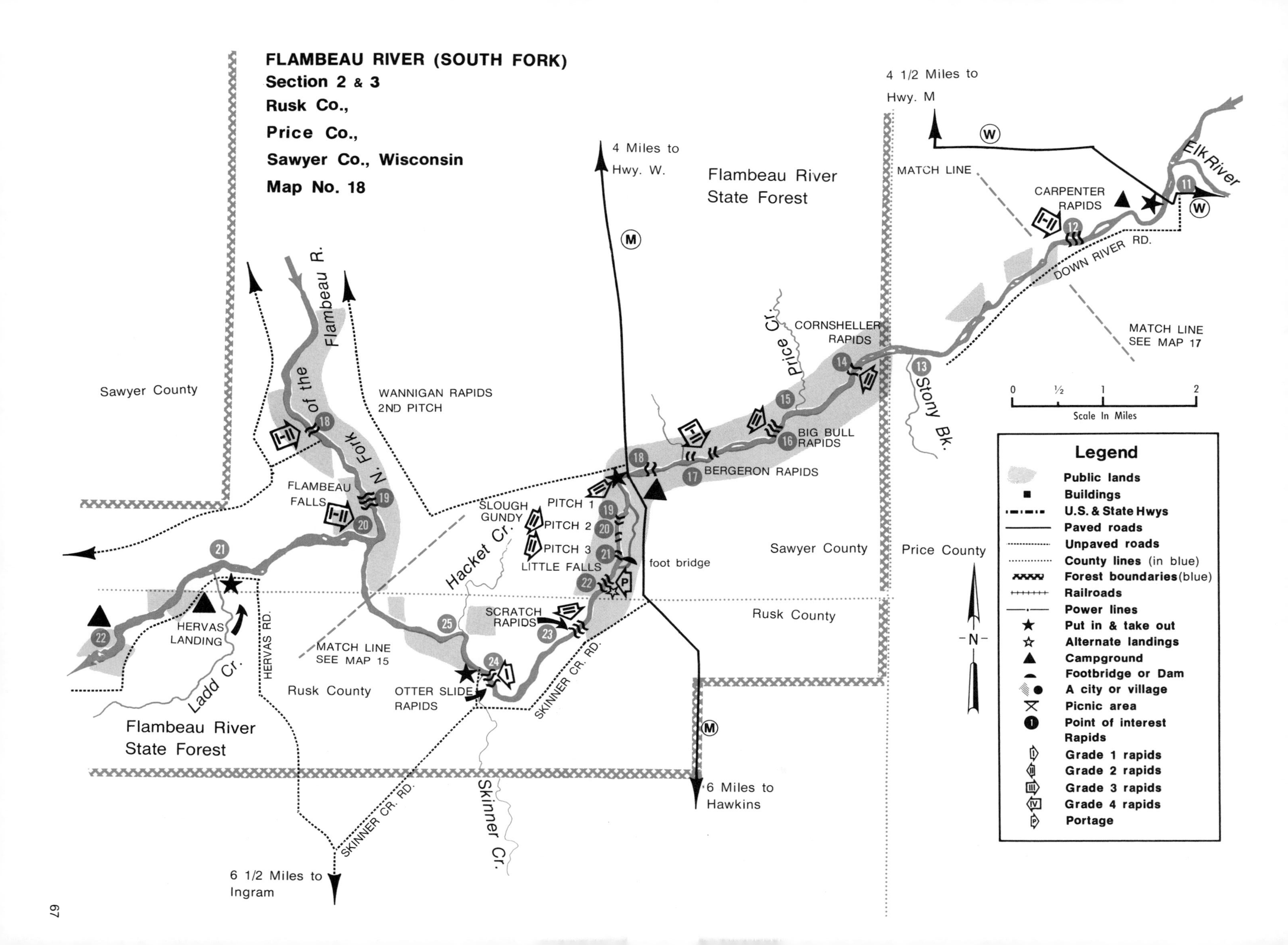
FLAMBEAU RIVER (SOUTH FORK)
Section 2 & 3
Rusk Co.,
Price Co.,
Sawyer Co., Wisconsin
Map No. 18
4 1/2 Miles to
Hwy. M
4 Miles to
Hwy. W.
Flambeau River
State Forest
MATCH LINE
CARPENTER
RAPIDS
Elk River
DOWN RIVER RD.
MATCH LINE
SEE MAP 17
CORNSHELLER
RAPIDS
Price Cr.
Stony Bk.
BIG BULL
RAPIDS
BERGERON RAPIDS
Sawyer County
Flambeau R.
of the
N. Fork
WANNIGAN RAPIDS
2ND PITCH
FLAMBEAU
FALLS
SLOUGH
GUNDY
PITCH 1
PITCH 2
PITCH 3
LITTLE FALLS
Hacket Cr.
foot bridge
Sawyer County
Price County
Rusk County
SCRATCH
RAPIDS
HERVAS
LANDING
HERVAS RD.
MATCH LINE
SEE MAP 15
Rusk County
OTTER SLIDE
RAPIDS
SKINNER CR. RD.
Ladd Cr.
Flambeau River
State Forest
Skinner Cr.
6 Miles to
Hawkins
6 1/2 Miles to
Ingram
Scale In Miles
0
½
1
2
Legend
Public lands
Buildings
U.S. & State Hwys
Paved roads
Unpaved roads
County lines (in blue)
Forest boundaries (blue)
Railroads
Power lines
Put in & take out
Alternate landings
Campground
Footbridge or Dam
A city or village
Picnic area
Point of interest
Rapids
Grade 1 rapids
Grade 2 rapids
Grade 3 rapids
Grade 4 rapids
Portage
N

FORD RIVER

Ford River: Delta County, Michigan.
Topo map: Escanaba (1:62,500) 1958.
Overview map: Escanaba (1954).
Public lands: Delta County highway map (1965).
Start: U.S. Highway 2 and 41 bridge at Hyde, Michigan.
End: Highway 35 bridge at the town of Ford River.

Difficulty (high water)	**II-III**
Difficulty (usual summer flow)	**not runnable**
Length	**8**
Time	**4**
Width	**50-200**
Gradient	**11**
Drainage area	**471**

Water Conditions: A U.S.G.S. gauging station is located not far upstream of Hyde at a point where the drainage area is 450 square miles. The flow of this river fluctuates greatly. It is only runnable during high water during the spring or after periods of unusually heavy rains. No maneuvering is required on the rapids of this river. There are waves but no rock outcroppings.

Scenery: There is good scenery along this section with minimal development. There is some cleared farm land.

Geology: The bedrock of this river consists of Plateville-Galena dolomite with some limestone.

Campgrounds: Fuller Park is a county park with six campsites located approximately eight miles south of the town of Ford River on Michigan Highway 35.

Points of Interest:

1. (0.0 miles) **U.S. Highway 2 and 41 bridge at Hyde.** This is the recommended put-in for this river.

2. (0.5 miles) **Five Mile and Finnland's Creeks.**

3. (4.0 miles) **Unnamed Rapids.** This rapids is preceeded by a large island at a point where the river bends to the left. It rates grade II-III because of the high waves that would probably swamp an open canoe. Boaters with open canoes should **scout** and perhaps **portage.**

4. (6.0 miles) **Unnamed Rapids.** Grade II.

5. (7.8 miles) **Highway 35 bridge at the town of Ford River.** This is the recommended take-out.

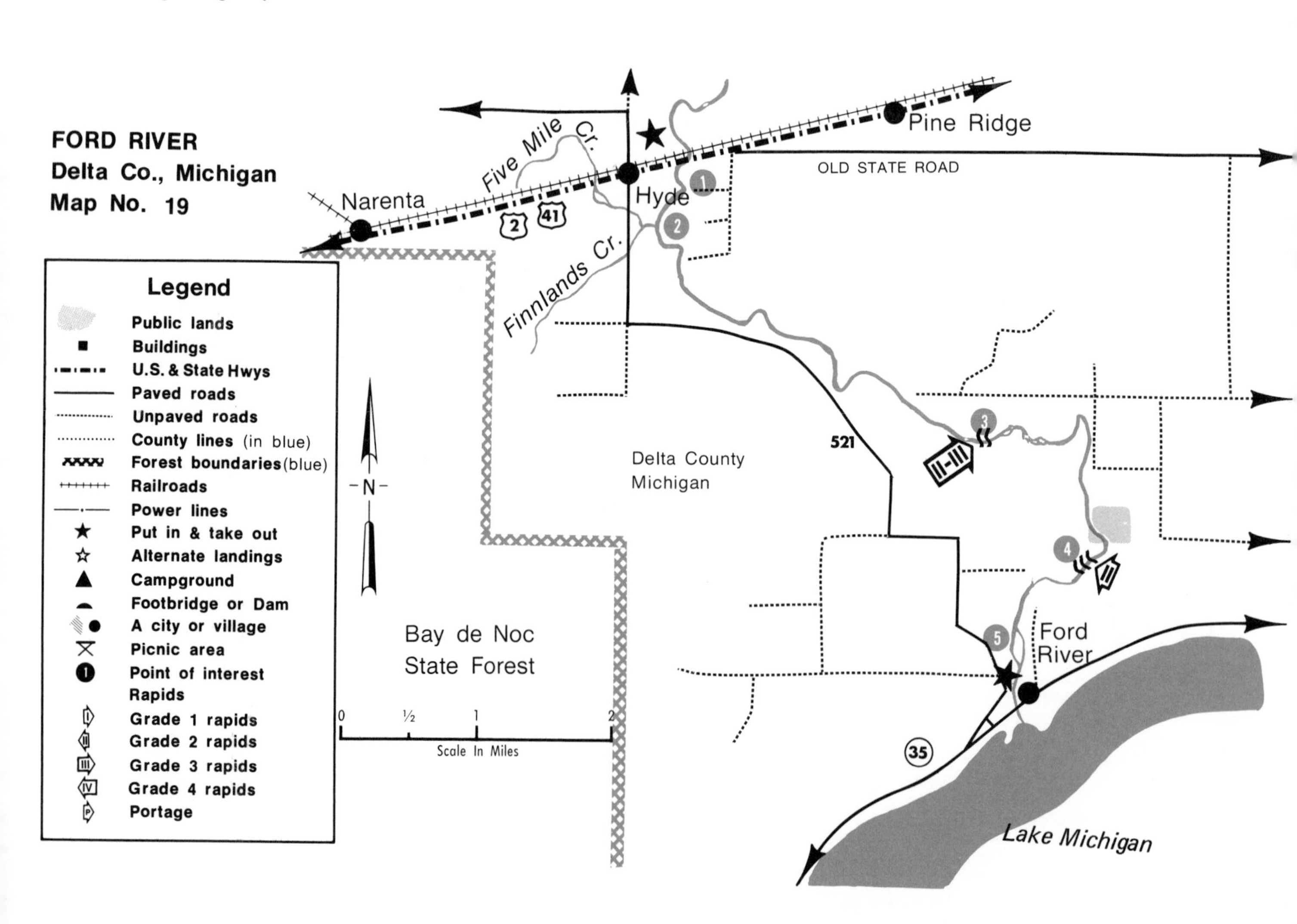

KETTLE RIVER

Kettle River: Pine County, Minnesota.
Topo map: Sandstone (1:62,500) 1961.
Overview map: Duluth (1953).
Public lands: not done.
Start: Highway 23 bridge.
End: Below Great Northern Railroad bridge at Sandstone.

Difficulty (high water)	**III-IV**
Difficulty (usual summer flow)	**II**
Length	**5**
Time	**2**
Width	**30-100**
Gradient	–
Drainage area	–

Water Conditions: See the bottom of the page accompanying map 10.
Scenery: This section is characterized by picturesque rock cliffs and steep banks throughout its length.
Geology: There are occasional exposures of ancient volcanic rock in the midst of sedimentary sandstone.
Campgrounds: There are campsites in Banning State Park.
Caution: We did not have access to recent maps of Banning State Park at the time our maps were prepared. Consequently we may have omitted some roads on our map and the location of those listed should be considered only as approximations.
Points of Interest:

1. (0.0 miles) **Highway 23 bridge.** This is the recommended put-in for this river. There is a half to one mile of quiet water before the action begins on this exciting river.

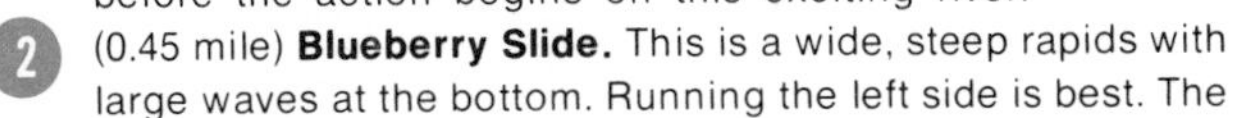

2. (0.45 mile) **Blueberry Slide.** This is a wide, steep rapids with large waves at the bottom. Running the left side is best. The right side is either too shallow or has a stopper wave. This rapids rates a grade II in low water and a grade III in high water. Blueberry patches may be seen on the left bank of the river. Shortly below this rapids are two easier grade II rapids.

3. (0.80 mile) **Mother's Delight.** This rapids is located 200 yards downstream from the last ledge of the above-mentioned rapids. This rapids is easier but also rates a grade II in low water and a grade III in high water. There is a very large and regular hydraulic on the left in high water which can easily retain boaters.

4. (1.4 miles) **Scenic overlook.** This provides a great opportunity to look over the river and do any required **scouting** before beginning the run.

5. (1.8 miles) **Dragon's Tooth.** This rapids should definitely be **scouted** at high water. The river is very narrow at this point (30 feet wide), and there are high cliffs on both sides of the river. Furthermore, most of the overhanging rocks have sharp surfaces. "Dragon's Tooth" is a large pointed rock toward the right side which creates large souse holes in high water. This rapids rates grade II in low water, grade III in high water (when the gauge is above 3), and grade IV in very high water (when the gauge is above 4).

6. (2.1 miles) **Old village ruins.** On the right bank below Dragon's Tooth is the site of the old village of Banning. This town was active during the stone mill era. Stone foundations and other symbols of the past still remain.

7. (2.6 miles) **Hell's Gate.** The river is very narrow at this point (30 feet wide) with high sandstone cliffs on either side of the river. Large waves develop here creating a grade II rating in low water. There are no other problems. High water (gauge above 3) makes the rapids a grade III.

8. (4.0 miles) **Sandstone.** The take-out is on the right bank not far downstream from the Great Northern Railroad bridge. There are pilings from an old bridge just below here.

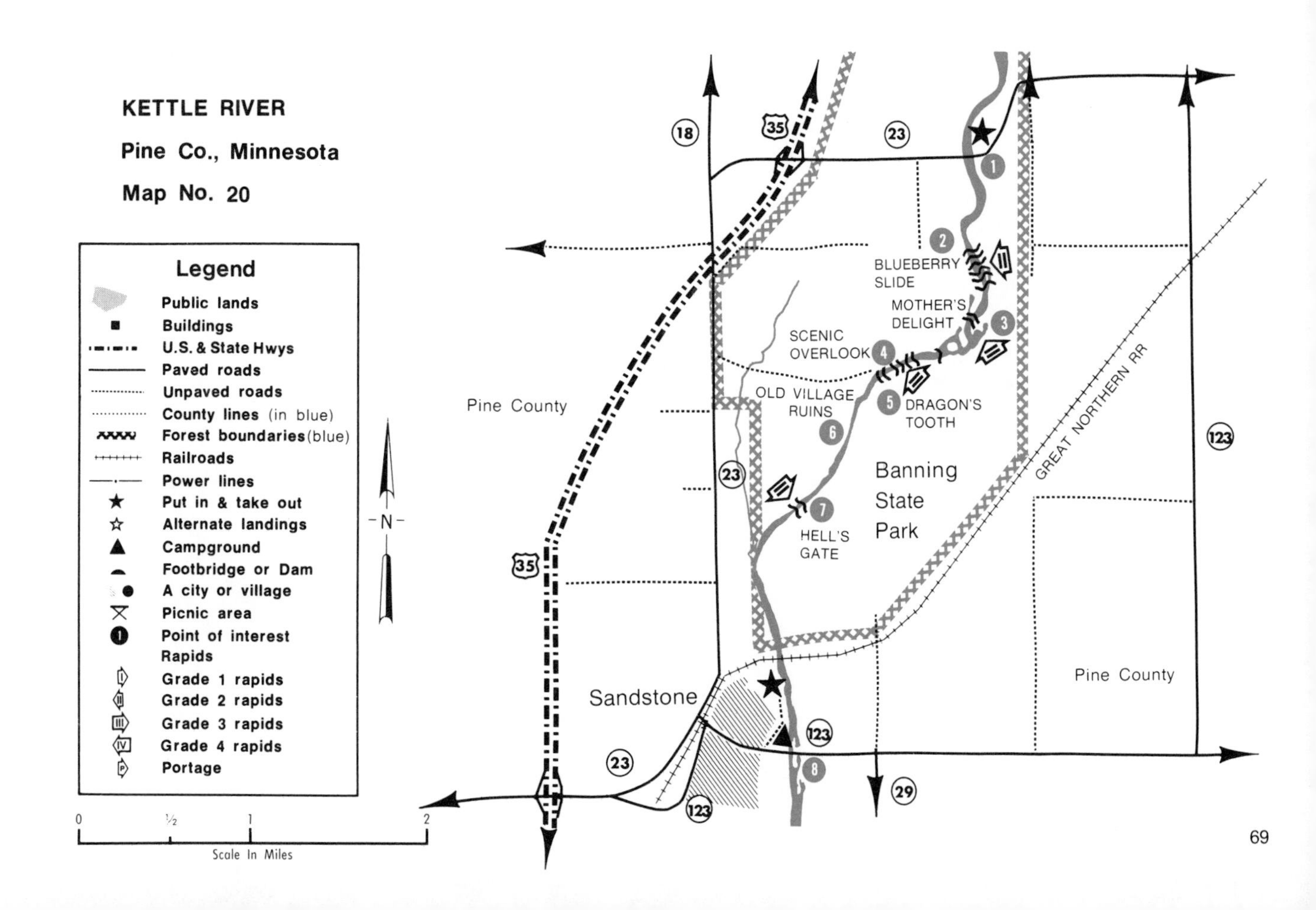

KICKAPOO RIVER

Kickapoo River: Vernon County, Wisconsin.
Topo map: La Farge (1:62,500) 1965.
Overview map: La Crosse (1955).
Public lands: Instead of public lands, the shaded area on this map shows the flood plain anticipated after installation of a proposed dam. This impoundment is ostensibly intended for flood control. Numerous legal maneuvers have been initiated in an attempt to halt this project. At this writing the future of this free flowing portion of the Kickapoo is in jeopardy.
Source of flood plain information: Army Corps of Engineers Impact Statement (1972).
Start: Highway 33 bridge at Ontario, Wisconsin.
End: Bridge 20 (Highway 82) west of La Farge, Wisconsin.

Difficulty (high water)	**Q**
Difficulty (usual summer flow)	**Q**
Length	**20**
Time	**10**
Width	**25-50**
Gradient	**3**
Drainage area	**800** at mouth

Water Conditions: There is generally enough water for a pleasant run. Too much water is a more likely problem as this river is noted for its floods. A U.S.G.S. gauge is located on the left bank 10 feet upstream of the Highway 82 bridge at La Farge.
Scenery: Nothing exceptional other than its ranking as one of the most scenic paddleways in the upper Midwest. Numerous fern-covered cliffs line the banks. The scene is reminiscent of the Wisconsin Dells area, but there are no offensive tour boats to contaminate the view.
Geology: The drainage area (800 sq. miles) of this river is the largest of all the Wisconsin River tributaries. This river basin lies within the driftless area of Wisconsin. The steep river banks are deeply eroded, revealing the sandstone outcroppings with its usual limestone capping. This river is subject to frequent floods.
Campgrounds: Wildcat Mountain State Park has 30 developed campsites. Wisconsin DNR charges a small user and admission fee. For more information write Wildcat Mountain State Park, Ontario, Wisc. 54651.
Fee camping is also permitted at the La Farge City Park.
Fish: The river has small mouth bass, pike, and some trout. Most tributaries are teeming with trout in this fisherman's paradise.

Note: Our points of interest have been numbered to coincide with the numbers already painted on the bridges.
Points of Interest:

1. (0.0 miles) **State Highway 33 bridge.** The Put-in is located 100 yards upstream on the left bank.
2. (0.5 miles) **A farm bridge.**
3. (1.9 miles) **State Highway 131 bridge.**
4. (2.8 miles) **State Highway 131 bridge.**
5. (5.9 miles) **Entrance to Wildcat Mountain State Park.** An alternate landing on the left bank has a trail leading to a scenic overlook. This makes a nice side trip and a good spot for a mid-morning snack.
6. (6.6 miles) **A farm bridge.**
7. (7.5 miles) **State Highway 131 bridge.**
8. (8.3 miles) **A farm bridge.**
9. (9.0 miles) **State Highway 131 bridge.**
10. (10.0 miles) **State Highway 131 bridge.** A half mile further downstream Warner Creek, a trout stream, enters from the left.
11. (11.0 miles) **A farm bridge.** Alternate landing.
12. (11.7 miles) **A farm bridge.** Another alternate landing.
13. (12.6 miles) **State Highway 131 bridge.**
14. (13.6 miles) **County Highway P bridge.**
15. (14.1 miles) **State Highway 131 bridge.**
16. (14.8 miles) **State Highway 131 bridge.**
17. (15.6 miles) **A farm bridge.**
18. (17.6 miles) **State Highway 131 bridge.**
19. (18.9 miles) **State Highway 131 bridge.** Recently an earthen dam has been constructed across the river at this site. The dam has several culverts, which are sometimes runnable, depending upon water level. Another half mile or so downstream there is an old power dam that must always be portaged. Heed the posted warnings and **portage left.** The low grade rapids below pose no special problems as long as the hazardous reversal immediately below the dam is avoided. Some canoeists prefer to take out at bridge 19 to avoid these portages.
20. (20.3 miles) **State Highway 82 bridge at La Farge.** This is the usual take out. The U.S.G.S. gauge is located here.

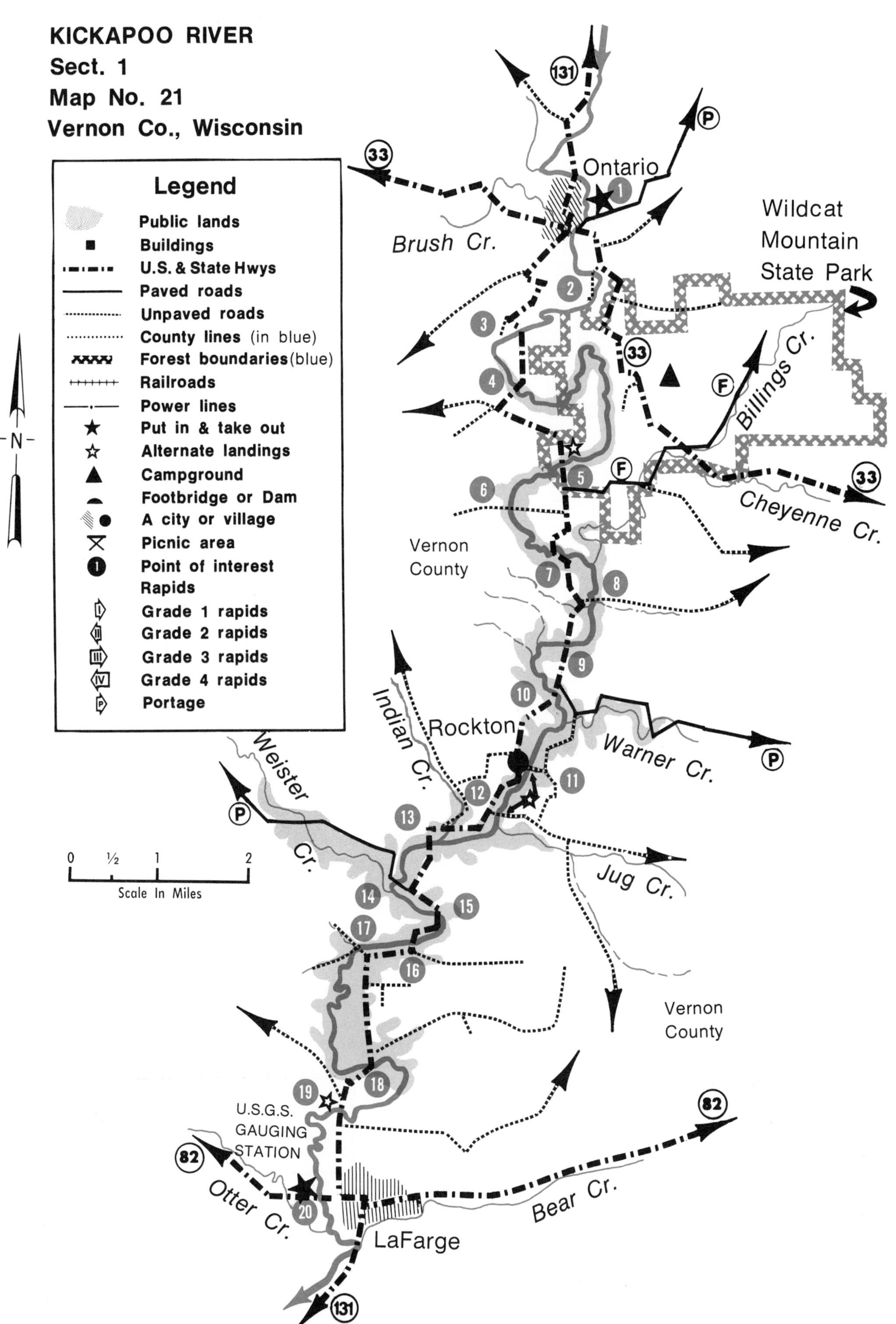
KICKAPOO RIVER
Sect. 1
Map No. 21
Vernon Co., Wisconsin
Legend
Public lands
Buildings
U.S. & State Hwys
Paved roads
Unpaved roads
County lines (in blue)
Forest boundaries (blue)
Railroads
Power lines
Put in & take out
Alternate landings
Campground
Footbridge or Dam
A city or village
Picnic area
Point of interest
Rapids
Grade 1 rapids
Grade 2 rapids
Grade 3 rapids
Grade 4 rapids
Portage
N
0 ½ 1 2
Scale In Miles
Ontario
Brush Cr.
Wildcat
Mountain
State Park
Billings Cr.
Cheyenne Cr.
Vernon
County
Rockton
Indian Cr.
Weister
Cr.
Warner Cr.
Jug Cr.
Vernon
County
U.S.G.S.
GAUGING
STATION
Otter Cr.
LaFarge
Bear Cr.

LITTLE WOLF RIVER

Described by Terry Spennetta
Little Wolf River: Waupaca County, Wisconsin.
Topo map(s): Tigerton (1:48,000) 1955 planimetric.
Overview map(s): Green Bay (1955).
Public lands: Waupaca County plat book (1968).
Start: Mud Lake Road Bridge.
End: County Highway C bridge at the town of Big Falls.

Difficulty (high water)	**II**
Difficulty (usual summer flow)	**II**
Length	**8**
Time	**5**
Width	**15-50**
Gradient	**13**
Drainage area	**175**

Water Conditions: A U.S.G.S. gauge was located near Royalton, Wisconsin, for 56 years until 1970, when it was removed. This river is generally only runnable during periods of high water, such as in the spring or after periods of prolonged heavy rains. There is a gauge on the right bank downstream of the County Highway P bridge, and upstream of the put-in. The old U.S.G.S. gauge heights are indicated on the canoeability chart, not those of the stage marker at the bridge. We do not have a correlation between these two markers. However, a stage marker reading of 4 on the Highway P bridge is minimal for enjoyable canoeing.

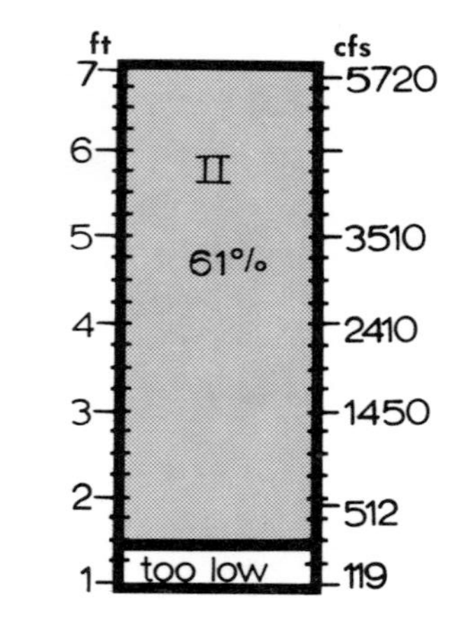

Canoeable Days Per Month

month	Apr	May	June	July	Aug	Sep
days	30	31	24	9	3	15

Scenery: The scenery is fair to good because there is a moderate amount of development along the shoreline. This little river has been described as having a certain "quaintness" about it due to the heavy brush, open fields, and mixed forest. More fishermen than wildlife are usually seen.
Geology: The bedrock of this river consists of granite and other igneous rocks.
Fish: This river is a trout stream that has brown and rainbow trout.
Campgrounds: At County Highway J, there is a state reserve which offers several undeveloped sites.
Points of Interest:

1. (0.0 miles) **Mud Lake Road Bridge.** Recommended put-in is developed access at Point 2, the end of the dirt road on the north side of the river.

2. (0.8 miles) **Comet Creek.** Trout stream enters from the right.

3. (2.0 miles) **Barbara Rapids.** This grade II rapids is typical of the boulder-strewn rapids found in this stretch of the river.

4. (2.4 miles) **Toy Boat Rapids.** This is similar to Barbara Rapids preceding it and rates a grade II. Downstream from here there are nearly continuous grade I-II rapids, with a few quiet pools in between.

5. (3.0 miles) **Mud Creek.** Outlet of Mud Lake enters from the left.

6. (3.7 miles) **County Highway J bridge.** This could be used as an alternate landing. There is unimproved parking space for up to 15 cars upstream of the bridge on the left bank. Camping is allowed, but there are only wilderness facilities. Except for the culverts and the canyon described below, there are no rapids to speak of below this bridge--only riffles. There is a trail on the left bank near the parking area. It heads upstream and can be used by fishermen and hikers. By taking out at County Highway J bridge it is possible to make many runs in a day and avoid the downstream quiet water.

7. (5.7 miles) **McNinch Road Bridge.** This bridge has several culverts underneath that are usually runnable. Occasionally, however, they are clogged with debris. **Scouting** from the bridge is **recommended.** The current in the culverts is fast, and the water drops. Small standing waves form below in high water and rate grade II.

8. (6.2 miles) **Canyon.** This miniature canyon is recognizable by an island which precedes it. There is fast current in the canyon and there are large waves. **Scouting** from the left bank is **advisable** for novices. This stretch normally rates grade II.

9. (7.5 miles) **County Highway C bridge** This is the recommended **take-out.** If you continue downstream portage the Big Falls Dam on the right.

10. (7.7 miles) **Big Falls Rapids.** These boulder-strewn rapids are runnable in very high water, at which time they rate IV. **Scouting is mandatory.**

Photo 17. The little Wolf in mid May.

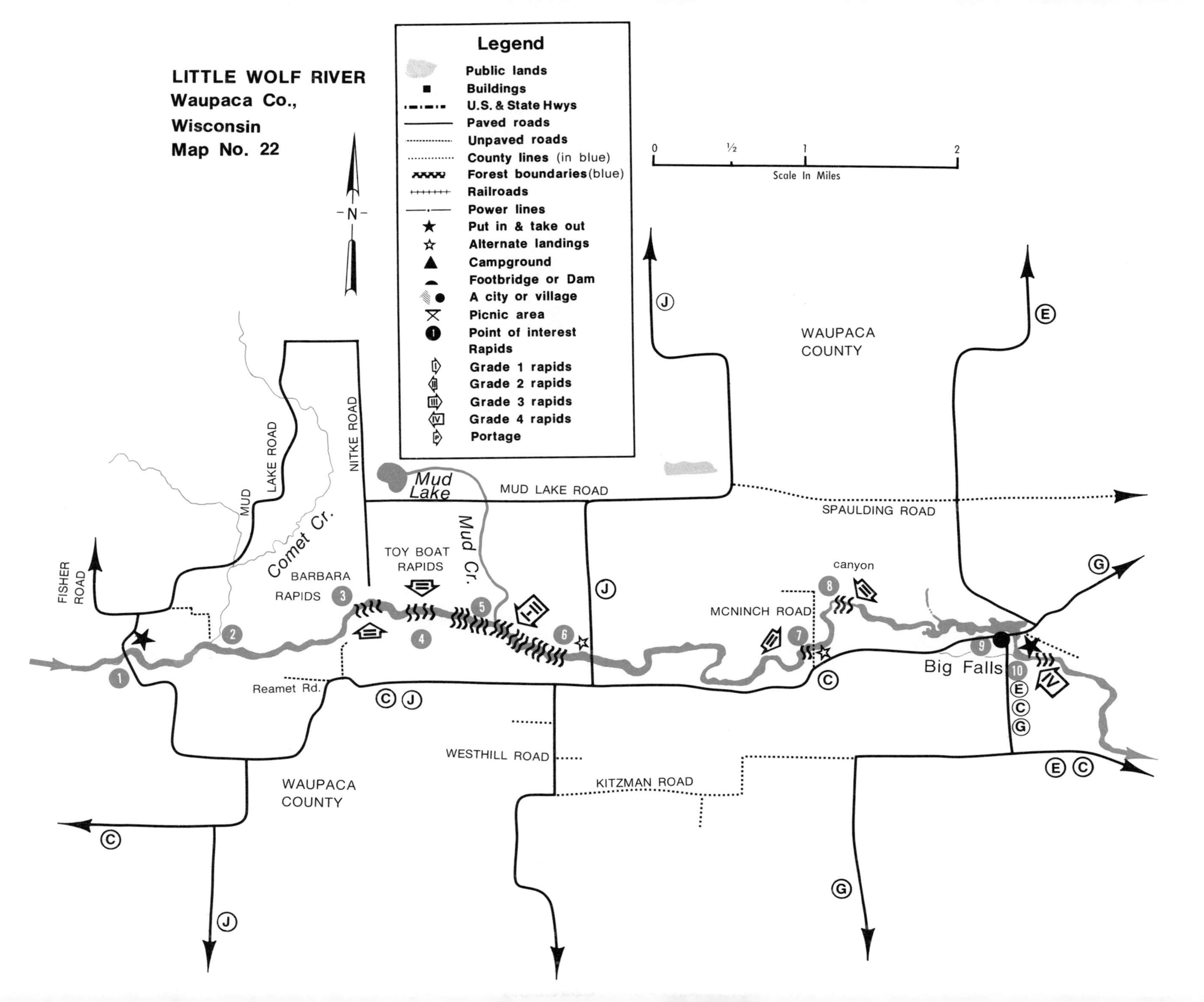
LITTLE WOLF RIVER
Waupaca Co.,
Wisconsin
Map No. 22
N
Legend
Public lands
Buildings
U.S. & State Hwys
Paved roads
Unpaved roads
County lines (in blue)
Forest boundaries (blue)
Railroads
Power lines
Put in & take out
Alternate landings
Campground
Footbridge or Dam
A city or village
Picnic area
Point of interest
Rapids
Grade 1 rapids
Grade 2 rapids
Grade 3 rapids
Grade 4 rapids
Portage
0 ½ 1 2
Scale In Miles
WAUPACA COUNTY
FISHER ROAD
MUD LAKE ROAD
NITKE ROAD
Mud Lake
Mud Cr.
Comet Cr.
BARBARA RAPIDS
TOY BOAT RAPIDS
Reamet Rd.
MUD LAKE ROAD
SPAULDING ROAD
WESTHILL ROAD
KITZMAN ROAD
MCNINCH ROAD
canyon
Big Falls
WAUPACA COUNTY

MARENGO RIVER TO THE BAD RIVER

Marengo River: Ashland County, Wisconsin.
Topo map(s): Mellen (1:62,500) 1967.
Overview map(s): Ashland (1953).
Public lands: Ashland County plat book (1969).
Section 1
Start: Bridge due north of town of Highbridge.
End: Elm Hoist Trail Bridge.
Section 2: See Bad River (map 1).

	SEC. 1
Difficulty (high water)	I-II
Difficulty (usual summer flow)	I
Length	12
Time	6
Width	20-100
Gradient	2
Drainage area	209

Water Conditions: The Marengo River is largely spring fed and is likely to be runnable during most of the summer. However, there is no convenient road access where the Marengo enters the Bad River. During the summer the Bad is generally too shallow to run. See the description accompanying map 1.
Geology: See description accompanying map 1.
Scenery: Excellent. There is virtually no development along the shoreline.
History: The village located near the put-in became known as Highbridge when the Wisconsin Central Railroad built a bridge some ninety feet high to cross a deeply cut ravine of Silver Creek. The Marengo River was supposedly named after the battle by that name where Napolean Bonapart defeated the Austrians. (For more history of this area see the description accompanying map 1.)
Fish: There are trout and walleye in the river.
Campgrounds: Copper Falls State Park has 34 developed campsites Wisconsin DNR charges a small fee for their use. For more information write Box 438, Mellen, Wisconsin 54546, or phone (715) 274-5123.
Points of Interest:
Section 1

1. (0.0 miles) **Bridge.** The recommended put-in is at a bridge located due north of the town of Highbridge.
2. (0.5 miles) **Silver Creek.** Just below the mouth of this creek, which happens to be a trout stream, there is a short grade I rapids. One of the problems most frequently run into here is that the narrow river is prone to having downed trees. Better watch out for these unexpected obstacles and portage when necessary.

Photo 18. Marengo River. "By golly, there really are trout in this river!"

3. (2.0 miles) **Billy Creek.** There is another grade I rapids located a short way downstream of the mouth of this creek. These grade I rapids may also suffer the misfortunes of downed trees, so **scout** first to make sure the way is clear.
4. (4.5 miles) **Confluence with the Bad River.** There is another grade I rapids just upstream of this spot. Since we have not yet run the Bad River upstream of this point, it would be wise to question our estimates which are based upon scouting and aerial photographs. There are two, definitely very difficult, **mandatory portages** at Copper and Brownstone Falls. The grade designations indicated on the map are primarily "guesstimates" and should be considered accordingly. If you want to put in, the only road access is located at Copper Falls State Park.
5. (7.2 miles) **Potato River.** Enters from the right.
6. (7.7 miles) **Soo Line RR trestle** crosses river.
7. (12.4 miles) **Elm Hoist Bridge.** This is the recommended take-out for this section. It is also the recommended put-in for Section 2 of the Bad River (map no. 1). There is a U.S.G.S. gauge here, plus a limited parking area. Elm Hoist Trail is really a dirt road, so its value is suspect for other than four-wheel drive vehicles, during the spring thaw and following prolonged periods of unusually heavy rains.

Photo 19. Bad River. "Somebody's been in our camp!"

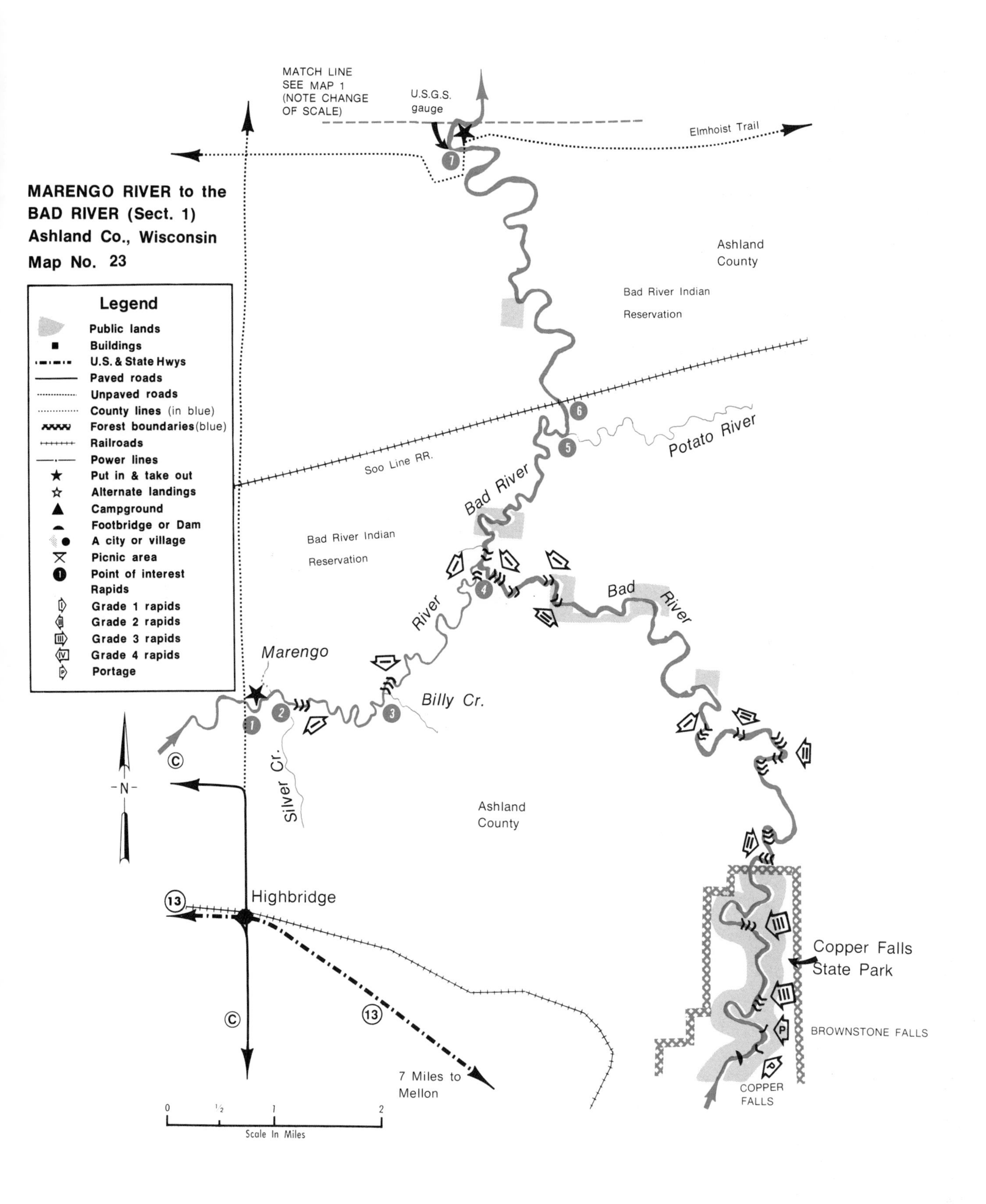

MARENGO RIVER to the
BAD RIVER (Sect. 1)
Ashland Co., Wisconsin
Map No. 23
Legend
Public lands
Buildings
U.S. & State Hwys
Paved roads
Unpaved roads
County lines (in blue)
Forest boundaries (blue)
Railroads
Power lines
Put in & take out
Alternate landings
Campground
Footbridge or Dam
A city or village
Picnic area
Point of interest
Rapids
Grade 1 rapids
Grade 2 rapids
Grade 3 rapids
Grade 4 rapids
Portage
MATCH LINE
SEE MAP 1
(NOTE CHANGE
OF SCALE)
U.S.G.S.
gauge
Elmhoist Trail
Ashland
County
Bad River Indian
Reservation
Soo Line RR.
Potato River
Bad River
Bad River Indian
Reservation
Bad
River
River
Marengo
Billy Cr.
Silver Cr.
Ashland
County
Highbridge
Copper Falls
State Park
BROWNSTONE FALLS
COPPER
FALLS
7 Miles to
Mellon
Scale In Miles

MENOMINEE RIVER

Menominee River: Marinette County, Wisconsin and Dickinson County, Michigan.
Topo map: Norway (1:62,500) 1955.
Overview map: Escanaba (1954).
Public lands: Marinette County, Wisconsin plat book (1970) and Dickinson County, Michigan map (1967).
Start: Below Little Quinnesec Falls Dam in Niagara.
End: U.S. Highway 8 bridge.

Difficulty (high water)	**IVp**
Difficulty (usual summer flow)	**IIIp**
Length	**4**
Time	**3**
Width	**75-350**
Gradient	**10**
Drainage area	**2,450**

Water Conditions: There is always enough water to run this section of river — however, at high water it may be too hazardous. This rapids has one of the greatest flows in the midwest; the hydraulics are somewhat similar to those of large western rivers. The rate of water flow is dependent on the volume of water that is released by the Little Quinnesec Falls Dam. This information can be obtained by calling (715) 251-3151.

Scenery: Currently the water is heavily polluted. We hope this situation will be improved in the near future. There is minimal development along the wooded shoreline.

Campgrounds: We don't know of any campgrounds on this river. We have usually camped at the sites that are recommended for the Pike and Peshtigo Rivers, which are near here.

Note: This section of river is one of the most difficult in the book and should be run only by experts in decked boats.

Points of Interest:

1 (0.0 miles) **Little Quinnesec Falls dam.** The recommended put-in for this river is located just downstream of this dam. Open canoes should never attempt this stretch unless **all** rapids are portaged.

2 (1.6 miles) **Sand Portage Falls.** At this point the river is obstructed by a large island. Sand Portage Falls is located in the right channel. This rapids rates grade II in low water but rates grade III at high levels because a backroller develops. This rapids was so named by the early Indian inhabitants of this region because they crossed over large amounts of sand as they portaged around the rapids.

3 (2.4 miles) **Misicot Falls PORTAGE!** This falls has a variety of names depending on the source. This is an eight-foot drop that has a runnable chute. It is located uncomfortably close downstream of a blind turn and is preceded by some grade I-II rapids. Although we know of many successful runs of this drop we also know of **many drownings** that have occurred at this location. A tipover is particularly dangerous because of the huge boulder and souse hole immediately downstream of the falls. This site is also referred to as Pier's Gorge. On the Michigan side of the river there is a foot path to this falls and the rapids below.

4 (2.5 miles) **Pier's Gorge.** This rapids usually rates grade IV. There are a number of souse holes that must be avoided. **Scouting** from the left bank is **strongly recommended.**

5 (2.6 miles) **Backroller. Caution.** At most water levels, there is a potentially dangerous backroller that develops here. It can be avoided by running on the right.

6 (4.0 miles) **U.S. Highway 8 bridge.** The recommended take-out is on the right side of the river, upstream of this bridge.

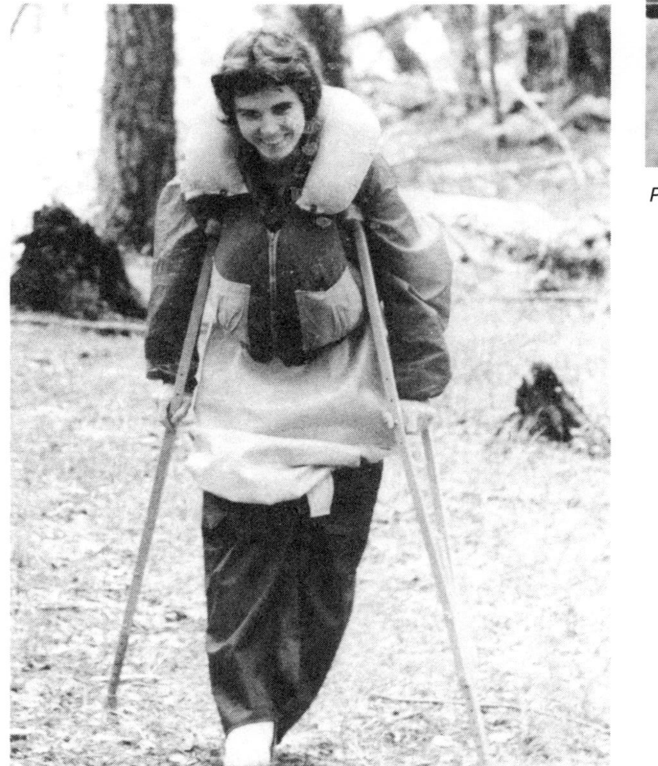

Photo 20. Deliverance II? Not really. Neither rain, nor sleet, nor snow, nor broken leg...

Photo 21. "Banzai - Charge!"

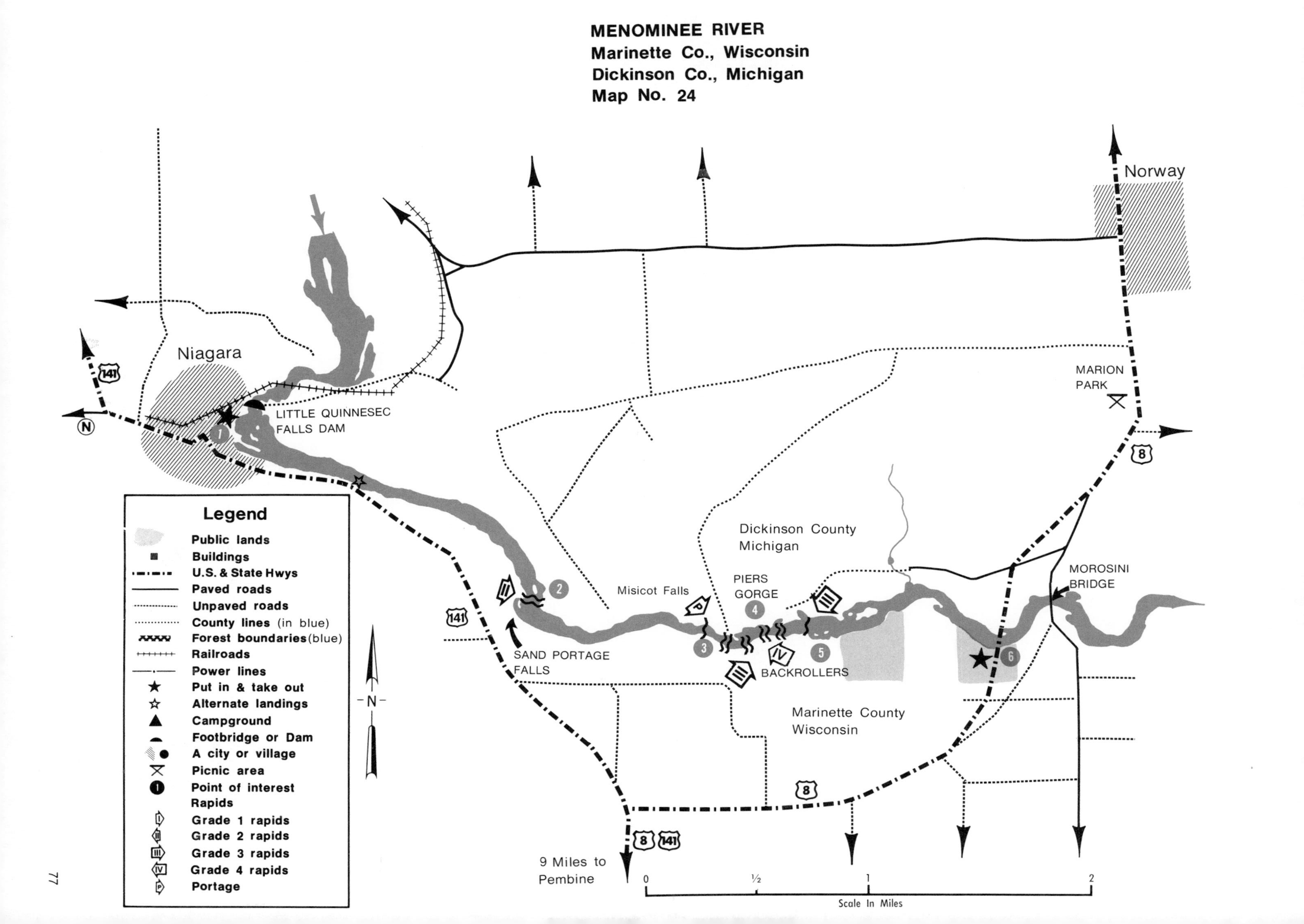
MENOMINEE RIVER
Marinette Co., Wisconsin
Dickinson Co., Michigan
Map No. 24
Norway
Niagara
141
N
LITTLE QUINNESEC
FALLS DAM
MARION
PARK
8
Dickinson County
Michigan
PIERS
GORGE
Misicot Falls
MOROSINI
BRIDGE
SAND PORTAGE
FALLS
BACKROLLERS
Marinette County
Wisconsin
9 Miles to
Pembine
0
½
1
2
Scale In Miles
Legend
Public lands
Buildings
U.S. & State Hwys
Paved roads
Unpaved roads
County lines (in blue)
Forest boundaries (blue)
Railroads
Power lines
Put in & take out
Alternate landings
Campground
Footbridge or Dam
A city or village
Picnic area
Point of interest
Rapids
Grade 1 rapids
Grade 2 rapids
Grade 3 rapids
Grade 4 rapids
Portage

MIRROR LAKE

Mirror Lake: Sauk County, Wisconsin.
Topo map(s): Wisconsin Dells (1:62,500) 1957.
Overview map(s): Madison (1957).
Public lands: Sauk County plat book (1970).
Start: State Highway 23 bridge.
End: Bridge and dam in town of Lake Delton.

Difficulty (high water)	**Q**
Difficulty (usual summer flow)	**Q**
Length	**3.8**
Time	**2**

Water Conditions: This is an excellent quiet-water trip. There is never the problem of insufficient water.

Geology: Bedrock of Upper Cambrian Potsdam sandstone.

Scenery: Although the shoreline is quite developed there are scenic sandstone bluffs resembling those found along the Upper Wisconsin.

Campgrounds: Mirror Lake State Park has 95 developed sites. A user fee is charged. This campground is located one mile southeast of Lake Delton on Highway 12. For more information write Mirror Lake, Rt. 3, Box 92, Baraboo, Wisc. 53913, or call (608) 254-7561.

Note: During the summer this is a busy resort area. If you seek privacy it is best to take this trip in September or October.

Points of Interest:

1. (0.0 miles) **Put in at the Highway 23 bridge.** In the first quarter mile you pass through dense reeds frequently inhabited by ducks. At the end of the first lake, the banks rise to form a canyon. After a mile, this opens into another lake. The right arm of the lake goes south. There is a large swimming beach and boat landing for Mirror Lake State Park. It is not uncommon to see many turtles sunning themselves on stumps along the shore here. Just past the arm, on the right bank of the "lake," is Ishnala, a famous restaurant.

2. (3.1 miles) After you have passed under the two bridges of **Interstate 90-94,** the banks begin to resemble the carved sandstone of the upper Wisconsin Dells.

3. (3.8 miles) **The recommended take-out** can be recognized by docks on the left bank and a dam. This dam can be portaged if you wish to continue to the end of Lake Delton. A rope is recommended for this portage as there is a 25-foot bank with a very steep decline.

4. (4.5 miles) **Highway 12 bridge.**

5. (6.0 miles) There is an alternate take-out on Highway A.

Photo 22. The Wisconsin River near Merrimac.

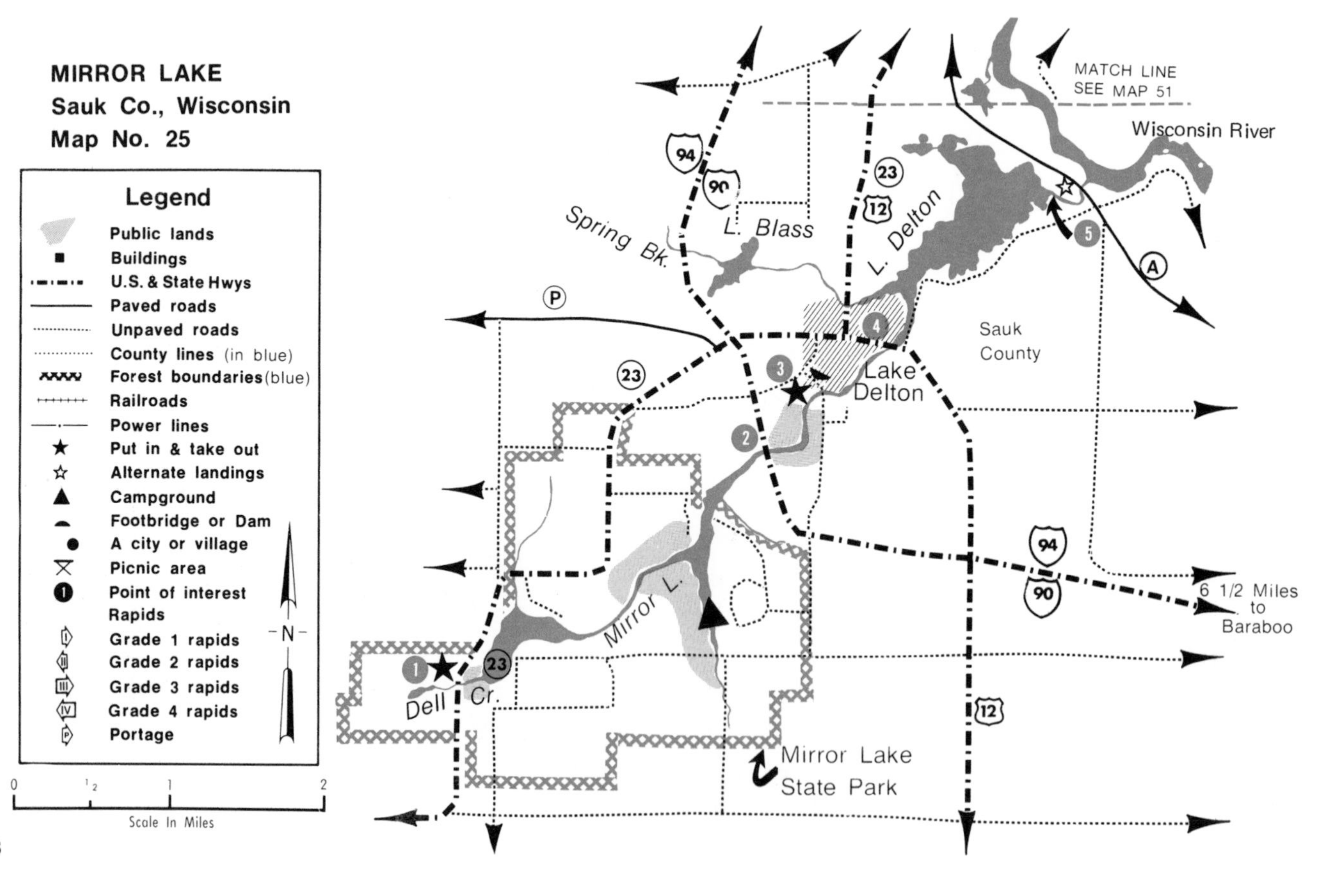

Photo 23. The Canyon of the Little Wolf.

MONTREAL RIVER

Montreal River: Iron County, Wisconsin, and Gogebic County, Michigan.
Topo Maps: Little Girls Point (1:62,500) 1956 and Ironwood, (1:62,500) 1955.
Overview map: Ashland (1953).
Public lands: Iron County plat book (1969) and Michigan DNR map of Gogebic County (West) 1968.
Section 1
Start: West Branch of Montreal River below Gile Flowage, at the Highway 77 bridge.
End: Wisconsin Highway 2 bridge.
Section 2
Start: Below Saxon Falls Dam, off of County Highway B.
End: Wisconsin Highway 122 (Michigan Highway 505) bridge.

	SEC. 1	SEC. 2
Difficulty (high water)	III	II
Difficulty (usual summer flow)	II-III	II
Length	5	4
Time	4	3
Width	6-80	20-100
Gradient	70	--
Drainage area	--	262

Water Conditions: Average flow for 32 years is 325 cfs. The gauge was located in Gogebic County, Michigan, on the right bank about 1.5 miles downstream of the Saxon powerhouse. **Section 1** is on the West Branch of the Montreal River, which is the outlet for the Gile Flowage. Check with the people at the dam to see if the gates are open before running the river. This is a sporty river with many challenges. The water level for Section 2 should be checked out with the people at the Saxon Dam.

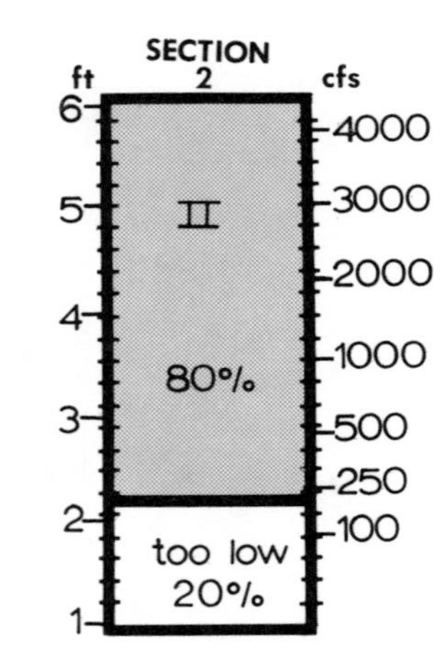

Canoeable Days Per Month

month	Apr	May	June	July	Aug	Sep
days	30	31	30	25	16	15

Scenery: Both sections described here are very beautiful. **Section 2** has a lovely canyon with sheer cliffs of weathered sandstone that makes it particularly outstanding.

Campgrounds: Saxon Harbor Park has developed sites. It is located off County Highway A on Lake Superior. This campground is run by the Iron County Parks Commission, Courthouse, Hurley, Wisc. 54534. Call (715) 561-2695. A user fee is charged.

Points of Interest:
Section 1

1 (0.0 miles) **Highway 77 bridge.** This is the recommended put-in. There is a park west of this bridge in Montreal where cars can be parked.

2 (1.2 miles) **Bridge.** From the put-in to this bridge, the water is fast, but there are no drops or rapids. Some large boulders mark the beginning of Railroad Bridge Rapids. Get out and **scout** when the railroad bridge is in sight. These rapids can be run, but they are wild. They consist of a series of ledges which are close together. **The whole stretch must be run once started. There is no way out in case of a capsize.** The left shore is a 60-foot high rock wall. **Width of rapids is 6 to 20 feet. Portage** on the right side and get up on the railroad tracks as quickly as possible. Carry on the tracks about 400 feet or so around a curve going west. Stop on the bridge and admire the roaring rapids--then walk to the beginning of the next curve. There you can slide the boats down a steep bank to the river. Put-in as soon as possible.

3 (2.4 miles) **Chicago & Northwestern Railroad bridge.** - A stretch of several hundred yards of good grade III rapids follows the bridge. Then there is a drop which should be **scouted.** Continuous rapids follow, but you can get in to shore occasionally. The next drop should be **scouted,** too. It is best to follow the main flow of water in the middle of the river. It is necessary to make some pretty sharp turns to avoid rocks and boulders. A mile or so below the railroad bridge, there is a park on the left shore.

4 (4.0 miles) **Steel bridge.** At the bridge, you hear the roar of a waterfall. The first drop is easy, but it is best to do some thorough **scouting.** The falls can probably be run but it has a high hazard rating. There are about 200 feet of white water with a turn to the left. The total drop is probably 15 feet or so, and there are some nice standing waves at the bottom. About a hundred yards below the falls, there is a four-foot drop which should be run very close to the right shore. The chute has a 90 degree turn to the left; be careful not to run into the rock on the right side. There is another mile and a half of continuous rapids to the take-out. There are a lot of rocks to dodge but no need for scouting. Access to shore is pretty good.

5 (5.1 miles) **U.S. Highway 2 bridge.** The recommended take-out is on the right bank upstream of the bridge. There is a gravel road on the west side of the river that goes back to Montreal (six miles).

Section 2

6 (15.2 miles) **Saxon Falls.** We have not run the 10 miles between the end of Section 1 and the start of Section 2. The put-in for **Section 2** is below this falls. The rapids in this section rate grade II and are tame in comparison to those in the previous section. To get to the put-in go north from Saxon on State Highway 122 and turn east onto County Highway B. Where B turns south, turn north onto a gravel road that goes to the Saxon Dam. There is a stairway that goes down to the river here, just below the powerhouse. Permission should be obtained before putting in here as this land is owned by the Lake Superior District Power Company. Saxon Falls is just upstream of the powerhouse.

7 (16.8 miles) **Montreal River Canyon.** This is a fantastically beautiful gorge with high sheer cliffs on both sides of the river. The upper part of the canyon consists mostly of dark volcanic basalt, while the lower canyon has walls of weathered sandstone conglomerate.

8 (8.8 miles) **Wisconsin Highway 122** (Michigan Highway 505) bridge. This is the take-out for this section.

Note: Difficulty levels for Section 1 at various water levels are in great dispute. Please use special precautions as locals have been known to obstruct this narrow stream with things such as logs and barbwire. The put-in to Section 2 is now posted as "No Trespassing", and there is no alternate put-in available. Therefore, Section 2 should no longer be considered runable.

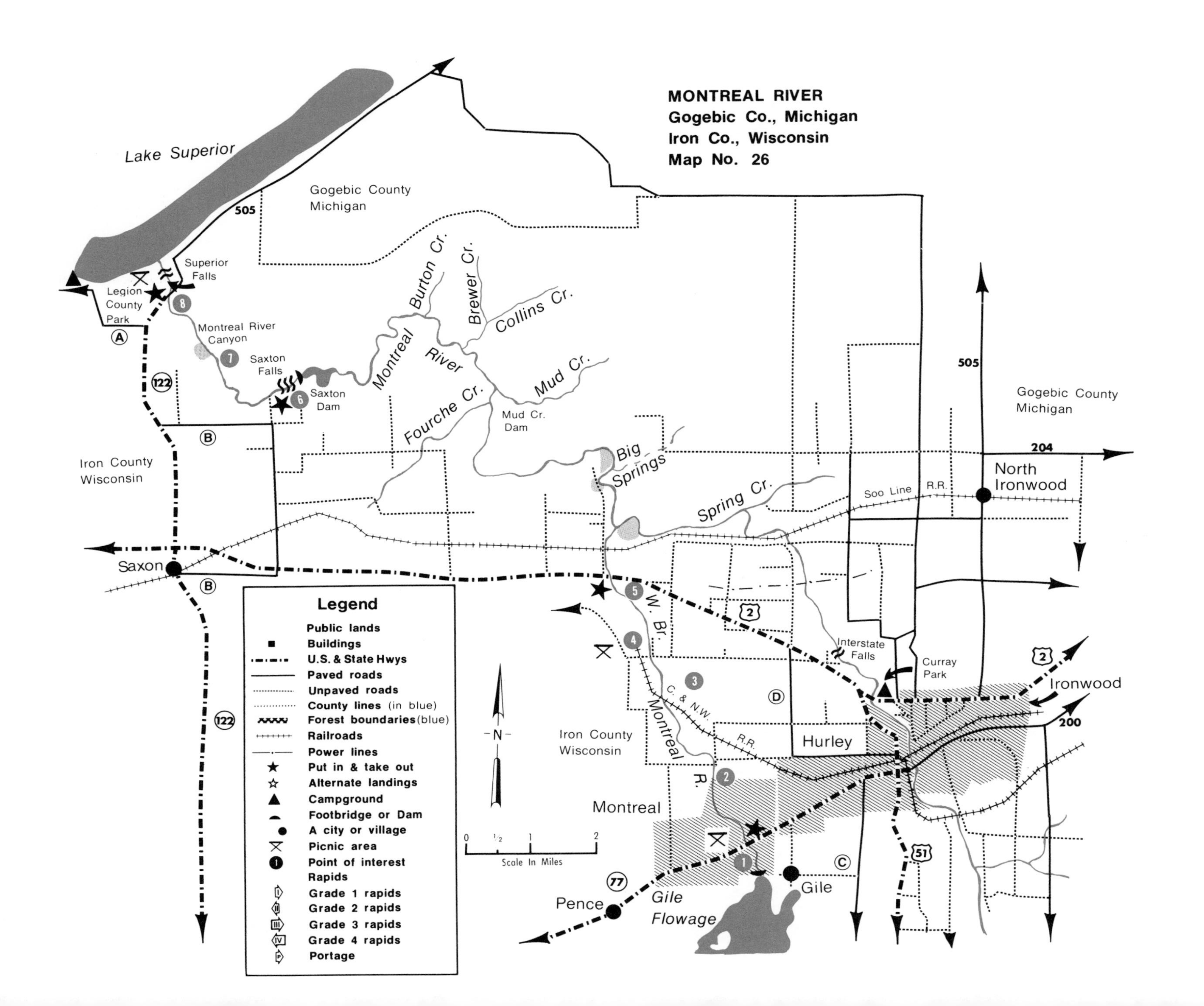

MONTREAL RIVER
Gogebic Co., Michigan
Iron Co., Wisconsin
Map No. 26
Lake Superior
Gogebic County Michigan
505
Superior Falls
Legion County Park
A
Montreal River Canyon
Saxton Falls
Saxton Dam
122
B
Iron County Wisconsin
Saxon
Montreal
River
Burton Cr.
Brewer Cr.
Collins Cr.
Mud Cr.
Fourche Cr.
Mud Cr. Dam
Big Springs
Spring Cr.
Soo Line R.R.
North Ironwood
204
Gogebic County Michigan
W. Br.
Montreal R.
C. & N.W. R.R.
Interstate Falls
Curray Park
2
Ironwood
200
D
Hurley
Iron County Wisconsin
Montreal
C
Gile
51
77
Pence
Gile Flowage
N
0
1/2
1
2
Scale In Miles
Legend
Public lands
Buildings
U.S. & State Hwys
Paved roads
Unpaved roads
County lines (in blue)
Forest boundaries (blue)
Railroads
Power lines
Put in & take out
Alternate landings
Campground
Footbridge or Dam
A city or village
Picnic area
Point of interest
Rapids
Grade 1 rapids
Grade 2 rapids
Grade 3 rapids
Grade 4 rapids
Portage

NAMEKAGON RIVER

SECTION 1

Namekagon River: Bayfield and Sawyer Counties, Wisconsin.
Topo map(s): Hayward (1:48,000) 1944 planimetric and Namekagon Lake (1:48,000) 1944 planimetric.
Overview map(s): Ashland (1953).
Public lands: Bayfield County plat book (1967) and Sawyer County plat book (1968).
Section 1
Start: Below the dam at Lake Namekagon.
End: Seely.

	SEC. 1
Difficulty (high water)	**Ip**
Difficulty (usual summer flow)	**Ip**
Length	**21**
Time	**6**
Gradient	**5**

Water Conditions: The river is generally runable all summer. The best source of information on water levels can be obtained by calling the Trego Dam between 7:00 A.M. and 3:00 P.M. on weekdays only. Highest flows occur between 7:00 A.M. and 2:00 P.M. The personnel at the dam can usually provide an estimate of the conditions to expect on the upper sections and a flow above 350 cfs. is considered minimal for Sections 5 and 6.

Name: Namekagon is an Ojibwa word meaning "where the sturgeons are plentiful."

Scenery: Most of this river has moderate development along the shoreline, as well as dams on the river itself. This river was one of the first rivers in the nation to be designated as a wild river by the National Wild and Scenic Rivers Act of 1968. It was a somewhat peculiar choice since the river doesn't meet most of the wild river requirements. It will be somewhat of a challenge to return the condition of the upper stretch of this river to that of a true wild river.

Geology: This area has undergone extensive glacial activity. The oldest rocks in the area are of Pre-Cambrian metamorphic and volcanic formations. These are found mostly as bedrock that is covered by Cambrian sandstone and various glacial sands, clays, silts, and gravels. There are numerous low marshy areas on this river.

Fish and Campgrounds: See the description accompanying map 29.

Points of Interest:

1. (0.0 miles) **Namekagon Lake Dam.** Put in below this dam on the right side of the river.

2. (1.0 miles) **Foot bridge.** Shortly downstream you leave the boundary of the Chequamegon National Forest. There are grade I riffles located in this stretch.

3. (7.0 miles) **County Highway M bridge.** Just upstream of Fivemile Creek there is a landing on the right bank. Fivemile Creek is a good stream for brook trout. The river from this bridge to Pacwawong Lake is good trout fishing for browns and rainbows.

4. (7.7 miles) **Cap Creek.** Enters from the left. The mouth of this creek is on the left bank. This is a good brook trout stream. About one and a half miles below Cap Creek on the left bank is the old Namekagon to Lake Owen portage trail. This ancient historic trail was used by Ojibwa Indians, traders, missionaries, and explorers. Dating back hundreds of years, this trail connected the Mississippi waterway with Lake Superior.

5. (10.5 miles) **Footbridge.** There is a footbridge at this location that **must be portaged** because it is too close to the river surface. Hopefully this obstacle will be eliminated soon.

6. (11.5 miles) **Landing.** There is an alternate landing on the right bank by the Phillippi Bridge.

7. (12.7 miles) **Chicago and Northwestern Railroad crossing.** Shortly downstream U.S. Highway 63 crosses the river.

8. (14.3 miles) **Big Brook.** This is another well-known trout stream.

9. (15.0 miles) **Undeveloped landing.** On right bank.

10. (16.5 miles) **County line.** This point marks the boundary of Bayfield and Sawyer Counties.

11. (17.6 miles) **Pacwawong Lake Dam. Portage** right or run the spillway, depending on your ability and the water level.

12. (20.9 miles) **Seely.** Take out at the landing on the right bank downstream of Seely.

Photo 24. Canoeing the Upper Namekagon.

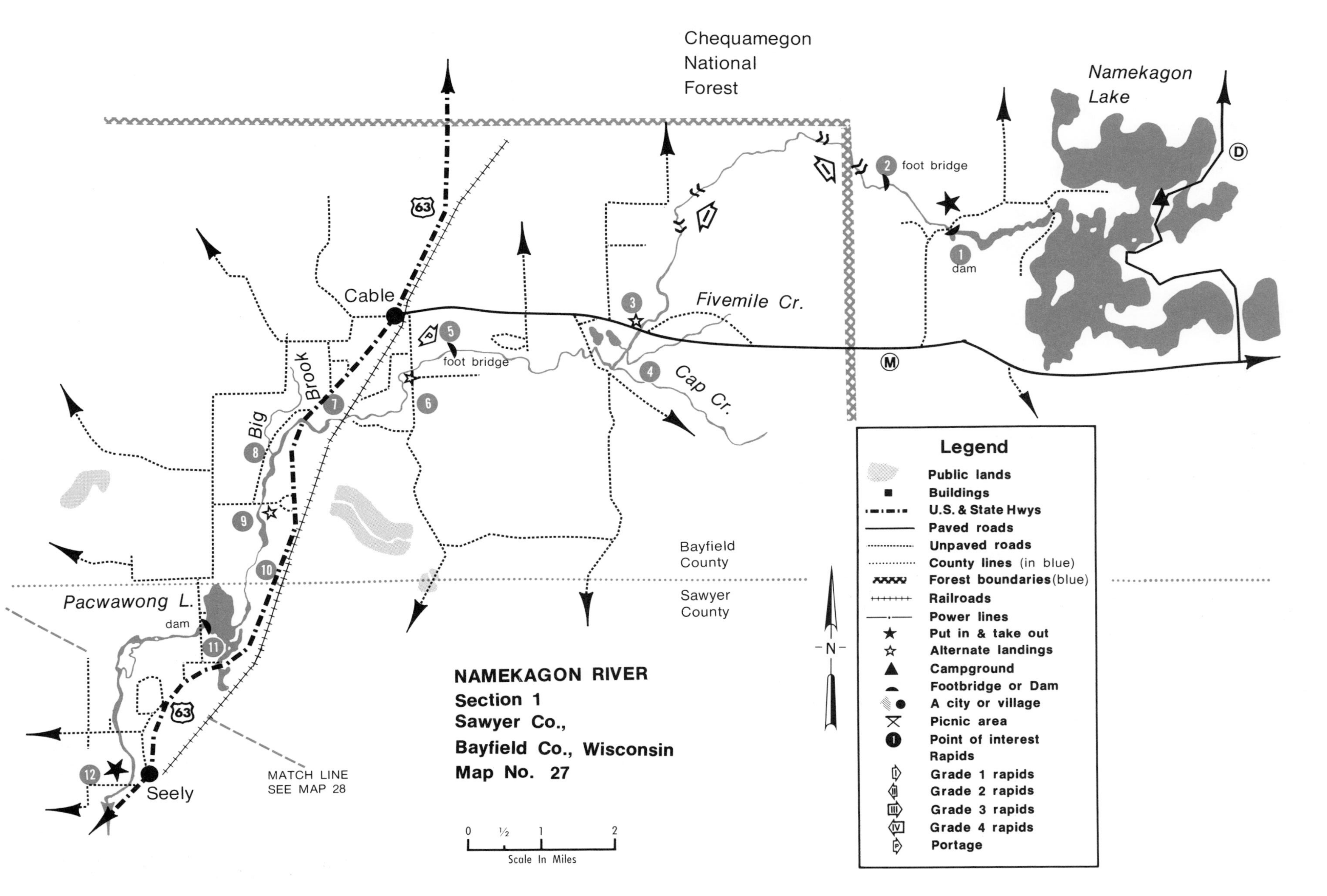

Chequamegon
National
Forest
Namekagon
Lake
D
foot bridge
dam
Cable
63
Fivemile Cr.
Cap Cr.
M
foot bridge
Big
Brook
Bayfield
County
Sawyer
County
Pacwawong L.
dam
Seely
MATCH LINE
SEE MAP 28
NAMEKAGON RIVER
Section 1
Sawyer Co.,
Bayfield Co., Wisconsin
Map No. 27
0 ½ 1 2
Scale In Miles
N
Legend
Public lands
Buildings
U.S. & State Hwys
Paved roads
Unpaved roads
County lines (in blue)
Forest boundaries(blue)
Railroads
Power lines
Put in & take out
Alternate landings
Campground
Footbridge or Dam
A city or village
Picnic area
Point of interest
Rapids
Grade 1 rapids
Grade 2 rapids
Grade 3 rapids
Grade 4 rapids
Portage

NAMEKAGON RIVER

SECTION 2

Namekagon River: Sawyer County, Wisconsin.
Topo maps: Hayward (1:48,000) 1944 planimetric.
Overview map: Ashland (1953).
Public lands: Sawyer County plat book (1968).
Section 2
Start: Seely.
End: Hayward.

Difficulty (high water)	**Q1**
Difficulty (usual summer flow)	**Q1**
Length	**11**
Time	**5**
Gradient	**7**
Drainage area	**503** (at Trego)

Water Conditions: The river is generally runnable all summer. (see description accompanying Map 27.

Points of Interest:

12 (20.9 miles) **Seely.** Put in on the right bank downstream of Seely. Brown and rainbow trout fishing is good in this area.

13 (22.3 miles) **Larson Bridge.** Alternate landing.

14 (23.1 miles) **Stone Bridge.** There are some grade I riffles located downstream of this location.

15 (24.2 miles) **McDermott Brook.** Trout stream enters from the left.

16 (25.5 miles) **U.S. Highway 63 bridge.** The next mile flows through the Phipps Flowage.

17 (27.5 miles) **Phipps Dam. Portage** left.

18 (27.8 miles) **Mosquito Brook.** Trout stream enters from the left.

19 (29.7 miles) **Chicago and Northwestern Railroad bridge.**

20 (30.8 miles) **Airport Bridge.**

21 (32.1 miles) **Highway 77 bridge.** The recommended take-out is on the right bank upstream of this bridge. Should you wish to paddle the one and one-half miles of the Hayward Dam Flowage through the city of Hayward, the dam can be portaged on the left.

Photo 25. "Do you think we'll catch anything?"

Photo 26. If you like fishing and camping too, the Namekagon is the river for you.

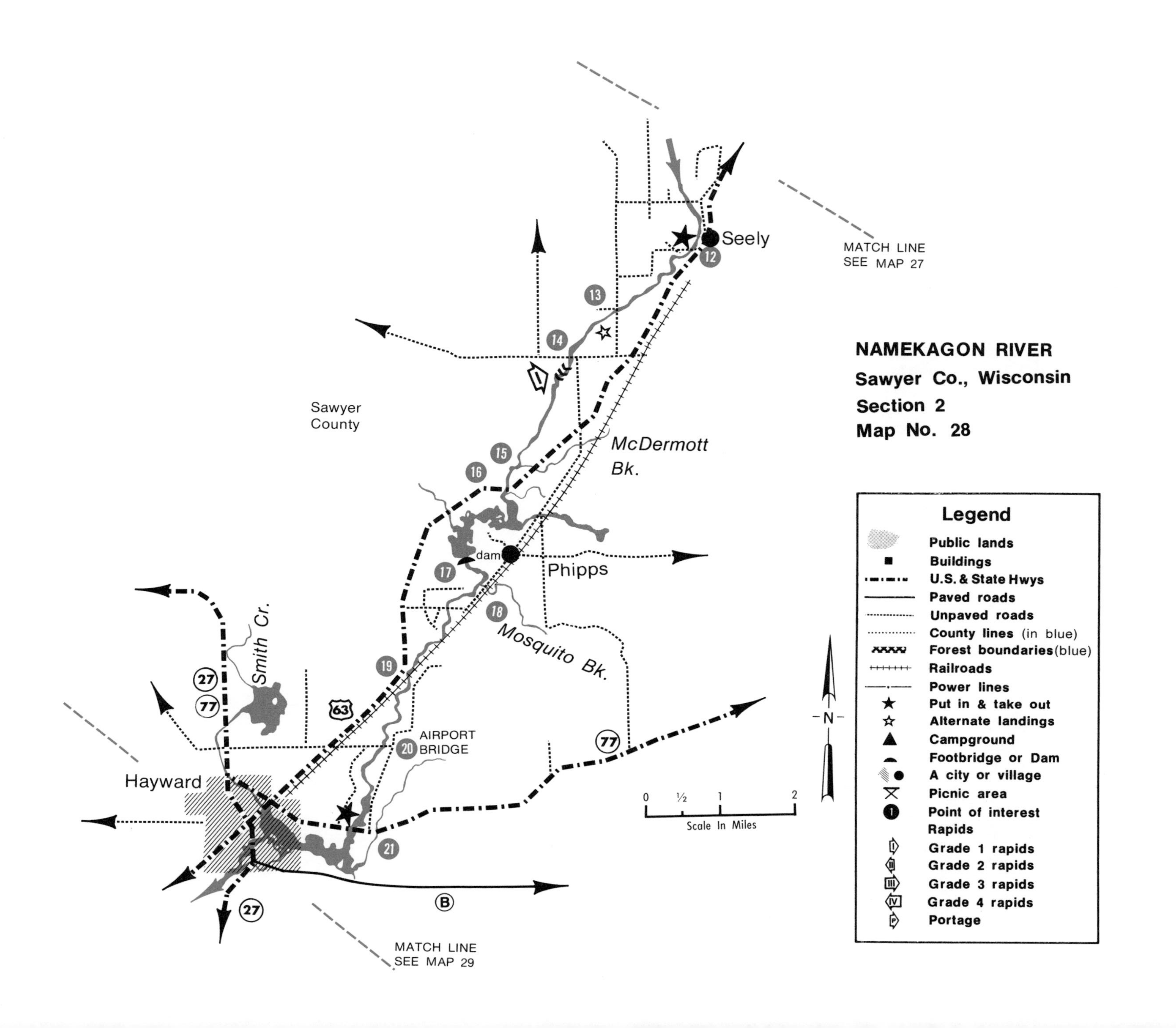

NAMEKAGON RIVER
Sawyer Co., Wisconsin
Section 2
Map No. 28
Legend
Public lands
Buildings
U.S. & State Hwys
Paved roads
Unpaved roads
County lines (in blue)
Forest boundaries (blue)
Railroads
Power lines
Put in & take out
Alternate landings
Campground
Footbridge or Dam
A city or village
Picnic area
Point of interest
Rapids
Grade 1 rapids
Grade 2 rapids
Grade 3 rapids
Grade 4 rapids
Portage
MATCH LINE
SEE MAP 27
MATCH LINE
SEE MAP 29
N
0
½
1
2
Scale In Miles
Seely
12
13
14
15
16
17
18
19
20
21
McDermott
Bk.
Phipps
dam
Mosquito Bk.
AIRPORT
BRIDGE
77
B
63
27
Sawyer
County
Smith Cr.
Hayward

NAMEKAGON RIVER

SECTION 3

Namekagon River: Sawyer and Washburn Counties, Wisconsin.
Topo maps: Hayward (1:48,000) 1944 planimetric and Stone Lake (1:48,000) 1948 planimetric.
Overview map: Ashland (1953).
Public lands: Sawyer County plat book (1968) and Washburn County plat book (1972).
Section 3
Start: Below Hayward Dam.
End: Spring Brook Landing.

Difficulty (high water)	**II**
Difficulty (usual summer flow)	**I²-II**
Length	**15**
Time	**6**
Gradient	**3**

Water Conditions: This river is generally runnable all summer. See description accompanying map 27.
Scenery: Not bad with some development, but a noisy highway nearby is a nuisance.
Geology: See description accompanying map 27.
Fish: There are smallmouth bass and trout in the rapids and certain tributary streams as indicated in the points of interest for this section.
Campgrounds: Hayward River Park. This Wisconsin DNR controlled campsite has 10 spaces. A small admission and user fee is charged. This campground is located just downstream of the Hayward Dam and across the road from the Hayward Ranger Station. For more information contact the Ranger Station, Hayward, WI 54843, or call (715) 634-2688.
Points of Interest:

1. (34.1 miles) **Hayward River Campground.** The put-in for Section 3 is on the left at this DNR developed campground located one-half mile below Hayward Dam.
2. (35.1 miles) **Warder's Rapids.** An easy grade II rapids that is typical of this stretch of river.
3. (36.6 miles) **Spring Lake Creek.** Enters the river from the left.
4. (37.6 miles) **Cadotte Trading Post.** This is the site of an old fur trading post established in 1784. About a mile downstream is the Sawyer-Washburn county line.
5. (39.0 miles) **Cranberry Bog** (or marsh). This is one of many cranberry marshes found along the river. After these berries are harvested they are processed and distributed to international markets.
6. (41.6 miles) **Rat River Campground.** There is a shelter and water available at this semi-primitive campground located on the right bank of the river.
7. (42.1 miles) **Old Stinnett Bridge.** There is an easy grade I rapids that begins at the bridge and continues for about 100 feet downstream. This location can be used as an alternate landing. The County Highway E bridge is just downstream.
8. (42.5 miles) **Soo Line Railroad bridge.** About half a mile downstream of the bridge there is an easy grade I rapids.
9. (44.5 miles) **Chippanazie Creek and Groat Landing.** Creek enters from the right. There is a landing on the left side of the river at the bridge located near this creek.
10. (44.6 miles) **Chippanazie Rapids.** This rapids is in two pitches. The first begins below the mouth of Chippanazie Creek and the second is slightly further downstream. They rate grade I-II.
11. (46.3 miles) **Unnamed rapids.** An easy grade I rapids located just downstream of a large island.
12. (46.8 miles) **State highway wayside.** Could be used as a picnic area by boaters, but the steep bank that must be climbed to get to it does not make this a convenient alternate landing.
13. (48.5 miles) **Spring Brook Rapids.** An easy grade I rapids that continues to the U.S. Highway 63 bridge. There is another easy, but rocky, grade I rapids 200 yards downstream.
14. (49.5 miles) **Spring Brook Landing.** About one-half mile downstream of the U.S. 63 bridge there is an old bridge not open to vehicular traffic. The recommended take-out is on the left bank of the bridge. There is ample parking and a nice swimming hole at this location.

Photo 27. What more could you ask for?

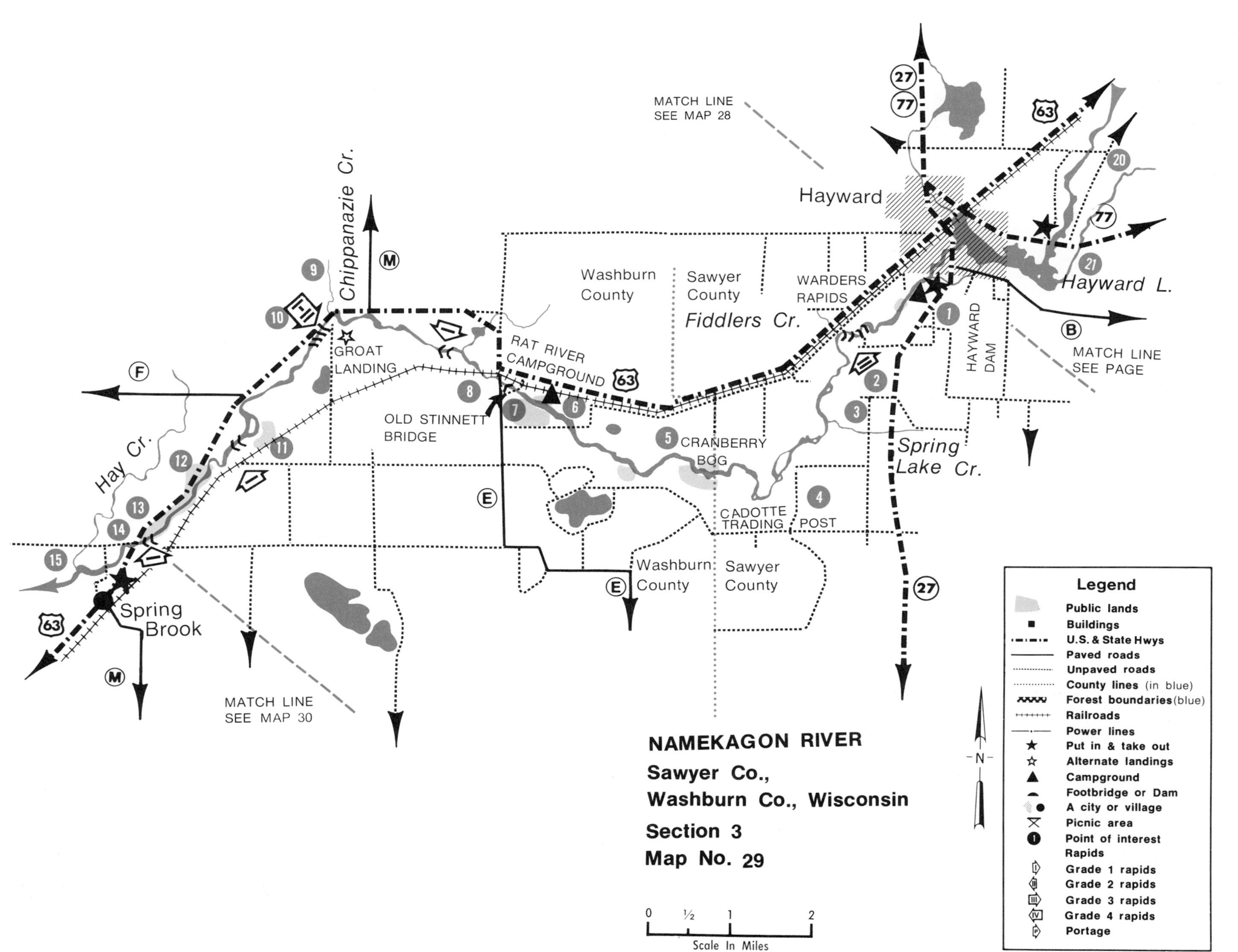
MATCH LINE
SEE MAP 28
Hayward
Hayward L.
MATCH LINE
SEE PAGE
HAYWARD
DAM
Chippanazie Cr.
Washburn
County
Sawyer
County
WARDERS
RAPIDS
Fiddlers Cr.
GROAT
LANDING
RAT RIVER
CAMPGROUND
OLD STINNETT
BRIDGE
CRANBERRY
BOG
Spring
Lake Cr.
CADOTTE
TRADING
POST
Hay Cr.
Washburn
County
Sawyer
County
Spring
Brook
MATCH LINE
SEE MAP 30
27
77
63
B
E
M
F
1
2
3
4
5
6
7
8
9
10
11
12
13
14
15
20
21
NAMEKAGON RIVER
Sawyer Co.,
Washburn Co., Wisconsin
Section 3
Map No. 29
0
½
1
2
Scale In Miles
N
Legend
Public lands
Buildings
U.S. & State Hwys
Paved roads
Unpaved roads
County lines (in blue)
Forest boundaries (blue)
Railroads
Power lines
Put in & take out
Alternate landings
Campground
Footbridge or Dam
A city or village
Picnic area
Point of interest
Rapids
Grade 1 rapids
Grade 2 rapids
Grade 3 rapids
Grade 4 rapids
Portage

NAMEKAGON RIVER

SECTION 4

Namekagon River: Washburn County, Wisconsin.
Topo map(s): Spooner (1:62,500) 1965 and Stone Lake (1:48,000) 1948 planimetric.
Overview map: Ashland (1953).
Public lands: Washburn County plat book (1972).
Section 4
Start: Spring Brook Landing.
End: Start of Trego Flowage.

Difficulty (high water)	**I**
Difficulty (usual summer flow)	**Q**
Length	**12**
Time	**5**
Gradient	**3**

Water Conditions: The river is generally runnable all summer. See description accompanying map 27.
Scenery: See the description accompanying map 29.
Geology: See the description accompanying map 27.
Fish: Nearly all of the tributary streams have trout. Smallmouth bass frequent the river itself.
Campgrounds: Earl County Park. There are six spaces at this campsite located north of Earl. A small user fee is charged. For more information write Spooner, Wisc. 54801, or call (715) 635-2997. Trego Park Campground. The private campground has 45 sites and is located north of Trego. There is a small user fee. For more information contact Cliff Peterson, Trego, Wisc. 54888, or call (715) 635-2997. Canfield's Log Cabin and Campground. There are 50 sites on the Namekagon River six miles north of Spooner. There is a small user fee. For more information contact Jack Canfield, Trego, Wisc. 54888, or call (715) 635-2959.

Points of Interest:

14 (49.5 miles) **Spring Brook Landing.** The recommended put-in is on the left bank.

15 (50.0 miles) **Hay Creek.** Brook trout stream enters from the right.

16 (50.8 miles) **Spring Creek.** Brook trout stream enters from the right.

17 (52.5 miles) **Gull Creek.** Trout stream enters from the right.

18 (53.0 miles) **Bean Brook.** Enters from the left. This trout stream is particularly famous for its brook and brown trout.

19 (57.0 miles) **Earl.** Campground.

20 (59.0 miles) **Whalen Creek.** Enters from the right. This trout stream has rainbow as well as brook and brown trout.

21 (60.5 miles) **U.S. Highway 63 bridge.** The Chicago and Northwestern Railroad bridge is one-tenth mile downstream.

22 (61.8 miles) **Trego Park Landing and Campground.** The recommended take-out is on the right shore at O'Brien Road.

23 **Trego Flowage.** The 6.5 mile stretch above the dam is intended to be developed as a multiple-use recreation area according to the National Park Service master plan for the Namekagon River. There are northern pike, walleye, bass, and pan fish in this man-made impoundment.

24 (66.5 miles) **Trego Dam.** There is a portage trail on the right bank. This is also an alternate landing.

Photo 28. Have Paddle - Will Travel.

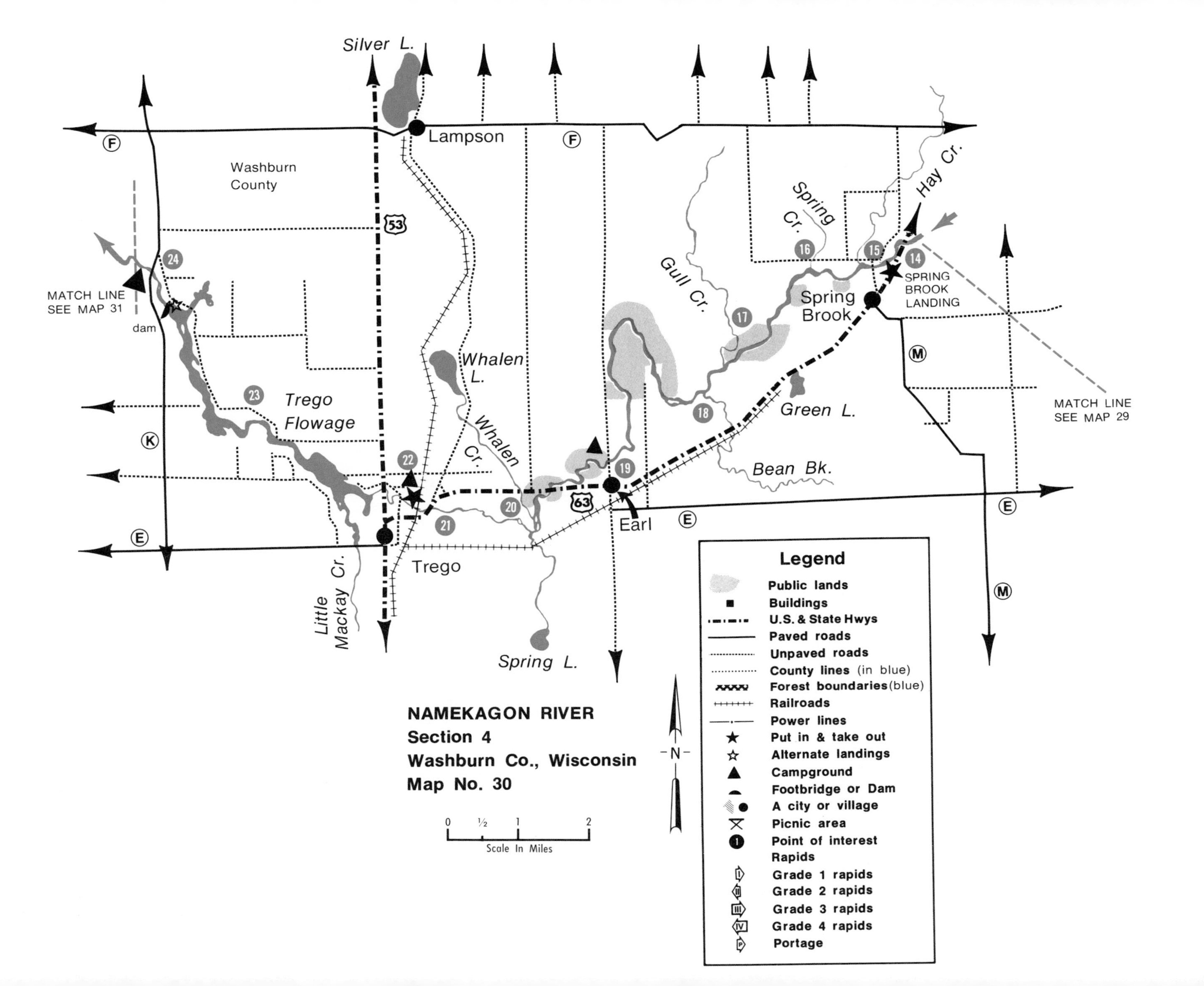

NAMEKAGON RIVER
Section 4
Washburn Co., Wisconsin
Map No. 30

NAMEKAGON RIVER

SECTIONS 5 & 6

Namekagon River: Washburn and Burnett Counties, Wisconsin.
Topo maps: Webb Lake (1:62,500) 1955, Minong (1:62,500) 1965, and Spooner (1:62,500) 1965.
Overview maps: Ashland (1953) and Duluth (1953).
Public lands: Washburn County (1972) and Burnett County (1971) plat books and National Park Service Master Plan (1971).
Section 5
Start: Below Trego Dam.
End: Fritz Landing.
Section 6
Start: Fritz Landing.
End: Riverside Landing on the St. Croix River (map 44).

	SEC. 5	SEC. 6
Difficulty (high water)	Q	Q
Difficulty (usual summer flow)	Q	Q
Length	16	15
Time	6	6
Gradient	6	3
Drainage area	503 (at Trego)	

Water Conditions: See description accompanying Map 27.
Scenery: Excellent. This section has very little development along the shoreline.
Geology: See the description accompanying map 27.
Fish: Walleye lurk in the river itself and trout in the tributary streams.
Campsites: Howell Bridge Park. This campground maintained by Washburn County is located 13 miles west of Minong on State Highway 77 and has nine campsites. There is overnight camping only. A small user fee is charged. For more information, contact County Extension Office, Spooner, Wisc. 54801, or call (715) 635-3192.
Points of Interest:
Section 5

1. (66.6 miles) **County Highway K bridge.** A campsite is located on the left shore at this recommended **put-in** for section 5. There are no real rapids on this stretch aside from some easy grade I riffles that continue for a mile or two below the Trego dam. From here downstream to the St. Croix is the least developed portion of the Namekagon River.

2. (76.5 miles) **Stuntz Brook.** Trout stream enters right.

3. (77.0 miles) **Byrkits Landing.** There are camping facilities at this alternate landing that is also known as Whispering Pines Landing. The current is rather fast, but there are no rapids.

4. (78.5 miles) **Mouths of the Casey and McKenzie Creeks.** Both enter from the left. McKenzie Creek is a trout stream.

5. (80.0 miles) **Old Howell Bridge.** This was an important river crossing in the early logging days. Now only the old pilings exist, the bridge itself has long since disappeared and it has not been replaced. Fee camping is permitted (overnight only).

6. (82.5 miles) **Highway 77 bridge.**

7. (83.0 miles) **Fritz Landing.** This is the recommended **take-out.** This landing is located on the left bank about a half mile downstream of Highway 77 bridge. The Washburn-Burnett County line is located an additional half mile further downstream.

Section 6

7. (83.0 miles) **Fritz Landing.** This is the put-in for this section.

8. (87.5 miles) **Mapru Landing.** The landing is on the right bank. There are primitive camping facilities here. This is also a good swimming hole.

9. (90.0 miles) **Webb Creek.** Enters from the left.

10. (90.5 miles) **Mouth of the Totogatic River.** Enters from the right. This river has numerous rapids and was once used to float logs.

11. (91.5 miles) **Namekagon Trail bridge.** This is an alternate landing.

12. (95.5 miles) **Dog Town Creek.** A trout stream enters left. Easy grade I riffles continue intermittently to take-out.

13. (97.5 miles) **Mouth of the Namekagon River.** Currently there is no public landing at this location. See map 44 for a description of the St. Croix River down to the recommended take-out at Riverside four miles downstream of the confluence of the Namekagon and St. Croix Rivers.

Photo 29. The Old Foot Brace.

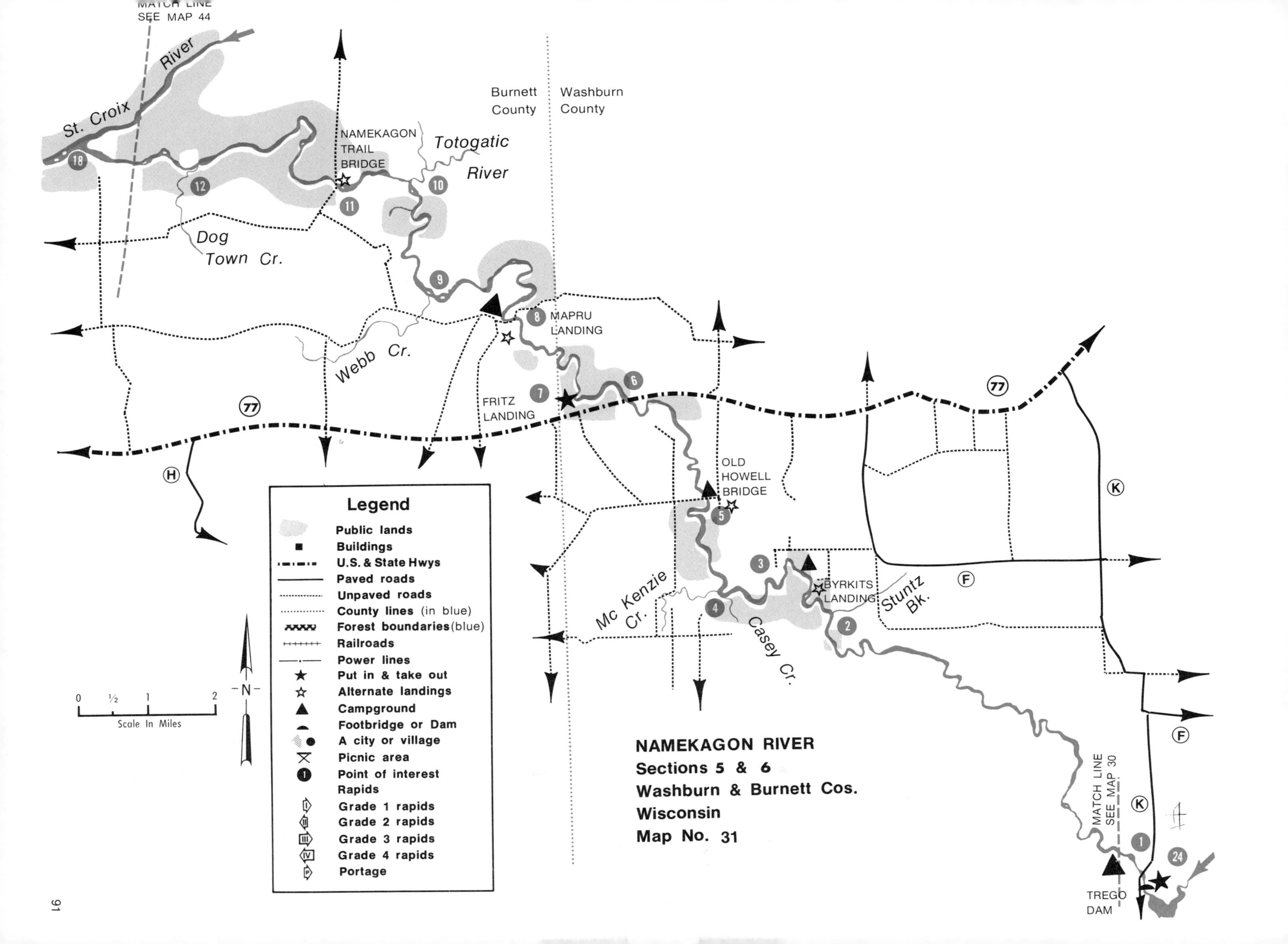
MATCH LINE
SEE MAP 44
St. Croix River
Burnett County
Washburn County
NAMEKAGON TRAIL BRIDGE
Totogatic River
Dog Town Cr.
Webb Cr.
MAPRU LANDING
FRITZ LANDING
OLD HOWELL BRIDGE
Mc Kenzie Cr.
Casey Cr.
BYRKITS LANDING
Stuntz Bk.
MATCH LINE
SEE MAP 30
TREGO DAM
77
H
K
F
Legend
Public lands
Buildings
U.S. & State Hwys
Paved roads
Unpaved roads
County lines (in blue)
Forest boundaries (blue)
Railroads
Power lines
Put in & take out
Alternate landings
Campground
Footbridge or Dam
A city or village
Picnic area
Point of interest
Rapids
Grade 1 rapids
Grade 2 rapids
Grade 3 rapids
Grade 4 rapids
Portage
N
0 ½ 1 2
Scale In Miles
NAMEKAGON RIVER
Sections 5 & 6
Washburn & Burnett Cos.
Wisconsin
Map No. 31

OCONTO RIVER (NORTH BRANCH)

Oconto River: (North branch) Oconto County, Wisconsin.
Topo Map(s): Thunder Mountain (1:48,000) 1951 planimetric and Langlade (1:48,000) 1952 planimetric.
Overview map(s): Iron Mountain (1954).
Public lands: Oconto County plat book (1967).
Section 1
Start: FS 2104 bridge.
End: Highway 32 and 64 bridge.
Section 2
Start: Highway 32 and 64 bridge.
End: County Highway W bridge.
Section 3
Start: County Highway W bridge.
End: Chute Pond.
(No map for Section 3.)

	SEC. 1	SEC. 2
Difficulty (high water)	II	II
Difficulty (usual summer flow)	(not runnable in low water)	
Length	4	4
Time	4	3
Width	20-50	20-80
Gradient	18	25
Drainage area	193	--

Water Conditions: This narrow river is generally runable only during high-water periods in the spring and early summer or after periods of unusually heavy rainfall. The drainage basin of this river parallels that of the Wolf River. Novice canoers should avoid this river at all times: the only time there is enough water to run it, the current is going to be extremely fast. In addition, both the lower and upper stretches are prone to downed trees. These hidden hazards will turn up around blind curves, along the banks, and even completely blocking the river. Anyone who is unfamiliar with the back ferry should not attempt the trip.
Scenery: Section 1 is very impressive, almost exceptionally beautiful. **Section 2** is hampered by shoreline development. The last mile of this section runs through alternating thickets and pastures. Although a majority of the shoreline is privately owned, both sections lie within the boundaries of the Nicolet National Forest. Note: watch out for **barbed wire** across the river.
Geology: The bedrock of this river consists of granite and other igneous rocks.
Fishing: Above Bagley Rapids, the entire river is one big, chock-full trout stream fairly teeming with browns, brooks, and rainbows.
Campgrounds: There is a developed U.S. Forest Service campsite at Bagley Rapids. There are 31 sites, and a user fee is required. For more information, write to the U.S. Forest Service, Lakewood, Wisc. 54138, or phone (715) 276-3313.

Points of Interest:
Section 1

1. (0.0 miles) **FS 2104 bridge.** Our recommended put-in is located on what is also known as Tar Dam Road.
2. (0.12 miles) **Unnamed Rapids.** This unnamed rapids rates grade II and is similar to most found on this run: it has numerous boulders and moderate current. No special difficulties unless there are downed trees. Windfalls often tend to be a problem on this narrow river, so be on the lookout.
3. (1.08 miles) **FS 2310 bridge.** This is another alternate landing. However, there is no developed parking area.
4. (1.32 miles) This is an easy unnamed grade II rapids.
5. (2.4 miles) **Loon Rapids.** This rapids also rates grade II, but is a bit harder than the others on this stretch. There are numerous grade I riffles and minor rapids between here and the railroad bridge.
6. (3.36 miles) **Chicago and Northwestern Railroad bridge.** About one-third of a mile downstream of this bridge, there is a long, rocky rapids that rates grade III in high water. **Scouting** is frequently advisable as occasionally there are downed trees around somewhat blind turns. These are often in areas where there are no eddies that can be used as stopping places.
7. (4.2 miles) **Highway 32 and 64 bridge.** This is the recommended take-out for **Section 1** and the suggested put-in for **Section 2.**

Section Two:

8. **Section 2** consists of relatively continuous rapids.
9. (5.3 miles) **Old Krammer Dam site.** The old dam has long ago been claimed by the river, so it cannot be used as a point of reference. However, there are several six-foot boulders on the bank that stand on the site. The river is less than 20 feet wide at this point and forms a natural point for flotsam to congregate, joined occasionally by a swamped canoe or two. This rapids only rates grade II, but the casuality rate should suggest scouting, from the right bank, just to make sure the chute is clear.
10. (5.8 miles) **Grade I riffles** alternate with quiet water below the Old Krammer Dam site. The river approaches placidity in some spots. Then it meanders through alternating thickets and pasture land. There have been reports of **barbed wire** strung across the river, so watch out.
11. (6.8 miles) **County Highway W bridge.** This is the recommended take-out for this stretch. No developed parking, however. It is suggested that those who wish to run Bagley Rapids or camp there paddle the next two miles of quiet water and take out there.
12. (7.8 miles) **Chicago and Northwestern Railroad bridge.**
13. (9.0 miles) **Bagley Rapids campground.** This National Forest Service campground has a boat landing. There are some ledge-type rapids here which rate grade II-III, but they are generally runnable only in relatively high water. The rest of the river downstream of Bagley Rapids to Chute Pond consists of one and a half mile of quiet water.

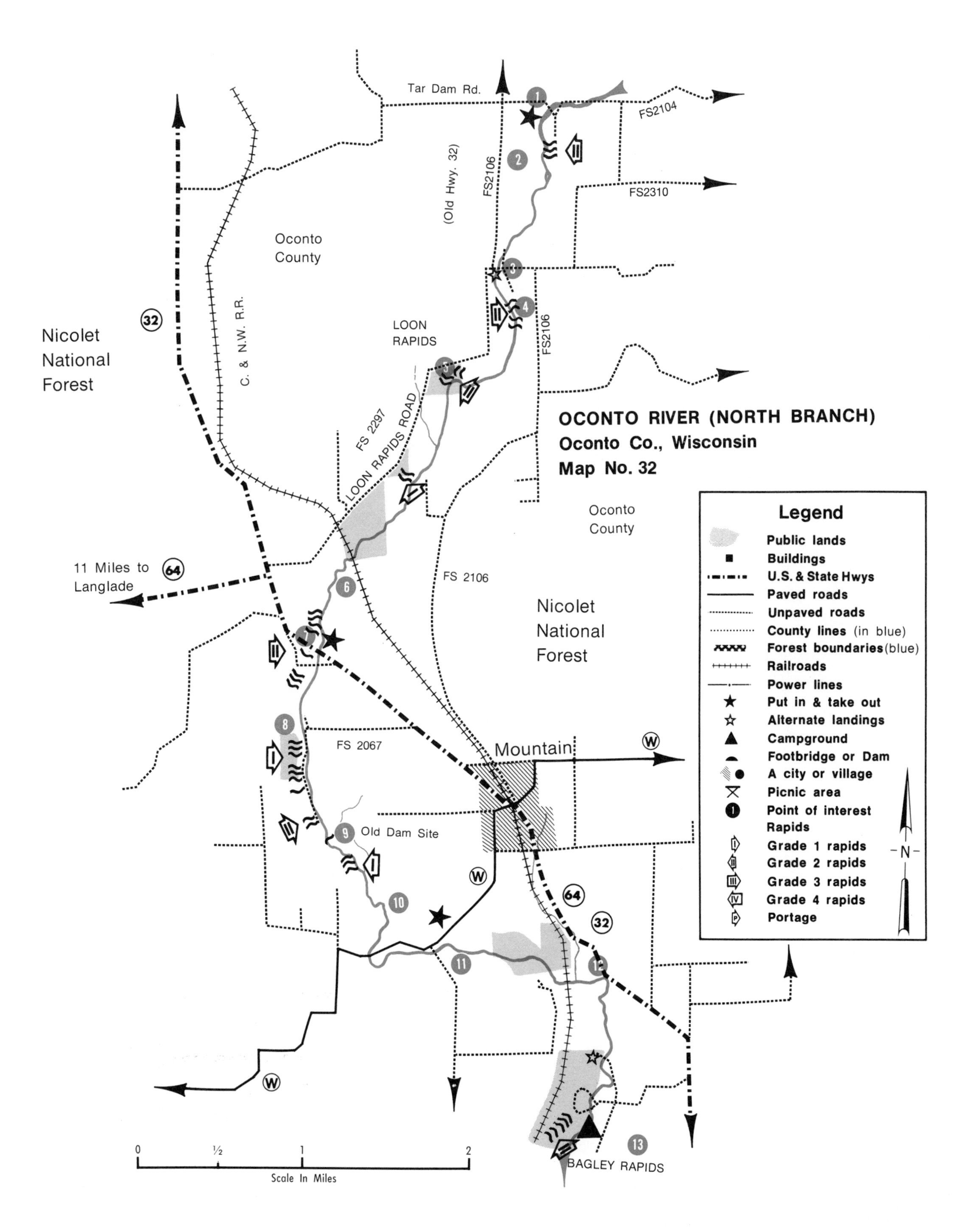

OCONTO RIVER (NORTH BRANCH)
Oconto Co., Wisconsin
Map No. 32
Legend
Public lands
Buildings
U.S. & State Hwys
Paved roads
Unpaved roads
County lines (in blue)
Forest boundaries (blue)
Railroads
Power lines
Put in & take out
Alternate landings
Campground
Footbridge or Dam
A city or village
Picnic area
Point of interest
Rapids
Grade 1 rapids
Grade 2 rapids
Grade 3 rapids
Grade 4 rapids
Portage
N
Tar Dam Rd.
FS2104
FS2310
FS2106
(Old Hwy. 32)
Oconto
County
Nicolet
National
Forest
C. & N.W. R.R.
LOON
RAPIDS
FS 2297
LOON RAPIDS ROAD
11 Miles to
Langlade
FS 2106
FS 2067
Mountain
Old Dam Site
BAGLEY RAPIDS
Scale In Miles
0
½
1
2

ONTONAGON RIVER (EAST BRANCH)

Ontonagon River (East Branch): Ontonagon County, Michigan.
Topo map(s): Rockland (1:62,500) 1949.
Overview map(s): Iron River (1958).
Public lands: Michigan DNR map (1969)

Section 1
Start: FS 208 (East Branch Road).
End: U.S. Highway 45 bridge (Military Bridge).
Section 2
Start: U.S. Highway 45 bridge.
End: Bridge near Rockland, Michigan.

	SEC. 1	SEC. 2
Difficulty (high water)	III	I
Difficulty (usual summer flow)	II-III	Q
Length	8	3
Time	4	2
Width	30-150	50-150
Gradient	29	8
Drainage area	265	671

Water Conditions: A U.S.G.S. gauge is located a few hundred yards below the put-in on land owned by Arthur Pihlaja. He will read the gauge for boaters who call him at (906) 883-3454. Section 1 has one of the longest stretches of continuous grade II-III rapids in the Midwest.

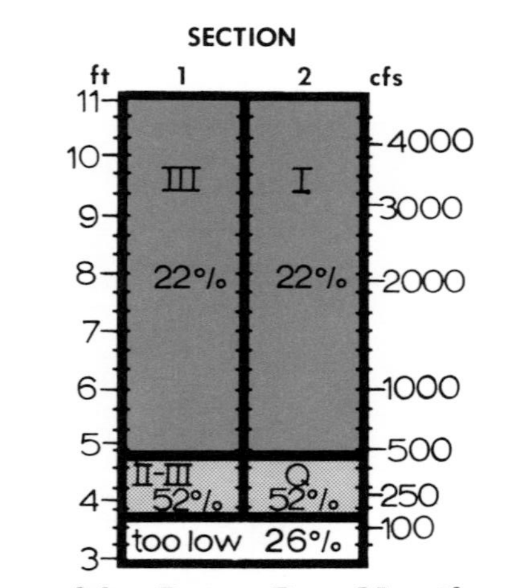

Canoeable Days Per Month

month	Apr	May	June	July	Aug	Sep
days	30	31	27	16	16	15

Scenery: Excellent. Wild and rugged with no development along the shoreline except at the put-in and take-out. Wildlife and wildflowers are abundant. In late spring, huge masses of showy ladyslippers are particularly attractive. The river is nestled in a deep valley with steep clay bluffs rising abruptly from the shore. These banks are highly susceptible to erosion and this creates some problems for river runners. The water is frequently muddy and the rocks are hard to spot. What's more, fallen trees often obstruct the river, particularly on the outside of turns.

Caution: Avoid a possible entanglement with protruding branches and the almost inevitable upset that would follow. Many of these downfalls are difficult to avoid. **Only experienced boating parties should attempt this run.**

Fish: The river and its many tributaries abound with trout.

Campgrounds: A scenic campground at Bob Lake in the Ottawa National Forest has 17 developed sites. Another campground with 19 developed sites is located at nearby Courtney Lake. Black bears are common in these U.S. Forest Service fee areas.

Shuttle (for section 1): Take U.S. highway 45 north to Michigan Highway 26 and then head east to Mass. In Mass take the main cross road south until it forks in about a mile. The right fork, East Branch Road, dead ends at the put-in.

Points of interest:

Section 1

1. (0.0 miles) **FS 208 bridge.** Don't look too hard for the bridge. It washed out in the flood of 1963 and hasn't been replaced. This landing is owned by Arthur Pihlaja. Seek permission before using it. Also make certain the gate is kept closed so his cattle don't stray. The river is deceptively calm both here and at the take-out, but there's plenty of action in between.
2. (0.6 miles) **Unnamed Creek.** Enters left. Grade II-III rapids begin near here and continue with little let up until about a mile above the take-out.
3. (6.0 miles) **Deer Lick Creek.** Trout stream enters right.
4. (7.0 miles) **Middle Branch of Ontonagon River.** Enters left.

Section 2

5. (7.2 miles) **U.S. Highway 45 bridge.** Also called the Military Bridge, this is the recommended take-out for Section 1 and put-in for Section 2. The landing is the wayside upstream of the bridge. This run is mostly quietwater with a few minor riffles.
6. (8.1 miles) **Rockland Creek.** Enters right.
7. (8.5 miles) **West Branch of the Ontonagon River.** This last branch of the Ontonagon enters left.
8. (9.7 miles) **Powerline.**
9. (10.8 miles) **Take-out.** A U.S.G.S. gauge is located here.

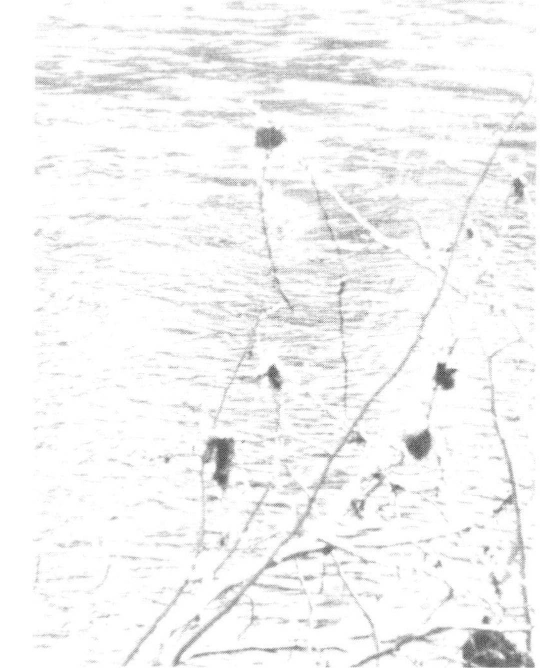

Photo 30. Deadfall in the fast current on the right. Shoals on the left.

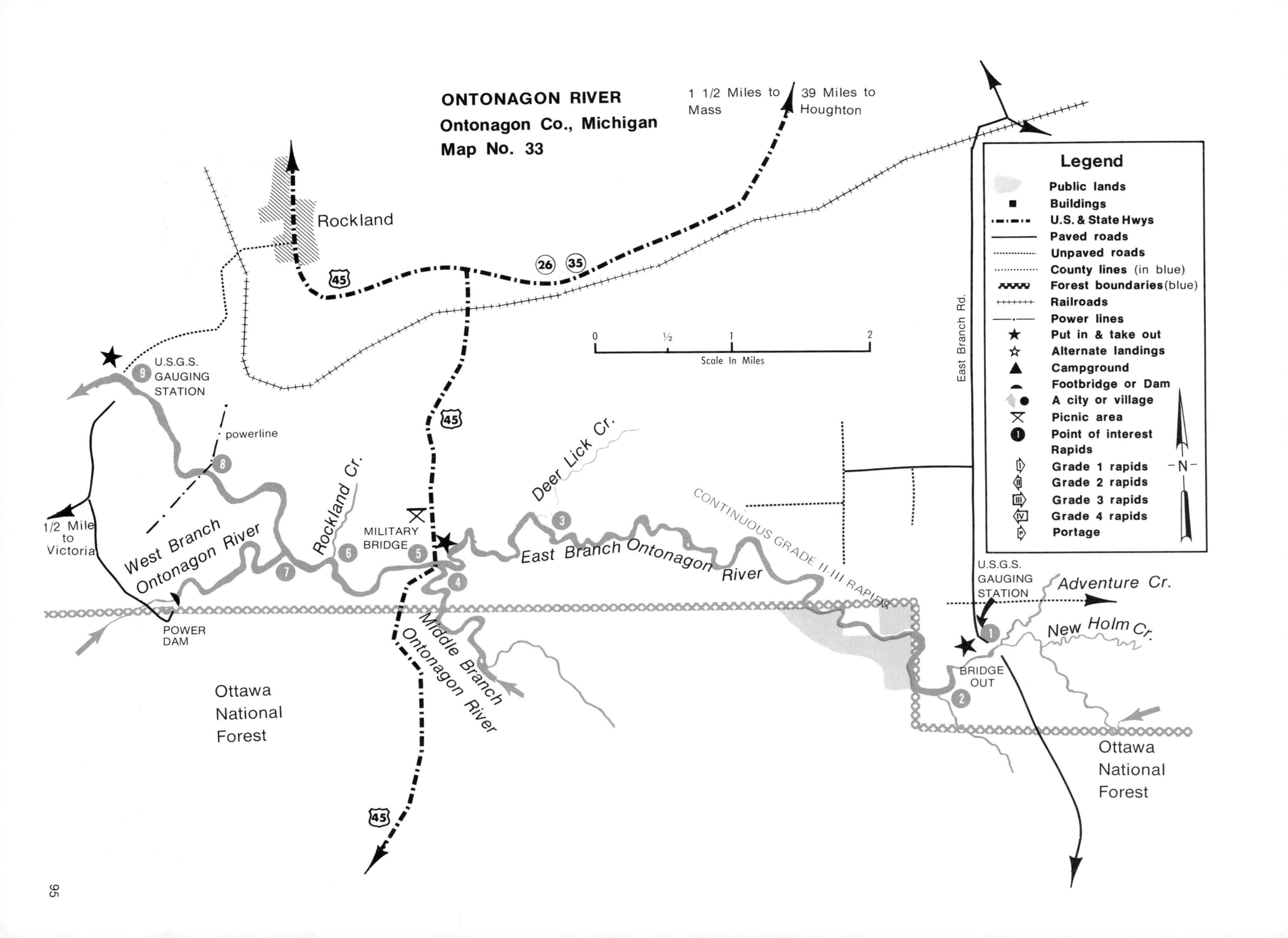
ONTONAGON RIVER
Ontonagon Co., Michigan
Map No. 33
1 1/2 Miles to Mass
39 Miles to Houghton
Rockland
26
35
45
Legend
Public lands
Buildings
U.S. & State Hwys
Paved roads
Unpaved roads
County lines (in blue)
Forest boundaries (blue)
Railroads
Power lines
Put in & take out
Alternate landings
Campground
Footbridge or Dam
A city or village
Picnic area
Point of interest
Rapids
Grade 1 rapids
Grade 2 rapids
Grade 3 rapids
Grade 4 rapids
Portage
N
0 ½ 1 2
Scale In Miles
East Branch Rd.
U.S.G.S. GAUGING STATION
powerline
Deer Lick Cr.
Rockland Cr.
MILITARY BRIDGE
CONTINUOUS GRADE II-III RAPIDS
1/2 Mile to Victoria
West Branch Ontonagon River
East Branch Ontonagon River
Middle Branch Ontonagon River
POWER DAM
Ottawa National Forest
U.S.G.S. GAUGING STATION
Adventure Cr.
New Holm Cr.
BRIDGE OUT
Ottawa National Forest

PESHTIGO RIVER

SECTION 1

Peshtigo River: Forest County, Wisconsin.
Topo map(s): Laona (1:48,000) 1939 planimetric.
Overview map(s): Iron Mountain (1954).
Public lands: Forest County plat book (1966).
Section 1
Start: FS 2131 Bridge below Cavour.
End: FS 2134 Bridge (Burnt Bridge Campground).

	SEC. 1
Difficulty (high water)	**III**
Difficulty (usual summer flow)	**II**
Length	**9**
Time	**6**
Width	**30-60**
Gradient	**14**
Drainage area	**175**

Water Conditions: The only remaining U.S.G.S. gauge on this river is located at the City of Peshtigo. However, since the water flow is greatly influenced by the numerous dams located upstream of this gauge, readings from that source are of little value to the canoeist. There is, however, a stage marker located on the left bank on the upstream side of the County Highway C bridge. This marker reads in inches.

SECTION

inches	1	2
20–40	II-III	II-III
10–20	II	II
0–10	too low	too low

This river is runable during periods of high flow during the spring runoff or after heavy rains.
Scenery: This is a beautiful undeveloped area. Sections 1 and 2 lie within the boundaries of the Nicolet Forest. There is minimal development along the heavily forested shoreline. Elms, ash, popple, and pines predominate.
Geology: The bedrock consists primarily of granite and other igneous rocks. The water, while unpolluted, has a rather dark color from the tamarack swamps in the area. This makes it a little more difficult than usual to detect many of the numerous rocks.
History: Nicolet National Forest was first established in 1933. Before this, the area was logged rather extensively.
Fish: Trout in rapids and numerous tributary streams.
Campgrounds: See descriptions accompanying maps 35 and 36.

Points of Interest:
Section 1

1. (0.0 miles) **U.S. Highway 8 bridge above Cavour.**

2. (0.40 miles) **Gruman Creek.** A trout stream, enters from the right.

3. (4.0 miles) **Whiting Creek.** A trout stream, enters from the right.

4. (6.0 miles) **U.S. Forest Service Highway 2131 bridge.** This is also known as the CCC bridge. This is the recommended **put-in.**

5. (7.0 miles) **Camp 12 Rapids.** Grade I. There is a campground located on the left bank of this rapids. There are two low-hazard rapids downstream of Camp 12 and above Catwillow Creek. They rate grade I-II and grade I.

6. (8.0 miles) **Catwillow Creek.** A trout stream, enters from the left.

7. (8.5 miles) **Upda Creek.** Enters from the right.

8. (9.0 miles) **Unnamed Creek** enters from the right. There is a grade I rapids downstream from here.

9. (10.0 miles) **Calamity Jane Rapids.** This is a fast and rocky grade I-II rapids.

10. (11.0 miles) **Unnamed rapids.** Grade I. FS 3787 has a locked gate one mile from the river. One mile downstream there is a grade I rapids.

11. (13.0 miles) **Unnamed rapids.** Grade I.

12. (13.8 miles) **Unnamed rapids.** This is a shallow, grade II rock garden.

13. (14.5 miles) **Unnamed rapids.** This short rapids rates grade II.

14. (15.0 miles) **Burnt Bridge Campgrounds.** This is the recommended take-out for Section 1 and the put-in for Section 2. The landing is below the bridge on the right bank. This is named for an old, partly burned railroad bridge that used to occupy this site, a reminder of the disastrous fires of the 1920's. The partially developed U.S. Forest Service campground is located on the right bank below the bridge. There is limited space here and no fee is charged.

Photo 31. Above Michigan Rapids just below the put-in for Section 2.

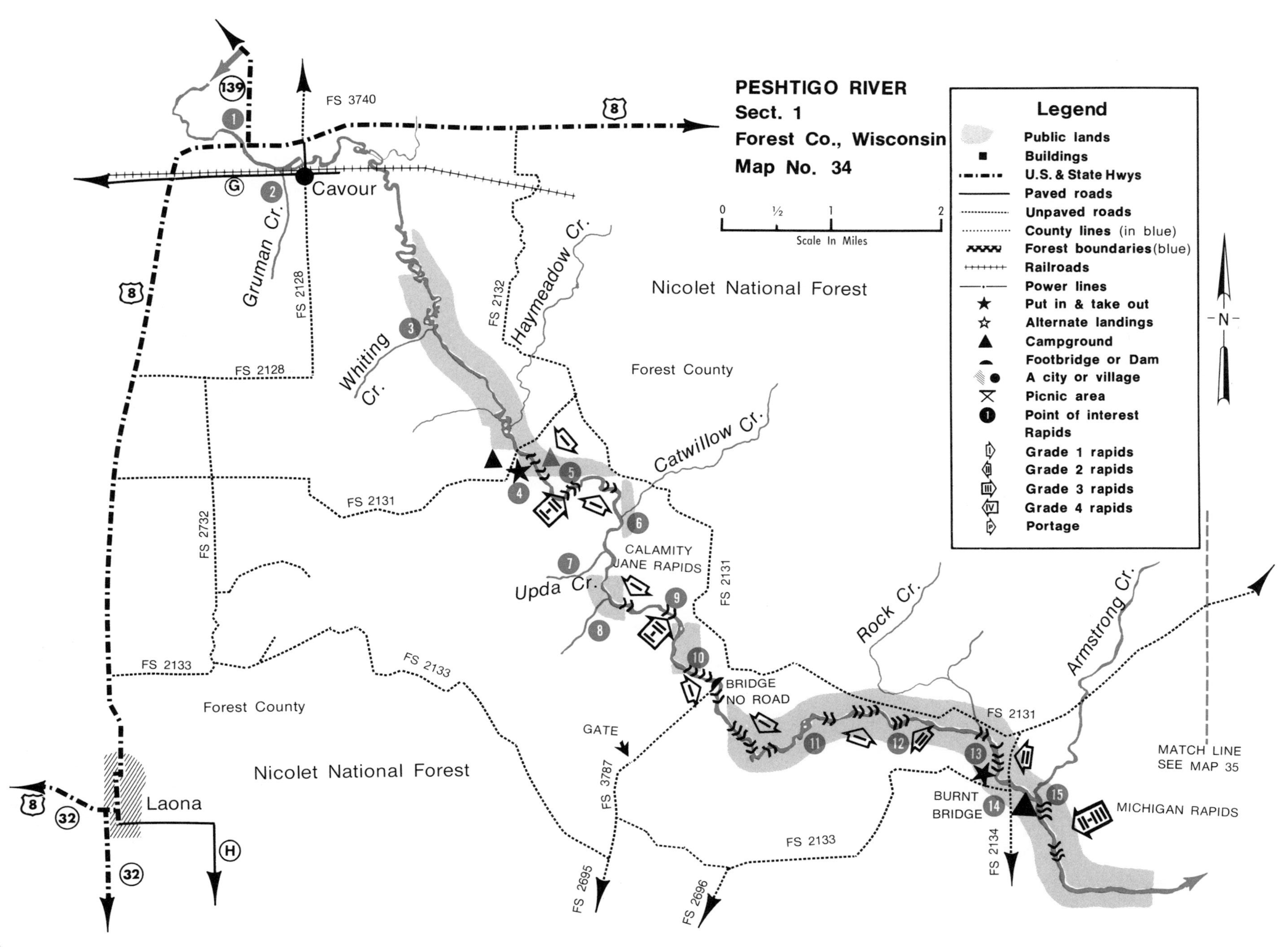
PESHTIGO RIVER
Sect. 1
Forest Co., Wisconsin
Map No. 34
0 ½ 1 2
Scale In Miles
Legend
Public lands
Buildings
U.S. & State Hwys
Paved roads
Unpaved roads
County lines (in blue)
Forest boundaries (blue)
Railroads
Power lines
Put in & take out
Alternate landings
Campground
Footbridge or Dam
A city or village
Picnic area
Point of interest
Rapids
Grade 1 rapids
Grade 2 rapids
Grade 3 rapids
Grade 4 rapids
Portage
N
Nicolet National Forest
Forest County
Cavour
Gruman Cr.
Whiting Cr.
Haymeadow Cr.
Catwillow Cr.
Upda Cr.
CALAMITY JANE RAPIDS
BRIDGE NO ROAD
Rock Cr.
Armstrong Cr.
BURNT BRIDGE
MICHIGAN RAPIDS
MATCH LINE SEE MAP 35
GATE
FS 3740
FS 2128
FS 2132
FS 2131
FS 2732
FS 2133
FS 3787
FS 2695
FS 2696
FS 2134
Laona
Nicolet National Forest
Forest County

PESHTIGO RIVER

SECTION 2

Peshtigo River: Forest and Marinette Counties, Wisconsin.
Topo map(s): Laona (1:48,000) 1939 planimetric and Goodman (1:48,000) planimetric.
Overview map(s): Iron Mountain (1954).
Public lands: Forest County Wisconsin (1966) and Marinette County Wisconsin (1970) plat book.
Section 2
Start: FS 2134 Bridge (Burnt Bridge Campground).
End: FS 2136 Bridge.

	SEC. 2
Difficulty (high water)	**II-III**
Difficulty (usual summer flow)	**II**
Length	**7**
Time	**6**
Width	**15-100**
Gradient	**14**
Drainage area	**265**

Water Conditions, Geology, History, Fish, and Scenery: See description accompanying map 34.

Campgrounds: Goodman Park is located 32 miles west of Wausaukee on County C, north to park on Peshtigo River. There are 15 campsites and a small fee. McClintock Park (not shown on the map) is located 28 miles west of Wausaukee on County C on the Peshtigo River. Ten campsites are available for a small fee. For more information on both of these campsites write: Forestry Office, Courthouse, Marinette, Wisc. 54143, or phone (715) 732-7530.
Burnt Bridge is located three miles north of Laona on U.S. Highway 8, and 12 miles east on Forest Service Road 2131 on the Peshtigo River. This site is open all year and run by the Forest Service. There is limited space available and no user fee is charged.

Points of Interest:
Section 2

14 (15.0 miles) **Burnt Bridge Campground.** The landing is on right bank below the bridge. This is the recommended take-out for Section 1 and the put-in for Section 2. See description accompanying map 34 for more information.

15 (15.5 miles) **Armstrong Creek.** Enters from the left. This is a trout stream. Shortly below the mouth of the creek, Michigan Rapids begins. This rapids rates grade II in summer and grade III in high water. Open canoes are a no-no in the spring because of the high waves. There is a 150 foot long portage around it on the right bank. This rapids is named after an Indian by the name of Frank Michigan.

16 (16.5 miles) **Michigan Creek.** A trout stream, enters from the right.

17 (17.0 miles) **Unnamed Rapids.** This is a short grade II rapids.

18 (18.5 miles) **Ralton's Rip Rapids.** The rapids is also known locally as the Dells. A large island divides the river; the left channel is too shallow to run; the right channel turns into a steep, fast, and narrow rapids. Length is 150 feet. It is 10 to 20 feet wide. This rapids should be avoided by open canoers in the spring. It normally rates grade II in summer, but is grade III in high water. There is a **portage** trail on the right bank, but **scouting** is better from the island.

19 (19.5 miles) **Mac Tackie Rapids.** This rapids rates grade I in two pitches. Half a mile downstream is a grade I-II rock garden.

20 (21.5 miles) **FS 2141 bridge.** This is our recommended take-out for this stretch. There is a landing with primitive camping facilities at the Burton Wells bridge. This is named after an old railroad bridge on the early logging era. The mouth of Halley Creek, a trout stream, is located just downstream of this location and enters from the right.

21 (24.5 miles) **Unnamed Creek.** Enters from the left. There are several (we have not run this stretch) rapids at this location which have not been rated.

22 (25.5 miles) **Taylor Rapids.** This is a long, difficult rapids that culminates with a six foot falls at Goodman Park. **A portage is mandatory.**

23 (26.5 miles) **Goodman Park.** This developed campground has been created and maintained by Marinette County. (We have not mapped the 19 miles downstream from Burton Wells bridge until the start of Section 3 of the Peshtigo (map 36). From observations of the river at various selected points along the shore, we found the rapids to be long, shallow, and unrunnable. This stretch would require a number of portages for the quiet-water paddler and offers no interesting rapids for the white-water boater.

Photo 32. "Ah! This looks easy."

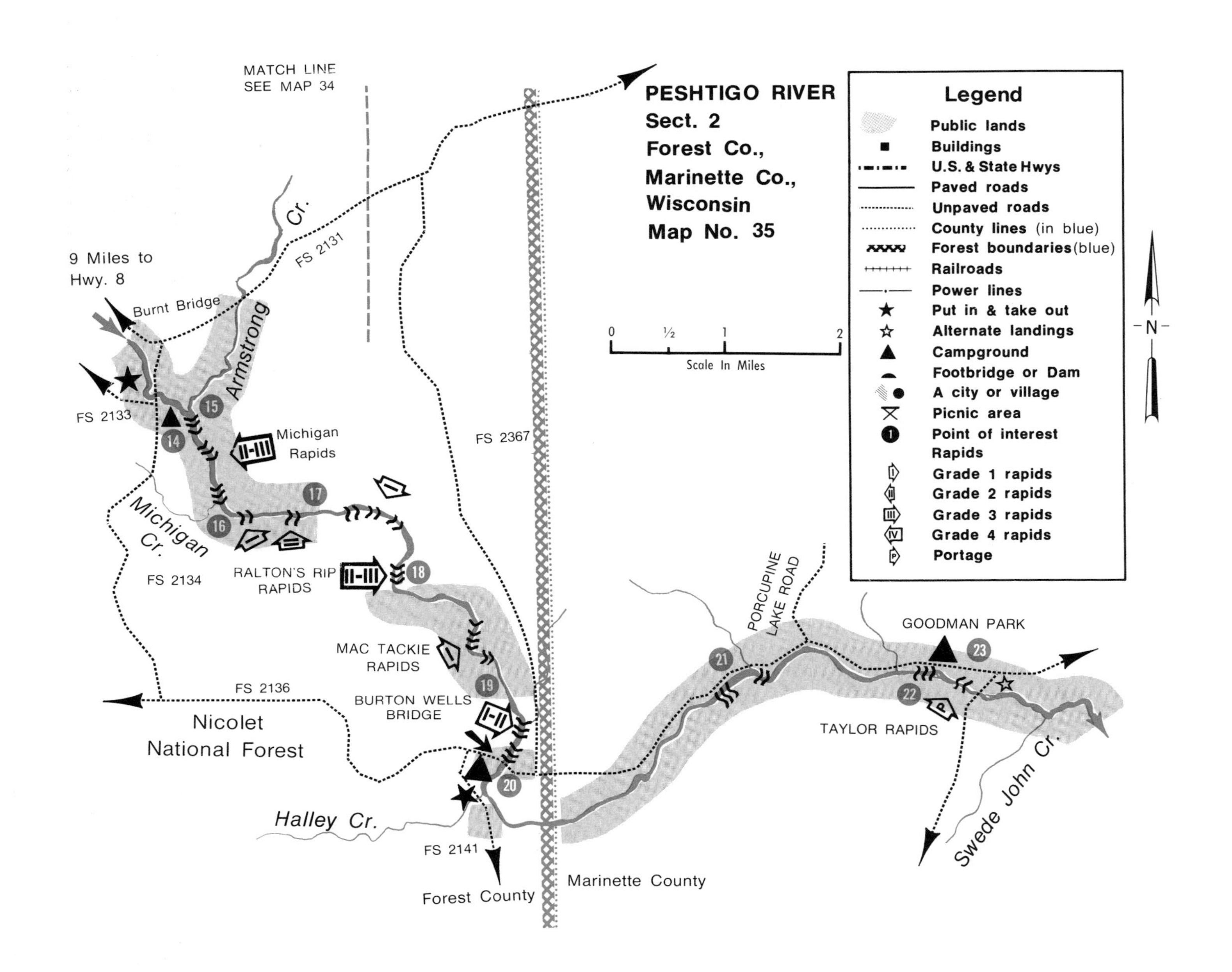
PESHTIGO RIVER
Sect. 2
Forest Co.,
Marinette Co.,
Wisconsin
Map No. 35
Legend
Public lands
Buildings
U.S. & State Hwys
Paved roads
Unpaved roads
County lines (in blue)
Forest boundaries(blue)
Railroads
Power lines
Put in & take out
Alternate landings
Campground
Footbridge or Dam
A city or village
Picnic area
Point of interest
Rapids
Grade 1 rapids
Grade 2 rapids
Grade 3 rapids
Grade 4 rapids
Portage
N
0
½
1
2
Scale In Miles
MATCH LINE
SEE MAP 34
9 Miles to
Hwy. 8
Burnt Bridge
Armstrong
Cr.
FS 2131
FS 2133
Michigan
Rapids
II-III
Michigan
Cr.
FS 2134
RALTON'S RIP
RAPIDS
II-III
FS 2367
MAC TACKIE
RAPIDS
BURTON WELLS
BRIDGE
I-II
FS 2136
Nicolet
National Forest
Halley Cr.
FS 2141
Forest County
Marinette County
PORCUPINE
LAKE ROAD
GOODMAN PARK
TAYLOR RAPIDS
Swede John Cr.
14
15
16
17
18
19
20
21
22
23

PESHTIGO RIVER

SECTION 3

Peshtigo River: Marinette County, Wisconsin.
Topo map(s): Thunder Mountain (1:48,000) 1951 planimetric.
Overview map(s): Iron Mountain (1954).
Public lands: Marinette County plat book (1966).
Section 3
Start: Farm Dam (town of Silver Cliff baseball area).
End: County Highway C bridge.

	SEC. 3
Difficulty (high water)	III-IV
Difficulty (usual summer flow)	II³-III
Length	4
Time	4
Width	20-120
Gradient	40
Drainage area	462

Water Conditions: This run is best known as the roaring rapids section of the Peshtigo. In spring and during other periods of high water, this stretch should be attempted only by experts using decked boats. At other times, this is a good intermediate run in decked boats, or expert run in open canoes. There is a stage marker at the County Highway C bridge that reads in inches. Both the gauge and the bridge were replaced in 1974. Don Kosir has agreed to read the new gauge for boaters if called at (715) 757-2371. Assuming a reasonable correlation with the old guage, the river is runnable in decked boats down to a reading of 1 or 2. Open canoes require about two more inches of water. At readings above 5 to 8 open canoes should avoid this run.

SECTION
inches 3
40
30 IV
20 decked boats only III
10
0 II-III 3

Geology, History, and Fish: See description accompanying map 34.

Scenery: Scenic value is excellent except for the development along the last mile of this section. THIS STRETCH OF RIVER HAS SOME OF THE MOST UNIQUE WHITE WATER IN THE ENTIRE MIDWEST AND DESERVES PROTECTION. It should be designated as a wild river.

Campgrounds: See Page 98.

Points of Interest:
Section 3

1 (0.0 miles) **Farm Dam.** This is the recommended put-in. Presently there is no dam at this location although a sluice dam once occupied this site. This area is recognized by a sign on County Highway C indicating "Silver Cliff Baseball" and by a fire number No. 22/58. Free camping is permitted at this primitive site. There are toilets and picnic tables, but there is no water supply. Fishing for northern pike is reportedly good here. This section of the Peshtigo River is aptly called the Roaring Rapids. From start to finish one encounters almost continuous rapids interrupted by very short, quiet pools. The first rapids are encountered 100 yards downstream of the put-in. For one and one-half miles, until First Drop, one encounters continuous grade II rapids. Frequent backferries are required to negotiate these shallow rapids.

2 (1.6 miles) **First Drop.** This is recognized by the cleared right-of-way for a recently installed natural gas pipeline, located just upstream of First Drop. **Scouting is recommended** (from the left bank) at all times, since this drop changes character greatly with the different water levels. The side curler on the right of the main chute has necessitated many a swim. Rafts are particularly prone to tipover at this drop. Pull out on the left bank just past the cleared pipeline area. This rapids rates grade II-III at low water and grade III at high water levels.

3 (1.7 miles) **Second Drop.** This rapids is within sight of First Drop. **Scouting** on the left bank is recommended. This rapids rates grade II at usual summer levels and grade III at higher flows. Brandywine Creek enters from the left just below here.

4 (2.3 miles) **Third Drop,** also called Kussokavitch. This drop rates grade III both because of its proximity to Five-Foot Falls, and because it has a rather uniform back-roller at higher water levels that could trap a boater. This drop is preceeded, in midstream, by a small, forested island that is followed by a rock island located close to the left bank. Do not go below the rock island in the right channel if you wish to **scout.** For this purpose the left bank is best.

5 (2.4 miles) **Five-Foot Falls.** Grade III at both low and high water levels. There is a runnable chute close to the left bank. Immediately below the drop and precariously close to the chute, there is a large boulder on the left which has stove in many a canoe. **Scouting from the left bank, is strongly advised.** A portage may be advisable for most parties. At high water some skilled boaters that are equipped with decked boats may elect to run another chute in the middle of the river although rescue is not readily available in case of upset, which is likely.

6 (2.5 miles) **Horserace Rapids.** This rapids is within sight of Five-Foot Falls, and it can be identified by a cabin located on the left bank midway downstream. It is a narrow constriction of the river that is about 100 yards long. This rapids gets more difficult as you proceed towards the end. **Scouting is strongly recommended.** Make sure you stop on the left bank well in advance of this drop, as it is rather easy to proceed to a point of no return where it becomes most difficult to reach the left bank. This is further complicated by the shallow rock garden on the left preceeding the rapids. Once committed, it may not be possible to scout. In high water this rapids develops rather large souse holes. Under these conditions this rapids should be attempted only by the most skilled boaters who are suitably equipped with decked craft. The most difficult part of this rapids is located at the end of the drop, where it is difficult to make a clean run even in low water. It is very easy to underestimate the difficulty of this rapids which rates grade III in low water and rates as high as grade IV in high water.

7 (2.6 miles) **S-Curve Rapids. Scouting** from the left bank **is recommended,** since critical maneuvering will be required. This rapids rates grade II in summer and grade III in high water. There is a mile-long stretch of continuous grade I-II rapids located downstream followed by a half mile of quiet water to the take-out.

8 (4.0 miles) **County Highway C Bridge.** Take out at the end of Landing 12 Road one-hald mile south of County Highway C. This landing is maintained by Wisconsin Public Service for both whitewater boaters and the fishermen who put in here to use the flowage downstream.

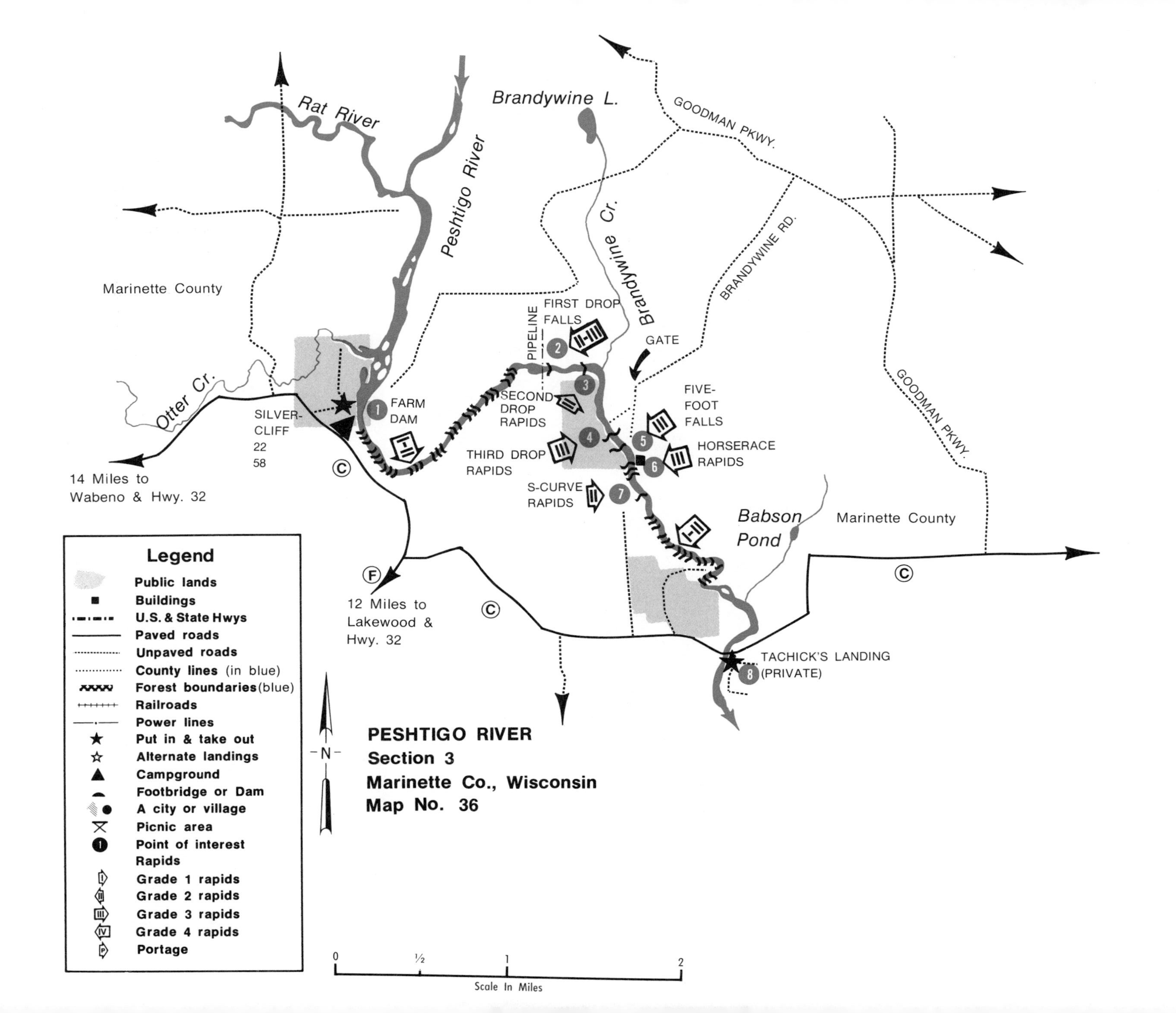

Rat River
Peshtigo River
Brandywine L.
Brandywine Cr.
GOODMAN PKWY.
BRANDYWINE RD.
GOODMAN PKWY.
Marinette County
Marinette County
Otter Cr.
SILVER-CLIFF
22
58
14 Miles to Wabeno & Hwy. 32
FARM DAM
PIPELINE
FIRST DROP FALLS
SECOND DROP RAPIDS
THIRD DROP RAPIDS
GATE
FIVE-FOOT FALLS
HORSERACE RAPIDS
S-CURVE RAPIDS
Babson Pond
TACHICK'S LANDING (PRIVATE)
12 Miles to Lakewood & Hwy. 32
Legend
Public lands
Buildings
U.S. & State Hwys
Paved roads
Unpaved roads
County lines (in blue)
Forest boundaries (blue)
Railroads
Power lines
Put in & take out
Alternate landings
Campground
Footbridge or Dam
A city or village
Picnic area
Point of interest
Rapids
Grade 1 rapids
Grade 2 rapids
Grade 3 rapids
Grade 4 rapids
Portage
N
PESHTIGO RIVER
Section 3
Marinette Co., Wisconsin
Map No. 36
0
½
1
2
Scale In Miles

Photo 33. First Drop of the Peshtigo - a decked boater's paradise.

Photo 34. "Wake up! It looks nasty up ahead." Third drop on Section 3 just above 5-Foot Falls.

Photo 35. 5-Foot Falls on the Peshtigo.

PIKE RIVER

WATER CONDITIONS (MAP NO. 37)

Water Conditions: There is a minimal pollution by current standards. The water flow is rather consistent. For 56 years, until mid 1970, there was a U.S.G.S. gauging station located at the County K bridge, which is the start of Section 2. The average flow for those years was 216 cfs. The mean flow for 7 days of highest flow in a typical year was 836, and a 10 year average of the mean flow in August was 159 cfs. The minimum flow for enjoyable canoeing on the most difficult section (2) is 123 cfs. Thus this section is virtually always runnable, even though you may scrape in a few shallow places when the river is at the lowest levels. When the flow exceeds 450 cfs. only decked boats are recommended for **Section 2.** - Currently the only gauge on this river is a stage marker at the U.S. Highway 141 bridge. At a reading of 2.5 on this gauge Section 2 becomes grade II-III. We have insufficient information to correlate the two gauges or to indicate the minimum water flow reading on the stage marker.

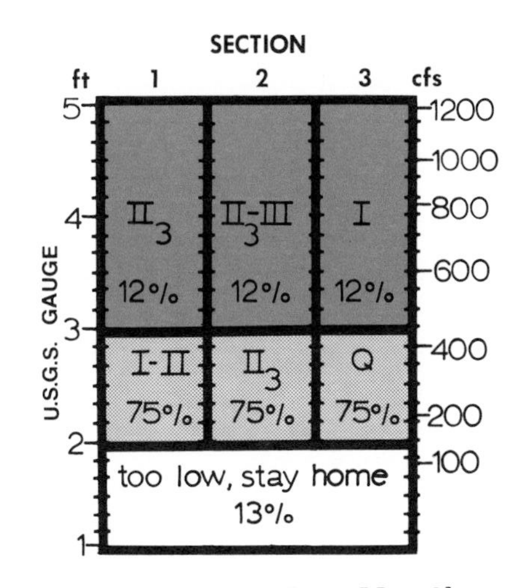

Canoeable Days Per Month

month	Apr	May	June	July	Aug	Sep
days	30	31	30	24	23	21

Photo 36. A typical scene on the Pike.

Photo 37. Yellow Bridge Rapids at high water - First Pitch.

PIKE RIVER

Pike River: Marinette County, Wisconsin.
Topo maps: Pembine (1;62,500) 1963 and Wausaukee (1:62,500) 1963.
Overview map: Escanaba, Michigan (1954).
Public lands: Marinette County plat book (1970), updated to Jan. 1973 with Wisconsin DNR records.

Section 1
Start: U.S. Highway 141 bridge, just east of Amberg.
End: County Highway K bridge.

Section 2
Start: County Highway K bridge.
End: Left bank approximately one-fourth mile below Yellow Bridge rapids.

Section 3
Start: Pike River Road bridge.
End: Right bank at the confluence with the Menominee River.

	SEC. 1	SEC. 2	SEC. 3
Difficulty (high water)	II3	II3-III	I
Difficulty (usual summer flow)	I-II	II3	Q
Length	6	3	4
Time	3	3	2
Width	20-70	20-70	50-100
Gradient	6	18	--
Drainage area	253	--	--

Scenery: Good to excellent. Large pines are in abundance on the shoreline of this river, which has thus far escaped most commercial development. This river, along with the Pine and Popple, are the only rivers included in the 1965 Wisconsin Wild Rivers Bill. Wisconsin DNR is currently starting to protect the entire shoreline of this river from commercial development. Current plans call for the allocation of ORAP-200 funds for either outright purchase or for the securement of scenic easements along the entire lower Pike River, starting from a point well above Amberg.

Geology: The bedrock consists of granite and other igneous rocks.

Fishing: Fishing is considered tops for brook and brown trout as well as for bass in **Sections 1 and 2.** Pike fishing predominates in **Section 3.**

Campgrounds: Goodman and McClintock Parks are located 32 and 28 miles west of Wausaukee on County Highway C, on the Peshtigo River. Both of these campgrounds have been developed and are maintained by Marinette County. There is a total of 15 sites between them. These campgrounds are open from May to November and there is a small daily user's fee. For further information, contact the Forestry Office, Marinette, Wisc. 54143, or phone (715) 732-7530.

Points of Interest:

1 (0.0 miles) **Daves Falls County Park.** This is an attractive picnic area. However, camping is not allowed. The falls have been run successfully in high water. However, **a portage is recommended,** since the falls are usually too shallow and steep to permit an elegant run. There is a portage trail on the right bank.

2 (0.6 miles) **U.S. Highway 141 Bridge.** This is the recommended put-in for **Section 1.** There is limited parking available on the left bank downstream of the U.S. Highway 141 bridge.

3 (1.0 miles) **Powerline Rapids.** This rapids takes its name from the powerline which crosses the river slightly upstream of its start. This rapids is atypically difficult for this section of river. **Scouting is recommended.** Open boats should avoid this rapids in high water.

4 (3.0 miles) **K.C. Creek.** Enters from the left. There is good trout fishing here.

5 (3.5 miles) **Slough Creek.** Enters from the left.

6 (5.0 miles) **Unnamed rapids.** An easy grade I rapids that begins about 1.5 miles below Slough Creek. This rapids and the quiet stretch below it are particularly good fishing spots.

Section 2

7 (6.2 miles) **County Highway K bridge.** There is a landing area on the left bank just upstream of the bridge. Limited parking is available. This landing serves as the **take-out** for Section 1 and the **put-in** for Section 2. There is an easy grade I rapids that begins upstream of the bridge and continues in several pitches below it.

8 (7.2 miles) **Scrounge Canyon.** The river narrows here producing a miniature gorge. Standing waves develop during high water levels, but since there are few rocks little maneuvering is necessary. This rapids should be avoided by undecked boats in high water. Immediately following this is a difficult rock garden that may have to be waded in low water.

9 (8.5 miles) **Horseshoe Falls.** This is an easy drop which can be recognized by a large island which forces most of the water abruptly to the right--Horseshoe Falls. **Scouting is recommended** since the chute is not readily obvious to those who have not seen this drop before. This rapids does not change significantly with different water levels. Although at very high flows, a small backroller develops below this drop.

10 (9.0 miles) **Yellow Bridge Rapids.** This series of drops is located just downstream of a bridge which for many years has had a yellow railing. This rapids is S-shaped and consists of two pitches separated by a small pool of quiet water. The upper pitch is shallow and rocky, but otherwise easy. The second pitch is the falls itself: this drop merits scouting by all, and portaging by most. This falls changes greatly with water level. Below Yellow Bridge Falls and continuing for about 250 yards downstream, there is a continuous boulder-bed rapids. If you dunk at the falls as many boaters do, you may be in for a long nasty swim, with high risk of damage to swamped open canoes, unless you have set up a good rescue team. This falls is the most difficult drop on this section.

Section 3

11 (9.4 miles) **Landing.** The recommended take-out for section 2 is an undeveloped landing where the Pike River Road comes close to the river shortly below the last rapids on this run.

12 (10.5 miles) **Unnamed Creek.** Enters from the right.

13 (12.2 miles) **Pike River Road Bridge.** There is a landing on the right bank. This is the logical starting place for Section 3 because there is easier access than at the take-out for Section 2. The three-mile stretch from here to the confluence with the Menominee River is noted for its good pike fishing. The current is rather slow and there are no rapids on this stretch of river.

14 (13.8 miles) **Mouth of the Pike River.** There is a landing on the right bank at the confluence of the Pike and Menominee Rivers.

Water Conditions: See preceding page.

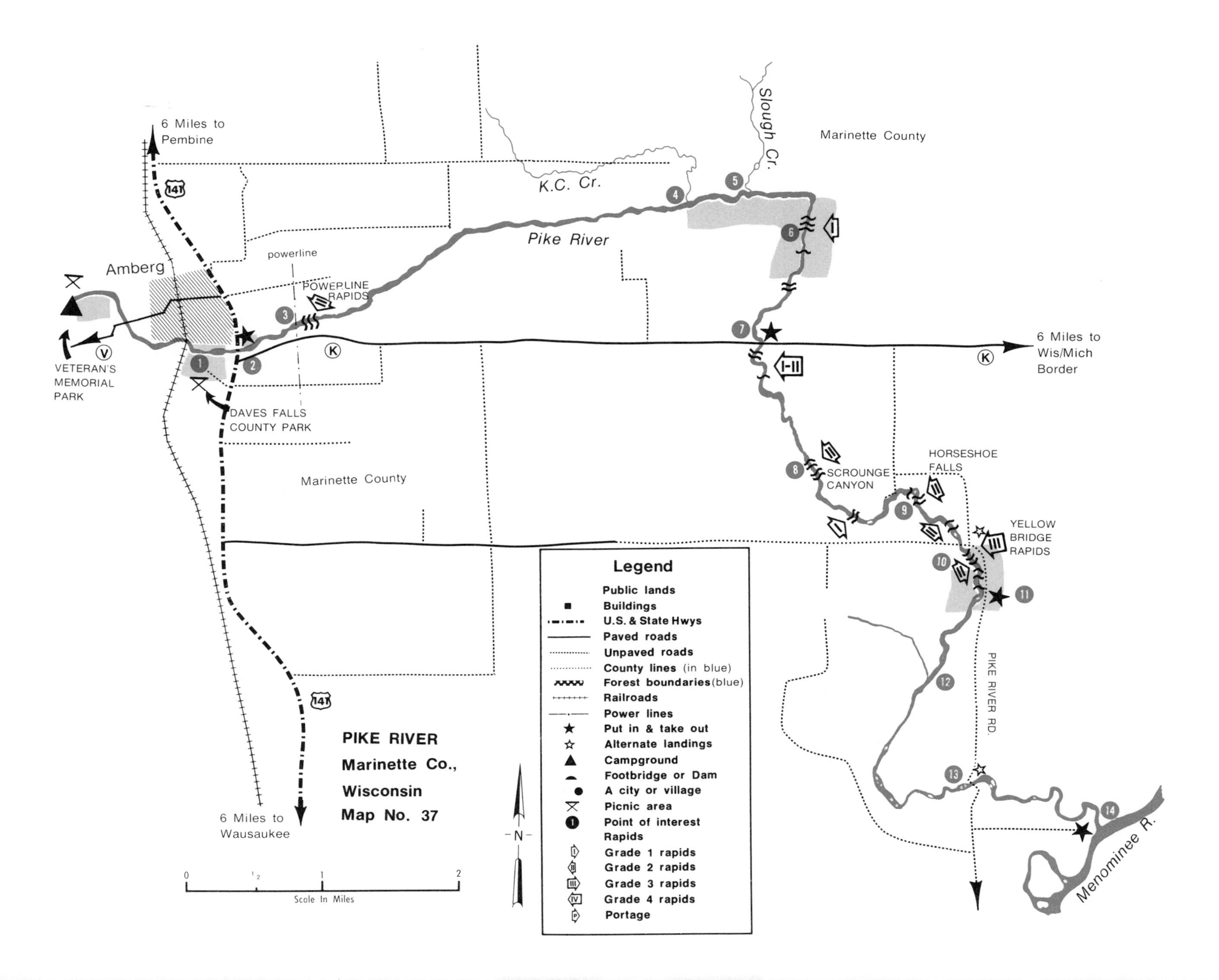
6 Miles to Pembine
141
K.C. Cr.
Slough Cr.
Marinette County
Amberg
powerline
POWERLINE RAPIDS
Pike River
VETERAN'S MEMORIAL PARK
V
K
6 Miles to Wis/Mich Border
K
I
I-II
DAVES FALLS COUNTY PARK
Marinette County
SCROUNGE CANYON
HORSESHOE FALLS
YELLOW BRIDGE RAPIDS
PIKE RIVER RD.
Menominee R.
141
6 Miles to Wausaukee
PIKE RIVER
Marinette Co.,
Wisconsin
Map No. 37
N
0
1/2
1
2
Scale In Miles
Legend
Public lands
Buildings
U.S. & State Hwys
Paved roads
Unpaved roads
County lines (in blue)
Forest boundaries (blue)
Railroads
Power lines
Put in & take out
Alternate landings
Campground
Footbridge or Dam
A city or village
Picnic area
Point of interest
Rapids
Grade 1 rapids
Grade 2 rapids
Grade 3 rapids
Grade 4 rapids
Portage
1
2
3
4
5
6
7
8
9
10
11
12
13
14

PINE RIVER

Section 1

Pine River: Florence and Forest Counties, Wisconsin.
Topo maps: Long Lake (1:48,000) 1939 planimetric and Alvin (1:24,000) 1938 planimetric.
Overview map: Iron Mountain (1954).
Public lands: Forest County (1966) and Florence County (1970) plat books, updated to January 1973 with Wisconsin DNR records.
Section 1
Start: Highway 55 bridge
End: Chipmunk Rapids Campground.

	Sec. 1
Difficulty(high water)	**II**
Difficulty (usual summer flow)	**I-II**
Length	**21**
Time	**10**
Width	**20-100**
Gradient	**8**

Water Conditions: There is a stage marker at the Highway 55 bridge. See the graph accompanying map 39 for more information.

Canoeable Days Per Month (Sec. 1)

month	Apr	May	June	July	Aug	Sep
days	24	31	12	3	0	3

Wild Rivers: The Pine and Popple Rivers, along with the Pike River, were declared wild rivers by the Wisconsin Legislature in 1965. The upper reaches of both of these rivers lie within the Nicolet National Forest. Wisconsin DNR is attempting to allocate ORAP-200 funds to secure outright fee titles or to obtain scenic easements on the Pine River starting at Snake Tail Rapids and continuing downstream to the confluence with the Monominee River. Similarly, Wisconsin DNR intends to purchase or obtain easements on the river frontage of the Popple from the mouth of Rock Creek near Fence to the confluence of the Popple and the Pine Rivers. Much information contained here was obtained from USGS Water-supply Paper 2006, "The Pine-Popple River Basin: Hydrology of a Wild River Area, Northeastern Wisconsin," by E. Oakes, S. J. Field, and L.P. Seeger. This report is available from the United States Government Printing Office Washington D.C. Additional information on canoeability was obtained from Bill Beverly of the John Muir chapter of the Sierra Club.
Scenery: For the most part, both the Pine and Popple Rivers have little commercial development along the shoreline. Red, white, and jack pine and aspen are the most common trees. Deer, bear, coyote, beaver, muskrat, woodcock, ruffed grouse, and various types of waterfowl inhabit this region. There are a number of active beaver lodges.
Geology: The bedrock in the Pine-Popple basin is a continuation of the Canadian Shield. There are igneous and metamorphic rocks of Pre-Cambrian age. Rapids and falls are located where the river flows over granite, gneiss, and metavolcanic rocks. The Pine River, where it flows over soft metasedimentary bedrock (Michigamme slate) below the Pine River flowage has it's lowest gradient and consequently is devoid of rapids and falls. The depth of the Pine River is from one to five feet. The river ranges from moderate current to deep quiet pools.
History: The area that now comprises the Nicolet National Forest was extensively logged during 1870-1920. The Nicolet National Forest was established in 1933.
Fish: There are native populations of brook trout in the Pine and Popple Rivers and their tributary streams. Brown and rainbow trout are also planted in these rivers periodically.
Campgrounds: Chipmunk Rapids Campground is four miles east of Tipler on State Highway 70 and three miles south on Forest Road (point of interest No. 12). There is no fee and six campsites are available. For more information, write U.S. Forest Service, Florence, Wis. 54121.
Points of Interest:
Section 1
The stretch of the Pine River above Highway 55 has not been described or mapped; this is because the river is rather narrow, and consequently beaver dams and logjams are commonly encountered. Furthermore, this portion of the river is usually only navigable during brief periods of high water, such as in early spring.

1. (0.0 miles) **U.S. Highway 55 bridge.** There is an improved landing with parking facilities. This is our recommended **put-in** for this section. About half a mile downstream there is a 100-yard-long unnamed grade I rapids in two pitches.

2. (4.3 miles) **FS 2170.** At this point FS 2170 approaches the river. Old bridge pilings can be found at this site. This is not a convenient landing, however, because the road has a locked gate approximately half a mile from the river. From here down to Kingstone Creek there are several grade II rapids which we could not locate from aerial photographs and therefore have not indicated on the map.

3. (5.6 miles) **An alternate landing** is located on the right bank. This is a side road off of FS 2168. There is a locked gate on the road at a point close to the river.

4. (9.3 miles) **Kingstone Creek.** Just downstream of this creek there is a grade II rapids in several pitches. About half a mile further downstream there are remnants of an old logging dam that require a short **portage** on the left bank.

5. (11.3 miles) **Unnamed rapids.** This is a 50-yard-long rapids with two pitches. The first pitch rates grade I, and the second is grade II.

6. (13.0 miles) **FS 2169 bridge.** This road serves as an alternate landing. Upstream of the bridge is a long grade I rapids.

7. (14.5 miles) **Stevens Creek.** Enters from the left. This is also the border of Forest and Florence Counties.

8. (15.6 miles) **Highway 139 bridge.** An alternate landing with ample room for parking.

9. (16.5 miles) **Johnson Creek.** Enters from the left. The Chicago and Northwestern Railroad bridge is just upstream of Johnson Creek.

10. (17.2 miles) **FS 2155 bridge.** Could be used as an alternate landing. Just above the bridge is a shallow rock garden that is a real pain in low water.

11. (20.0 miles) **Fay Lake outlet.** Enters from the left.

12. (21.1 miles) **Chipmunk Rapids. FS 2150.** This grade 1 rock garden barely qualifies as a rapids. Two developed U.S. Forest Service campgrounds are located here. Chipmunk Rapids Campground is located on the river and Lost Lake Campground is just to the south. This area marks the end of **Section 1** and the start of **Section 2.**

Photo 38. A long grade II rapids on the Pine.

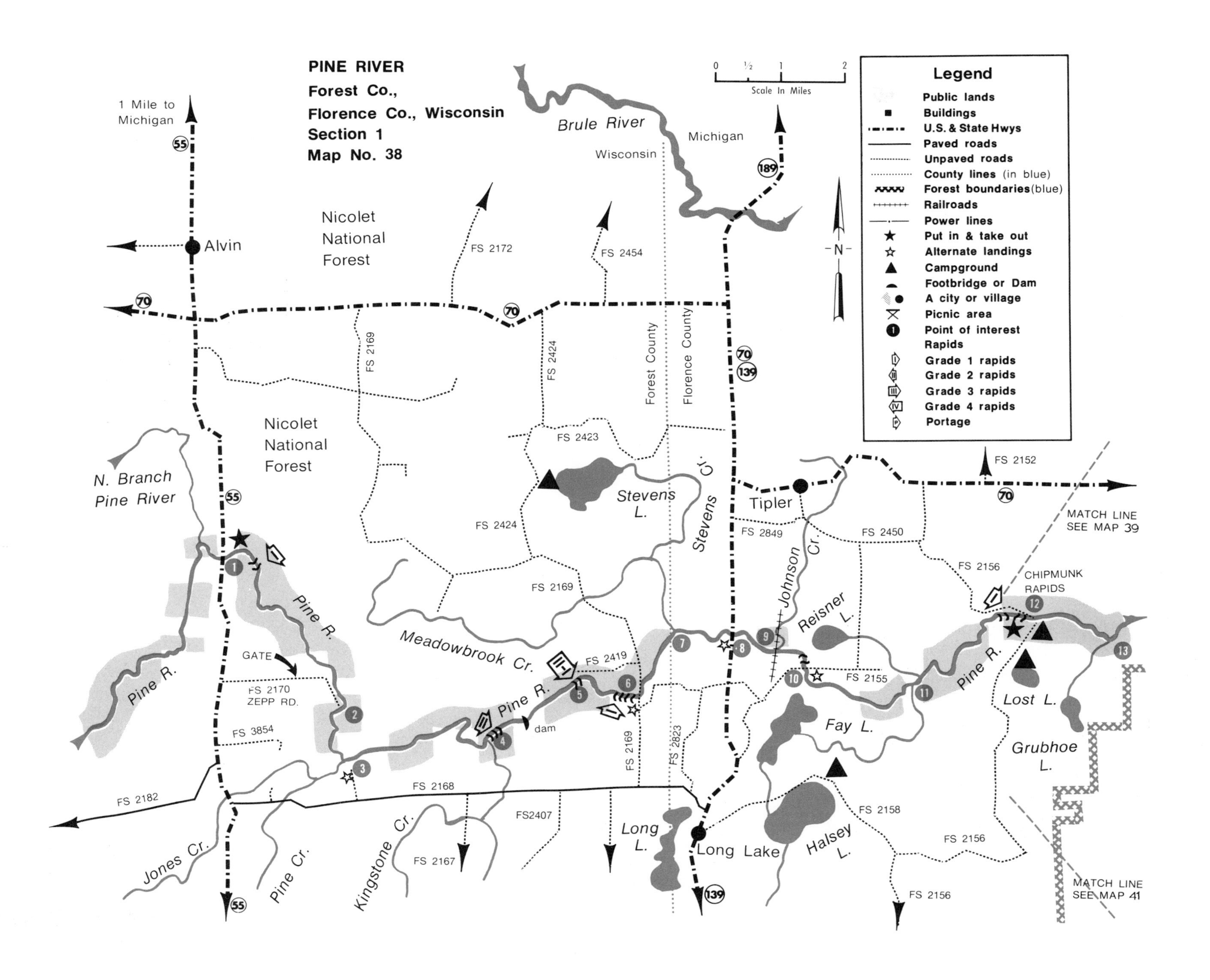
PINE RIVER
Forest Co.,
Florence Co., Wisconsin
Section 1
Map No. 38
Legend
Public lands
Buildings
U.S. & State Hwys
Paved roads
Unpaved roads
County lines (in blue)
Forest boundaries(blue)
Railroads
Power lines
Put in & take out
Alternate landings
Campground
Footbridge or Dam
A city or village
Picnic area
Point of interest
Rapids
Grade 1 rapids
Grade 2 rapids
Grade 3 rapids
Grade 4 rapids
Portage
Scale In Miles
0
½
1
2
N
1 Mile to Michigan
Alvin
Nicolet National Forest
Nicolet National Forest
Brule River
Michigan
Wisconsin
Forest County
Florence County
FS 2172
FS 2454
FS 2169
FS 2424
FS 2423
Stevens L.
Stevens Cr.
Tipler
FS 2849
FS 2450
FS 2152
FS 2156
MATCH LINE
SEE MAP 39
CHIPMUNK
RAPIDS
N. Branch
Pine River
Pine R.
Pine R.
GATE
FS 2170
ZEPP RD.
FS 3854
Meadowbrook Cr.
FS 2419
Pine R.
dam
Johnson Cr.
Reisner L.
FS 2155
Pine R.
Lost L.
Fay L.
Grubhoe L.
FS 2182
FS 2168
FS2407
FS 2823
FS 2167
Long L.
Long Lake
Halsey L.
FS 2158
FS 2156
FS 2156
MATCH LINE
SEE MAP 41
Jones Cr.
Pine Cr.
Kingstone Cr.

PINE RIVER

SECTIONS 2 & 3

Pine River: Florence County, Wisconsin.

Topo maps: Long Lake (1:48,000) 1939 planimetric, Florence SE (1:24,000) 1962, and Florence SW (1:24,000) 1962.

Overview map: Iron Mountain (1954).

Public lands: Florence County (1966) plat book, updated to January 1973 with Wisconsin DNR records.

Section 2

Start: Chipmunk Rapids Campground.

End: Goodman Grade.

Section 3

Start: Goodman Grade.

End: Highway 101 bridge.

	Sec. 2	Sec. 3
Difficulty (high water)	II^4	II
Difficulty (usual summer flow)	II^3	I-II
Length	10	9
Time	5	6
Width	20-100	20-100
Gradient	14	--

Water Conditions: There is a gauge on the Highway 55 bridge.

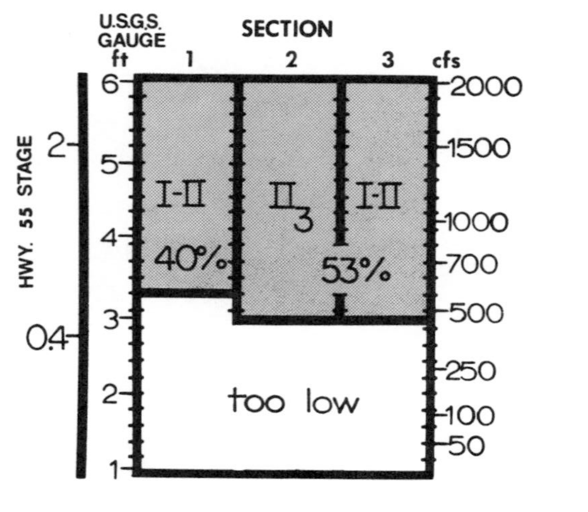

Canoeable Days Per Month (Sec.'s 2, 3 & 5)

month	Apr	May	June	July	Aug	Sep
days	26	29	18	8	6	10

Flow, Scenery, Campgrounds, Geology, and Fish: See the description accompanying map 38.

Points of Interest:

Section 2

12 (21.1 miles) **Chipmunk Rapids.** This grade I rock garden barely qualifies as a rapids. There is a developed U.S. Forest Service campground at this location. This is the **put-in** for this section.

13 (22.8 miles) **Outlet of Grubhoe Lake.** Enters from the right.

14 (24.8 miles) **FS 2154. Snake Tail Rapids.** This is a shallow rapids in 2 pitches separated by a quiet pool. If necessary, **portage** the upper pitch on the left and the lower pitch on the right. This is the western boundary of the Wisconsin Wild River section of the Pine River.

15 (25.0 miles) **Unnamed creek.** Enters from the left.

16 (25.6 miles) **Lautermans Creek.** Enters from the right.

17 (28.0 miles) **Outlet of Rubago Lake.** Enters left. Kieper Creek enters right.

18 (30.0 miles) **Meyers Falls.** A shallow grade III drop half a mile upstream of Wakefield Creek, which enters from the left. There is a cabin on the left near the major drop of the rapids. A large island divides the river into two channels. The right channel is so small that the island may not be recognized as an island from the river. Meyers Falls is in the left channel. Land canoes 100 yards upstream of the falls on the right (on the island) to **scout and/or portage.**

Section 3

19 (30.6 miles) **Goodman Grade.** This is the recommended **take-out** for **Section 2** and **put-in** for **Section 3.** This is the right of way of an old logging railroad.

20 (31.6 miles) **Bull Falls Rapids.** Rates grade II-III.

21 (34.5 miles) **Seven Mile Creek.** Enters from the left. From here to the outlet of Bessie Babbet Lake, the river is very shallow. In low water you may have to walk your canoe through this stretch.

22 (36.0 miles) **Outlet of Bessie Babbet Lake.** Enters from the left.

23 (37.8 miles) **Outlet of Sea Lion Lake.** Enters from the left.

1 (39.8 miles) **Highway 101 bridge.** This is the recommended **take-out** for **Section 3.** There is no developed landing at this point.

17 (41.1 miles) **Confluence with the Popple River,** which enters from the right. This is the main landing for the last section of the Popple River and could be used as an alternate landing for **Section 3** of the Pine; however, the Highway 101 bridge mentioned above is more accessable.

Photo 39. Bottom of Meyer's Falls.

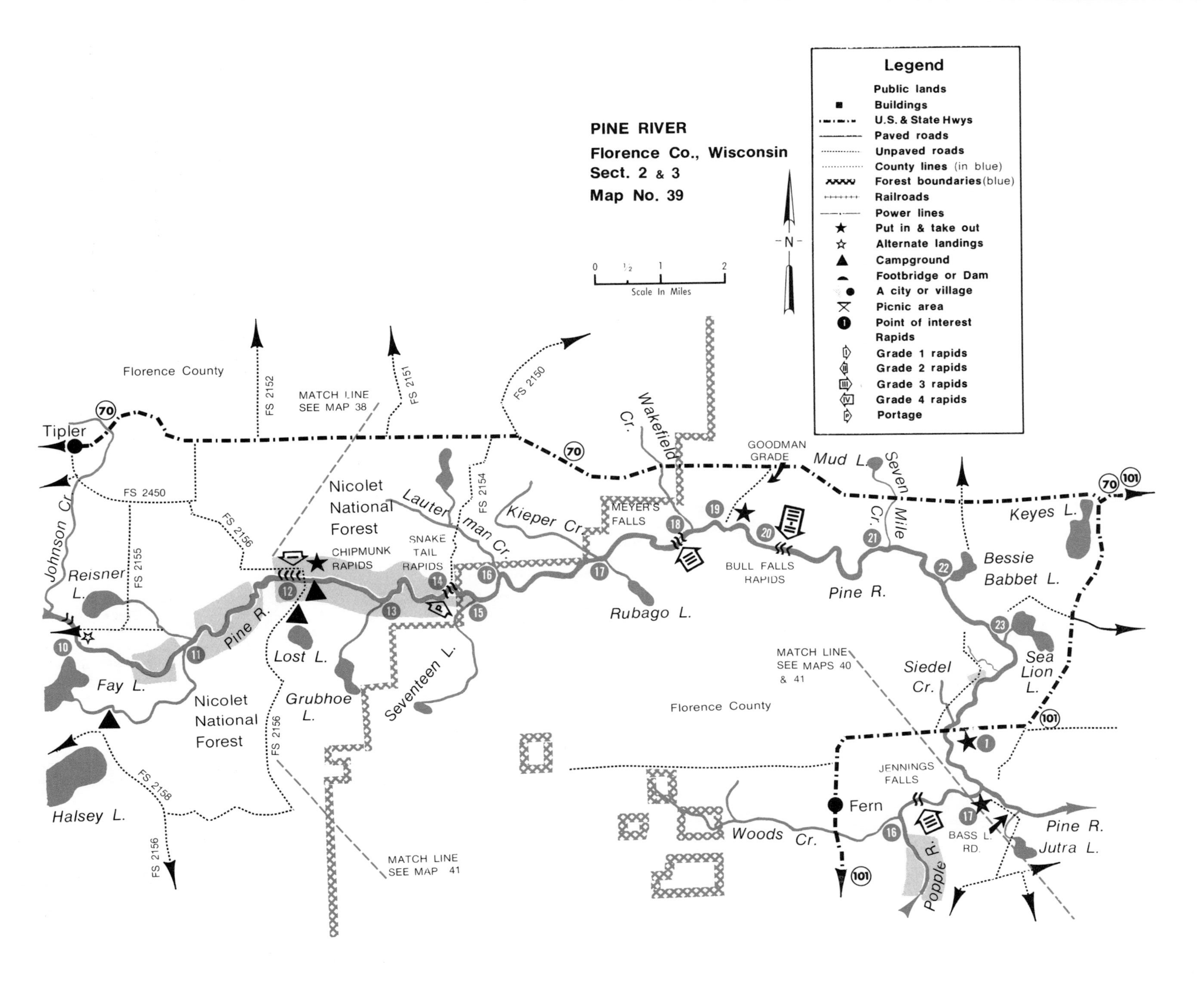
PINE RIVER
Florence Co., Wisconsin
Sect. 2 & 3
Map No. 39
0 ½ 1 2
Scale In Miles
N
Legend
Public lands
Buildings
U.S. & State Hwys
Paved roads
Unpaved roads
County lines (in blue)
Forest boundaries (blue)
Railroads
Power lines
Put in & take out
Alternate landings
Campground
Footbridge or Dam
A city or village
Picnic area
Point of interest
Rapids
Grade 1 rapids
Grade 2 rapids
Grade 3 rapids
Grade 4 rapids
Portage
Florence County
Tipler
70
FS 2152
MATCH LINE
SEE MAP 38
FS 2151
FS 2150
FS 2450
FS 2156
FS 2155
FS 2154
Johnson Cr.
Reisner L.
Nicolet National Forest
Lauterman Cr.
Kieper Cr.
CHIPMUNK RAPIDS
SNAKE TAIL RAPIDS
Pine R.
Lost L.
Fay L.
Grubhoe L.
Seventeen L.
Halsey L.
FS 2158
MATCH LINE
SEE MAP 41
Wakefield Cr.
MEYER'S FALLS
Rubago L.
GOODMAN GRADE
Mud L.
Seven Mile Cr.
BULL FALLS RAPIDS
Keyes L.
Bessie Babbet L.
101
Sea Lion L.
Siedel Cr.
MATCH LINE
SEE MAPS 40 & 41
Florence County
JENNINGS FALLS
Fern
Woods Cr.
BASS L. RD.
Popple R.
Jutra L.
10
11
12
13
14
15
16
17
18
19
20
21
22
23
1

PINE RIVER

SECTIONS 4 & 5

Pine River: Florence County, Wisconsin.
Topo map(s): Florence SE (1:24,000) 1962, Iron Mountain SW (1:24,000) 1962, and Iron Mountain (1:24,000) 1955.
Overview map(s): Iron Mountain (1954).
Public lands: Florence County (1966) plat book, updated to January 1973 with Wisconsin DNR records.
Section 4
Start: Highway 101 bridge.
End: Pine River flowage.
Section 5
Start: County Highway N.
End: Lake Ellwood landing (half a mile above the confluence with the Menominee River).

	Sec. 4	Sec. 5
Difficulty (high water)	Q_P	Q
Difficulty (usual high water)	Q_P	Q
Length	10	7
Time	6	6
Width	50-150	50-200

Drainage area 528 at the Pine River Dam

Water Conditions: The gauge is located on the Highway 101 bridge. The river is rather winding and sluggish downstream from the dam. There are no rapids, but this makes a great float fishing trip. The water is highest from 10:00 a.m. to 4:00 p.m. when power production is greatest.
The water level for Section 4 is primarily determined by the release of water from the dam. The Pine River Power plant starts operation at 8:00 a.m.; before canoeing, it is best to find out the water conditions for the lower stretch of the river by calling the Pine Station of the Wisconsin-Michigan Power Company, (715) 582-4757.

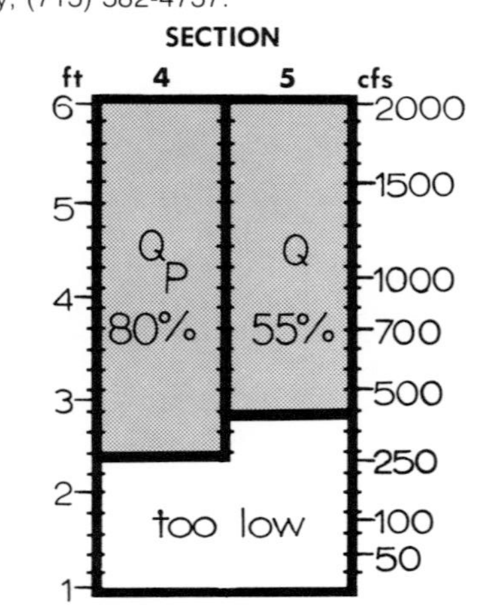

Canoeable Days Per Month (Sec. 4)

month	Apr	May	June	July	Aug	Sep
days	30	31	28	18	19	21

Scenery and Geology: See the descriptions accompanying map 38.
Fish: There are pike and bass present in the flowage and in the section of the river below the flowage.
Campgrounds: Pine Station of the Wisconsin-Michigan Power Company has a limited number of primitive campsites. There is no fee.
Points of Interest (Section 4): Because of the extremely difficult portage around LaSalle Falls, we have considered this stretch as a separate section. The rapids below this unrunnable falls and the very scenic falls itself make this section very worthwhile.
Points of Interest:
Section 4

1. (39.8 miles) **Highway 101 bridge.** This is the **put-in** for **Section 4.**
2. (44.5 miles) **LaSalle Falls. Take-out** as early as possible, for rapids preceed the falls. **This is a mandatory portage at all times.** There are portage trails on both sides of the river. The portage on the right bank is long, but there is a better view of this most attractive falls. The rapids below are quite challenging and are runnable. If you choose to run the stretch below the falls, use the portage trail on the left, because there is a large eddy on the right that can take you back into the falls if you **put-in** too early. Access is rather difficult, as you must lower your boat down steep canyon walls. Sightseers use a footpath to the falls from the road. You can also paddle up river from the flowage if you wish to see this spectacular drop.
3. (46.0 miles) **Halls Creek.** Enters from the right. This creek marks the start of the Pine River flowage.
4. (46.6 miles) **Pine River** flowage. There are camping facilities at this location. This is the recommended **take-out** for **Section 4.** Otherwise, **the dam must be portaged** on the right.
5. (47.5 miles) There is an alternate landing just below the dam.

Section 5

6. (49.5 miles) **County Highway jn.** There is a wayside. located at this **put-in** for **Section 5.** Note: the river makes a large oxbow that doubles back on itself. This permits you to paddle for about two hours and still be within a five to ten minute walk of your car if you park it at this location. The downstream landing is recognized by a field with a ridge parallel to the road and a narrow cut through the ridge. Since the Pine River Power Plant starts operation at 8:00 a.m. it is best to start canoeing this stretch at 10 or 11 o'clock when there is sufficient water.
7. (54.0 miles) **Pine Creek.** Trout stream enters from the right.
8. (54.6 miles) **Lepage Creek.** Trout stream enters from the left.
9. (56.2 miles) **Lake Ellwood landing.** This is the recommended **take-out** for this section of the Pine. The landing is on the left bank.
10. (57.1 miles) **Confluence with the Menominee River.** There is no take-out here. You can continue below this point on the Menominee and **take out** at Aurora, Wisconsin, after portaging the Henry Ford Dam.

Photo 40. The gentle Pine - but where are the pine?

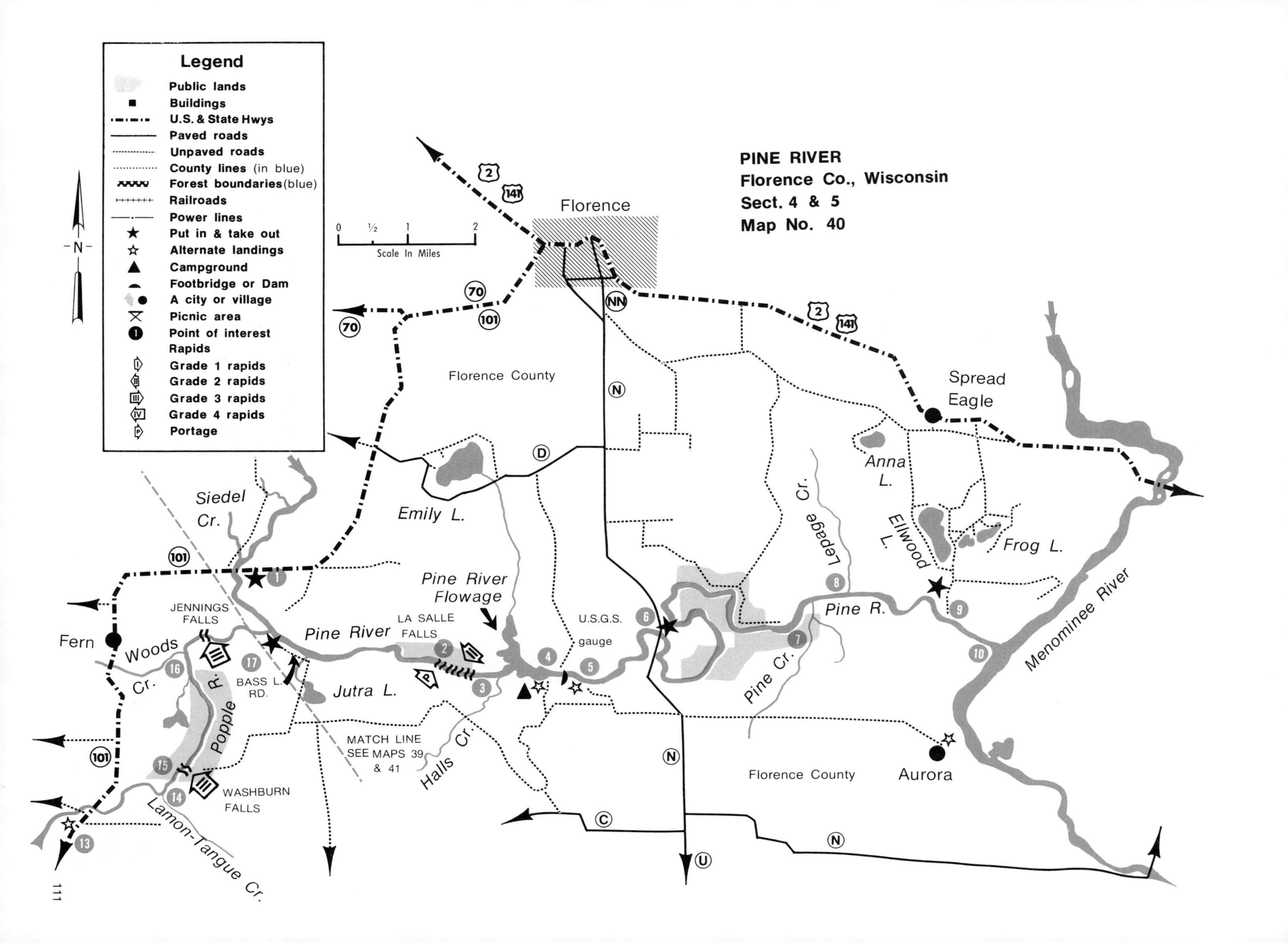
PINE RIVER
Florence Co., Wisconsin
Sect. 4 & 5
Map No. 40
Legend
Public lands
Buildings
U.S. & State Hwys
Paved roads
Unpaved roads
County lines (in blue)
Forest boundaries (blue)
Railroads
Power lines
Put in & take out
Alternate landings
Campground
Footbridge or Dam
A city or village
Picnic area
Point of interest
Rapids
Grade 1 rapids
Grade 2 rapids
Grade 3 rapids
Grade 4 rapids
Portage
N
0
½
1
2
Scale In Miles
Florence
Spread Eagle
Florence County
Emily L.
Siedel Cr.
Pine River Flowage
LA SALLE FALLS
Pine River
U.S.G.S. gauge
JENNINGS FALLS
Woods Cr.
Fern
BASS L. RD.
Jutra L.
Popple R.
MATCH LINE SEE MAPS 39 & 41
Halls Cr.
WASHBURN FALLS
Lamon-Tangue Cr.
Anna L.
Ellwood L.
Frog L.
Lepage Cr.
Pine R.
Pine Cr.
Menominee River
Florence County
Aurora
1
2
3
4
5
6
7
8
9
10
13
14
15
16
17

POPPLE RIVER

Popple River: Florence County, Wisconsin.
Topo Map(s): Florence SW (1:24,000) 1962 and Florence SE (1:24,000) 1962.
Overview map(s): Iron Mountain (1954).
Public lands: Florence County plat book (1970), updated to January 1973 with Wisconsin DNR records.
Section 1
Start: FS 2398 bridge.
End: FS 2159 bridge.
Section 2
Start: FS 2159 bridge.
End: Confluence with Pine River.

	Sec. 1	Sec. 2
Difficulty (high water)	II	III
Difficulty (usual summer flow)	I-II	II3
Length	9	10
Time	5	8
Width	15-100	15-100
Gradient	10	16
Drainage area	131 at gauge	

Water Conditions:

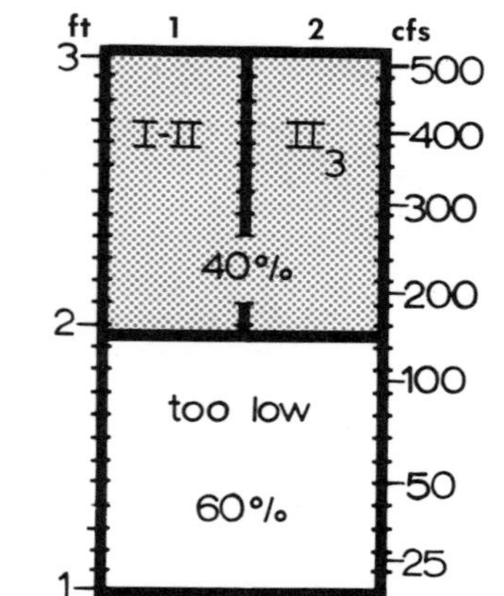

Canoeable Days Per Month

month	Apr	May	June	July	Aug	Sep
days	21	21	13	5	4	9

The Popple River is not runnable after mid-May unless there is a lot of rain. If the rock garden at the wayside at the Highway 101 bridge is runnable, the Popple is O.K. If not, don't bother to start. There is a stage marker at this location. For a rough approximation, you can multiply the stage marker reading by 100 to get the cfs.

Scenery: Excellent. Wild, wooly, and undeveloped.

Campgrounds: Burnt Dam Rapids and Washburn Falls both have primitive camping areas. Morgan Lake has 10 developed sites and a user fee is required. For more information write U.S. Forest Service, Florence, Wisc. 54121, or call (715) 528-4464.

Points of Interest:

Section 1

1 (0.0 miles) **FS 2398 bridge.** This is the recommended **put-in** for **Section 1.** In the area above this point there are many beaver dams and logjams as the river meanders through sedge-alder marshes. The only rapids of merit upstream of the recommended put-in is McDonald Rapids which is nearly 400 yards of shallow rock garden at normal water levels.

2 (0.5 miles) **Unnamed Rapids.** This rapids is a very shallow rock garden and rates grade I.

3 (2.1 miles) **Riley Creek.** Enters from the left. The river is 50 to 75 feet wide here and canoeing is easy. Further downstream the river becomes rocky; the water here is dark-colored and the rocks are difficult to spot.

4 (4.2 miles) **Burnt Dam Rapids.** There are 2 short grade I rapids located near the mouth of Morgan Creek. A primitive campsite is located here.

5 (4.6 miles) **FS 2159 bridge.** There is a primitive campsite located at this unimproved landing. Just upstream is Goodman Grade, an old railroad right of way.

6 (4.8 miles) **Confluence with the South Branch of Popple River,** which enters from the right. This branch is usually shallow and full of obstacles such as beaver dams and logjams.

7 (6.8 miles) **Rock Creek.** Enters from the right. Just above this creek there is an unnamed rapids in two pitches. The second pitch is shallow and rocky. This is the start of the Wisconsin Wild River section.

8 (8.5 miles) **FS 2159 bridge.** This is the recommended **take-out** of **Section 1** and **put-in** for **Section 2.** A U.S.G.S. gauging station is located at the bridge.

Section 2

Caution: This section recommended for experts with decked boats only.

8 (8.5 miles) **FS 2159 bridge.** This section has four grade III drops, making it the most difficult run on the Popple River. It is also the most interesting run on this watershed, since the stream and the vegetation change character many times.

9 (9.2 miles) **Little Bull Falls.** A grade III drop preceded by some relatively easy rapids. **Scouting** and possible **portage** are **recommended** to avoid the deceptively difficult hole in this four foot drop. A tip-over here could result in a long swim.

10 (10.0 miles) **Big Murphy Rapids.** This rapids has 2 pitches. The first rates grade I, and the second rates grade II.

11 (11.0 miles) **Nine-Mile Rapids.** This is a shallow grade I-II rock garden. This rapids is 9 miles downstream of Riley Creek, and was probably a major run to the Popple-Pine waterway during the logging era.

12 (12.4 miles) **Big Bull Falls.** A six to eight foot drop divides around a small island. The left channel is nasty and should be avoided. The right drops over a series of ledges and rates grade III. **Scouting recommended.** Left bank best for a carry.

13 (13.2 miles) **Highway 101 bridge.** This may be used as an alternate landing.

14 (14.8 miles) **Lamon-Tangue Creek.** Enters from the right. A half mile downstream of the mouth of this

15 (15.3 miles) **Washburn Falls.** The river drops some 25 feet in a hundred yards, ending with a 6 to 8 foot drop. Two huge boulders mark the spot. The holes above the lower drop could easily be a stopper at higher flows. Grade IV. **Portage** on the established trail to the **right.**

16 (17.0 miles) **Jennings Falls.** This grade III drop is downstream of a left turn. **Scout and/or portage** on the right. Woods Creek has brown trout.

17 (18.5 miles) **Confluence with Pine River.** The recommended **take-out** is at the end of Bass Lake Road on the right bank.

Photo 41. Scene on the Popple.

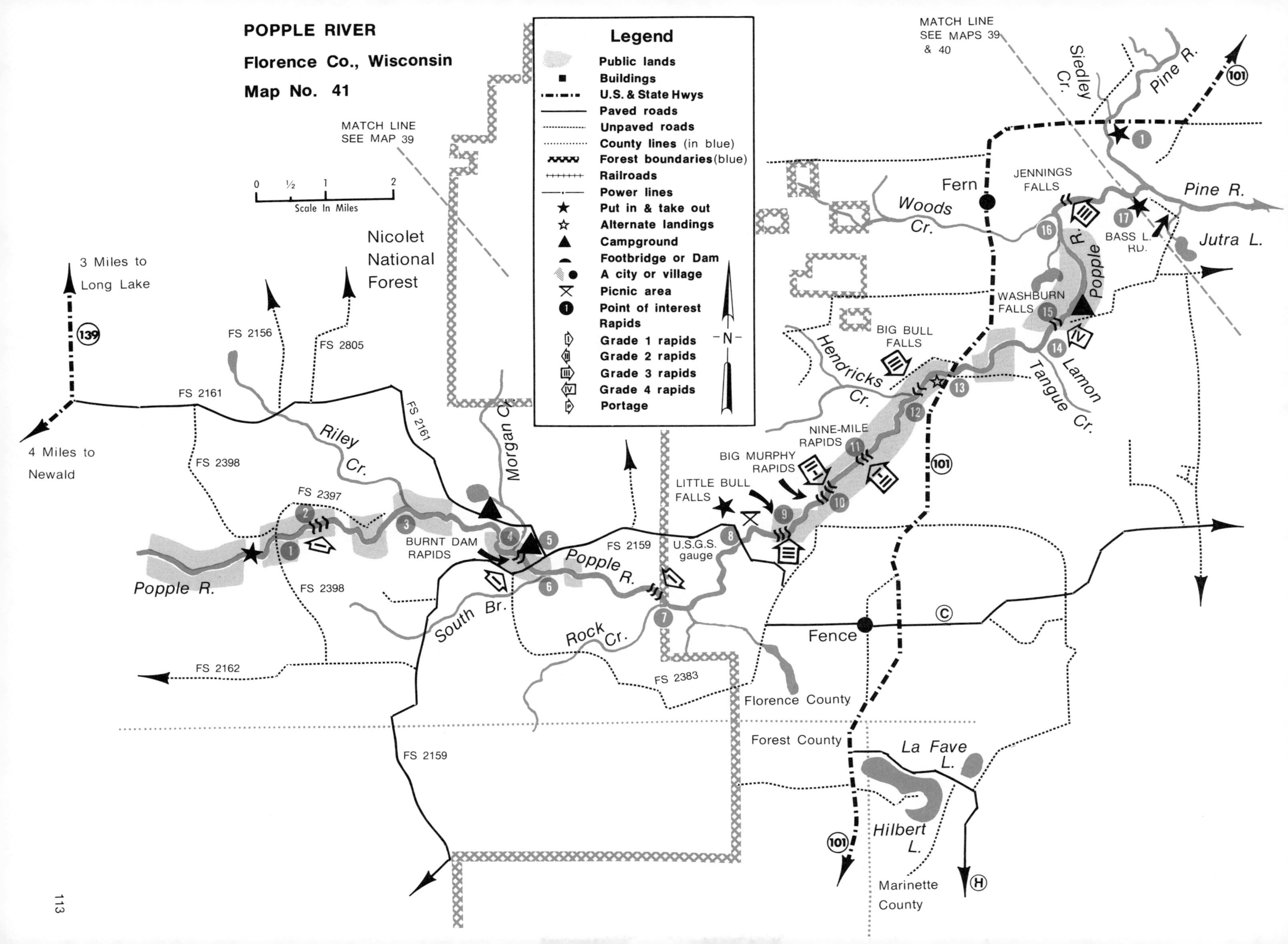
POPPLE RIVER
Florence Co., Wisconsin
Map No. 41
MATCH LINE SEE MAP 39
0 ½ 1 2
Scale In Miles
Nicolet National Forest
3 Miles to Long Lake
4 Miles to Newald
Legend
Public lands
Buildings
U.S. & State Hwys
Paved roads
Unpaved roads
County lines (in blue)
Forest boundaries (blue)
Railroads
Power lines
Put in & take out
Alternate landings
Campground
Footbridge or Dam
A city or village
Picnic area
Point of interest
Rapids
Grade 1 rapids
Grade 2 rapids
Grade 3 rapids
Grade 4 rapids
Portage
N
MATCH LINE SEE MAPS 39 & 40
FS 2156
FS 2805
FS 2161
FS 2398
FS 2397
Riley Cr.
Morgan Cr.
BURNT DAM RAPIDS
Popple R.
South Br.
Rock Cr.
FS 2159
FS 2162
FS 2383
U.S.G.S. gauge
LITTLE BULL FALLS
BIG MURPHY RAPIDS
NINE-MILE RAPIDS
BIG BULL FALLS
Hendricks Cr.
Woods Cr.
Fern
JENNINGS FALLS
WASHBURN FALLS
Lamon Tangue Cr.
BASS L. RD.
Jutra L.
Pine R.
Siedley Cr.
Fence
Florence County
Forest County
La Fave L.
Hilbert L.
Marinette County

RED RIVER

Red River: Schawano County, Wisconsin.
Topo map(s): Gresham (1:62,500) 1964 and Shawano (1:48,000) 1954 planimetric.
Overview map: Green Bay (1955).
Public lands: Shawano County plat book (1968).
Section 1
Start: Where the road closely approaches the left bank of the river, one-third of a mile above the west branch of Red River.
End: Bridge on road that runs due south of Morgan.
Section 2
Start: 1.3 miles southeast of Gresham, just downstream from the dam and powerhouse.
End: County Highway A bridge in the town of Red River.

	SEC. 1	SEC. 2
Difficulty (high water)	II4	II4
Difficulty (usual summer flow)	–	I3
Length	6	4
Time	4	3
Width	8-35	6-40
Gradient	12	–
Drainage area	134	–

Water Conditions: Section 1 is only runnable during periods of high water such as early spring or after periods of prolonged rain. **Section 2** is runnable in the spring and summer. There is no gauge on this river. The upper part of the Red River, from Phlox through Menominee County, is not runnable because numerous portages are required around fallen logs and the river dissipates into numerous small unrunnable channels.

Scenery: The scenery is rather good, but there are numerous cabins and other development along the shoreline. Beavers are common in this area.

Geology: The bedrock of this river consists of granite and other igneous rocks.

Fish: This river has both brook and brown trout.

Points of Interest:

Section 1

1 (0.0 miles) **Landing.** The recommended put-in is at a point where the road approaches the river.

2 (0.6 miles) **Confluence with West Branch of Red River.** - Just upstream from this junction is a short steep rapids that ends in a ledge. This is easy to spot since only about 50 feet of rapids separate this drop from the preceeding quiet water. A narrowing of the river, a slight bend to the left, rising rocky banks, and a small footbridge across the river also help in identification of this spot from upstream. **Portaging is recommended. Caution: About 10 yards below this rapids is a steel cable** that stretches across the river not much above the surface.

3 (1.5 miles) **Slicky Creek.** Enters from the left.

4 (1.7 miles) **Unnamed Rapids.** At this point a large island divides the river into two channels; both have rapids. **Scouting is recommended.** The rapids in the left channel ends in a falls that **must be portaged.** The rapids in the right channel is tricky grade III but has been run successfully in high water.

5 (2.4 miles) **Unnamed Rapids.** Once more an island signals an imminent rapids. This island has a cabin on it. The right channel is too narrow to run. The water in the left channel flows over a steep sloping ledge that is runnable in moderately high water. (We located this rapids on the aerial photos, but we don't recall it. It probably rates a grade II.)

6 (3.3 miles) **Rapids.** This is a long grade II rapids which is marked by a farm on the left side of the river.

7 (4.0 miles) **Rapids.** The first in this pair of rapids is a small grade II-III rapids that ends in a three-foot drop. The second grade II rapids, is not difficult, but it includes a sharp blind turn in the river that on numerous occasions has held a fallen tree, thereby forcing a portage.

8 (4.7 miles) **Smith Creek.** The outlet of Smith Lake enters from the right.

9 (5.5 miles) **Bridge.** This is the recommended take-out.

10 (7.7 miles) **County Highway G bridge.**

Section 2

This section makes a good beginning trip if Alexian and possibly Zeimer's Falls are portaged.

11 (9.5 miles) **Red River Flowage landing.** Put-in on the gravel bar just below the powerhouse.

12 (9.8 miles) **Unnamed rapids.** Grade I with standing waves. Open canoes could ship water here at higher flows.

13 (10.0 miles) **Gardner Creek.** Nice catches of brook and brown trout have been taken here.

14 (10.4 miles) **Rapids.** Grade I.

15 (11.2 miles) **Alexian Falls. Scouting recommended.** About 50 yards below some grade I-II rapids, the river forms a quiet pool before narrowing down to a 6' wide slot which marks the falls. A large boulder in the middle and generally tight quarters, prompts most boaters to **portage** this one on the **left.** This is clearly the most difficult drop on this run. A picturesque spot, the novitiate overlooking this drop received widespread national publicity in the winter of 1975 when it was forcefully occupied by a group of dissident Menominee Indians.

16 (11.5 miles) **Rock Garden.** Some maneuvering is required to avoid the rocks.

17 (12.1 miles) **Ziemers Falls. Scouting recommended.** The river divides into two channels, each no more than 8 to 10 feet wide. The left channel is sometimes runnable on this grade II rapids. Maneuvering is required. **Portage left** if so inclined.

18 (12.5 miles) **Rapids.** Grade I. Standing waves form here as the river deepens into a pool. At high flows open canoes may take on water.

19 (12.9 miles) **Mill Dam ruins.** All that remains are some concrete abutments of the former dam. At times the right channel can be run if care is taken to avoid the rocks.

20 (13.5 miles) **Rapids.** Grade I.

21 (13.8 miles) **County Highway A bridge.** Take-out at the landing upstream of the bridge in the village of Red River.

Note: Leaving cars unattended at various spots along this river has resulted in vandalism. Access may also be a problem.

Photo 44. Large boulder bed on the Red.

Photo 42. Oops!

Photo 43. Running Meyer's Falls. Pine River.

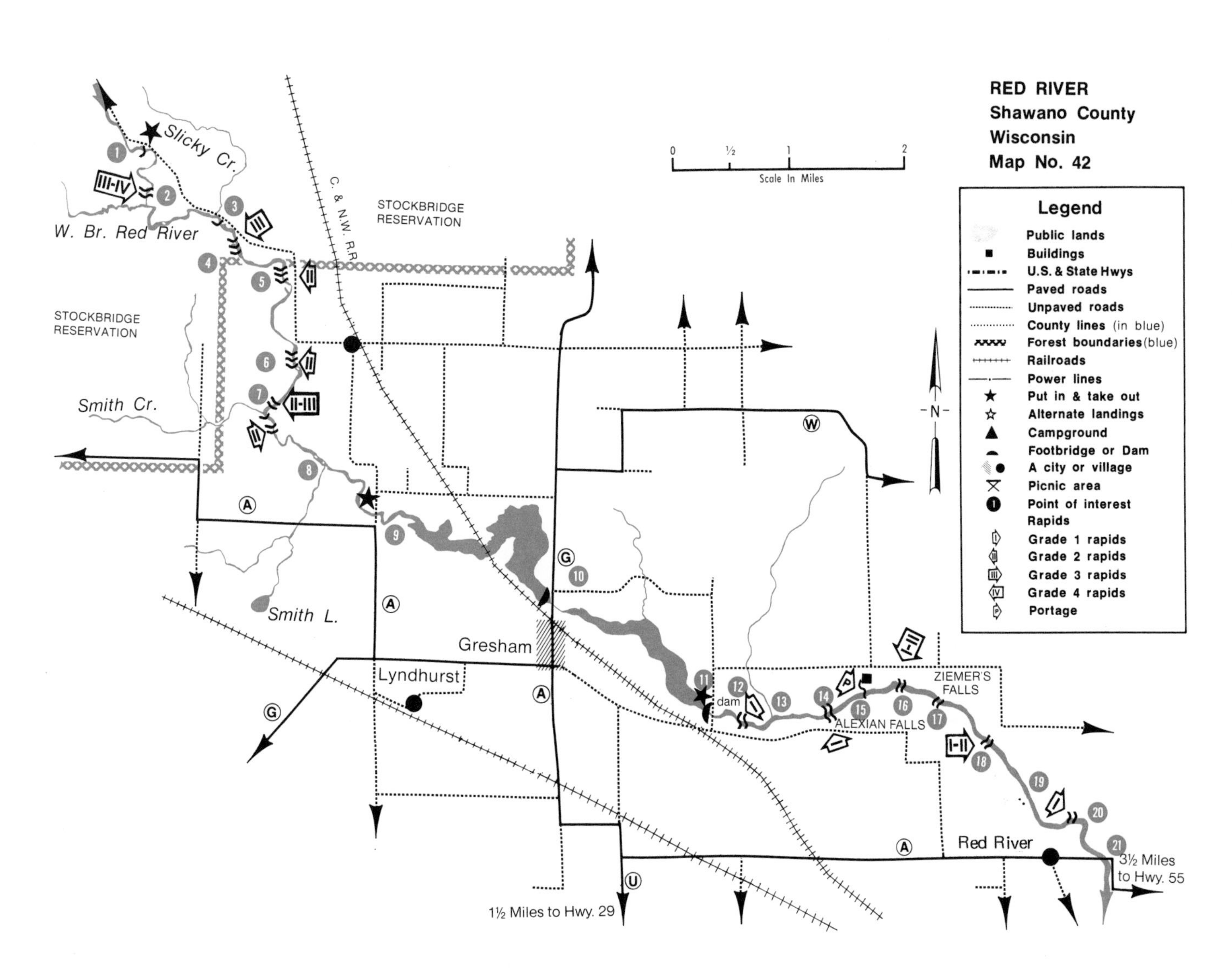

ST. CROIX RIVER

SECTION 1

St. Croix River: Douglas and Burnett Counties, Wisconsin.
Topo map(s): Solon Springs (1:62,500) 1961, Minong (1:62,500) 1965, and Webb Lake (1:62,500) 1955.
Overview map(s): Ashland (1953) and Duluth (1953).
Public lands: Douglas County plat book (1973), Burnett County plat book (1971), and National Park Service Master plan (1971).
Section 1
Start: Below Gordon Dam.
End: CCC bridge.

	SEC. 1
Difficulty (high water)	**II-II3**
Difficulty (usual summer flow)	**I-II**
Length	**16**
Time	**7**
Width	**50-100**
Gradient	**5**
Drainage area	**224**

Water Conditions: This section and section 4 have significant areas of grade I-II rapids, unlike the other three sections of the St. Croix which are essentially quiet water. The nearest gauge is located near Danbury; consequently, flow rates are presented with map 44.

Scenery: Good to excellent. Much of the shoreline has escaped extensive development. The river banks are primarily forested with relatively mature, second-growth hardwoods, such as oak, sugar maple, birch, and aspen. There are also pines and basswood.

Geology: This area has undergone extensive glacial activity. The oldest rocks are Pre-Cambrian metamorphic and volcanic formations. In most places this bedrock is covered by Cambrian sandstone and other glacial sands, clays, silts, and gravels. In some areas there are outcroppings of sandstone which can be seen along the river banks. Rapids are located where the river passes over harder rocks of Pre-Cambrian lava origin. Springs are common in this area.

History: Evidence of early inhabitation by Indians goes back to at least 1000 B. C. There are numerous Indian mounds and other remnants of early civilization to be found in this region. During the fur trading era of the 1700's, the Chippewa lived here. The Chippewa were allied with the French who supplied them with firearms. There were many bloody battles fought over the control of this early trade route, which extended from Lake Superior via the Bois Brule River, the St. Croix, and Mississippi Rivers down to the Gulf of Mexico. This trade route was first discovered by Daniel Greysolon in 1679. The British took over control of this area in 1763 when France ceded Canada to England. By the end of the 18th century John Jacob Astor and his American Fur Company had established a strong foothold in the territory. Following a treaty in 1837, the Indians surrendered to the United States control of all lands east of the Mississippi, except for small areas of reservation lands near the start of the St. Croix and Chippewa Rivers. The last main group of Indians in the area were Sioux. Near the end of the 19th century the railroad was introduced to this area, and along with it came the loggers. Lumber production reached its peak in 1899. By 1920, the big logging boom had tapered off considerably.

Fish and Campgrounds: See description accompanying map 44.

Wild Rivers: The St. Croix downstream from Riverside Dam continuing to just above Taylor Falls, Minnesota, is included in the National Wild Rivers Act of 1968.

Points of Interest:

1. (0.0 miles) **Gordon Dam.** Below this dam is the put-in for **Section 1.** There is ample parking at this improved landing. There is also a campground at this location.

2. (0.5 miles) **Scout Chute.** This is a grade I-II rapids that begins at a large island and continues downstream. There is a primitive campsite on the island.

3. (1.0 miles) **Scott Rapids.** This is a small grade I rapids located about one-quarter mile upstream of Scott Bridge.

4. (1.6 miles) **Scott Bridge.** The Moose River enters the St. Croix from the right just above this bridge. The left bank next to the bridge can be used as an alternate landing.

5. (2.5 miles) **Sheosh Creek.** Enters from the right.

6. (5.6 miles) **Crotte Creek.** Enters from the right. A half-mile upstream of this creek, there is a landing on the left bank.

7. (6.8 miles) **Buckley Creek.** Enters from the left.

8. (7.0 miles) **Copper Mine Sluice Dam.** This is the partial ruins of an early logging dam. **Scouting is recommended** since logs and other debris can become lodged in the remaining supports. There is a good portage trail on the right bank.

9. (7.5 miles) **Shelldrake Rapids.** An island divides the river into two channels. These grade I rapids are located in the right channel.

10. (8.8 miles) **Highway T bridge.** Due to lack of a developed parking area, this is a possible, but less desirable, alternate landing.

11. (9.0 miles) **Bear Trap Rapids.** This rapids begins just downstream of the County Highway T bridge. This is a shallow rapids that has numerous boulders to dodge. Its rating is grade I-II. This rapids gradually fades out into a long continuous stretch of alternating riffles and quiet water that extends to just below Louis Park.

12. (10.0 miles) **Louis Park.** This primitive campground is located on the right bank at the mouth of Beaver Creek. There is road access to this area, and thus it can be used as an alternate landing.

13. (11.6 miles) **Shone Park.** This is a primitive campground with limited room. It has road access. Rock Creek enters from the right just downstream of this location.

14. (12.5 miles) **County line landing.** This alternate landing is located on the Douglas and Burnett County line. There is road access on the left bank.

15. (14.5 miles) **Big Fish Trap Rapids.** This is the most difficult rapids on the upper St. Croix. It rates grade II. If you choose not to run this rapids, you can line down a canoe on the right bank.

16. (15.5 miles) **Little Fish Trap Rapids.** This grade I rapids begins just upstream of the CCC bridge. Clemeng Creek enters on the left. The CCC bridge is the recommended take-out for Section 1 and put-in for Section 2. There is a primitive campsite at this location.

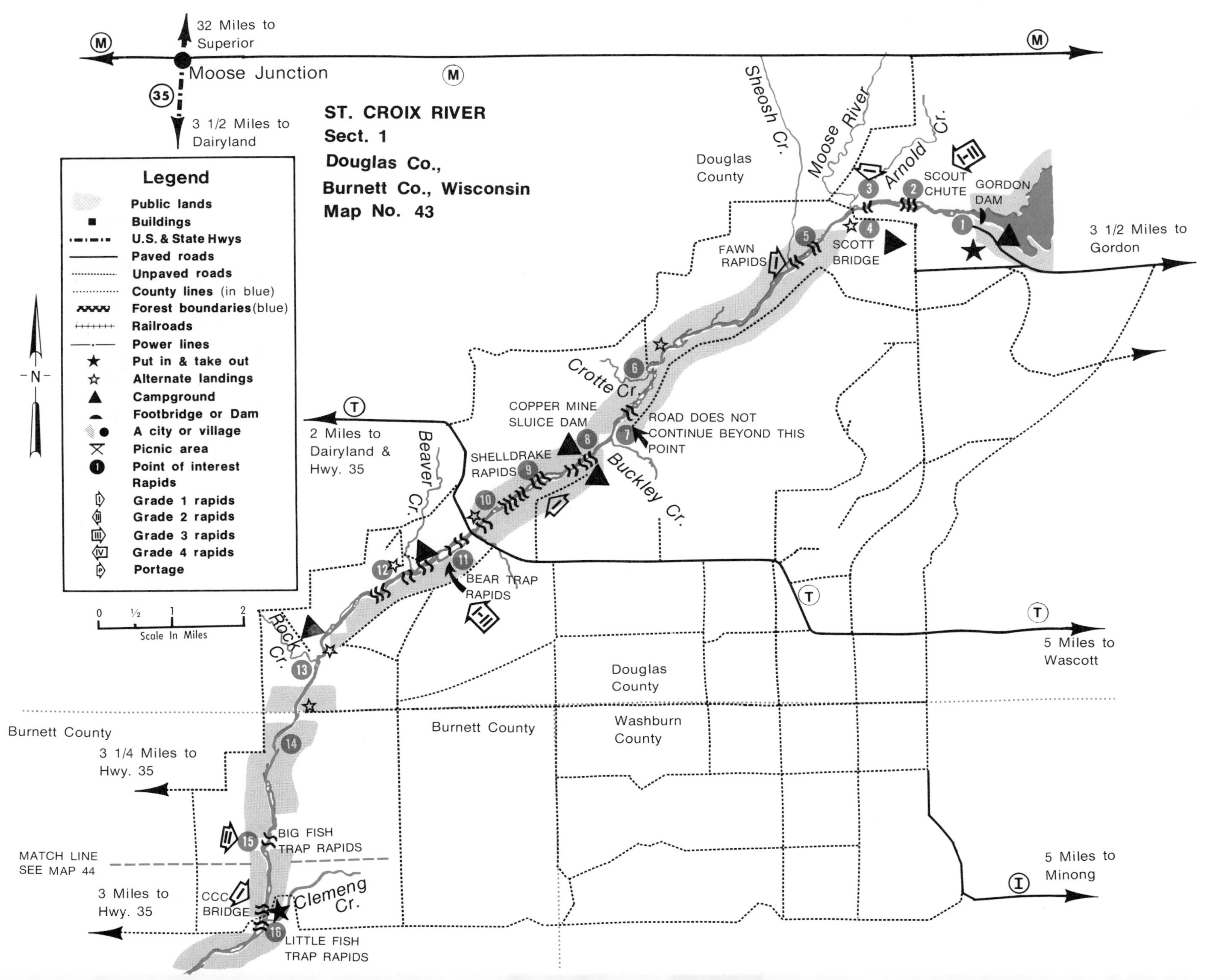

ST. CROIX RIVER
Sect. 1
Douglas Co.,
Burnett Co., Wisconsin
Map No. 43
32 Miles to Superior
Moose Junction
3 1/2 Miles to Dairyland
Legend
Public lands
Buildings
U.S. & State Hwys
Paved roads
Unpaved roads
County lines (in blue)
Forest boundaries (blue)
Railroads
Power lines
Put in & take out
Alternate landings
Campground
Footbridge or Dam
A city or village
Picnic area
Point of interest
Rapids
Grade 1 rapids
Grade 2 rapids
Grade 3 rapids
Grade 4 rapids
Portage
Scale In Miles
N
Douglas County
Sheosh Cr.
Moose River
Arnold Cr.
SCOUT CHUTE
GORDON DAM
SCOTT BRIDGE
FAWN RAPIDS
3 1/2 Miles to Gordon
Crotte Cr.
COPPER MINE SLUICE DAM
ROAD DOES NOT CONTINUE BEYOND THIS POINT
SHELLDRAKE RAPIDS
Buckley Cr.
2 Miles to Dairyland & Hwy. 35
Beaver Cr.
BEAR TRAP RAPIDS
Rock Cr.
5 Miles to Wascott
Douglas County
Washburn County
Burnett County
Burnett County
3 1/4 Miles to Hwy. 35
BIG FISH TRAP RAPIDS
MATCH LINE SEE MAP 44
3 Miles to Hwy. 35
CCC BRIDGE
Clemeng Cr.
LITTLE FISH TRAP RAPIDS
5 Miles to Minong

ST. CROIX RIVER

SECTION 2

St. Croix River: Burnett County, Wisconsin and Pine County, Minnesota.
Topo map(s): Danbury (1:62,500) 1962 and Webb Lake (1:62,500) 1955.
Overview map(s): Duluth (1953).
Public lands: Burnett County plat book (1971), National Park Service Master plan (1971), and NSR book.
Section 2
Start: CCC bridge.
End: Danbury, Wisconsin.

	SEC. 2
Difficulty (high water)	I
Difficulty (usual summer flow)	Q-I
Length	15
Time	7
Width	50-200
Gradient	2
Drainage area	449

Water Conditions: The U.S.G.S. gauge is located in Burnett County, Wisc. on the left bank of the Highway 35 bridge at Riverside, 3.5 miles downstream of the confluence of the Namekagon River.

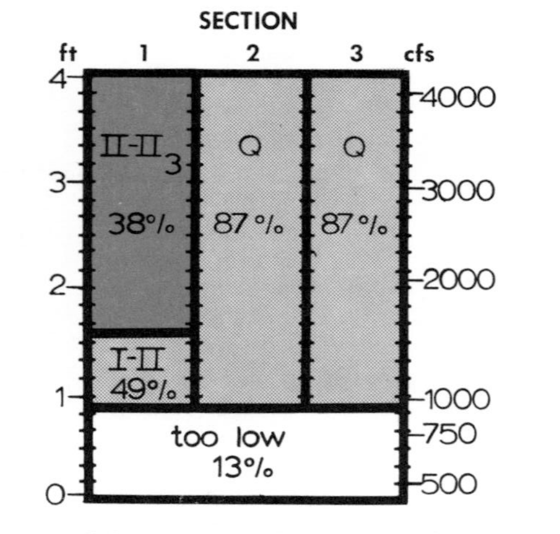

Canoeable Days Per Month

month	Apr	May	June	July	Aug	Sep
days	30	31	30	23	20	25

Scenery, Geology, History: See description accompanying map 43.

Fish: Trout can be found in the rapids areas and in numerous cold water tributary creeks. Muskie and smallmouth bass are common in other parts of the river.

Campgrounds: Gordon Dam Park has been developed by Douglas County. There are 40 spaces that frequently are filled on weekends in summer. There is a small user fee. For more information contact the County Clerk, Superior, Wisc. 54880, or call (715) 394-6611. There are numerous primitive campsites along the river. There is no fee required for their use, but camping is limited to overnight. There are primitive campsites with road access at Louis and Shone Parks.

Points of Interest:

16 (15.5 miles) **CCC bridge.** This is the recommended put-in for Section 2.

17 (17.7 miles) **Moore Farm Creek.** Enters from the left.

18 (18.7 miles) **Mouth of Namekagon River.** Enters from the left. For an account of the upstream portions of the Namekagon River see maps 27-31 and the accompanying descriptions. There are some riffles here. Since the watershed of the Namekagon at this point is twice that of the St. Croix, the river becomes larger downstream here.

19 (19.2 miles) **Perkins Creek.** Enters from the right.

20 (20.0 miles) **Big Island.** This inhabited island is approximately one mile long and one-half mile wide. Both the right and left channels around this island are navigable.

21 (22.0 miles) **Hay Creek.** Enters from the right. Just downstream of this creek is an optional landing at a developed campground.

1 (22.7 miles) **Riverside State Roadside Park.** This is a suitable and alternate landing with developed camping facilities.

2 (23.2 miles) **Chase Creek.** Enters from the right.

3 (23.4 miles) **Hen and Chicken Islands.** This area received its name during the logging era when it was the site of numerous logjams.

4 (24.7 miles) **Ginger Island.** This large island signals the start of State Line Rapids. This rapids rates grade I and is located in the right channel around the island. Downstream of this location, the right bank of the river lies within the state of Minnesota. From this point until its mouth, the St. Croix forms the boundary of Wisconsin and Minnesota.

5 (25.9 miles) **Mouth of the Upper Tamarack River.** Enters from the right. There is an alternate landing located slightly downstream from here on the opposite side of the river.

6 (26.5 miles) **Trout Brook.** Enters from the right.

7 (28.2 miles) **Crystal Creek.** Enters from the right.

8 (30.2 miles) **Mouth of Yellow River.** The drainage area of the Yellow River is 310 square miles at its mouth. This makes the total drainage area of the St. Croix River 2,084 square miles just below this location.

9 (30.4 miles) **Minneapolis-St. Paul Railroad Crossing.** This railroad crossing signals landings which are located slightly downstream of here on both the Wisconsin and Minnesota banks of the river. These landings are the recommended **take-outs** for this section.

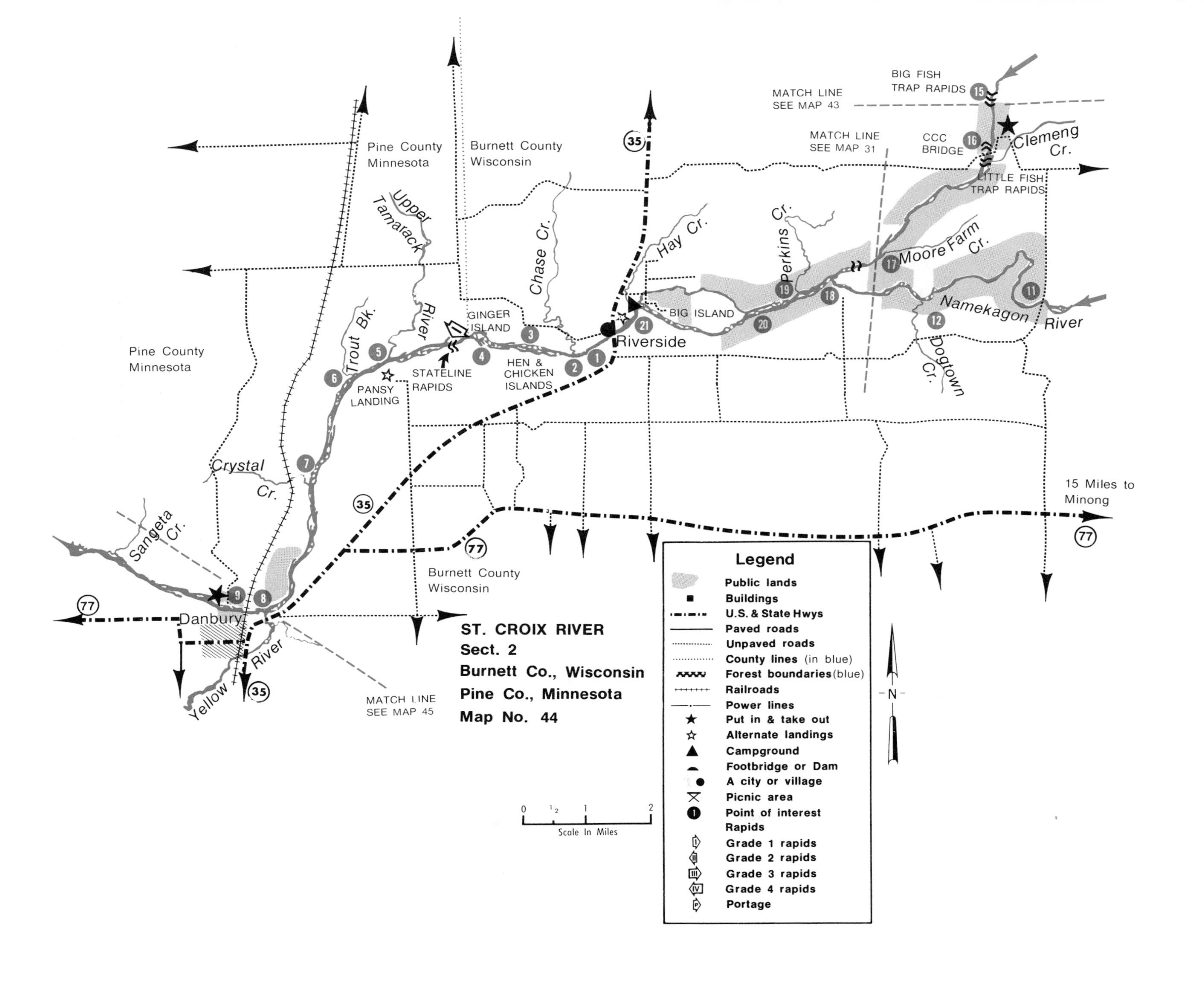

ST. CROIX RIVER
Sect. 2
Burnett Co., Wisconsin
Pine Co., Minnesota
Map No. 44
Legend
Public lands
Buildings
U.S. & State Hwys
Paved roads
Unpaved roads
County lines (in blue)
Forest boundaries (blue)
Railroads
Power lines
Put in & take out
Alternate landings
Campground
Footbridge or Dam
A city or village
Picnic area
Point of interest
Rapids
Grade 1 rapids
Grade 2 rapids
Grade 3 rapids
Grade 4 rapids
Portage
N
0 1/2 1 2
Scale In Miles
MATCH LINE SEE MAP 43
BIG FISH TRAP RAPIDS
MATCH LINE SEE MAP 31
CCC BRIDGE
Clemeng Cr.
LITTLE FISH TRAP RAPIDS
Pine County Minnesota
Burnett County Wisconsin
Upper Tamarack River
Chase Cr.
Hay Cr.
Perkins Cr.
Moore Farm Cr.
Namekagon River
Dogtown Cr.
BIG ISLAND
Riverside
GINGER ISLAND
HEN & CHICKEN ISLANDS
STATELINE RAPIDS
PANSY LANDING
Trout Bk.
Pine County Minnesota
Crystal Cr.
15 Miles to Minong
Sangeta Cr.
Burnett County Wisconsin
Danbury
Yellow River
MATCH LINE SEE MAP 45
35
77

ST. CROIX RIVER

SECTION 3

St. Croix River: Burnett County, Wisconsin and Pine County, Minnesota.
Topo map(s): Grantsburg (1:62,500) 1962, Webster (1:62,500) 1955, and Danbury (1:62,500) 1962.
Overview map(s): Duluth (1953) and Stillwater (1953).
Public lands: Burnett County plat book (1971) and National Park Service Book (1971).
Section 3
Start: Danbury.
End: Norway Point.

	SEC. 3
Difficulty (high water)	**Q**
Difficulty (usual summer flow)	**Q**
Length	**19**
Time	**8**
Gradient	**1**
Drainage area	**2,084**

Water Conditions, Scenery, Geology, History and Fishing: See descriptions accompanying maps 43 and 44.
Campgrounds: Big Yellow Banks and Little Yellow Banks campgrounds are in Pine County, Minnesota. We have no information on these sites. See point of interest 16.
Points of Interest:

9 (30.4 miles) **Danbury.** This is the put-in for **Section 3.** There are landings on both the Wisconsin and Minnesota sides of the river. Since the river is rather large at this point, allow extra time if there are appreciable headwinds from the west. There are no rapids on this section.

10 (32.6 miles) **Sangeta Creek.** This creek enters from the right.

11 (33.2 miles) **Lower Tamarack River.** Enters from the right. Remains of a primitive Indian village are located on the right bank near the mouth of this river.

12 (34.8 miles) **Wisconsin Highway 77** (Minnesota Highway 48) bridge. There is a parking area and public landing on the right bank just downstream of this bridge. This point marks the start of the St. Croix River State Forest.

13 (37.9 miles) **Sioux Portage Creek.** This was the main travel route to Yellow Lake used by the Indians and fur traders.

14 (40.4 miles) **Crooked Creek.** Enters from the right. There is a landing on the right bank just downstream of this location at the site of an old logging camp.

15 (43.9 miles) **Mouth of Clam River.** Enters from the left. The drainage area of this river is 416 square miles.

16 (44.4 miles) **Little Yellow Banks.** On the right bank just downstream of the mouth of the Clam River, there is a landing and campground.

17 (46.4 miles) **Kohler Peat Bog.** There are approximately 4,000 acres of conifer swampland in public ownership. There is a large deer population in this region, which is a public hunting ground.

18 (47.1 miles) **Big Yellow Banks.** There is a landing and campground located at these ruins of the old logging era. The Old Flemming logging railroad brought white pine to the river at this point and from here the logs were floated downstream.

19 (48.6 miles) **Mouth of Clover and Sand Creeks.** Both enter from the right.

20 (49.4 miles) **Norway Point.** This is the **take-out** for Section 3 and **put-in** for Section 4. There is an improved landing located on the right bank. There are primitive camping facilities. A U.S.G.S. gauging station was located at this site from 1923 until 1970 when it was discontinued. The drainage area at this location is approximately 2,820 square miles. In times past, this was the site of a small mill and a ferry crossing.

Photo 45. All quiet on the St. Croix.

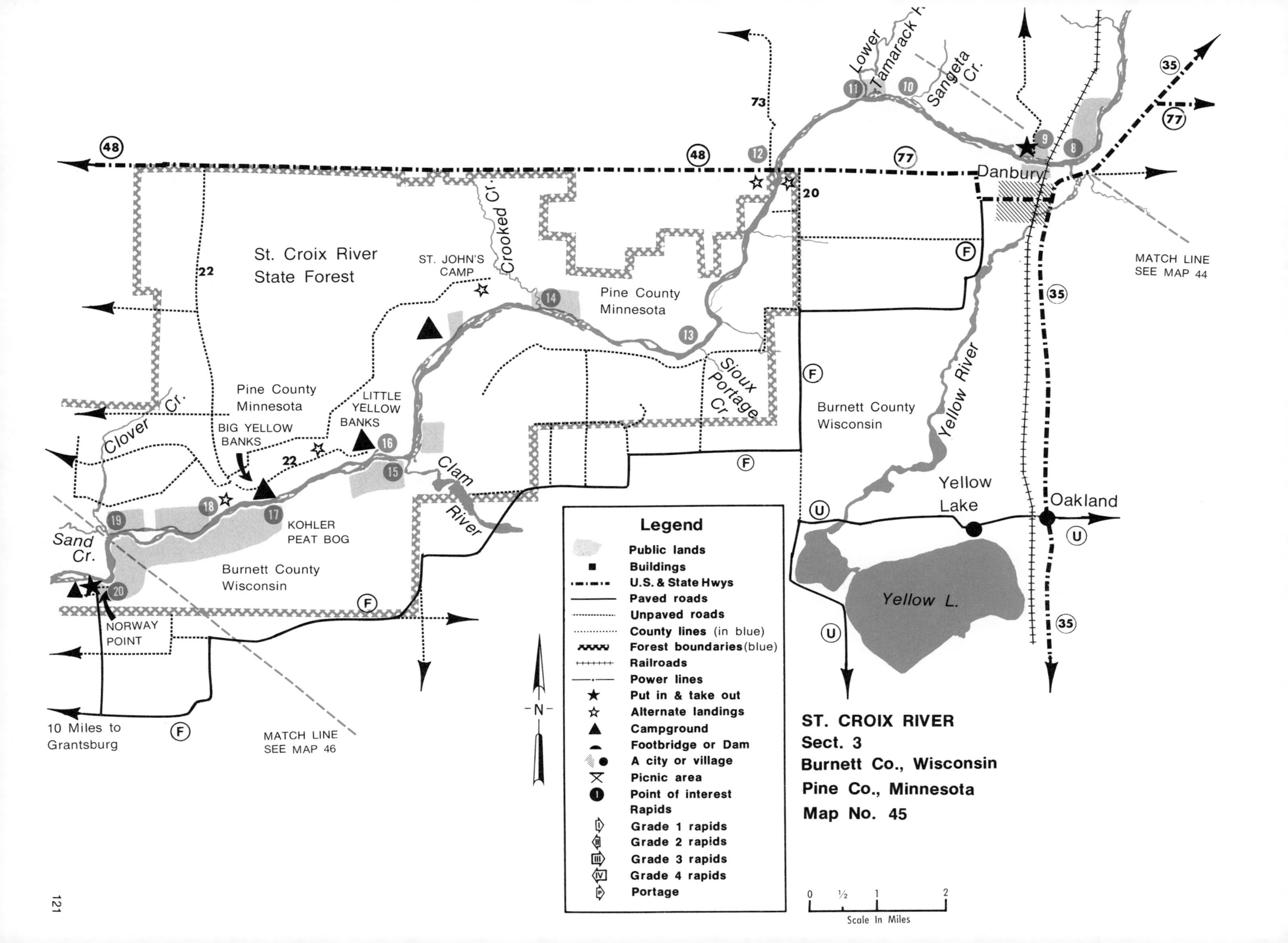

ST. CROIX RIVER
Sect. 3
Burnett Co., Wisconsin
Pine Co., Minnesota
Map No. 45
Legend
Public lands
Buildings
U.S. & State Hwys
Paved roads
Unpaved roads
County lines (in blue)
Forest boundaries (blue)
Railroads
Power lines
Put in & take out
Alternate landings
Campground
Footbridge or Dam
A city or village
Picnic area
Point of interest
Rapids
Grade 1 rapids
Grade 2 rapids
Grade 3 rapids
Grade 4 rapids
Portage
0 ½ 1 2
Scale In Miles
-N-
St. Croix River
State Forest
Pine County
Minnesota
Burnett County
Wisconsin
ST. JOHN'S
CAMP
Crooked Cr.
LITTLE
YELLOW
BANKS
BIG YELLOW
BANKS
KOHLER
PEAT BOG
NORWAY
POINT
Clover Cr.
Sand Cr.
Clam River
Sioux Portage Cr.
Lower Tamarack R.
Sangeta Cr.
Yellow River
Yellow Lake
Yellow L.
Danbury
Oakland
10 Miles to
Grantsburg
MATCH LINE
SEE MAP 44
MATCH LINE
SEE MAP 46
48
77
35
73
20
22
F
U
8
9
10
11
12
13
14
15
16
17
18
19
20

ST. CROIX RIVER

SECTION 4

St. Croix River: Burnett County, Wisconsin and Pine County, Minnesota.
Topo map(s): Grantsburg (1:62,500) 1962 and Pine City (1:62,500) 1961.
Overview map(s): Stillwater, Minnesota (1953).
Public lands: Burnett County plat book (1971) and National Park Service Master Plan (1971).
Section 4
Start: Norway Point.
End: Soderbeck Landing.

	SEC. 4
Difficulty (high water)	**II**
Difficulty (usual summer flow)	**I-II**
Length	**10**
Time	**5**
Width	**50-250**
Gradient	**5**
Drainage area	**2,820**

Water Conditions: The U.S.G.S. gauge is located in Burnett County, Wisc. on the left bank of the Highway 35 bridge at Riverside. Both Sections 4 & 5 are nearly always runnable. At a gauge reading of 1.5 Section 4 becomes a grade II.

SECTION
ft 4 5 cfs
4 3 2 1 0
II 38%
I-II 49%
too low 13%
Q 87%
4000 3000 2000 1000 750 500

Canoeable Days Per Month

month	Apr	May	June	July	Aug	Sep
days	30	31	30	23	20	25

Campgrounds: See description accompanying map 47.
Scenery, Geology, History, Fish: See description accompanying maps 43 and 44.
Points of Interest:

20 (49.4 miles) **Norway Point.** This is the put-in for **Section 4.** This section has numerous I-II rapids. Iron Creek enters from the left.

21 (50.5 miles) **Bear Creek.** Enters from the right.

22 (51.5 miles) **Nelson Landing.** There is a landing on the left bank with primitive camping facilities. This is the last chance to exit before the rapids (grades I and I-II) that begin downstream. There is a good parking lot which holds 20 cars.

23 (51.7 miles) **Pike Rapids.** This is a short easy grade I rapids. About 100 yards downstream there are a series of very large islands that divide the river into two channels. These channels are described separately below.

Left Channel: This channel has fewer rapids than the right channel.

24 (52.5 miles) **Big Beef Rapids.** This is a rather long grade I-II rapids.

25 (53.6 miles) **Main cut across channel.** This marks the nearly halfway point to where the right channel joins the left one. In normal and low water levels this is a 25-minute walk towing the boat around rocks -- if you want to change channels.

26 (55.7 miles) **August Olson Rapids.** This is a shallow-but-easy grade I-II rapids that begins in both channels just above their confluence with one another.

Right Channel:

27 (52.5 miles) **Bearpaw Creek.** Enters from the right. Near this location, loggers are alleged to have blasted away the river to clear logjams. During high water periods in subsequent years this channel increased to its present size.

28 (52.7 miles) **Upper Kettle Rapids.** This is a shallow grade I rapids.

29 (55.0 miles) **Mouth of Kettle River.** Enters from the right. The Kettle River has a total drainage area of 1,093 square miles. This river is regarded as a Wild River by the state of Minnesota. Just downstream of this location there is a long grade I-II rapids. This is followed by August Olson Rapids at the point where the left and right channels join.

30 (58.5 miles) **Redhorse Creek.** About a half mile downstream there are landings on both sides of the river. These landings are the recommended **take-outs** for this section. There is a small parking area for six to eight cars. Note: Some rapids on the map are not graded.

Photo 46. The St. Croix. This river was included in the National Wild and Scenic Rivers Act of 1968.

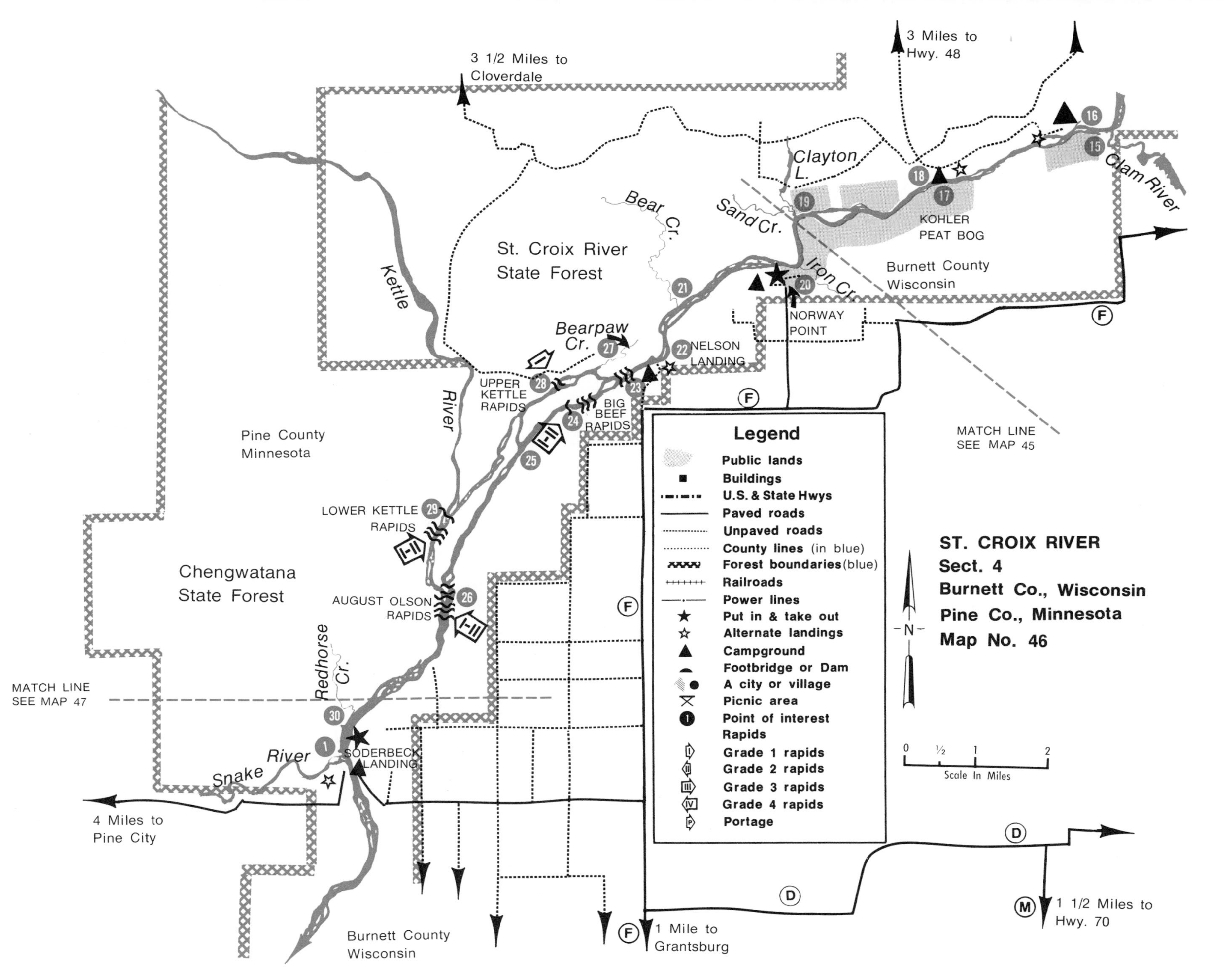
ST. CROIX RIVER
Sect. 4
Burnett Co., Wisconsin
Pine Co., Minnesota
Map No. 46
Legend
Public lands
Buildings
U.S. & State Hwys
Paved roads
Unpaved roads
County lines (in blue)
Forest boundaries (blue)
Railroads
Power lines
Put in & take out
Alternate landings
Campground
Footbridge or Dam
A city or village
Picnic area
Point of interest
Rapids
Grade 1 rapids
Grade 2 rapids
Grade 3 rapids
Grade 4 rapids
Portage
N
0 ½ 1 2
Scale In Miles
3 1/2 Miles to Cloverdale
3 Miles to Hwy. 48
Clayton L.
Bear Cr.
Sand Cr.
Iron Cr.
Clam River
KOHLER PEAT BOG
Burnett County Wisconsin
St. Croix River State Forest
Kettle
River
Bearpaw Cr.
NORWAY POINT
NELSON LANDING
UPPER KETTLE RAPIDS
BIG BEEF RAPIDS
LOWER KETTLE RAPIDS
AUGUST OLSON RAPIDS
Pine County Minnesota
Chengwatana State Forest
MATCH LINE SEE MAP 45
MATCH LINE SEE MAP 47
Redhorse Cr.
Snake River
SODERBECK LANDING
4 Miles to Pine City
Burnett County Wisconsin
1 Mile to Grantsburg
1 1/2 Miles to Hwy. 70

ST. CROIX RIVER

SECTION 5

St. Croix River: Burnett County, Wisconsin and Pine and Chisago Counties, Minnesota.
Topo map(s): Rush City (1:62,500) 1955, Pine City (1:62,500) 1961, and Grantsburg (1:62,500) 1962.
Overview map(s): Stillwater (1953).
Public lands: Burnett County plat book (1971) and National Park Service Master Plan (1971).
Section 5
Start: Soderbeck Landing (Wisc.)--Mouth of Snake River (Minn.)
End: Old Rush City Ferry Crossing (County Highway 0).

	SEC. 5
Difficulty (high water)	Q
Difficulty (usual summer flow)	Q
Length	11
Time	6
Width	100-400
Gradient	10
Drainage area	5,097

Water Conditions: See description accompanying map 46.
Scenery, Geology, History: See description accompanying map 43.
Campgrounds: Interstate Park is located on the St. Croix River (see point of interest 3). There is a user fee for camping at this large DNR campground. For more information write DNR Interstate Park, St. Croix Falls, Wisc. 54024, or call (715) 483-3747.
Points of Interest:

1. (59.2 miles) **Soderbeck Landing.** Downstream from this point there are numerous agricultural areas. The put-in for this quiet stretch of river is on either the Wisconsin or Minnesota side of the river immediately downstream of the Snake River. The Snake River is a State of Minnesota Wild River. There are primitive camping facilities on both sides of the river.
2. (62.3 miles) **Sandstone Cliff.** The top of this cliff provides a panoramic view of the river valley. There is road access, but this area is not a convenient landing.
3. (63.2 miles) **Interstate Park.** There is a landing with a developed camping area on the left bank immediately downstream of the Interstate (Highway 70) bridge.
4. (63.6 miles) **Mouth of Wood River.** Enters from the left.
5. (64.2 miles) **Raspberry Landing.** There is road access on the Wisconsin side of the river.
6. (65.7 miles) **Riffles.** In this area there are a few grade I riffles.
7. (66.0 miles) **Stevens Creek.** Enters from the right. This creek marks the border of Pine and Chisago Counties on the Minnesota side of the river.
8. (66.2 miles) **Unnamed creek.** Enters from the left.
9. (67.5 miles) **Rock Creek.** Enters from the right.
10. (68.5 miles) **Benson Landing.** There is a primitive campsite at this landing which has road access, a U.S.G.S. gauging station is locating on the Minnesota side of the river.
11. (70.0 miles) **Old Rush City Ferry Crossing.** There is a take-out for this stretch on either side of the river. The ferry ceased operation in 1940. If you are headed downstream you might be interested to know that it is approximately 16 river miles to Nevers Dam and 24 miles to St. Croix Falls.

Photo 47. St. Croix River Overview.

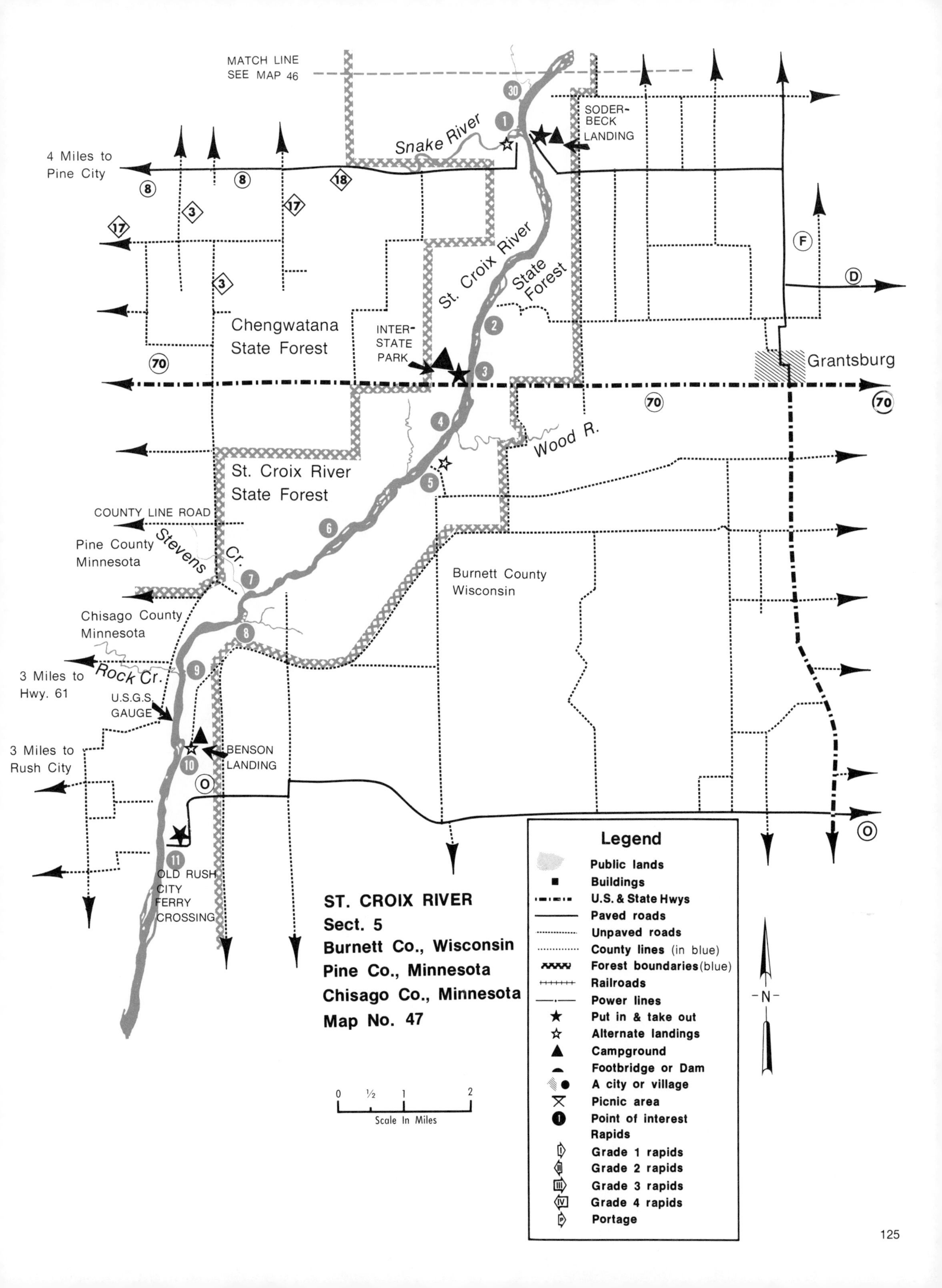
MATCH LINE
SEE MAP 46
SODER-
BECK
LANDING
Snake River
4 Miles to
Pine City
St. Croix River
State Forest
Chengwatana
State Forest
INTER-
STATE
PARK
Grantsburg
Wood R.
St. Croix River
State Forest
COUNTY LINE ROAD
Pine County
Minnesota
Stevens Cr.
Burnett County
Wisconsin
Chisago County
Minnesota
3 Miles to
Hwy. 61
Rock Cr.
U.S.G.S.
GAUGE
3 Miles to
Rush City
BENSON
LANDING
OLD RUSH
CITY
FERRY
CROSSING
ST. CROIX RIVER
Sect. 5
Burnett Co., Wisconsin
Pine Co., Minnesota
Chisago Co., Minnesota
Map No. 47
Legend
Public lands
Buildings
U.S. & State Hwys
Paved roads
Unpaved roads
County lines (in blue)
Forest boundaries (blue)
Railroads
Power lines
Put in & take out
Alternate landings
Campground
Footbridge or Dam
A city or village
Picnic area
Point of interest
Rapids
Grade 1 rapids
Grade 2 rapids
Grade 3 rapids
Grade 4 rapids
Portage
0 ½ 1 2
Scale In Miles
N

TOMAHAWK RIVER

Tomahawk River: Oneida County, Wisconsin.
Topo maps: McCord (1:48,000) 1940 planimetric and Heafford Junction (1:62,550) 1946.
Overview map: Iron Mountain (1954).
Public lands : Oneida County platbook (1968).
Start: Willow Dam.
End: Prairie Rapids Road Bridge upstream of Lake Nokomis.

Difficulty (high water)	**Q3**
Difficulty (usual summer flow)	**Q2**
Length	**18**
Time	**10**
Gradient	**3**
Drainage area	**543**

Water Conditions: The ease of this trip depends on water level and on the release from the Willow Dam. The dam has one gate. A gate height of 15" produces a flow of 350 cfs. which is about minimum for an enjoyable run, although Halfbreed Rapids is too shallow unless there is an 18" gate (450 cfs.).

History: The Willow Dam was constructed in 1924 by the Wisconsin Valley Improvement Company.

Scenery: There is moderate development along the shoreline particularly in areas where there are cottages. However, there is an abundant variety of wildlife including bald eagles.

Points of Interest:

1. (0.0 miles) **Willow Dam.** The recommended **put-in** is just below this dam. There is limited parking available at this site.
2. (1.5 miles) **Oelhafen Creek.** This creek enters from the right.
3. (3.0 miles) **County Highway Y Bridge.** Not far upstream of this bridge Bear Creek enters from the left. Brown trout are found in this creek.
4. (5.0 miles) **Half-Breed Rapids.** This is the most difficult of the two rapids on this stretch of river. It rates grade II-III; these rapids require a lot of maneuvering and a sharp eye for rocks. **Scouting is recommended.** The island that is located near the left shore at the end of the rapids can usually be run on either side, but don't wait until the last minute to decide. The portage trail is on the left bank, along an old road (quarter mile). If you choose to line your boat through, the right side is usually best.
5. (6.0 miles) **Swan Creek.** This creek enters the river from the left. There is a private landing located here. Seek permission from the owner beforehand if you wish to use it.
6. (6.1 miles) **Rocky Run.** This trout stream has brook trout.
7. (7.9 miles) **Johnson Creek.** This trout stream also has brook trout.
8. (10.2 miles) **Swamp Lake Road Bridge.**
9. (14.5 miles) **Swamp Creek.** There is a landing on the right bank shortly downstream of the mouth of this creek.
10. (17.3 miles) **Prairie Rapids.** This is an easy grade II rapids in two pitches. The upper pitch is shallow and rocky, the lower pitch has a rather obvious chute. There is also a landing here on the right bank. So if you elect not to run this rapids you can take out here rather than **portage** on the right bank.
11. (17.6 miles) **Prairie Rapids Road Bridge.** This is the recommended **take-out.**

Photo 48. Amidst the birch and pine lies the silent Tomahawk.

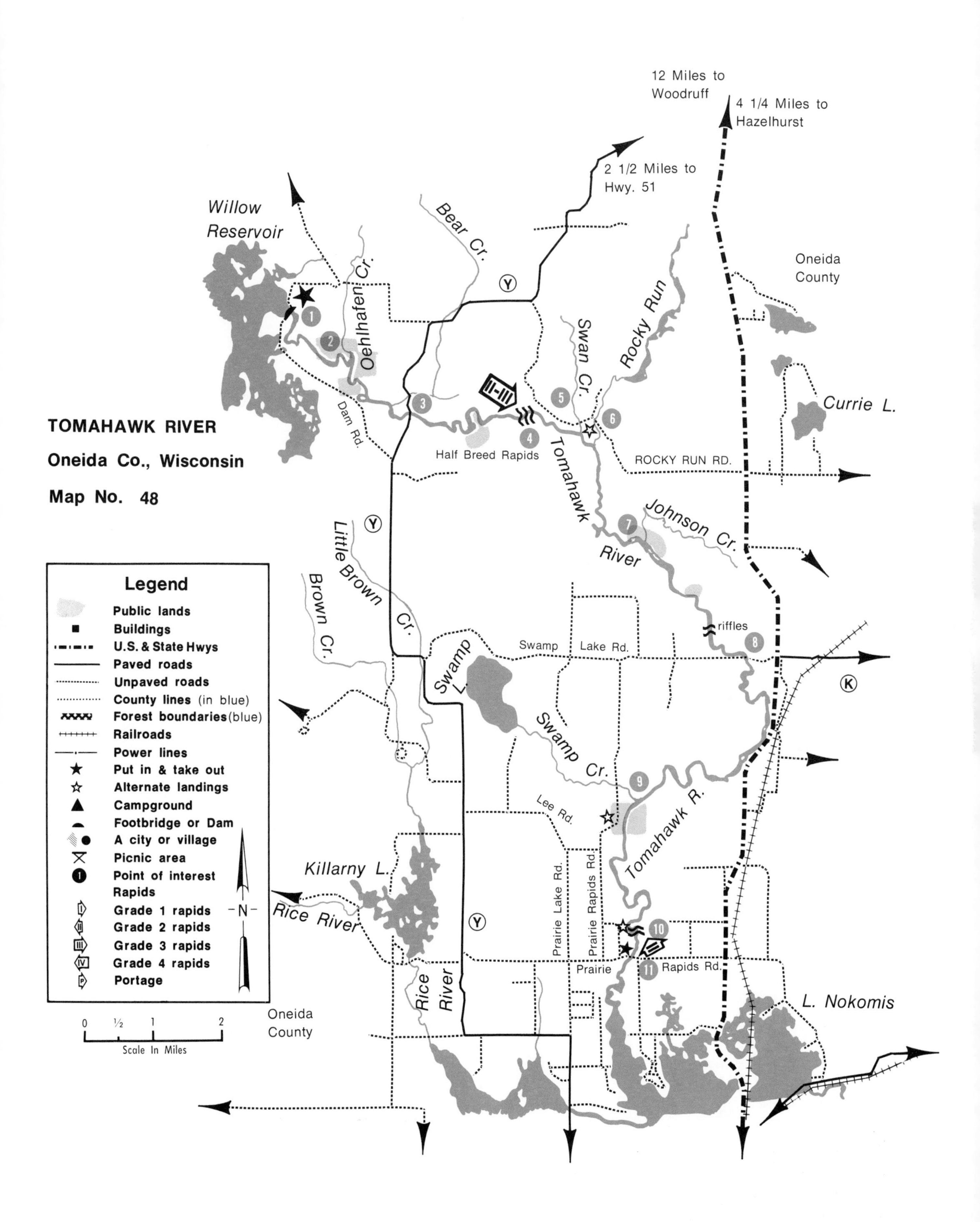
TOMAHAWK RIVER
Oneida Co., Wisconsin
Map No. 48
Legend
Public lands
Buildings
U.S. & State Hwys
Paved roads
Unpaved roads
County lines (in blue)
Forest boundaries (blue)
Railroads
Power lines
Put in & take out
Alternate landings
Campground
Footbridge or Dam
A city or village
Picnic area
Point of interest
Rapids
Grade 1 rapids
Grade 2 rapids
Grade 3 rapids
Grade 4 rapids
Portage
N
0 ½ 1 2
Scale In Miles
12 Miles to Woodruff
4 1/4 Miles to Hazelhurst
2 1/2 Miles to Hwy. 51
Willow Reservoir
Oehlhafen Cr.
Bear Cr.
Swan Cr.
Rocky Run
Oneida County
Currie L.
Dam Rd.
Half Breed Rapids
Tomahawk River
ROCKY RUN RD.
Johnson Cr.
Little Brown Cr.
Brown Cr.
riffles
Swamp Lake Rd.
Swamp L.
Swamp Cr.
Lee Rd.
Tomahawk R.
Killarny L.
Rice River
Prairie Lake Rd.
Prairie Rapids Rd.
Prairie Rapids Rd.
L. Nokomis
Oneida County
Y
K

WHITE RIVER

White River: Ashland and Bayfield Counties, Wisconsin.
Topo map(s): Grandview (1:48,000) 1944 planimetric and Marengo (1:62,500) 1967.
Overview map(s): Ashland (1953).
Public lands: Ashland County (1969) and Bayfield County (1967) plat books.
Start: Town Road due east of the town of Mason.
End: Highway 112 bridge.

Difficulty (high water)	**II**
Difficulty (usual summer flow)	**I-II**
Length	**14**
Time	**6**
Width	**30-100**
Gradient	**10**
Drainage area	**243**

Water Conditions: There is a U.S.G.S. gauge located downstream of the Highway 112 bridge at the take-out. The average flow has been 286 cfs for the past 22 years. There is nearly always enough water for a pleasant run. The water is rather muddy so it is difficult to see the many rocks. This entire stretch is nearly a continuous grade I-II rapids. See canoeability chart.

ft / cfs
3 — 1250
1000
750
2 — 500
250
1 — 150
100
I-II
>90%
too low
< 10%

Scenery: An excellent trip. There is virtually no development on the shoreline except for brief stretches near the put-in and take-out. Wildlife and wild flowers predominate.
Geology: The bedrock of this river is similar to that of the Bois Brule. As with the lower part of the Bois Brule, the banks of the river are steep cliffs of red clay. Erosion is common, so the water is frequently muddy. Occassionally there are downed trees to avoid.
Fish: The entire river is noted for its excellent trout fishing.
Campgrounds: Ranch Park is a private campground owned by Edward J. Sander. There are 15 sites. Write Rt. 1, Ashland, Wisc. 54806, or call (715) 746-2424 for more information. There is also a Wisconsin DNR campground located at Copper Falls State Park near Mellen, Wisconsin. See map 1 for the location of this park and additional information on camping.

Points of Interest:

1. (0.0 miles) **Town Road Bridge.** The recommended put-in is at a bridge on a town road located due east of the village of Mason.
2. (1.0 miles) **Landing.** There is a privately owned landing that has very limited parking available. Access is obtained by climbing down a very steep, wooded hillside.
3. (4.2 miles) **Schrumm Creek.** Enters from the left.
4. (13.4 miles) **County line.** The border of Ashland and Bayfield Counties. The rest of the river consists of quiet water.
5. (14.2 miles) **White River Dam.** The recommended take-out is at the public access on the left side of the flowage and is maintained by the Lake Superior District Power Company.

Photo 50. Structures such as this abandoned barn are reminders of the agricultural, mining and lumbering activity that once prevailed in northwestern Wisconsin.

Caution: Make certain the reservoir at the take-out is holding water before making this run. At certain times, especially in late fall, the dam is opened and the flowage drained. What once was a quiet flowage becomes a raging torrent of continuous standing waves through a narrow channel that ends in a grade VI-plus drop. To escape the potential disaster, it would be necessary to slog out through foot-deep mud flats, a rather unpleasant alternative.

Photo 49. Although photographed elsewhere, add more water and you have the White River.

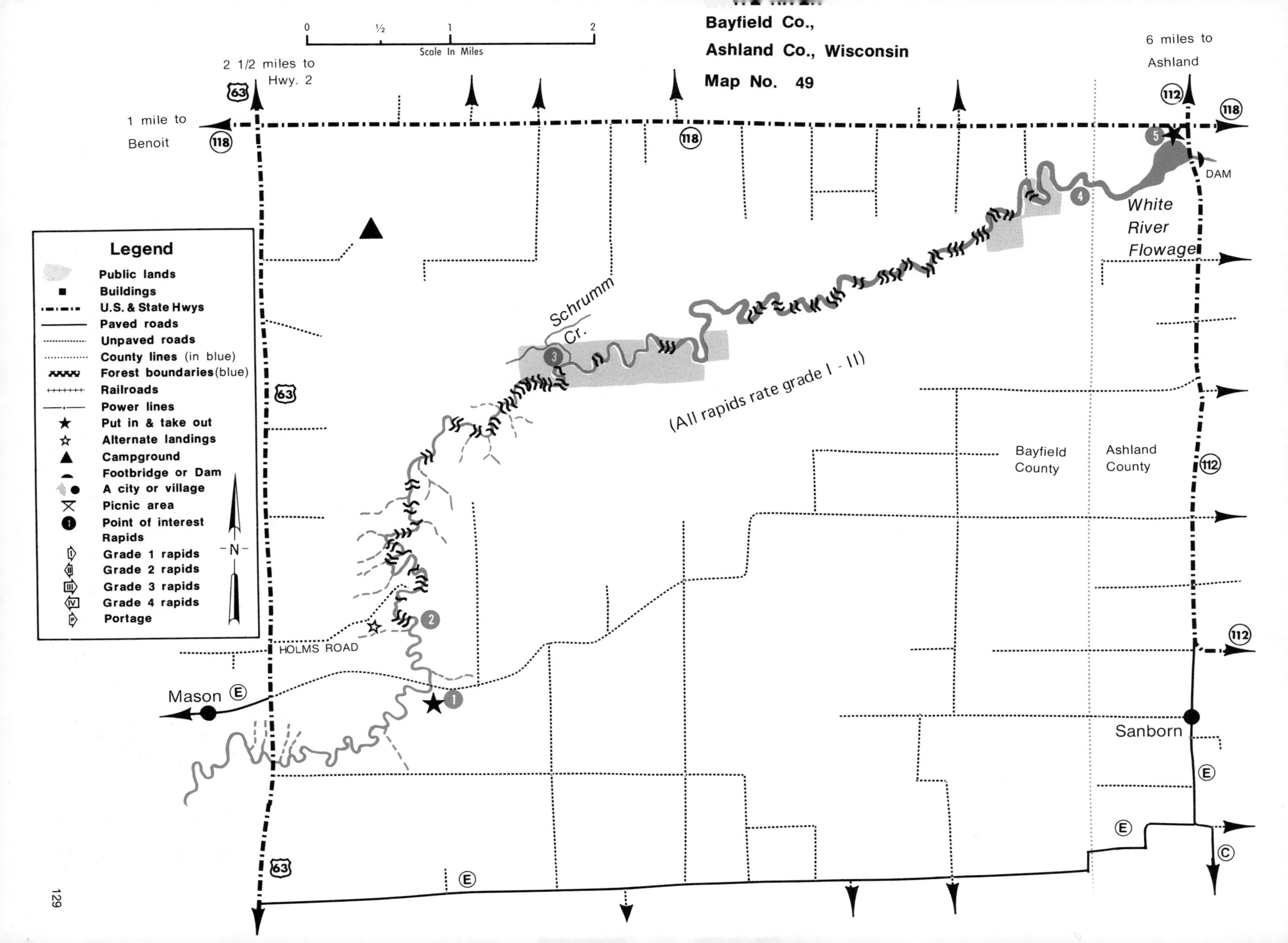

Bayfield Co.,
Ashland Co., Wisconsin
Map No. 49
0
½
1
2
Scale In Miles
2 1/2 miles to
Hwy. 2
1 mile to
Benoit
6 miles to
Ashland
63
118
112
DAM
White
River
Flowage
Schrumm
Cr.
(All rapids rate grade I - II)
Bayfield
County
Ashland
County
HOLMS ROAD
Mason
E
Sanborn
C
Legend
Public lands
Buildings
U.S. & State Hwys
Paved roads
Unpaved roads
County lines (in blue)
Forest boundaries (blue)
Railroads
Power lines
Put in & take out
Alternate landings
Campground
Footbridge or Dam
A city or village
Picnic area
Point of interest
Rapids
Grade 1 rapids
Grade 2 rapids
Grade 3 rapids
Grade 4 rapids
Portage
N

WISCONSIN RIVER

Wisconsin River: Dane, Sauk and Iowa Counties, Wisconsin.

Topo maps: Baraboo (1:62,500) 1959, Cross Plains (1:62,500) 1962, Blue Mounds (1:62,500) 1962, Spring Green (1:62,500) 1960.
Overview maps: Madison (1957) and La Crosse (1955).
Public lands: Plat books, Dane Co. (1971), Sauk Co. (1970), Iowa (1971).
Section 1
Start: Prairie du Sac Dam.
End: Prairie du Sac Dam.
Section 2
Start: Municipal parking lot in Sauk City (on the river, just upstream of the Highway 12 bridge.
End: Arena (River Road).
Section 3
Start: Arena.
End: Lone Rock. State Highway 130 bridge.

	SEC. 1	SEC. 2	SEC. 3
Difficulty (high water)	I-II	Q	Q
Difficulty (summer)	I-II	Q	Q
Length	1/2	15	19

Time: Section 1 is a practice area, you can spend as much or as little time here as you wish. **Sections 2 and 3** are one day trips. The time required to run them depends on how fast you paddle.
Scenery: Very beautiful. This section of river is amazingly remote and peaceful for southern Wisconsin.
Geology: The bedrock is Upper Cambrian sandstone covered with alluvial sand and gravel in the river valley.
History: Tower Hill State Park is one of the most historic sites in southern Wisconsin. In 1832 the American troops crossed the river here in pursuit of Chief Black Hawk. It was here where the shot industry of southern Wisconsin was started (with lead from mines at Mineral Point). This industry drew many settlers into Wisconsin after the Black Hawk War. Nearby Helena was once a prosperous and fairly well sized village, which at one time rivaled Madison as a proposed location for the state capital. This village disappeared after the Civil War.
Campgrounds: Tower Hill State Park. This developed campground with 22 sites is located on County Highway C south of Spring Green on the Wisconsin River. It is open year round and a user fee is charged. Write Tower Hill State Park, Rt. 3, Spring Green, WI 53588 or call (608)588-2116.

Prairie du Sac Village Park. Exactly 2 miles north on Highway 78 from the stop and go light in Sauk City turn right. Located on the river, it is marked by two cement flower pots and two inconspicuous signs on the left side of the road "River St." and "Free Boat Landing." There are a number of free sites here.
Section 1: The rapids below Prairie du Sac dam provide the boaters in south-central Wisconsin with a convenient practice area. To get to the dam, go 2 1/2 miles north from the intersection of Highways 12 and 78 in Sauk City, turn right onto a paved road marked by a sign "Allen's Typewriter Service." When the road forks go right. The rapids are located on the right half of the river just below the dam turbines. Put in at the Wisconsin Power and Light Company parking lot on the right shore just below the dam. The rapids are about 100 yards long and are about as wide. The grade of difficulty depends on the number of turbines in operation at the dam. When only one or two of the turbines are in operation, there are several exposed rocks which create eddies extending halfway across the rapids. This is a good place to practice rapids maneuvers such as eddy turns, ferrying and surfing -- which are necessary for safe and pleasurable rapids boating. There is a large eddy that extends the entire length of the rapids along this shore. By traveling up river in the eddy, "peeling out" into the current, riding the haystacks, and turning back into the eddy, the boater can complete a clockwise course with a minimum of exertion. Since the rapids are quite wide, the novice is advised to stay close to the right shore. The current is very strong and a tipover in the center of the river will result in a very long swim downstream. **(On this as on all other rapids, you should always wear a life jacket.)** Avoid the backroller that extends across the rapids just below the turbines. This is a long regular back wave which conceals numerous iron pilings and will hold a canoe or kayak indefinitely with little or no chance of escape unless the turbines are shut down. During periods of peak power demand, when 3 or more of the turbines are operating, most of the rocks in the center of the rapids are subjerged and the eddies below them disappear. The eddy along the right shore remains however and a long train of standing waves develops to the left of the eddy. These waves can reach 3-4 feet in height and provide an exciting ride.

During the summer months the shoreline is lined with fishermen usually along the lower half of the rapids and the washout below. To avoid the wrath of the fishermen and their fish hooks it is best to stay clear of them.
Sections 2 and 3: A boater can vary the length of this trip according to his own desires. One put-in is just below the Prairie du Sac power dam (see Section 1). Our suggested put-in is at the municipal parking lot on the river just upstream of the Highway 12 bridge in Sauk City. It is an easy one-day paddle from the dam to Arena and a two-day paddle to Lone Rock. Caution: If you camp on the islands pull your canoes far out of the water. Water level can fluctuate as much as two feet overnight.

Points of Interest:

1. (0.0 miles) **Prairie du Sac dam.** Put in on the west side.
2. (1.4 miles) **Highway 60 bridge.**
3. (3.0 miles) **Highway 12 bridge in Sauk City.** Put in the west bank above the bridge at the municipal parking lot.
4. (3.4 miles) **R. R. bridge. Caution: Beware of severe current differentials at this bridge.**
5. (8.5 miles) **Ferry bluff** on right bank.
6. (15.0 miles) **Arena.** Houses on left bank. Take-out here at boat ramp. River Road leads directly to this landing.
7. (22.0 miles) **R. R. bridge.**
8. (22.5 miles) **Highway 14 bridge.**
9. (24.0 miles) **Tower Hill State Park** on left bank.
10. (24.5 miles) **Highway 23 bridge.** Take-out on right bank just above bridge.
11. (34.0 miles) **Highway 130 bridge.** This is also a possible take-out.

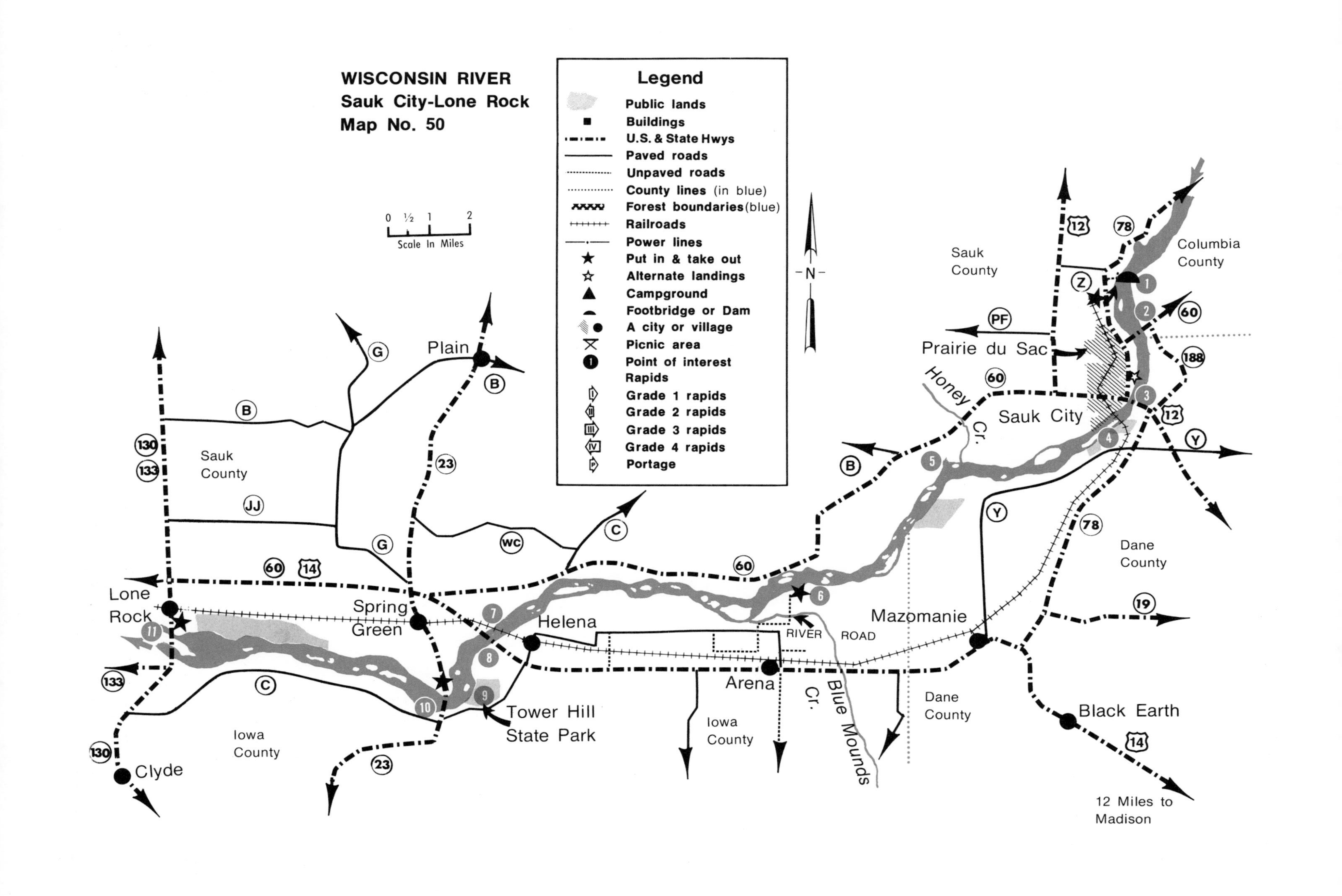
WISCONSIN RIVER
Sauk City-Lone Rock
Map No. 50
0 ½ 1 2
Scale In Miles
Legend
Public lands
Buildings
U.S. & State Hwys
Paved roads
Unpaved roads
County lines (in blue)
Forest boundaries (blue)
Railroads
Power lines
Put in & take out
Alternate landings
Campground
Footbridge or Dam
A city or village
Picnic area
Point of interest
Rapids
Grade 1 rapids
Grade 2 rapids
Grade 3 rapids
Grade 4 rapids
Portage
N
Sauk County
Columbia County
Prairie du Sac
Sauk City
Honey Cr.
Dane County
Mazomanie
RIVER ROAD
Blue Mounds Cr.
Arena
Iowa County
Black Earth
12 Miles to Madison
Helena
Tower Hill State Park
Spring Green
Plain
Lone Rock
Clyde

WISCONSIN RIVER

THE DELLS

Wisconsin River (The Dells): Sauk, Juneau, Adams, and Columbia Counties, Wisconsin.
Topo map: Wisconsin Dells (1:62,500) 1957.
Overview map: Madison (1957).
Public lands: Plat books, Sauk Co. (1970), Juneau Co. (1972), Columbia Co. (1968), Adams Co. (1970).
Start: Pine Ridge Campgrounds on County Highway N.
End: Lake Lee.

Difficulty (high water)	**Q**
Difficulty (usual summer flow)	**Q**
Length	**4.5**
Time	**3**

Water Conditions: The river varies in width from 50 to 1,000 feet and up to 150 feet in depth.
Scenery: The wind and weather have aided the rock outcroppings and sheer cliffs in developing a unique character not seen elsewhere in Wisconsin in such an overwhelming display. The softer elements, being more submissive to the weathering, have left behind intricate and gargoylic sculptures of the harder rock.
Geology: The bedrock is upper Cambrian Potsdam sandstone with overlying alluvial sand and glacial drift.
History: In the 1830's, some 30 years before he became president of the Southern Confederacy, Jefferson Davis was an officer at Fort Winnebago near Portage. Davis and a group of soldiers went north of the Dalles and did some logging for the construction of buildings at the fort, then rafted the logs through what is known today as the Dells of the Wisconsin River. Few people visited the Dells until the 1890's, when it had been deserted by lumbermen.
Campgrounds: Pine Ridge Campground. On County Highway N about one half mile north of Stand Rock, where the road makes an S bend. This is a privately owned campground with a few primitive sites. A small user fee is charged. For more information call (414) 254-7190. Camping is also allowed on the sandy beaches below (not on) Blackhawk Island. However, permits are required to camp here and they are sold by the people patroling the beaches by motor boat. Also see the description accompanying map 25.

It is important to remember that there are commercial boats operating in this area. Please try not to get in their way or tie up their dock space. Also watch out for the large waves produced by these boats, they could swamp an open canoe.

Points of Interest:

1 (0.0 miles) This is an **alternate put-in** where Highway 13 crosses Corning Creek, which enters from the left, approximately six and a half miles north of Wisconsin Dells. There are also several possible put-ins north of this one. However, the usual southerly wind is very strong. The disadvantage of these landings is the hard work required to canoe the four-mile flowage. Among the advantages in the autumn are the beautiful colors. There is also an alternate put-in at a bar just below Gilmore Creek, but there is a charge to put in there.

2 (0.6 miles) **Trout Creek.** Enters from the right.

3 (2.0 miles) **Plainville Creek.** Enters from the left.

4 (2.9 miles) **Shadduck Creek.** Enters from the left.

Our suggested put-in is at Pine Ridge Campground (see "Campgrounds"). The owners will charge a nominal fee to put in. This put-in is just upstream and across the river from Witches Gulch.

5 (4.2 miles) **Witches Gulch. Note the funnel-like entrance.** If it is at all windy, the waves tend to build as you enter the canyon, and you may not make it out. **Beware: Land on the rocks under the walkway.** This is a high-walled sandstone canyon carved out by water erosion. The trail into the gulch is highlighted by small falls, unique erosion patterns, and abundant flora. (Be prepared to pay to get out of your boat here.)

On the west side of the river, directly across from Witches Gulch and just downstream of the suggested put-in, is Stand Rock. Land on the sand beach below the walkway. The walkway is a circular route to the amphitheater and various rock formations. Fees are charged to land here, also.

This is a word of warning about the canyon which goes from Witches Gulch to below Blackhawk Island: **It is a narrow canyon with rock walls. There are large commercial boats using this route during the summer months. The wake of these boats can rebound off the rocks and a canoeist is suddenly faced with waves coming at him from both directions.**

6 (4.8 miles) **Roode's Glen** is small and easy to miss. It is on the east side of the river, just above Steamboat Rock Island. This glen is particularly worthwhile as the commercial tour boats bypass it. Pull up to the end. The top of the cliff makes a nice place to eat lunch with a scenic view of the river. This one is free.

7 (6.2 miles) **Coldwater Canyon** is essentially like Witches Gulch. If you land, try pulling up past the docks. There are no really good landings, so you may have to walk in the mud.

After the narrows near Blackhawk Island, the river widens and there are several nice swimming beaches. Be sure to see the swallow nests under the cliffs on the east side. You need a permit to camp on these sandy beaches. Blackhawk Island is private property.

8 (8.0 miles) **Take-out at Lake Lee.** To get to Lake Lee by car from the suggested put-in follow Highway N south until it changes to Highway A, take Highway 13 east across the river to the first stop and go light, and turn left onto Superior Street. This becomes River Road after several blocks. A few blocks later turn left onto Illinois Avenue. Park near the railroad tracks about two blocks down.

Alternate Trip. *If you have only one car and would like to paddle a circular route, you can put-in from County Highway N at Blackhawk Island. The road comes very close to the river at this point and it's an easy climb down the bank to put in. From here you can paddle upstream, where there is no noticeable current, as far as you wish, and then paddle the return trip on the opposite side of the island. Also, there are possible trips on the lower Dells where there are several caves along the river that are worth paddling into.*

Photo 51. Although taken elsewhere, the cliffs (and "pleasure craft") are reminiscent of the Wisconsin Dells.

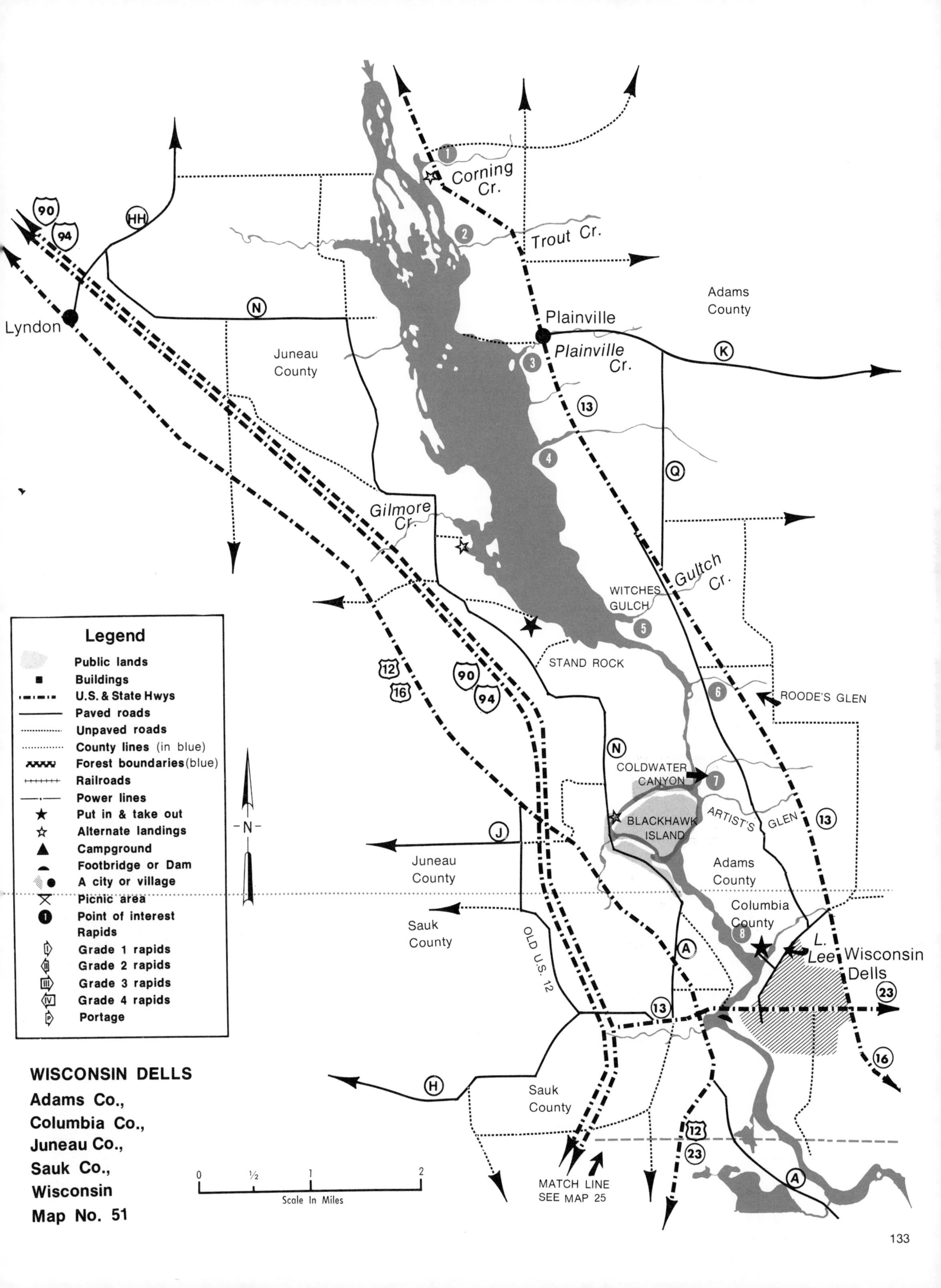
Corning Cr.
Trout Cr.
Plainville
Adams County
Lyndon
Juneau County
Plainville Cr.
Gilmore Cr.
WITCHES GULCH
Gulch Cr.
STAND ROCK
ROODE'S GLEN
COLDWATER CANYON
BLACKHAWK ISLAND
ARTIST'S GLEN
Juneau County
Adams County
Columbia County
Sauk County
OLD U.S. 12
L. Lee
Wisconsin Dells
Sauk County
MATCH LINE
SEE MAP 25
Legend
Public lands
Buildings
U.S. & State Hwys
Paved roads
Unpaved roads
County lines (in blue)
Forest boundaries (blue)
Railroads
Power lines
Put in & take out
Alternate landings
Campground
Footbridge or Dam
A city or village
Picnic area
Point of interest
Rapids
Grade 1 rapids
Grade 2 rapids
Grade 3 rapids
Grade 4 rapids
Portage
0 ½ 1 2
Scale In Miles
WISCONSIN DELLS
Adams Co.,
Columbia Co.,
Juneau Co.,
Sauk Co.,
Wisconsin
Map No. 51

WOLF RIVER

SECTION 1

Wolf River: Langlade County, Wisconsin.
Topo maps: Lily (1.48,000) 1950 planimetric and White Lake (1:48,000) 1952 planimetric.
Overview map: Iron Mountain (1954).
Public lands: Langlade County plat book (1971), updated to January 1973 with Wisconsin DNR records.
Section 1
Start: Highway 55 bridge in Lily.
End: Hollister.

	SEC. 1
Difficulty (high water)	II-III
Difficulty (usual summer flow)	II
Length	7
Time	4
Width	20-100
Gradient	10
Drainage area	460

Water Conditions: For current information on levels, call Whitewater Specialty in White Lake at (715) 882-5400.

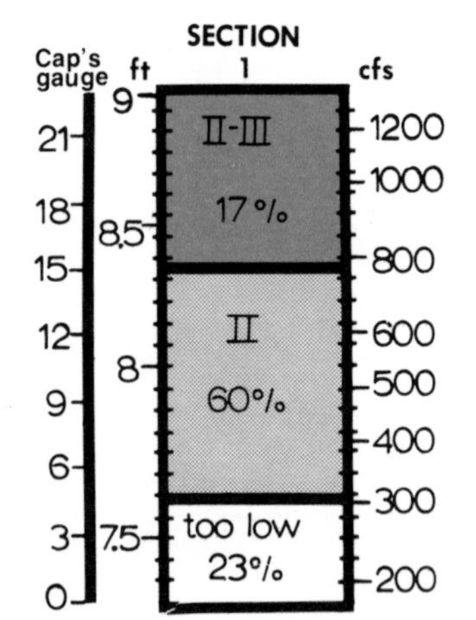

Canoeable Days Per Month

month	Apr	May	June	July	Aug	Sep
days	30	31	30	20	14	16

Scenery: The scenery is very good to excellent. The Wisconsin DNR is currently attempting to acquire land (under the ORAP-200 program) along the entire shoreline of the Wolf River from a location slightly upstream of Pearson and continuing downstream to Menominee County.

Geology: The bedrock of this river is composed of granite and other igneous rock, which comprise the boulders in the rapids. The extensive quiet-water sections are found where the river flows through areas with shallow sand and gravel beds.

Fishing: If you want to fish a nationally renowned trout stream--brown, brook, rainbow--then this section and the entire Wolf River upstream of Keshena is just what you're looking for.

Campgrounds: See description accompanying map 55.

If you wish to extend this stretch by 12 miles you could put in at the County Highway A bridge near Pearson. That portion of the river is most suitable in high water. There are only a few minor rapids in that stretch.

Points of Interest:

1. (0.0 miles) **Lily.** The put-in is on the right bank of the Lily River above Highway 55 bridge in Lily. This short stretch of the Lily River until its confluence with the Wolf may be quite shallow. A half mile downstream there is what appears to a permanent logjam; usually the opening in the center is runnable. Eagle Rapids, a grade I rock garden, is located one-half-mile downstream from the logjam. Between this rapids and the Big Slough Gundy, there are three minor rock gardens, none of which rate above grade I.

2. (2.5 miles) **Big Slough Gundy Rapids.** This is a relatively easy, grade I-II rapids.

3. (3.0 miles) **Little Slough Gundy Rapids.** This grade II rapids is a bit harder than Big Slough Gundy and may rate grade III in very high water. There is a landing located here on the left bank. Several hundred yards downstream, there is a rock garden that is known as Little Sheen Rapids. Below this, there are four miles of quiet water until you reach the rock garden at Hollister.

4. (6.8 miles) **Hollister.** This is the take-out for Section 1 and the put-in for Section 2. There is a small grade I rock garden here.

Photo 52. A rock garden on the upper Wolf.

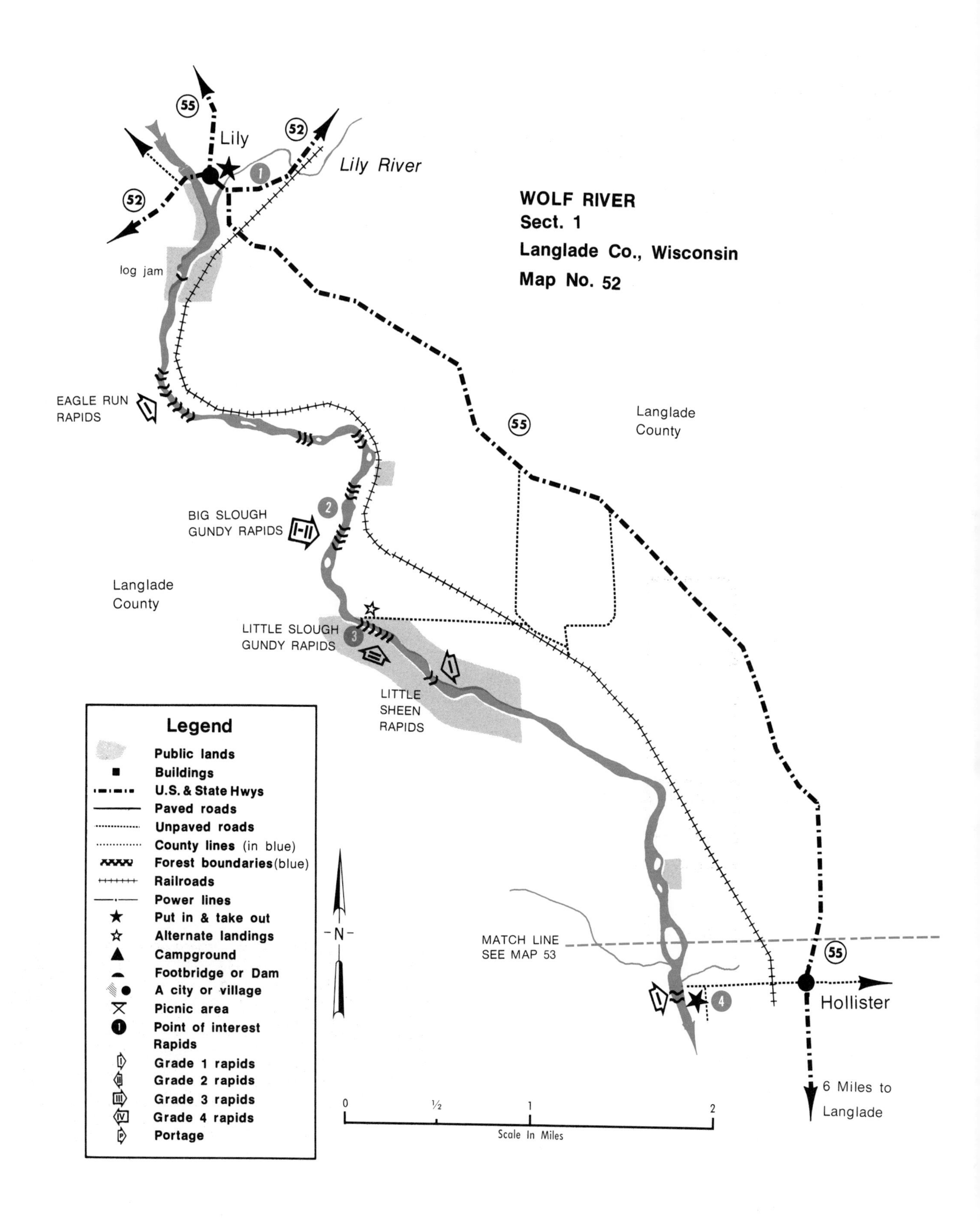
WOLF RIVER
Sect. 1
Langlade Co., Wisconsin
Map No. 52
Lily
Lily River
55
52
log jam
EAGLE RUN
RAPIDS
BIG SLOUGH
GUNDY RAPIDS
I-II
Langlade
County
LITTLE SLOUGH
GUNDY RAPIDS
LITTLE
SHEEN
RAPIDS
Langlade
County
MATCH LINE
SEE MAP 53
Hollister
6 Miles to
Langlade
Legend
Public lands
Buildings
U.S. & State Hwys
Paved roads
Unpaved roads
County lines (in blue)
Forest boundaries(blue)
Railroads
Power lines
Put in & take out
Alternate landings
Campground
Footbridge or Dam
A city or village
Picnic area
Point of interest
Rapids
Grade 1 rapids
Grade 2 rapids
Grade 3 rapids
Grade 4 rapids
Portage
-N-
0
½
1
2
Scale In Miles

WOLF RIVER

SECTION 2

Wolf River: Langlade County, Wisconsin.

Topo maps: Lily (1:48,000) 1950 planimetric, White Lake (1:48,000) 1952 planimetric, and Langlade (1:48,000) 1952 planimetric.

Overview map: Iron Mountain (1954).

Public lands: Langlade County (1971) plat book updated to January 1973 with Wisconsin DNR records.

Section 2

Start: Hollister.

End: Highway 64 bridge in Langlade.

	SEC. 2
Difficulty (high water)	II-III
Difficulty (usual summer flow)	II
Length	8
Time	4
Width	30-100
Gradient	14
Drainage area	469*

*This calculation is at the junction with Nine Mile Creek about one mile downstream of the start of this section.

Water Conditions: For current information on levels, call Whitewater Specialty in White Lake at (715) 882-5400.

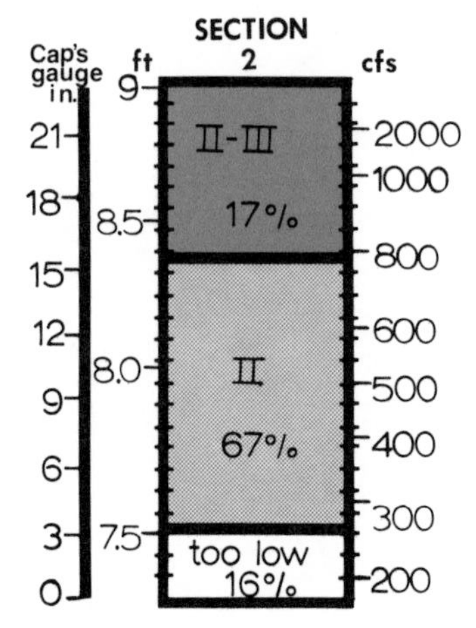

Canoeable Days Per Month

month	Apr	May	June	July	Aug	Sep
days	30	31	30	22	20	21

Scenery, Geology, Fish: See description accompanying map 52.
Campgrounds: See map 54 and accompanying description.

Points of Interest:

4 (6.8 miles) **Hollister.** This is the take-out for Section 1 and the put-in for Section 2. There is a small grade I rock garden at this location.

5 (10.0 miles) **Oxbow Rapids.** This is the first real rapids on this stretch. This is a rather long, grade II rapids, with five pitches. It is not particularly difficult.

6 (10.4 miles) **Nine Mile Rapids.** A rather long, grade II rapids.

7 (10.7 miles) **Fly fishing only.** Most of the Wolf River is excellent trout water. In this stretch fishermen are restricted to the use of flies as bait.

8 (12.3 miles) **Dierck's Landing.** This location is also known as the Irrigation Ditch. There is an island at that point. The irrigation pump is visible from the left channel however, the right channel is most frequently run. This is a convenient landing with limited parking available. Some of the finest rapids on the Wolf are located in the next 25 miles downstream from here.

9 (13.2 miles) **Cedar Rapids.** This short grade II rapids is laced with granite boulders and is very typical of most rapids on this river. At a reading of 800-1000 cfs (15-18 on Cap's gauge), large waves develop in these rapids and at Sherry and Lazelere Rapids below. At this higher water level, these three rapids rate a grade III for open canoes.

10 (13.7 miles) **Sherry Rapids.** Another long grade II rapids with lots of rocks to dodge. This rapids may rate grade III in high water.

11 (14.1 miles) **Lazelere Rapids.** A grade II rapids that is very similiar to Sherry Rapids but is not as long. Its approach is signaled by a large island upstream. It may also rate grade III in high water.

12 (15.2 miles) **Langlade.** Take-out is below the Highway 64 bridge on the left bank.

Photo 53. Rafting on the Wolf.

Photo 54. Playing in Hanson's Rips.

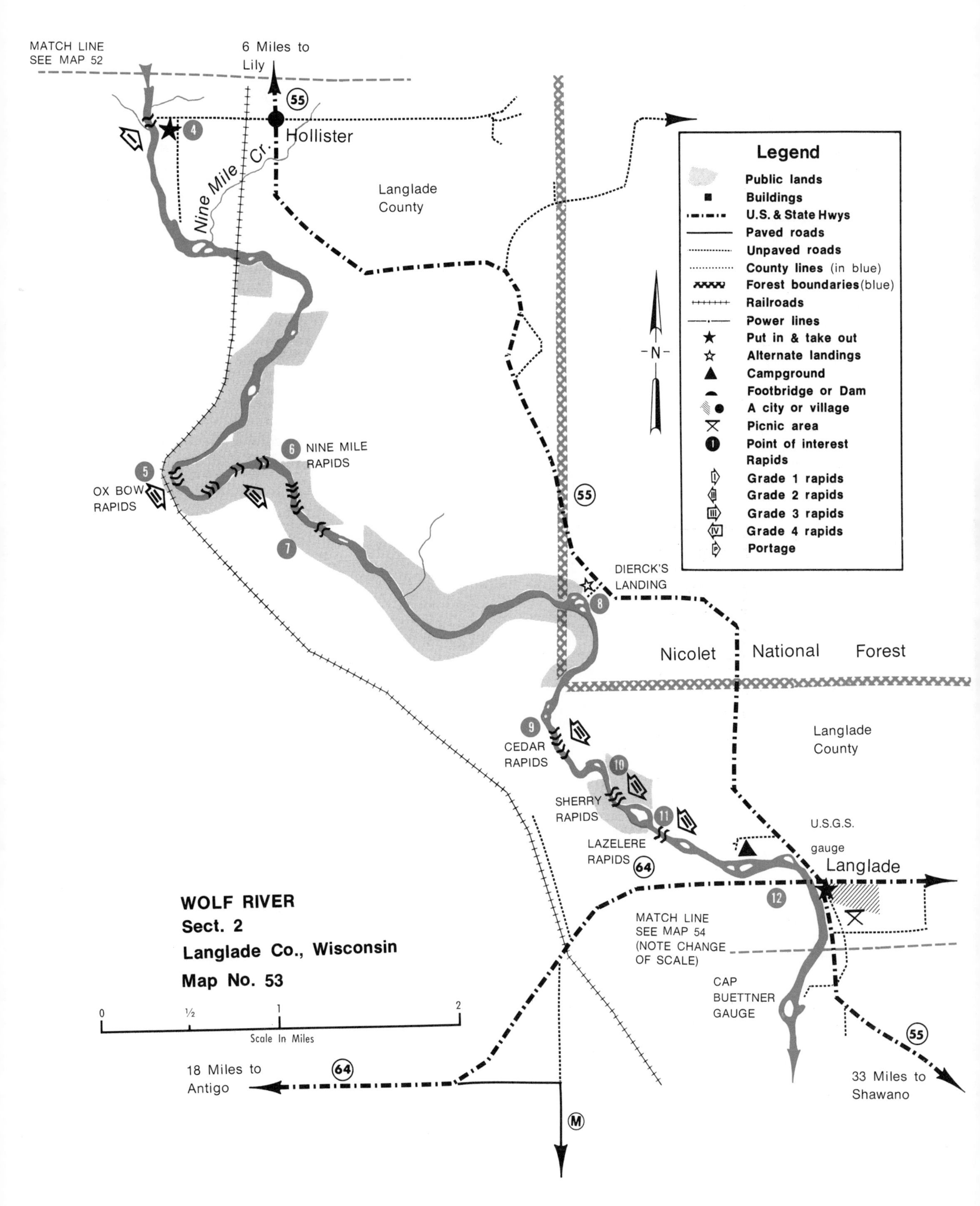
MATCH LINE
SEE MAP 52
6 Miles to
Lily
55
4
Hollister
Nine Mile Cr.
Langlade
County
Legend
Public lands
Buildings
U.S. & State Hwys
Paved roads
Unpaved roads
County lines (in blue)
Forest boundaries(blue)
Railroads
Power lines
Put in & take out
Alternate landings
Campground
Footbridge or Dam
A city or village
Picnic area
Point of interest
Rapids
Grade 1 rapids
Grade 2 rapids
Grade 3 rapids
Grade 4 rapids
Portage
N
6 NINE MILE
RAPIDS
5
OX BOW
RAPIDS
7
55
DIERCK'S
LANDING
8
Nicolet
National
Forest
Langlade
County
9
CEDAR
RAPIDS
10
SHERRY
RAPIDS
11
LAZELERE
RAPIDS
64
U.S.G.S.
gauge
Langlade
12
MATCH LINE
SEE MAP 54
(NOTE CHANGE
OF SCALE)
CAP
BUETTNER
GAUGE
55
33 Miles to
Shawano
WOLF RIVER
Sect. 2
Langlade Co., Wisconsin
Map No. 53
0
½
1
2
Scale In Miles
18 Miles to
Antigo
64
M

WOLF RIVER

Section 3

Wolf River: Langlade and Menominee Counties, Wisconsin.
Topo map(s): White Lake (1.48,000) 1952 planimetric and Langlade (1:48,000) 1952 planimetric.
Overview map: Iron Mountain (1954).
Public Lands: Langlade County (1971) plat book.
Section 3.
Start: Highway 64 bridge in Langlade.
End: Menominee County Highway WW bridge.

Difficulty (high water)	**III**
Difficulty (usual summer flow)	**II**
Length	**14**
Time	**8**
Width	**20-100**
Gradient	**18**
Drainage area	**479**

Water Conditions: For current information on levels, call Whitewater Specialty in White Lake at (715) 882-5400.
Scenery, Geology, Fish: See description accompanying map 52.
Campgrounds: See description accompanying map 55.

Points of Interest: This section is harder than the above stretches. It usually rates grade III in high water.

12 (15.5 miles) **Highway 64 bridge at Langlade.** The left bank downstream of the bridge is the **put-in** for Section 3 and the **take-out** for Section 2. The U.S.G.S. gauge is located immediately upstream of the bridge. The Cap Buettner gauge is located on the left bank, several hundred yards downstream of the bridge. There is also a grade I rock garden at this location.

13 (16.1 miles) **Crowle Rapids.** This grade II rapids is located downstream of a large island and several smaller ones.

14 (17.0 miles) **Horserace Rapids.** This grade II rapids is similar to Crowle Rapids.

15 (19.5 miles) **Twenty Day Rapids.** This grade II rapids is shallower than the first two on this stretch. It's real rock garden in low water.

16 (23.8 miles) **Boy Scout Rapids.** Schneck's Landing is the optional put-in and is on the right bank about one and a half miles above Boy Scout rapids. Raft trips often put in here. Boy Scout Rapids is also known as Gardner Dam or Garfield Rapids. This rapids begins below the first of two footbridges on the Valley Council Boy Scout Grounds. It is a long rapids with no special visibility problems, but because of its length, rescue can be difficult following an upset. This rapids rates grade II at low water and grade III at higher flow. **A canoeist drowned here in 1961. Scouting is recommended.** A large eddy on the right, just downstream of the first bridge, is a convenient stopping place for scouting. Secure permission from the Boy Scouts if you stop here for scouting or use this as an alternate landing. The lower rapids is usually scouted from the second footbridge. In low water, less than 300 cfs, this rapids is too shallow to run: In this case, many boaters use the alternate landing (No. 18) at the wayside near Markton as the put-in for this section. There are numerous un-named grade II rapids between Boy Scout and Hanson's Rips.

17 (24.8 miles) **Hanson's Rips.** Since 1968 this has been the site of the annual University of Wisconsin Hoofers' canoe and kayak slalom. This rapids usually rates grade II, as does another un-named rapids located upstream from here. Scouting from the right bank is optional. Huge haystacks rating grade III develop in high water. There is a spring on the left bank 100 feet or so above the County Highway M bridge and an alternate landing on the right bank just below the bridge.

18 (25.3 miles) **Wayside near Markton.** This is located along side of Highway 55, downstream of County Highway M bridge. This is a convenient landing with ample parking and picnicing facilities.

19 (26.0 miles) **Gilmore's Mistake Rapids.** The river, which is atypically wide above this point, is constricted to a channel that is only 20 feet wide. In high water, there are large standing waves in the upper part and there are large rollers and numerous souse holes associated with the lower ledge. At such levels this is the most difficult rapids on this stretch. This rapids rates grade III in high water and is rated at grade II in summer. **Scouting** from the left bank is **recommended.** The lower ledge can be tricky, because the proper chute is not always obvious from upstream. Although there are conflicting stories as to how this rapids got its name, we feel the following is the most plausible: A lumber company scout named Gilmore was sent to explore the feasibility of using the Wolf River to transport logs downstream to a saw mill. He reported that the river was too constricted at this spot, and he predicted that logjams would block the river. Based on this recommendation his superiors decided not to acquire timber rights to the land upstream. Their competitors, using dynamite, enlarged the passage and made a fortune. And that was Gilmore's mistake.

Take out on river left below **Gilmore's Mistake Rapids** at the landing developed by the Wild Wolf Inn.

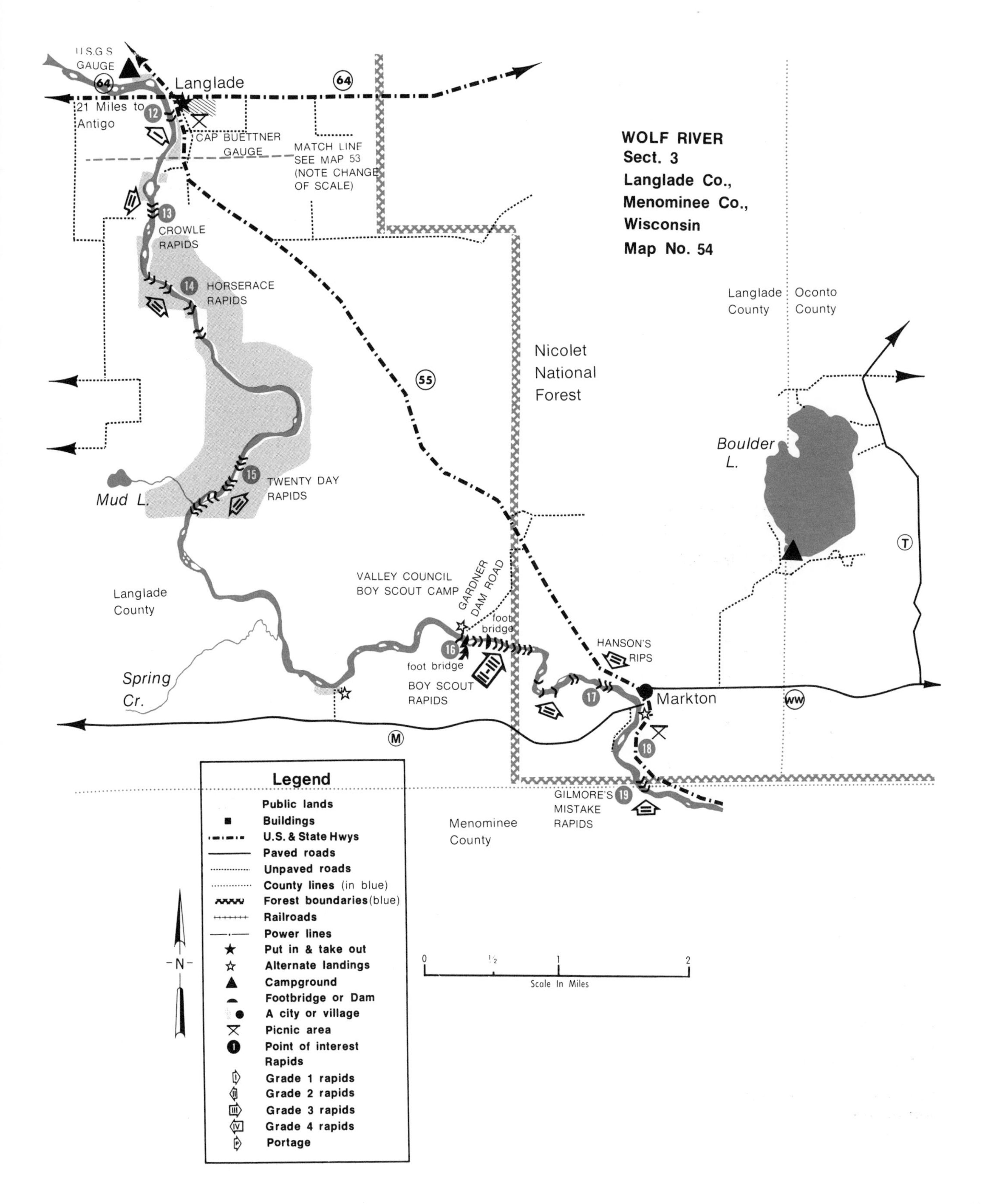

U.S.G.S.
GAUGE
64
Langlade
64
21 Miles to
Antigo
12
CAP BUETTNER
GAUGE
MATCH LINE
SEE MAP 53
(NOTE CHANGE
OF SCALE)
WOLF RIVER
Sect. 3
Langlade Co.,
Menominee Co.,
Wisconsin
Map No. 54
13
CROWLE
RAPIDS
14
HORSERACE
RAPIDS
Langlade County
Oconto County
Nicolet
National
Forest
55
Boulder
L.
15
TWENTY DAY
RAPIDS
Mud L.
T
VALLEY COUNCIL
BOY SCOUT CAMP
GARDNER DAM ROAD
Langlade
County
foot
bridge
16
foot bridge
HANSON'S
RIPS
Spring
Cr.
BOY SCOUT
RAPIDS
17
Markton
WW
M
18
GILMORE'S
19
MISTAKE
RAPIDS
Menominee
County
Legend
Public lands
Buildings
U.S. & State Hwys
Paved roads
Unpaved roads
County lines (in blue)
Forest boundaries (blue)
Railroads
Power lines
Put in & take out
Alternate landings
Campground
Footbridge or Dam
A city or village
Picnic area
Point of interest
Rapids
Grade 1 rapids
Grade 2 rapids
Grade 3 rapids
Grade 4 rapids
Portage
N
0
1/2
1
2
Scale In Miles

WOLF RIVER

SECTION 4

Wolf River: Menominee County, Wisconsin.

Topo map: Langlade (1:48,000) 1952 planimetric.
Overview Map: Iron Mountain (1954).
Public lands: We have not indicated the location of public lands on this stretch of river. On an annual basis the DNR has leased land from Menominee Enterprises at Pissmire Rapids, Lower Ducknest Rapids, the Dalles and Big Smoky Falls. There is also public access where the right of way of Highway 55 approaches the river.
Section 4
Start: Menominee County Highway WW bridge.
End: Big Smoky Falls.

Difficulty (high water)	**IV**
Difficulty (usual summer flow)	**III**
Length	**9**
Time	**7**
Width	**10-75**
Gradient	**12**
Drainage area	**517**

Water Conditions: This section of the river is always runnable but should be restricted to experts with decked boats only.

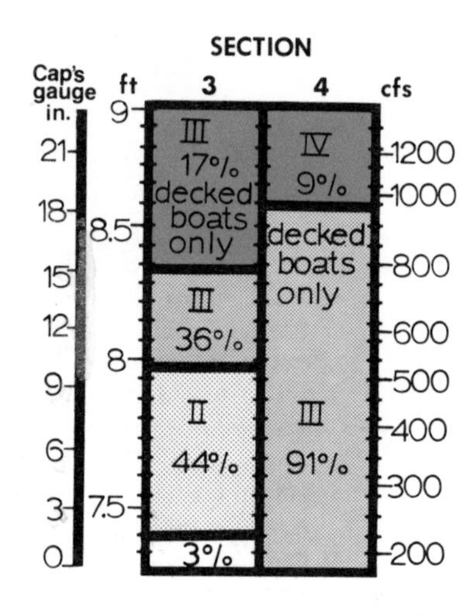

Scenery, Geology, Fish: See description accompanying Map 52.

Campgrounds: There is a developed Nicolet National Forest campground located at Boulder Lake. It has 53 campsites, and a user fee is charged. For more information write to the U.S. Forest Service, Lakewood, Wisc. 54138.

Note: This section of the river is in the Monominee Indian Reservation. The Monominee have changed their policy on access to this stretch of river on several occasions. Before any attempt is made to run this section, please contact Whitewater Specialty in White Lake at (715) 882-5400.

This section is recommended only for experts with decked boats at all times.

Points of Interest:

22 (30.0 miles) **Pissmire Falls.** The put-in for Section 4 is below the falls. In addition there is access to the river at places where Highway 55 approaches the river in the next few miles downstream.

23 (34.0 miles) **Sullivan Falls. This drop must be portaged.** A large island divides the river into two channels. The falls is located in the left channel about 250 yards downstream. Evergreen Rapids is formed in the right channel. Sullivan Falls is preceeded by 200 feet of rapids, Evergreen Rapids is shallow (not runnable when Caps' gauge reads below 6) and often has downed trees. So if you choose the right channel, **scouting is recommended** from the right bank. The recommended approach is to scout Evergreen Rapids and either run it, if possible, or line your boat through. Another alternative is to make the shorter **portage** on the left bank around Sullivan Falls.

24 (34.0 miles) **Evergreen Rapids.** This grade II rapids (described above) is also called Runaround Rapids.

25 (34.2 miles) **Ducknest Rapids.** This is a dilly that rates grade III. **Scouting** from the left bank is **strongly recommended.** There are two pitches separated by a boulder-strewn rapids. Even in low water, there are souse holes in this stretch that must be avoided. Large haystacks develop at the bottom of Lower Ducknest and these are followed by a shallow rocky area that has bruised many a boater. Under such conditions this rates grade IV. There is road access to Lower Ducknest that can serve as an alternate landing. About a half mile downstream there is an unnamed grade II rapids.

26 (35.5 miles) **Tea Kettle Rapids.** This rapids is grade III and is also known as Upper Dalles. An Indian tee-pee has been erected on the left bank. A small rocky island signals the start of this rapids which is a series of ledges located between steep rock cliffs. **Scouting is recommended** from the left bank. There are many boulders and sidecurlers which cannot be seen from upstream. The last ledge is located just below an island. In high water, both the right and left channels are runnable. In low water, the left channel is generally too shallow.

27 (36.0 miles) **The Dalles. Scouting and portage strongly recommended** on the left bank. This area is quite beautiful. However, in the event of upset, rescue is difficult because of the sheer rock cliffs located on both sides of the river. This grade III-IV rapids follows 200 feet of easy rapids that continue downstream of the island. The most difficult pitch of this rapids is at the start of the gorge. At high-water levels there is a back-roller here that can trap a dunker or his boat. A tip-over here can mean a pretty long swim. There is a grade II rapids at the end of the gorge. There is road access here, but a nominal user fee is usually required. **There have been reports that a person using a raft drowned here recently.**

28 (38.0 miles) **Big Smoky Falls. A portage is very strongly recommended** and thus the hazard rating is P. There are two channels both of which are spanned by footbridges. The best take-out is in the left channel just above the footbridge. There is road access here and this is our recommended take-out. **Do not under any curcumstances attempt to run the left channel.** The right channel should be run only by the most highly experienced boaters. But this is not recommended, as this very steep chute drops at least 15 to 20 feet within 50 yards. It culminates with a six-foot sheer drop. There is a roller near the middle of this channel which could cause trouble. (We have seen boaters shoot through the air like they were jumping off a ski jump.) A tip-over could be most unpleasant.

29 (39.0 miles) **Optional take-out.** Wayside.

(We have not run and therefore have not mapped the rest of the Wolf downstream from here until it enters Lake Winnebago. Numerous sources indicate that there are several rapids and falls located between Big Smoky Falls and Keshena. If traveling downstream, you should particularly avoid the sharp ledges of Big Eddy Falls: they can trap a swimmer.)

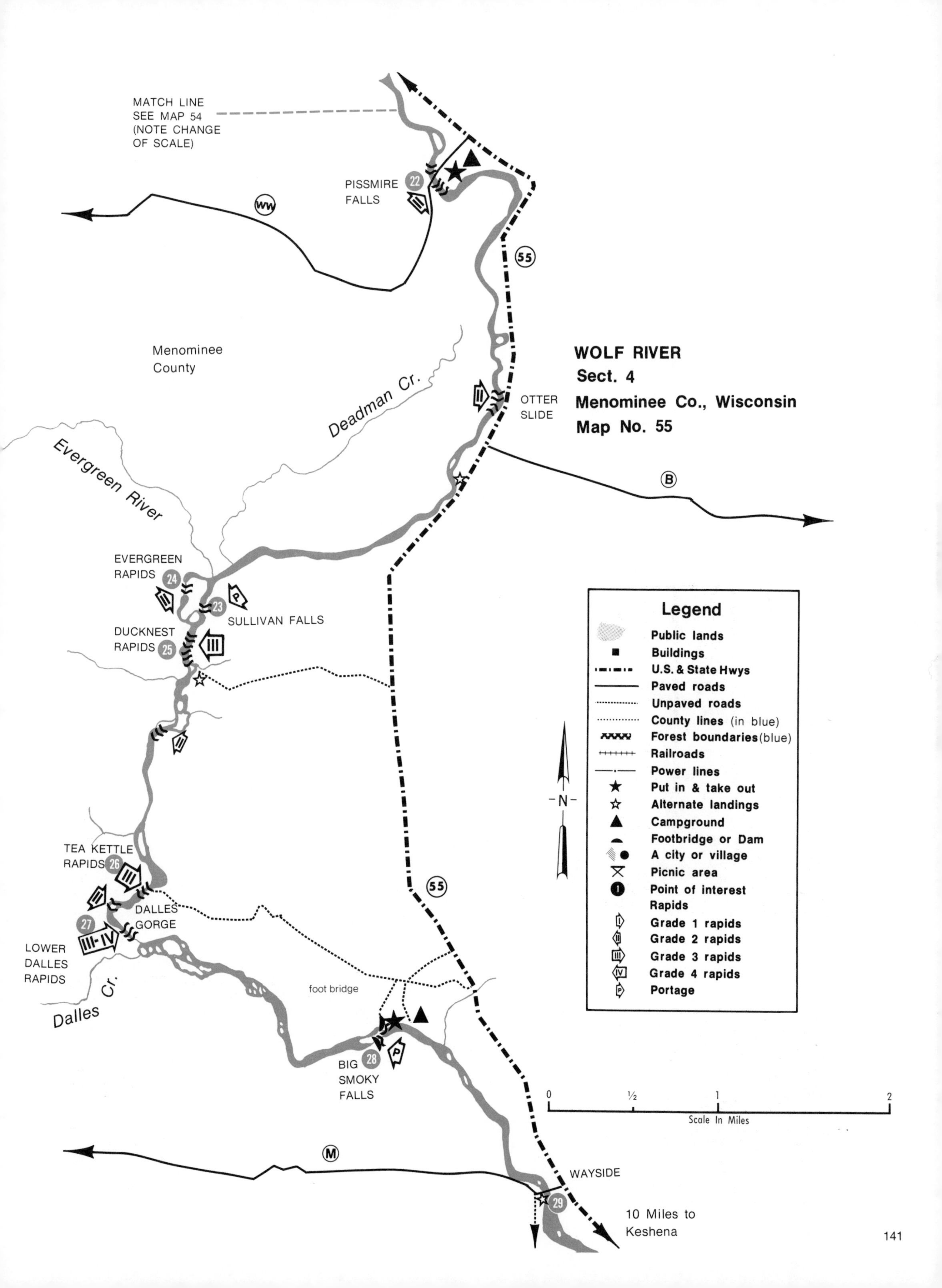
MATCH LINE
SEE MAP 54
(NOTE CHANGE
OF SCALE)
PISSMIRE
FALLS
22
WW
55
Menominee
County
WOLF RIVER
Sect. 4
Menominee Co., Wisconsin
Map No. 55
Deadman Cr.
OTTER
SLIDE
Evergreen River
B
EVERGREEN
RAPIDS
24
23
SULLIVAN FALLS
DUCKNEST
RAPIDS
25
Legend
Public lands
Buildings
U.S. & State Hwys
Paved roads
Unpaved roads
County lines (in blue)
Forest boundaries(blue)
Railroads
Power lines
Put in & take out
Alternate landings
Campground
Footbridge or Dam
A city or village
Picnic area
Point of interest
Rapids
Grade 1 rapids
Grade 2 rapids
Grade 3 rapids
Grade 4 rapids
Portage
N
TEA KETTLE
RAPIDS
26
DALLES
GORGE
27
III-IV
LOWER
DALLES
RAPIDS
Dalles Cr.
foot bridge
BIG
SMOKY
FALLS
28
0
½
1
2
Scale In Miles
M
WAYSIDE
29
10 Miles to
Keshena

Photo 55. The Dalles - one last lingering glance.

Photo 56. Sullivan Falls at high water - an unrunnable drop - for most.

9 Unmapped Rivers

BAPTISM RIVER

Described by Fred Young
N 47° 20' W 91° 12' ; 60 miles northeast of Duluth, Minnesota, on U.S. 61, 4-5 miles from Silver Bay.
Topo maps: Silver Bay (1:62,580) Finland (1:24,000) and Illgen City (1:24,000). Also, Superior National Forest map obtainable at Boundary Water check points.

	SEC. 1	SEC. 2
Difficulty	I-V6	I-VI
Length	6 1/2	4 1/4
Time	4 1/2	3 1/2
Width	5-55	15-65
Gradient	50	110

The Baptism River draining approximately 150 square miles in Lake County, Minnesota typifies many of the North Shore streams. For upstream one encounters conglomerate rock type rapids with shale, ledge-type drops being encountered more frequently toward the lake. Along the lake, one sees evidences of many felsite flows while farther upstream the basaltic diabase dikes thrust up to create the picturesque High Falls and Illgen Falls.

Section 1
The put-in for **Section 1** is reached by taking Minnesota 1 to Finland. Just before the junction of the road and river in town, bear left until the road crosses Hockamin Creek. Boats can be run through the culvert if there is sufficient water to run this small creek. The trip to the junction of the West Branch of the Baptism is extremely secluded. An alternate put-in is on the West Branch or East Branch in town. The East Branch appears to be a series of Beaver ponds farther up. The West Branch remains to be explored but offers more hope on the topographic maps. Approximately 3 miles below Finland we came upon a 15'-20' drop which almost tempted us. Grade V or VI? After this there were several milder rapids which presented little difficulty. There is a Forest Service campground located at the take-out.

Section 2
Commencing at the intersection of Highway 1 and the Baptism River, some three miles North of Highway 61, the intrepid boater will encounter progressively more difficult water. One quarter or perhaps 1/8 of a mile below the bridge, a fun grade III rapids occurs in a small, narrow canyon. Take-out on the right just above where a small stream enters; there is a sign "special upstream trout boundary." Scout on the right. A boulder midway down offers no problem. At times of high water the entire canyon is filled to the brim. About 1 1/2 miles down, the river forms a dandy low grade IV rapids. The difficulty here is a large boulder which forces the boater right or left. A pool below offers a chance to roll. Another 1/4 of a mile down, two ledge drops with chutes provide only moderate challenge, although high water may make them tough. A little distance beyond lies the half-way point to the Lake. Illgen Falls is a convenient point of egress. The Falls area is a sheer drop of about 35' and is easily noted from above. This spot makes an excellent campsite, as a short gravel road leads in from highway here. Two-thirds of a mile downstream the river pools slightly at a left bend. Here the river, plunges over a diabase dike commonly known as High Falls. There is an arduous carry around the left side of this beautiful drop. The river courses on to a double drop of 12 and 15 feet respectively. Both drops rate grade V and should be **portaged** on the **left.** About one third of a mile further downstream, the river constricts and picks up considerable velocity as it plunges through two, narrow crevices, each less than a boat length in width. The river drops about 30 feet in a relatively short distance. **Proceed with extreme caution as the tendency is to go past the point of no return on this grade VI drop. Caution: Take out well in advance!**
Portage this river left and admire the chasm. In the soup below, cautiously lower your boat to the water around the grade V portage. From here, there are several more grade III+ rapids which require your attention. The first has a boulder and pillow that must be avoided. Take-out at the lake carrying up to the parking lot on the south side of the road at the old bridge. There are several campsites along the river and nearby shoreline. Check the Superior National Forest map.

BRULE RIVER

This river should be run only by experts in decked boats.
Brule River: 120 miles northeast of Duluth, Minnesota, on U.S. 61.
Section 1
U.S.G.S. topographic maps: Two Harbors, (Minn.) (1:250,000); Tom Lake (Minn.) (1:24,000) Marr Island (Minn.) (1:24,000); Superior National Forest map obtainable at Boundry Waters check point centers.
Gradient: Estimated 0-80 feet/mile
Difficulty: I-IV.
Length: 15-18 miles to Sauna Bath Rapids.
Time: 7 hours.
Width of rapids: 200'-35'.
Water flow: 600 cfs.
Campgrounds: Judge D. R. Magney State Park is located at the mouth of the river. Kimball Lake is also a state-owned park; it is located along Minnesota Highway 140 about two miles east of the Gunflint Trail.
Section 2
Recommended for Whitewater Decked Boats Only.
Gradient:120'/mi. 160'/mi. 80'/mi. 120'/mi. 80'/mi. 180'/mi.
Difficulty: II through VII* (*Denoting probable loss of life)
Length: 6 1/4 miles with portages
Time: 3 1/2 hours.
Width of rapids: 15'-120'.
Water flow estimated: 900 cfs.

SECTION 1
Put-in at Northern Light Lake about 12 miles north of Lake Superior on the Gunflint Trail (Minn. 12). There may be alternate put-ins further down the river-lake chain; if you wish, explore gravel roads No. 382, No. 141, or improved No. 309. This would eliminate a good deal of quiet water, if the roads are passable. Putting in at Northern Lights Lake, we paddled a good deal of relatively quiet water. The scenery proved interesting, and we noted only one canoe and one boat on the lake. Further along the trip we saw no evidence of man. Especially indicative of the lack of civilization was the fact that we encountered seven moose. They apparently had had little or no contact with man; they allowed us to approach so closely to the cows and calves that I became nervous for our safety. Also we saw much beaver activity, ducks, and other wildlife.
Following each lake or slow section of river, we encountered rapids which became progressively longer and more difficult; none exceeded low grade III, except the final rapids above which

it was possible to takeout. The river bed was typically conglomerate gravel with small rocks. In some spots there were small waves that added to our enjoyment. There were no visibility problems nor drops.

Shortly after the last flat section, we noticed an old cabin on the left in the trees. To the right some distance away, perhaps three miles, was a fire lookout tower. Not too far after this, we came upon an old wooden bridge which had obviously been washed out for some time. One could take-out or put-in here from the east, but it's doubtful that even a four-wheel-drive vehicle could negotiate the final stretch of road. From three -fourths of a mile above this point down, the river becomes continuous rapids and falls -- each progressively more difficult.

The obvious take-out for this section and put-in for Section 2 is reached as described in **Section 2.** The terminal rapids is grade IV, V. It is possibly 75 yards long, preceded by lots of grade II, III stuff. Best scouting and portaging is on the left, though we elected to look from the right and eddy-out there. The end of the rapids occurs at a short pool marked by a small shack used as a sauna bath. The river is narrow, choked with rocks, frothy, and drops steeply. Midway down, it drops over a large rock into lots of foam which could be a stopper hole at a higher water level. There is another smaller, three-foot drop below this five-foot drop. A swim in this rapid would be real mean and conceivably quite dangerous.

SECTION 2

Along most of the North Shore area, Keweenanwan lava is the predominant rock. This Algonkian-age material ranges from basalt to rhyolite and has minor sediments intercalculated. Several large intrusives, also of Algonkian age, are embedded through a section of red rock, and upper granitic phase of the basic intrusives in the Keweenawan lava, and also just touches the edge of a large mass of Duluth gabbro. The first few miles of river have sharp sedimentary formations on the northeast bank while the other bank is more rounded Keweenawan lava.

In the first canyon, the river drops over a series of small ledges as it cuts down through the sedimentary layers.*

*Description from USGS geologic map of Minnesota.

We suggest that the Brule River be run only by a team of experts utilizing decked, whitewater boats and maximum safety precautions. The continuous nature of the river demands a sure roll. Because of the difficult portages, boaters should be in good physical condition.

Most North Shore rivers have relatively small drainage areas and steep gradients, and consequently have a fast run-off. Without any comprehensive flow date, we believe the recommended time for running is during spring run-off and after rainfall before about mid-June.

To reach the start, take County 69 (which is the first road to the left past the junction of the Brule and U.S. 61) past the second junction of the Flute Reed River until you reach County 70. Follow along 70, keeping to the left, until the road becomes impassable just before Mons Creek. In 1972, we were able to drive 200 yards further over Mons Creek. A potential four-wheel-drive road continues up stream to the site of an old washed-out bridge approximately one mile further up the river. From here, it is about one-third of a mile walk across private land to the river. Please ask permission to carry down from the young couple living in the cabins. Cross over the creek and keep to the left fork of the road until you reach a path leading off to the right past the first cabin and down to the river. You will hear the river before you can see it. This is one-eighth of a mile below Sauna Bath Rapids, which can be reached by portaging the boats a bit further up the river.

The river above the cabin swarms over a series of ledges to the point where we entered in 1971. Sauna Bath Rapids would undoubtedly make a hot warmup.

There is plenty of action on this run. The river drops 120 feet in the first mile. The water surface is almost completely white, and it is necessary to scramble a little to make the eddies. About 25 yards below the second wooded island, there is a five to eight foot waterfall that is not readily visible from above. Although we have run this drop successfully on the right, sharp protruding rocks, a potential stopper 10 yards downstream, and two mandatory portages another 300 yards beyond that, cautions most boaters to **portage** this one on the **left.**

About 300 yards downstream, the river narrows and enters a gorge. Following a short, fast-moving pool after the first drop, the river bends sharply to the right and cascades over a sloping drop that easily rates grade VI. The water piles up against a jagged, possibly undercut, wall on the left bank before dropping 40 feet. **Extreme caution is required to prevent a potential disaster.**

Portaging was extremely difficult and tiring as we had to climb an incline of 55-70° for 120 feet to the ridge top. At the top, we discovered a narrow trail which we followed for one-fifth of a mile to where it precipitously tumbled back down to the river. If the ridge path comes up from the river further upstream, the carry on the left might be much easier than beating through the bush. The other bank offered a shorter route, but it required a very difficult ferry and landing in order to pull out. On the 1972 trip, the portage on the right proved less difficult with a smaller initial climb. The brush was just as thick as on the other side. Terrain was steep with lots of bushes and trees to avoid. The decline back to the river was twice the climb and a lot steeper due to the falls. We put in below the falls in the froth. Strong backs, muscles, and ropes would be helpful on this arduous climb. After experiencing this lift, we looked back through the clouds of sweat and thought perhaps the falls were possible. . . .

The next mile slowed its descent to 80 feet per mile of continuous grade II to III rapids rushing over a bed of small rocks. As with the first and second mile, the water remained practically white because of the velocity and shallow depth. Very few eddies were apparent. Those we did catch were small and moving downstream. We did scrape a bit, but it was enjoyable nonetheless. The water moves through this section faster than it does through the Roaring Rapids of the Peshtigo in Wisconsin. We were told that the water level was a foot higher one week earlier. The gradient in the fourth mile picked up to 120 feet. Partway through, a small island, runnable on the right, appeared. The fifth mile tossed about at 80 feet per mile, and also contained a small island, runnable on the right.

The sixth and last mile abruptly became challenging to the limit. It commenced with Devil's Kettle a 40-foot drop named Harv's Delight by us after we lost an 80-pound C-1, without its paddler fortunately, over it. Shortly after this drop was another sloping falls. We named the 45' drop Harv's Boat Cemetery. The best trail around the drops is on the left bank. Below the falls, we put back in and ran down through what is known as lower falls. Running a narrow chute in it down the middle, we plunged about 15-16 feet within about 20-30 feet into a hole at the bottom. The acceleration going down the chute was fantastic, and we stopped even more abruptly in the backwash below. There was plenty of water moving through and we flushed through with no danger. This drop was succeeded by a small pool sufficient for a roll. There were mild rapids for the next 200 yards. At this point, the river enters a steep canyon with one more small falls, a five-to seven-foot drop, which we named Sewer Pipe. From here on to the lake there were a series of grade III rapids, starting above Sewer Pipe about one-fourth of a mile. These were a real delight. They may be runnable at lower water as the channel is more constricted.

This run would be fantastic during spring run-off and was terrific even at our low levels. A dependable roll should be prerequisite. Due to the inaccessibility from the road, I would grade the water one grade higher than the actual difficulty. Continuous rapids make boat rescue tough while wearing down the boater. The dunker would make it to shore with many bumps. The water is shallow, rocky and fast. **Exercise caution.**

Excellent trout fishing, good backpacking opportunities, hiking, and camping help to make this an enjoyable area. Campgrounds are available at the Lake Superior river mouth, Kadunce Creek along U.S. 61, and back from the lake on the side roads.

CASCADE RIVER

Described by Fred Young
110 miles northeast of Duluth, Minnesota on US Highway 61.
USGS topographic maps Two Harbors, Minn. 1:250,000; Deer Yark Lake 7.5 min. 1:24,000 and quadrangle directly north; Superior National Forest map obtainable at BWCA checkpoints.

	SEC. I	SEC. II
Gradient:	56'/mile (mean)	170', 150', 160', 320'
Difficulty	II5	II-VII (7 probable death)
Length	4 1/2 mi.	3 1/2 mi.
Approx. time	45 min.	?
Width of rapids	20'/100"	?

Conglomerate rocks; igneous base material (see geology of the Brule River, Minnesota.)
Estimated flow 300 CFS

Section 1 was generally low and scrapy, but with good depth in many parts. The bottom 1/3 of the run was more rocky and shallow. The put in is reached by taking the first intersection north of the junction of the Cascade and US 61; turning left on highway 7 to the second cross road marked Highway 45 turn west to the Cascade. This bridge is the take out for Section 1 and put in for Section 2. Continuing past the river, turn north, right on no. 159, to first junction to the right. East on 157 for about two miles to the river. This section started out with fairly mild water about 2/3 1/2 feet deep. A short distance below the bridge a series of logs were anchored in the water across the stream apparently to improve the fish habitat. All of these stretches were navigable, while the shallow sections downstream were somewhat more rocky. Several small streams join during this stretch improving the flow slightly. Not enough to justify starting at a low level, as the final part of the run widens and gets pretty shallow.

Halfway down, the boater approaches an island which marks the beginning of two unrunnable, falls - the first being 10'-15' and the second being about a 20' drop. Unfortunately, the river is relatively wide at this point and the drop is over a shallow ledge with rocks obstructing all possible channels. A small channel to the right of the island provides a good place to line boats down from the island bank as the drop is in two stages. Below the island, portage on the right avoid the second drop of 20'. A pool below it provides a good return to the water. The succeeding stretch was very enjoyable though only of moderate difficulty - grade II rapids.

Section 2

We did not run Section 2 to the lake, as a preview showed us a series of contiguous waterfall slides dropping perhaps 70/90' in 3/16 of a mile. Careful study of a topographic map indicated the rest of the section would be unnavigable also. Note gradients were 170'/mi, 150'/mi, 160'/mi, and 320'/mi. **Do Not Attempt This Section.**

Campsites at the section 1 take-out and mouth of river at Lake Superior, also Pike Lake. The lower section should make a very scenic hike as I am sure the Cascades are very beautiful.

CRYSTAL RIVER AND THE WAUPACA CHAIN OF LAKES

Location: Waupaca County, Wisconsin.

Put-in at Ding's Dock, located on County Highway Q at the bridge between Columbia and Limekiln Lakes. Free maps of this area are available here. However there is a charge for the use of this landing. A shuttle and boats are available for a fee. For additional information call (715) 258-2612.

If you paddle west through Columbia, Beasley, Lorland, Knight, Manomin, and Pope Lakes until you get to Marl Lake, you will end up in an exceptionally beautiful area. The water has a unique blue-green hue and there is virtually no development of the shoreline with the exception of the Whispering Pines Lodge. This resort has an interesting little museum open to the public. Retrace your steps back to Beasley Lake. Beasley Creek, between Lorland and Beasley Lakes, generally is quite shallow, and you may have to drag your boat some distance. Travel south through Lorland, Beasley and Long Lakes until you get to the Crystal River. The start of this river may be difficult to spot as tall reeds provide camouflage. There are a few shallow rock gardens followed by a small marshy area. Although there are occasional riffles, these low hazard "rapids" rarely cause serious difficulty even for the most inexperienced person. There is a low bridge near Rural. Portage right. Refreshments can be obtained at a small store on the left. After a few more rock gardens you will encounter the Smith Road Bridge at Parfreyville. Our recommended take-out is the picnic area at this site.

Allow about 5 to 6 hours for the total trip. It's an hour less if you skip the side trip to Marl Lake.

EMBARRASS RIVER

Embarrass River: Shawano County, Wisconsin.
Topo map(s): Tigerton (1:48,000) 1965 planimetric.
Overview map(s): Green Bay (1955-1967).
Start: Highway 45 bridge at Tigerton.
End: County Highway M bridge approximately two miles out of Tigerton.

Difficulty (high water)	II-III
Difficulty (usual summer flow)	(not runnable in low water)
Length	3
Time	2
Width	15-50
Drainage area	395 (at gauge)

Water Conditions: This river is runnable only in high water typical of spring flows. There is a U.S.G.S. gauge located on the left bank 10 feet downstream from the bridge on a county road, 1.3 miles downstream from Mill Creek and 4 miles northwest of Embarrass.

Scenery: The shoreline consists of pasture land and areas with second-growth timber. The dells are quite beautiful with high rock walls and steep banks.

Geology: The bedrock in this area consists of Pre-Cambrian crystalline rock and Cambrian sandstone.

The first two miles of the run are mostly quiet water with a few small, grade I rapids. However, **watch for fallen trees and barbed**

wire strung across the river. At the second 90° bend, on the left, the rapids begin with a genuine "embarrass" or logjam -- thus this river's name, from the French. This obstacle may be portaged on either bank. Shortly downstream there is a drop that rates grade II-III. At lower water levels this drop is very rocky. Scouting is mandatory, since novices frequently end up wedged broadside on the rocks. In high water passage is easier. However, there is a large souse hole just to the right of center which can detain a boater. After another stretch of quiet water, the approach to the dells proper begins. It is marked by high banks and the remains of an old shack on the right. The first two-pitch drop is narrow and difficult to navigate without hitting rocks. **Scouting is strongly advised.** Less experienced boaters should portage during high water, because it is immediately followed by a very wide and regular souse hole that may trap a boater or swimmer. The souse hole can only be avoided by staying on the extreme left and using precise, rapid maneuvers. The river then bends right and enters the main part of the dells, which consists of about a half mile of continuous grade II-III rapids in a steep canyon. The upper part is very rocky, and it is difficult to find clear passage in lower water. Near the end, there are several "surfing" waves that decked boats play on. The take-out immediately follows this canyon.
The dells may be easily scouted from a trail along the right bank to determine if the river is runnable before putting in.

Because of the shortness of the shuttle and the ease of put in and take out, this short run may be combined with a run on the Little Wolf if the party takes out early at the County J bridge.

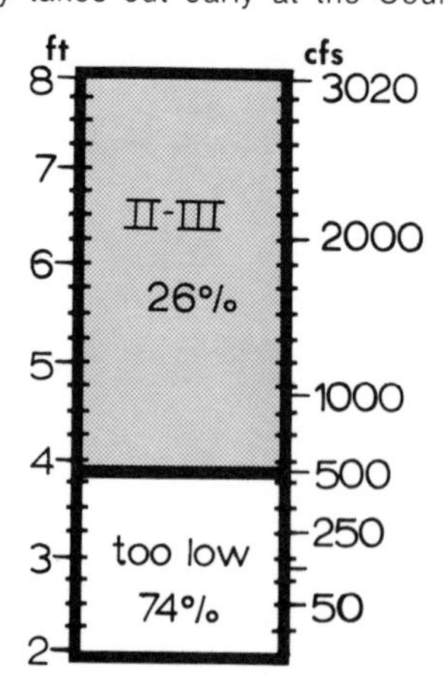

Canoeable Days Per Month

month	Apr	May	June	July	Aug	Sep
days	24	12	6	2	0	3

JUMP RIVER

Jump River: Rusk, Price, and Taylor counties, Wisconsin.

Topo maps: Sheldon (1:48,000) 1947 planimetric and Jump River Fire Tower (1:48,000) 1949 planimetric.
Overview map: Rice Lake (1953).
Section 1
Start: 12 miles southeast of Ogema at Oxbow landing 1.5 miles west on Highway I from the Highway M junction.
End: Big Falls.
Section 2
Start: Big Falls.
End: State Highway 73 bridge east of the town of Jump River.

	Sec. 1	Se. 2
Difficulty (high water)	II^3	II^3
Not runnable in low water.		
Length	10	10
Time	6	5
Width	10-80	---

Drainage area **574 at gauge**

Water Conditions: This river has extreme flow fluctuations. Little Falls and the mile of continuous rapids below Big Falls are usually too low to run except shortly after the ice goes out in the spring.

ft cfs
10
9 — II_3 — 5000
8 — 15% — 3000
7
6 — 1800
1000
5 — too low — 500
4 — 85% — 100
3

Canoeable Days Per Month

month	Apr	May	June	July	Aug	Sep
days	15	9	3	0	0	0

Scenery: This river provides rapids and wildlife for those who enjoy canoeing off the beaten track.
Section 1
Shuttle: The **put-in** for Section 1 is located 12 miles southwest of Ogema at a point where the river doubles back on itself forming an oxbow. To get to this location take State Highway 13 two miles south from Ogema and turn west on County Highway I. Follow Highway I to the river (S. Fork of Jump River), two miles past the junction with County Highway M.

Downstream of the Oxbow landing there is moderate current and occasional stretches of low hazard rapids until Little Falls is encountered about a mile above County Highway N. This grade II-III drop **should be scouted and portaged** right as prudence dictates. After about another 2 miles, Big Falls is encountered. A stand of pine trees on a grassy knoll signals one of the picnic areas of a county park and the recommended **take-out.** The river makes a "S" turn, first left then right, with a rock garden between the bends. Big Falls and a mile of continuous rapids begin here. There is no turning back below the rock garden. **Scouting is mandatory.** The county park at this site is the **take-out** for Section 1 and the **put-in** for Section 2. Camping is permitted. **Caution:** The dirt road leading to this site may be marginal in the spring.
Section 2

Big Falls is scenic due to its unique rock outcroppings. Most would do well to limiting efforts to viewing the falls. However, experts with decked boats may wish to attempt this grade III drop. Others should **portage** right. After the mile-long continuous rapids downstream of Big Falls, there are occasional riffles. The river flows through farm country for a few miles. The take-out at the State Highway 73 bridge is east of the village of Jump River. The landing is on the left side of the river just downstream of the bridge. There is ample parking and a picnic area.

ST. LOUIS RIVER

Described by Fred Young

20 miles west of Duluth, Minnesota on Highway 23/210. USGS topographic map Duluth, Minnesota, 1:250,000, Cloquet Quadrangle (1:24,000). Also, Jay Cooke State Park Map obtainable at Park Headquarters. Experts in decked boats only - Park officials and power company people may deny permission to run the river in the future for safety reasons if they get wind of our runs. Exercise caution and discretion.

Gradient	**80'-40'-100'**
Difficulty	**II-VI**
Length	**2 1/4 Mi.**
Approx. Time	**1 Hour**
Width rapids	**5'-200'**

Note: The St. Louis River is an extremely interesting river both from a geologic view-point and a boater's perspective. The put-in is reached by following Minnesota 210 3/4 a mile west of Thomson, where the bridge crosses the river just below the dam at the Thomson Reservoir. Regrettably, the river is obviously polluted by effluents from, we guess, paper mills, probably located in Cloquet a few miles upstream. Possibly the water may be contaminated by sewage also.

Right above the bridge there is a nice rapids which gobbled up a kayak blade at 1500 cfs. At high flow, the area would be a raging torrent. We noticed much foam generated by the residual material dumped in the water above. The odor was somewhat offensive too. For the first mile the river drops over a series of ledges growing progressively more difficult until approximately 3/4 a mile downstream, we encountered a grade V-VI, twisting, steep drop which appeared to be a possible invitation for disaster. We portaged river left putting in below, running a difficult drop on the left some 25 yards below. The ledges are caused by black diabase dikes which have intruded the slate and graywacke. In many places, the river drops through cleavages in this Thomson Slate formation and quartzite. It is interesting to note the massive folding in the slate beds and the basaltic dikes, while realizing the interesting rapids they produce.

Another 3/4 of a mile downstream, the river divides into two channels and drops steeply just 100 yards above the Swinging Bridge. After exhausting study, five of us decided to attempt the narrow chutes extreme river left. The first drop was probably 8'-10' down a tongue of water into long narrow pool. A small hole at the bottom did not prove to be a stopper. A rescue station was stationed below the drop as a succeeding drop was just 20 yards farther. It, too, was extreme river left and was similar in that it was very narrow and steep. It had several rocks midway down which almost caught one boater. At the bottom, one had to make an abrupt right manuever to avoid being wedged in a motch of rocks at the end. Just above the swinging bridge, a very small, ledge-type drop appeared deceptively easy trapping a boater so that he required assistance to escape its tenacious grip on his boat and bod. The section below the bridge awaits exploration. We did venture 1/8 of a mile down, where we encountered a number of grade IV, V and VI drops which looked very potent indeed. **Exercise utmost caution on this river due to sharp rocks, steep drops, possible pollution and high water.**

STURGEON RIVER

Baragara County, Michigan

Although some sections have been run successfully by experts using decked boats, this river is best appreciated from the shore. At two locations there are rapids-filled canyons below picturesque falls. The first falls has yet to be named. It can be reached by a footpath leading from a wayside on the north side of the Michigan Highway 41 Bridge, 10 miles south of L'Anse. A short hike will lead you to a series of ledges and a dramatic 25-foot falls. This falls marks the beginning of a long rapids-filled canyon which is very beautiful when viewed from atop the cliffs. The hike to the end of the canyon and back to the highway is about one mile.

A second scenic portion of this river lies within the Ottawa National Forest. Just east of Sidnaw, take F.S. 191 north from Michigan Highway 28 to the Sturgeon River Gorge. The gorge is well marked. There is a trail on the right bank. Shortly downstream there is an 18-foot ledge followed closely by Sturgeon Falls, an awesome sight. Immediately downstream of the falls, the river drops through a beautiful gorge with 400 foot high shear rock cliffs.

The hikes to both of these scenic areas are well worth the effort. Such scouting will undoubtably discourage most boaters from running this river.

TEMPERANCE RIVER

Described by Fred Young

Experts with decked boats only.

85 miles northeast of Duluth, Minnesota on U.S. Highway 61
Topo maps: Two Harbors (1:250,000), and Tofte (1:62,500). Also, Superior National Forest map obtainable at BWCA checkpoints.

	SEC. 1	**SEC. 2**
Gradient:	**36'/mi. (mean)**	**60'/mi, 70'/mi 20'/mi, 20'/mi 80'/mi, 60'/mi, 70'/mi, 80'/mi* the last 1/2 mile to the lake drops over 160**
Difficulty:	**I-II**	**I thru VII (7 death wishes)**
Length:	**7 1/2**	**8 1/2**
Time:	**1 1/2-3 hrs.**	**3 1/2 hrs.**
Width of rapids	**30'-100'**	**15'-100'**

See description of the geology of the Brule (Minn.) River. Bedrock in the lower reaches is Cambrian igneous rock with sedimentary formations upstream probably due to depositions from the meadow areas through which the river meanders. Estimed flow (200 CFS 7/4/70) I think it was more like 300 CFS 6/5/70. **Section 1:** Fellow University of Chicago paddlers say it contains eight miles of continuous shallow, rocky grade I and II water. This portion of the river should be definitely avoided at low water, though boaters can get through with much poling and scrapping into July. This section starts where Sawbill Trail (Minn. 2) crosses the river for the first time approximately 12 miles above the lake. There is a campsite close by. Take-out is the first bridge above Highway 61 (Minn. 166).

Section 2: The put-in is Minn. 166 bridge over the Temperance River to the Lake or where Minn. 343 approaches the river for the first time. A small park is located 1/2 - 3/4 mile down from the put-in on the left side. Since this campsite is not used very much, the boater may wish to camp there and put-in due to the convenience. It is a scenic sight located on a bluff overlooking the river. It could also be used as a take-out for **Section 1.** The river bends North and then southwest as a prelude to several miles of meandering through low terrain, though little is swampy. The stream valley here is rather wide and quite pretty. A number of small feeder brooks enter along this stretch. Several paths are evident leading away from the river and are probably used by fishermen for access or egress. Many spots along the river would make excellent campsites for remote camping, and early season bugs would be no problem. Fishing for trout no doubt would be superb, providing water conditions were right. After several miles of slow water, one enters a gorge about one hundred feet high characterized by a bedded shale-like rock, often jagged and sharp. Shortly after this, the river quickens its tempo. A three-foot waterfall is runnable straight down the center and provides some grade III excitement. A small hole at the bottom which engulfs the boater to the waist is refreshing though not likely to be dangerous even at higher levels. After 1/2 a mile, the valley widens, allowing the river to hunt its way through the typical, small, rocky, shallow stretches that follow. About 1 1/2 miles of easy grade II water precede the approach of Highway 343, which is marked by a guard rail 50' above the right bank. A short distance below, the river plunges over some small falls. The first drop is divided by a small island which may be practically submerged at high water. The river's left chute was too constricted and too steep to run. The right side offered an acceptable, although difficult, passage at 300-400 cfs. The boiling pit at the bottom is devoid of rocks and a rescue station may be easily set up. About 50 yards below, the river drops over a 16-foot horseshoe ledge on a 60° incline. **After racking up a boat and dinging my bod, I can authoritatively recommend caution.** I attempted to run from river right with a slight left cant to brace on the rock face under the sheer part of the waterfall. Instead I was engulfed by the undercut ledge, sucked out of the boat by the undertow, scraped along sharp rocks on the bottom and ledge face and unceremoniously tumbled around upside-down under water for 30 yards, subsequently swimming through a good portion of the canyon. The boat fared poorly, also sustaining numerous pressure fractures and contusions. Of the other two boaters with me, one ran right down the center and experienced no torque until the bottom hole forced a roll. The final boater stated he ran clean, though we were not witnesses. From that point the river was runnable through a narrow grade III gorge followed by another shallow rocky stretch about 1/3 mile long. The end of this rocky portion signals the start of the Cauldron Falls drop to Lake Superior, some 280 feet in about 1/4 mile. **Portage on the left bank to Highway 61.** It is a short distance, 1/3 mile to the road. One may take out at the Highway 343 approach to avoid this last carry. Campsites are available at the mouth of the river as well as along the Sawbill Trail. Unquestionably the Temperance would be a terrific run during spring runoff.

VERMILION RIVER

Vermilion River: La Salle County, Illinois.
Topo maps: Streator (1:62,500), Ottawa (1:62,500), and La Salle (1:62,500).
Overview map: Aurora.
Start: Camp Ki-Shau-Wau Boy Scout Camp.
End: Eastern end of Oglesby.

Difficulty (high water)	**II-III**
Difficulty (usual summer flow)	**not runnable**
Length	**9**
Time	**4**
Width	**25-200**
Gradient	**8**
Drainage area	**1218**

Water Conditions: A U.S.G.S. gauging station was located at the State Highway 178 bridge. It has been replaced by a stage marker. This section is runnable at 290 cfs, although the ledge by the cement plant must be portaged. On the other extreme, 5,000 cfs provides a fast run at a difficulty rating of II-III, with large waves predominating.

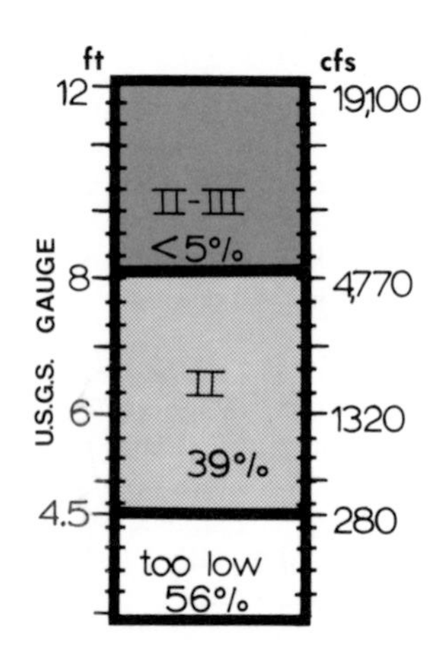

Canoeable Days Per Month

month	Apr	May	June	July	Aug	Sep
days	24	23	19	11	0	3

Scenery: Somewhat industrial. For the most part the banks are wooded, and in some places there are picturesque rock cliffs. The water is muddy though not visibly polluted.
Geology: The bedrock is of Pennsylvanian age.
Put-in: Camp Ki-Shau-Wau Scout Reservation, approximately 1.5 miles upstream from the State Highway 178 bridge. Within one mile south of Lowell along State Highway 179, the first in a series of signs indicates the direction to the Boy Scout Camp. Seek permission before using this privately owned landing.

This river is ideal for the novice. The gradient is uniformly distributed over many easy rapids instead of a few steep and difficult ones. Ledges and boulders provide variety and an opportunity to practice various maneuvers.

Wildcat Rapids is located just above Bailey Creek and about four miles below the State Highway 178 bridge. This rapids is the most difficult on this run. Its character changes greatly with different discharge, making **scouting advisable** even for boaters who have seen it before. Recognition from upstream is easy; after a gentle bend to the right the river narrows to a few yards forming the main drop. There are large boulders on both banks. This drop empties out into a quiet pool.

About one mile downstream from Wildcat Rapids, a cement plant becomes visible on the left bank. An abrupt man-made ledge at this location is the shallowest spot on this section. It is runnable on the right bank if the water is high. Caution: At same water levels a potentially **hazardous backroller** may develop here.

Since this narrow river is only runnable during periods of high flow, downed trees and other obstructions are possible hazards.

Take-Out: The third bridge upstream of the confluence with the Illinois River. This site is on the east side of Oglesby. The second upstream bridge is easier to find but has a less desirable landing.

Appendices

APPENDIX A

Summary Table of Mapped Rivers

River	Section	Map	Hazard Rating		Gradient (ft./mi.)	10/90 Ratio°	Length (miles)	Time (hours)
			Summer	Spring				
Bad	1	23						
	2	1	Q$_p$	Q$_p$	3	11.7	19	10
Black (Mich.)	1	2	I^2	I^2	8	15.6	8	6
	2	2	II	II-III	20		1.5	0.5
	3	3	nr	III	--		4	3
	4	3	nr	IV$_p$	60		6	5
Black (E. Fork)	1	4	II	II^3	4	--	8	6
	2	4	II	II	--		11	7
Bois Brule	1*	5	I	I	4	2.2	9	4
	2*	5	I-II	II	17		4	2
	3*	6	Q	Q	5		8	4
	4*	6	II	II-III	25		8	5
	5*	7	Q	I	15		7	4
Brule	1*	8	I	I	13	2.8	14	8
	2*	8	I-II	II	17		11	6
	3*	9	I-II	II	22		14	6
	4*	9	II-III	III	8		6	3
Cloquet (Minn.)		10	I	I-II	7	--	11	4
Eau Claire (Douglas Co.)		11	I	I-II	6	--	14	7
Eau Claire	1	12	II	II	18	8.2	3	3
(Marathon Co.)	2	12	II^3	II^3	19		5	4
Escanaba (Mich.)	1*	13	I	I-II	9	(4.3)	11	4
	2*	13	I	II^3	15		7	4
	3*	13	I	I-II	7		10	4
Flambeau	1*	14	I	I	3	(2.0)	9	5
(N. Fork)	2*	14	I	I	4		7	4
	3*	15	I-II	I-II	3		14	6
	4*	16	I-II	II	6		15	7
Flambeau	1*	17	I-II	II	5	9.3	10	6
(S. Fork)	2*	18	II	II-III	7		10	5
	3*	18	II$_p$	III$_p$	--		4	2
Ford (Mich)		19	nr	II-III	11	(11.4)	8	4
Kettle (Minn.)		20	II	III-IV	--	(20.4)	5	2
Kickapoo		21	Q	Q	3	--	20	10
Little Wolf		22	II	II	13	(6.0)	8	5
Marengo (to Bad)		23	I	I-II	2	--	12	6
Menominee		24	III$_p$	IV$_p$	10	3.8	4	3
Mirror Lake		25	Q	Q	--	--	4	2
Montreal	1	26	II-III	III	70	13.6	5	4
	2	26	II	II	--		4	3
Namekagon	1*	27	I$_p$	I$_p$	5	2.6	21	6
	2*	28	Q^1	Q^1	7		11	5
	3*	29	I^2-II	II	3		15	6
	4*	30	Q	I	3		12	5
	5*	31	Q	Q	6		16	6
	6*	31	Q	Q	3		15	6
Oconto	1	32	nr	II	18	--	4	4
(N. Branch)	2	32	nr	II	25		4	3
	3	32	nr	Q$_p$	--		2	--
Ontonagon	1	33	II-III	III	29	3.9	8	4
(Mich.)	2	33	Q	I	8		3	2
Peshtigo	1	34	II	III	14	--	9	6
	2	35	II	II-III	14		7	6
	3	36	II^3-III	III-IV	40		4	4
Pike	1	37	I-II	II^3	6	4.0	6	3
	2	37	II^3	II^3-III	18		3	3
	3	37	Q	I	--		4	2
Pine	1*	38	I-II	II	8	6.0	21	10
	2*	39	II^3	II^4	14		10	5
	3*	39	I-II	II	--		9	6
	4*	40	Q$_p$	Q$_p$	0.5		10	6
	5*	40	Q	Q	--		7	6
Popple	1*	41	I-II	II	10	(7.6)	9	5
	2*	41	II^3	III	16		10	8

Appendix A Continued

Summary Table of Mapped Rivers

River	Section	Map	Hazard Rating Summer	Hazard Rating Spring	Gradient (ft./mi.)	10/90 Ratio°	Length (miles)	Time (hours)
Red	1	42	nr	II[4]	12	--	6	4
	2	42	I[3]	II[4]	--		4	3
St. Croix	1*	43	I-II	II-II[3]	5	3.1	16	7
	2*	44	Q[1]	I	2		15	7
	3*	45	Q	Q	1		19	8
	4*	46	I-II	II	5		10	5
	5*	47	Q	Q	10		11	6
Tomahawk		48	Q[2]	Q[3]	3	--	18	10
White		49	I-II	II	10	2.9	14	6
Wisconsin	1	50	I-II	I-II	--	--	0.1	--
	2	50	Q	Q	--		15	6-8
	3	50	Q	Q	--		19	6-8
Wisconsin Dells	1	51	Q	Q	--	--	4	3
	2	51	Q	Q	--		4	2
Wolf	1*	52	II	II-III	10	3.3	7	4
	2*	53	II	II-III	14		8	4
	3*	54	II	III	18		14	8
	4*	55	III	IV	12		9	9

nr not runnable

* This section can be combined with other sections for a trip of 3 days or longer.

° Measured at the U.S.G.S. gauging station (see Chapter 5, seasonal variations in canoeability for a discussion). Numbers in parentheses were estimated from (30 days of highest flow)/(30 days of lowest flow).

APPENDIX B

Summary Table of Unmapped Rivers

River	Section	Hazard Rating Spring	Gradient (ft./mi.)	10/90 Ratio	Length (miles)	Time (hours)
Baptism (Minn.)	1	I thru V[6]★	50	28.6	6.5	4.5
	2	I thru VI★	110		4	3
Brule (Minn.)	1	I thru IV★	--	--	18	7
	2	II thru VII★	125		6	4
Cascade (Minn.)	1	II[5]	56	--	4.5	1
	2	II thru VII★	200		3.5	--
Crystal		Q	--	--	--	6
Embarass		II-III	--	8.1	3	2
Jump	1	I-II[3]	--	37.6	10	6
	2	I-II	--		10	6
St. Louis (Minn.)		II-VI	75	7.7	2	1
Sturgeon (Mich.)		•	--	--	--	--
Temperance (Minn.)	1	I-II	36	--	8	3
	2	I thru VII★	73		8.5	4
Vermillion		II-III	8	35.5	9	5

★ This hazard rating deviates from the standard format. The rapids consist mainly of high grade III and IV with some easy rapids and some very difficult falls which rate grade V and VI. Some of the falls are unrunnable (grade VII !).

• This River is very difficult and has not been rated. We have recommended it as a hiking trip rather than a boating trip although the sections we describe have been run - at least once. Our source of information got cold feet and has since refused to run the river again!

APPENDIX C

International Scale of River Difficulty

Prepared by Guidebook Committee - AWWA (From "American White Water," Winter, 1957)

PTS	Factors Related Primarily To Success in Negotiating SECONDARY FACTORS			Factors Affecting Both Success & Safety PRIMARY FACTORS				Factors Related Primarily To Safe Rescue SECONDARY FACTORS			
	Bends	Length, feet	Gradient, ft./mile	Obstacles, rocks trees	Waves	Turbulence	Resting or rescue spots	Water Velocity	Width, depth	Temp.	Acces-ibility
0	Few, Very Gradual	Less than 100 feet	Less than 5. Regular slope.	None	Few inches high. Avoidable	None	Almost anywhere	Less than 3 mph.	Narrow <75' & Shallow <3'	>65° F.	Road along river.
1	Many, gradual	100-700	5-15 Regular slope	Few. Passage almost straight through	Low (up to 1 ft.) Regular. Avoidable	Minor eddies		3-6 mph.	Wide >75' <3'	55°-65° F.	<1 hr. travel by foot or water
2	Few, sharp blind. Scouting neces.	700-5,000	15-40 ledges or steep drops	Courses easily recognizable	Low to med. (up to 3') reg. Avoidable.	Medium eddies		6-10 mph.	<75' >3'	45°-55° F.	1 hr. to 1 dy. tra. ft. or wa.
3		>5,000	>40 steep drops. small falls	Maneuvering. Course not easily recognizable.	Med. to large (up to 5') Mostly regular Avoidable	Strong eddies and cross currents.	A good one below every danger spot	>10 mph. or Flood	>75' >3'	<45° F.	>1 dy. tra. by ft. or water
4				Intricate maneuvering. Course hard to recognize.	Large irreg. avoid. or med. to large unavoidable	Very strong eddies, strong cross currents.					
5				Course torturous Frequent scouting.	Large, irreg. unavoidable	Lge. scale eddies & cross C's. sme. up & dn					
6				Very torturous. Always scout from shore.	Very large >5', irreg. unavoidable. spec. equip.		Almost none.				

RATING	APPROXIMATE DIFFICULTY	TOTAL POINTS (from above)	APPROXIMATE SKILL REQUIRED
I	Easy	0-7	Practiced Beginner
II	Requires Care	8-14	Intermediate
III	Difficult	15-21	Experienced
IV	Very Difficult	22-28	Highly Skilled (Several years with organized group)
V	Exceedingly Difficult	29-35	Team of Experts
VI	Utmost Difficulty-Near Limit of Navigability	36-42	Team of Experts taking every precaution

APPENDIX D

SAFETY EQUIPMENT CHECK LIST

The recommended equipment for a river trip where rapids are expected (in addition to the obvious: spare paddles, lifejackets, etc.):

a) first aid kit
b) boat repair kit (e.g. grey tape)
c) matches
d) maps and compass
e) flashlight
f) an extra change of clothes or a blanket
g) rescue lines

Items a, b, c, d, e, and f should be carried in a completely waterproof container. If the water is cold at least one extra change of clothes should also be carried. See chapter 6 for a discussion of the dangers of cold water. Item g should be tied in with a quick release knot. Without rescue lines rescue is often impossible.

ON-THE-RIVER ORGANIZATION

1. Never boat alone. The minimum party should have at least three boats.

2. Never boat after dark. Establish a reasonable timetable. Trips should be planned so that there is ample time to complete a day's run well before sunset.

3. Each boater should know the group plans, expected hazards, number of rapids that are likely to require scouting, location of special equipment, and expected rescue procedures.

4. The river leader should determine the order and spacing of boaters and who may run any given rapids.

5. The lead boat should be manned by a very experienced boater who sets the pace. He should never be passed, since he is on the lookout for possible hazards and has the delegated authority of the river leader to make all decisions in the interest of safety.

6. Each boater is responsible for keeping the one behind in sight, stopping to wait when necessary. This is particularly important after negotiating a series of rapids that contain potential hang-up areas or in places where it would be helpful to guide the next boat through an imminent danger spot (e.g. where fallen trees obstruct the river).

7. The sweep boat is equipped for rescue and is always in the rear.

APPENDIX E

INFORMATION DIRECTORY

We have compiled the following information for general reference only. Inclusion in this partial listing is not intended as an endorsement of any group, product, publication, or supplier over those not included.

ORGANIZATIONS

NATIONAL

American Canoe Association, P.O. Box 248, Lorton, VA 22079. Membership includes the publication ***Canoe*** (bimonthly).

American River Conservation Council, 323 Pennsylvania Ave., SE, Washington, DC 20003.

American Whitewater Affiliation, Box 1483, Hagerston, MD 21740. Membership includes the publication ***American Whitewater*** (bimonthly).

Friends of the Earth, 124 Spear St., San Francisco, CA 94105. Membership includes the publication ***Not Man Apart*** (semi-monthly).

National Organization for River Sports, Box 6847, Colorado Springs, CO 80924. Membership includes monthly publication ***Currents*** (Mar.-Aug.).

Sierra Club, National Office, 530 Bush St., San Francisco, CA 94108.

United States Canoe Association, 606 Ross St., Middletown, OH 45042.

United States International Slalom Canoe Association, P.O. Box 45, Elwyn, PA 19063. Souvenir programs and racing schedule (annually). Proceeds go to support the U.S. Slalom and Wildwater Racing Team.

Wilderness Society, 1901 Pennsylvania Ave. NW, Washington, DC 20006.

REGIONAL

Belleville Whitewater Club, #3 Oakwood, Belleville, IL 62223.

BIG Water Associates, 10009 Oxborough Rd., Bloomington, MN 55437.

Cascaders Canoe and Kayak Club, 3128 W. Calhoun Blvd., Minneapolis, MN 55416.

Chicago Whitewater Assoc., 5460 Ridgewood Ct., Chicago, IL 60629.

Illinois Paddling Council, 2316 Prospect Ave., Evanston, IL 60201.

Minnesota Canoe Assoc., P.O. Box 14177, Minneapolis, MN 55414. Membership includes the publication **Hut!** (bimonthly).

Raw Strength & Courage Kayakers, 2185 Mershon Dr., Ann Arbor, MI 48103.

Sierra Club—John Muir Chapter, River Touring Section, 10261 N. Sunnycrest Dr., Mequon, WI 53092. Membership includes the publication **Muir Views** (bimonthly). **Molds.**

Wisconsin Canoe Assoc., 9021-F N. 91st St., Milwaukee, WI 53224. Includes newsletter **Wisconsin Waters**.

Wisconsin Hoofers Outing Club, Wisconsin Union, 800 Langdon St., Madison, WI 53706. **Molds.**

Wolf River Canoe Club, R. Charles Steed, Wolf River Lodge, White Lake, WI 54491.

INFORMATION SOURCES

MAP SUPPLIERS

The U.S. Geological Survey publishes a wide variety of topographic maps for the U.S. Prices range from $1.25 for the 1:24,000 and 1:62,500 scale maps to $2.00 for the 1:250,000 scale. **The Canadian Dept. of Energy, Mines & Resources** publishes topo maps of Canada in 1:250,000 and 1:50,000 scales. These maps are available from the following sources.

Clarkson Map Co., 724 Desnoyer St., Kaukauna, WI 54130. Publish guides to Mich. & Wisc. which include county maps and other info.

Hudson Map Co., 1506 Hennepin Ave., Minneapolis, MN 55113.

Map Distribution Office, Dept. of Energy, Mines & Resources, 615 Booth St., Ottawa, Ontario K1A OE9, Canada.

Milwaukee Map Co., 4519 W. North Ave., Milwaukee, WI 53208.

Rand McNally & Co., 39 S. La Salle St., Chicago, IL 60603.

U.S./Canadian Map Service Bureau, Ltd., Hy. 41, Box 249, Neenah, WI 54956. Publish in 2 vols. a unique collection of map & chart indexes for entire U.S. & Canada.

U.S. Geological Survey, Branch of Distribution, 1200 S. Eads St., Arlington, VA 22202. Maps for areas east of the Miss. River, including Minn.

Wisconsin Geological Survey, 1815 University Ave., Madison, WI 53706. Topo maps for Wisc. only.

PERIODICALS

Canoe magazine, P.O. Box 10748, Des Moines, IA 50349 (bimonthly).

Wisconsin Sportsman magazine, P.O. Box 1307, Oshkosh, WI 54901 (bimonthly).

BOOKS

A Boatbuilder's Manual, Charles Walbridge. Wildwater Designs, Penllyn, PA 19422. How to build fiberglass canoes & kayaks. Diagrams & photos, paperback.

A Whitewater Handbook for Canoe and Kayak, John Urban. Appalachian Mtn. Club, 5 Joy St., Boston, Mass. 02108. Basic canoe & kayak technique. 76 pg., diagrams & photos, paperback.

The All-Purpose Guide to Paddling, Dean Norman. World Publications, Box 366, Mtn. View, CA 94042. Basic info on various paddling skills, 218 pg., illus.

Basic River Canoeing, Robert McNair. American Camping Assn., Bradford Woods, Martinsville, Ind. 46151. Basic canoe & kayak techniques. 97 pg., diagrams, paperback.

Canoe Poling, Al & Syl Beletz. A.C. Mackenzie River Co., Box 9301, Dept. 12, Rich. Heights, MO 63117. 180 photos & illus..

Kayaking, Jay Evans & Robert Anderson. The Stephen Greene Press, Brattleboro, VT 05301. 192 pg., diagrams & photos, paperback.

Whitewater Coaching Manual, Jay Evans. Ledyard Canoe Club, 201 McNutt, Hanover, NH 03755. Training guide for the serious whitewater coach & competitor. 56 pg., paperback.

Whitewater Rafting, William McGinnis. Quadrangle/New York Times Books, New York. All aspects of rafting. 361 pg.

Wildwater Touring, Scott & Margaret Arighi, MacMillan, New York. A guide to extended touring by canoe, kayak, & raft. 334 pg., photos & maps, hardbound.

EQUIPMENT SOURCES

Dealers and suppliers have been arbitrarily grouped into the following general categories: boats, paddles, general outing equipment, river touring equipment, and other specialty items. Multiple listings have been avoided, even where appropriate, with each source listed once only. This incomplete listing is biased in favor of those sources that supply catalogs or other information.

With the exception noted, the "paddles" listing includes sources of paddles with aluminum shafts and plastic or fiberglass blades, or ones of all laminated-wood construction.

Under general outing equipment, we have listed dealers that carry an extensive line of tents, packs, sleeping bags, and similar camping supplies. Sources for canoes, kayaks, paddles, lifejackets, flotation bags, and other boating accessories are listed under river touring equipment. The final category, specialty items, lists sources for items not generally available elsewhere.

BOATS

Alumacraft, 315 W. St. Julien, St. Peter, MN 56082.
Easy Rider, 10013 51st Ave. SW, Seattle, WA 98146.
Grumman Boats, Marathon, NY 13803.
Hollowform, Inc., 6345 Variel Ave., Woodland Hills, CA 91364.
Hyperform, 25 Industrial Park Rd., Hingham, MA 02043.
Klepper, 35 Union Sq. West, New York, NY 10003.
Old Town Canoes, Old Town, ME 04468.
Plasticrafts, 2800 Speer Blvd., Denver, CO 80211.

PADDLES

Blue Hole, Sunbright, TN 37872.
Borealis Kayak Works, Box 245, Ann Arbor, MI 48107.
Cannon, 2345 NW 8th Ave., Faribault, MN 55021.
Carlisle Au Sable, P.O. Box 150, Grayling, MI 49738.
Clement, P.O. Box 134, Markesan, WI 53946.
Great Canadian, 45 Water St., Worcester, MA 01604.
Hauthaway, 640 Boston Post Rd., Weston, MA 02193.
Hurka Industries, One Charles St., Newberryport, MA 01950.
Illiad, 55A Washington St., Norwell, MA 02061.
Kruger, 243 S. Webb Rd., DeWill, MI 48820.
Nona, 977 W. 19th St., Costa Mesa, CA 92627.
Norse, P.O. Box 77, Pine Grove Mills, PA 16868.
Sawyer Woodworking, P.O. Box 524, Rogue River, OR 97537.
Sports Equipment, Box T Dept. C, Mantua, OH 44255.
Swanson Boat Oar, Albion, PA 16401 (custom wood).

RIVER TOURING EQUIPMENT

Chicagoland Canoe, 4019 N. Narragansett, Chicago, IL 60634.
EMS Kayaks, 1041 Commonwealth Ave., Boston, MA 02215.
Great World, P.O. Box 250, W. Simsbury, Conn. 06092.
Hike Out, 2189 Abraham Lane, Oshkosh, WI 54901.
Kayak Specialties, Box 83, Buchanan, MI 49107.
Ketter Canoeing, 101 79th Ave. North, Mpls, MN 55430.
Moor and Mountain, Chelmsford, MA 02215.
Pack & Paddle, 701 E. Park Ave., Libertyville, IL 60048.
Rutabaga Whitewater Supply, 1002 S. Park St., Madison, WI 53715.
Seda Products, P.O. Box 997, Chula Vista, CA 92010.
Watermeister, P.O. Box 5026, Ft. Wayne, IN 46805.
Whitewater West, 622 Bancroft Way, Berkeley, CA 94710.

GENERAL OUTING EQUIPMENT

Alpine Designs, 6185 Arapahoe, Boulder, CO 80303.
Class V, 2010 7th St., Berkeley, CA 94710.
Eddie Bauer, 1737 Airport Way South, Seattle, WA 98134.
Gokey, 21 W. Fifth St., St. Paul, MN 55102.
Hoigaard's, 3550 S. Hwy 100, Mpls, MN 55416.
Laake and Joys, 1433 N. Water St., Milwaukee, WI 53202.
North Face, 2804 Telegraph Ave., Berkeley, CA 94704.
Northern Prairie Outfitters, 206 NW Hwy, Fox River Grove, IL 60021.
Recreational Equipment, 1525 11th Ave., Seattle, WA 98122.
Sierra Designs, 4th and Addison, Berkeley, CA 94710.
Ski Hut, 1615 University Ave., Berkeley, CA 94703.
Waters, 111 E. Sheridan St., Ely, MN 55731.

SPECIALTY ITEMS

Country Ways, 3500 Hwy 101, Minnetonka, MN. Boat and camp kits.
Canoes West, P.O. Box 61, Kentfield, CA 94904. Waterproof bags.
Leisure Imports, 104 Arlington Ave., St. James, NY 11780. Rafts.
Milwaukee Cutting, 1987 W. Purdue, Milwke, WI 53209. Ethafoam.
Quick-N-Easy, 934 W. Foothill Blvd., Monrovia, CA 91016. Car rks.
Rubatex, Box 245, Costa Mesa, CA 92627. Wet suits & nylon-coated neoprene.
Seuyon, 4476 E. Wash. Blvd., Los Angeles, CA 90023. Rafts.
Sundown, Box 10237, Burnsville, MN 55337. Camp kits.
Trailcraft, Box 60680, Concordia, KS 66901. Boat kits.
Voyageur, P.O. Box 512, Shawnee Mission, KS 66201. Wtrprf bags.
White Stag, 5100 S.E. Harney Dr., Portland, OR 97206. Wet suits.
Wildwater Designs, Penllyn, PA 19422. Spray & wet suit kits.

Glossary of River Terms

Backroller: A wave at the bottom of a ledge which curls back on itself. Water enters the trough of the wave from the upstream and downstream sides. See souse hole.

Block and Tackle: Recommended auxiliary aid whenever an open canoe is used on stretches of water that we recommend for decked boats only.

Bow: The front of a boat.

Broaching: A boat that is sideways to the current and usually out of control.

C-1: One-man decked canoe equipped with a spray skirt. Frequently mistaken for a kayak by the uninitiated. The canoeist kneels in the boat and uses a single-bladed paddle.

C-2: A two-man decked canoe. Frequently mistaken for a two-man kayak.

CFS: Cubic feet per second; a unit of water flow. See discharge.

Chicken Route: Need not be degrading. It is simply a conservative (less risky) path through a complex rapids.

Chute: A clear channel between obstructions that has faster current than the surrounding water.

DNR: Department of Natural Resources.

Daredevils: Our name for persons who boat above their ability. Also it is the term given to expert boaters by hackers and most locals.

Deck: The top portion of a decked boat.

Decked Boat: A completely enclosed canoe or kayak fitted with a spray skirt. When boater is properly in place, this forms a nearly waterproof unit.

Discharge: Volume of water in cubic feet per second that passes a given point. (One cubic foot per second is approximately 7.48 gallons per second or 449 gallons per minute.)

Downstream Ferry: A technique for moving sideways in the current while facing downstream. Can also be done by surfing on a wave.

Drainage Area or Watershed: The official definition is area measured in a horizontal plane, enclosed by a topographic divide from which direct surface runoff from precipitation normally drains by gravity into the stream above the specified point. In other words, this is area that has provided the water on which you are paddling at any given time. Accordingly the drainage area increases as you go downstream. The drainage basin of a river expressed in square miles.

Drop: A small portion of river where the water drops freely. Both rapids and falls fit into this category.

Dunker: A boater suddenly turned swimmer following a tipover.

Dynamic Clunk: A person who does the wrong thing in a critical situation.

Eddy: The water behind an obstruction in the current. The water may be relatively calm or actually flow upstream.

Eddy Line: The sharp boundary at the edge of an eddy between two currents of different velocity or direction.

Eddy Out: An involuntary eddy turn.

Eddy Turn: Maneuver used to get into an eddy.

Eskimo Roll: NOT AN ICE CREAM BAR! Rather it is the technique used to upright an overturned decked canoe or kayak by the occupant while remaining in the craft. This is done by coordinated body motion and usually facilitated by the proper use of the paddle.

Expert Boater: A person with extensive experience and good judgment who is familiar with up-to-date boating technique, practical hydrology, and proper safety practices. An expert boater never paddles alone and always uses the proper equipment.

Falls: A portion of river where the water falls freely over a drop. This designation has nothing to do with hazard rating or difficulty. See rapids.

Gauge Reader: A person in the area who reads the level of a stage marker and provides this information to others. See Good Guys/Gals.

Good Guys/Gals: Personnel of U.S.G.S., Wisconsin DNR, and any of our other public agencies that support wild and scenic rivers legislation. Also includes gauge readers, conservationists, and friendly locals. Could also include mining and power companies that donate river acreage to state or federal agencies (e.g., as the Northern States Power Company has done along the Namekagon and St. Croix Rivers).

Grab Loops: Loops (about 6 inches in diameter) of nylon rope or similar material attached to the bow and stern of a boat to facilitate rescue.

Gradient: Drop of river expressed in feet per mile.

Grey Tape: A cloth backed tape noted for its stickiness and grey color and useful as an emergency "band-aid" for damaged boats. The novice whitewater boater all too soon learns of its virtue and the expert is never without it. Alias heating duct tape.

Hacker: A person who doesn't know what he is doing but thinks of himself as an expert. Usually a person who has run a grade I or perhaps a grade II rapids without drowning, but has had so much difficulty in the endeavor that he feels that those who try more difficult things are fools. If he is also a bit too foolhardy he may move into the class dynamic clunk.

Hang Up: When a boat becomes stranded on a rock or other obstacle.

Damitol: A new non-prescription tranquilizer. Also a variation of frequently used boating terminology.

Haystack: Large standing waves which accompany deceleration of current.

Heavy Water: Fast current, large waves, usually associated with holes and boulders.

Hole Cover: A waterproof cover for the unused cockpit(s) of a three-holed C-2.

Hull: Bottom portion of a boat.

Hydraulic: General term for souse holes and backrollers, where there is a hydraulic jump (powerful current differential).

K-1: One-man decked kayak equipped with spray skirt. In this guide this category does not include non-decked kayaks. The kayakist sits in the boat with both feet extended forward. A double-bladed paddle is used.

K-2: A two-man kayak. An uncommon, unwieldy craft on rapids that will not be considered in this book.

Leap Year: Every fourth year there are 366 days instead of the usual 365. The extra day is February 29 which is no big deal for canoeists in this region.

Ledge: The exposed edge of a rock stratum which acts as a low natural dam or as a series of such dams.

Left Bank: Left side of river when facing downstream.

Lining: A compromise between portaging and running a rapids. It is a handy technique used to get a boat through a rock garden. By the use of a rope, a boat can be worked downstream from the shore.

Locals: Persons indigenous to a canoe area who are usually most hospitable, but who often have interesting notions as to the sanity of whitewater boaters.

Maximal Flotation: Plastic air bags and/or waterproof bulkheads placed in decked boats to prevent water from filling the boat in the event of an upset. A boat so equipped is less likely to be damaged following an upset because it floats higher and is much easier to get to shore.

Moving Wave: A large wave that moves slowly downstream. See standing wave.

ORAP 200: Outdoor Recreation Act Program. This is the legal authorization under which the Wisconsin DNR acquires and manages much of its public outdoor recreation holdings.

Open Canoe: Any non-decked (partial decking does not count) canoe constructed of aluminum, fiberglass, canvas covered wood, birch bark, etc.

Paddle Brace: A canoe stroke in which the boater uses his paddle as an outrigger to lean toward the side on which he is tipping. The brace gives added stability to prevent or recover from a potential tipover.

Painter: A line attached to the bow or stern of a canoe. It is handy for tying a boat to the shore and it can be used to facilitiate rescue of an overturned boat.

Pitch: A section of rapids usually steeper than the surrounding portions; a drop.

Pool: A quiet section of water that is usually deep and quiet. Frequently found below rapids and falls.

Power-face: The working side of a paddle blade.

Raft: Not a large life jacket.

Rapids: Portion of a river where there is appreciable turbulence usually accompanied by obstacles. See falls.

Riffles: Slight turbulence with or without a few rocks tossed in; they are not worthy of a grade on the International Scale of River Difficulty.

Right Side: The right bank of the river as you progress downstream.

Rock Garden: Shallow grade I-II rapids that has many exposed or partially submerged rocks necessitating intricate maneuvering or an occasional carry over shallow places.

Rocker: A good place for the retired boater. Also the curvature of the boat keel from bow to stern. The affects the turning characteristics; the greater the rocker the easier the boat turns.

Roller: Also called curler or backroller. It is a wave that falls back on itself.

Scout: To look at a rapids from the shore in order to decide whether or not to run it or to facilitate selection of a suitable route through the rapids.

Section: A portion of river located between two points. See stretch.

Shock Cord: An elastic cord made of a core of parallel rubber strands enclosed in a mantle of cotton cloth.

Sidecurler: Similar to a backroller except the wave is parallel to the main current; formed by a side current passing over a rock as it enters the main channel.

Shuttle: Movement of at least two vehicles to the take-out and one back to the put-in. Used to avoid having to paddle back upstream at the end of the run.

Souse Hole: Similar to a backroller except the water enters the hole from the sides as well as from the upstream and downstream direction.

Spray Skirt: A hemmed piece of waterproof material resembling a mini-mini skirt, having an elastic hem fitting around the boater's waist and an elastic hem fitting around the cockpit rim of a decked boat.

Stage Marker: A gauge placed along a river shoreline that is calibrated in feet or fractions thereof, starting with an arbitrary zero point. With appropriate conversion tables these readings can be converted into discharge (water flow in cfs), or more important into canoeability.

Standing Wave: An upright female member of the U.S. Navy. Also a regular wave downstream of submerged rocks which does not move relative to the riverbed as opposed to a moving one such as an ocean wave.

Static Clunk: A person who does nothing in a critical situation. See dynamic clunk.

Stern: The rear of a boat.

Stopper: A plug for the jug required to prevent loss of precious fluids. Also a sufficiently large backroller capable of stopping a boater "dead in his tracks" as he attempts to paddle through it.

Surfing: The technique of sitting on the upstream face of a wave or traveling back and forth across the wave when ferrying.

Stretch: A portion of river located between two points. See section.

Technique Manual: For our purposes this has nothing to do with sexual prowess. That subject is beyond the scope of this book, but it may be included in future editions. This subject deals with proper boat paddling techniques, equipment, safety procedures, and a practical understanding of river hydrology.

Thwart: Cross pieces used to reinforce the gunwales of an open canoe.

Trim: Paddlers and duffel should be positioned so the waterline is even from bow to stern and the boat does not list to the side.

Upstream Ferry: Similar to downstream ferry except the paddler faces upstream. Also see surfing.

U.S. Army Corps of Engineers: An unscrupulous group that seems to think that the only good river is a dam(n)ed river.

Virgin Boater: A person who has not canoed before, but one who may have done other things.

WITH A LITTLE HELP FROM OUR FRIENDS

This guidebook was prepared to fill what we considered to be a void on the canoeing scene. We have mapped over 750 miles of river and several thousand miles of roadways. Over a thousand rapids, falls, landings, campgrounds, and other points of interest have been described. With much of this material continuously subject to change, we hope you will bear with us if you come across anything that is inaccurate, misleading, or otherwise out-of-date. Better yet, we would be most grateful if you would take the time and trouble to point out any such matters directly to us.

Many of the changes that appear in this edition were prompted by helpful suggestions from our readers. Future modifications and revisions will be influenced by your responses.

Have you found **Whitewater; Quietwater** to be accurate? Easy to use?

Is there any material in this book that you feel should be expanded? Clarified? Deleted?

Have you run any river stretches that are not included here that you think should be?

Please drop us a note at Menasha Ridge Press, Post Office Box 59257, Birmingham, Alabama 35259. The more detailed and specific your comments and suggestions, the better. Thank you and happy paddling.

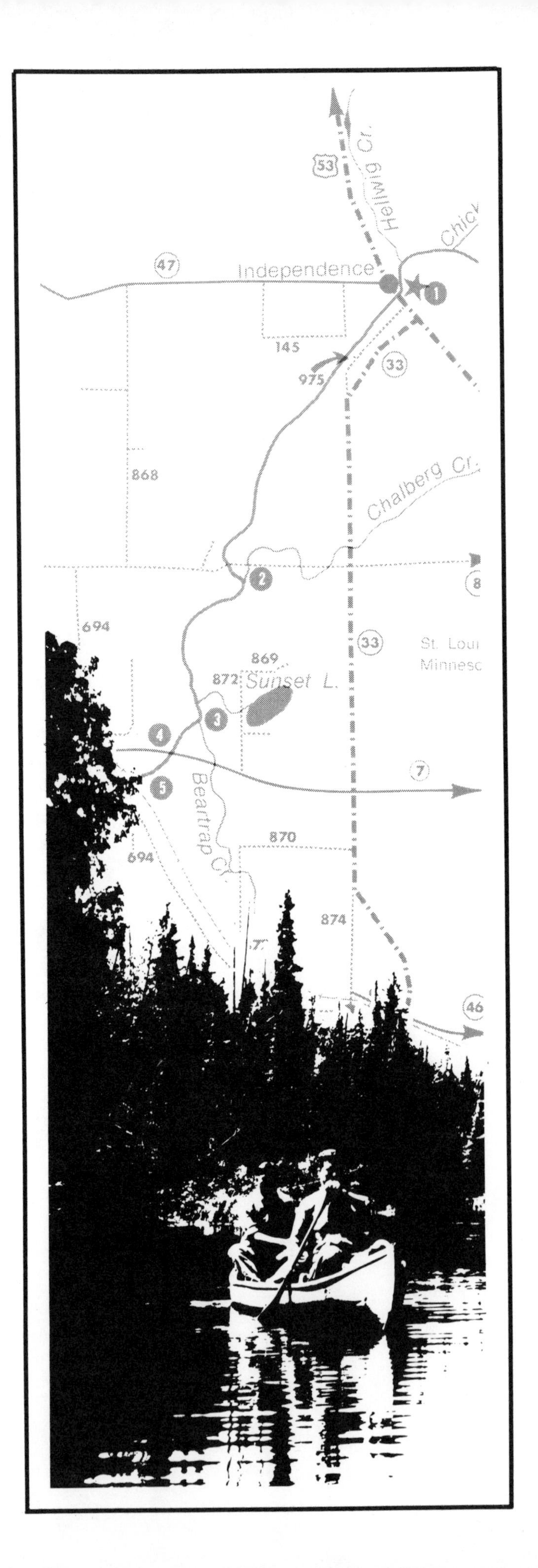